When
CHRIST
Lives
in
Us

A Pilgrimage of Faith

Justo L. González

Abingdon Press
NASHVILLE

WHEN CHRIST LIVES IN US

Copyright © 1995 by Abingdon Press

ISBN 0-687-01560X

Scripture quotations in this publication, unless otherwise indicated, are from the New Revised Standard Version of the Bible, copyrighted © 1989 by the Division of Christian Education of the National Council of the Churches of Christ in the USA. Used by permission. All rights reserved.

William A. Woods, Designer

Abingdon Press

CONTENTS

PREFACE

When The United Methodist Publishing House approached me about writing this book, I undertook the task with both excitement and trepidation. Excitement, because this project would give me the opportunity to express coherently, and in book form, some of the deepest concerns with which I have been struggling in recent years—concerns both for my own life and for the life of the church. Trepidation, because I know better than anyone else how far short I am from the fullness of Christ's presence of which this book speaks. Excitement, because this is a unique opportunity to call myself and the entire church to fuller discipleship. Trepidation, because this is a task that I dare undertake only as a fellow pilgrim with the many others whom I must now call to follow along the way. Excitement, because we are dealing with things holy. And trepidation, because we are dealing with things holy.

I therefore invite the reader to approach, not this book, but the Word that it seeks to express, with similar enthusiasm and apprehension. Be excited, because God is calling you to great things. And be fearful, also because God is calling you to great things. Above all, seek to be open to God's Word; and read this book in prayer both for yourself and for me, knowing that it has been written in prayer both for myself and for you.

Justo L. González
Princeton, New Jersey
June 5, 1995

4

INTRODUCTION

"I have been crucified with Christ; and it is no longer I who live, but it is Christ who lives in me" (Galatians 2:19-20).

"My little children, for whom I am again in the pain of childbirth until Christ is formed in you" (Galatians 4:19).

The title for this book is drawn from the words of the apostle Paul in the first of the quotes above. They are radical words; for they describe the Christian life, not just in terms of following an ethical teaching or even in terms of believing certain theological doctrines, but rather in terms of having Christ living in us. Even more radical, they imply that there is a correspondence between Christ living in us and our being crucified with Christ. The words indicate that along with the positive side of having Christ living in us, there is also the negative aspect of our being crucified with him.

The second quote is also intriguing, because here Paul reverses his most common metaphor. As we read his letters, we frequently hear Paul saying that believers are (or should be) "in Christ." Probably the best-known passage in this regard is 2 Corinthians 5:17: "So if anyone is *in Christ* [italics added], there is a new creation; everything old has passed away; see, everything has become new!" There, as in many other passages where Paul speaks of freedom "in Christ" or of being made alive "in Christ" or of all being one "in Christ" or even of boasting "in Christ," the image suggests that it is the believers who are to be "in Christ" and that their lives are to be shaped by Christ.

In the passage in Galatians 4, by contrast, it is Christ who is being "formed" in the believers. Moreover, in this context the image is that of a womb in which a child is taking shape. Of course, Paul does not literally mean that there is no Christ until he is formed in us, in the same way that there is no child until he or she is formed in the mother's womb. What Paul does mean is that Christ, having come into the lives of believers in an initial way, almost as a seed, must now grow and take shape in those lives. One might think here also of the manner in which a child being shaped in his or her mother's womb in turn shapes the mother herself. Thus, as Christ is being formed in us, it is we who are at the same time being shaped by Christ.

The dual Pauline metaphor of believers being "in Christ" and of Christ being shaped in believers helps us understand how it is that our lives are to be patterned after him—or, in the other set of metaphors, how it is that we are to be crucified in order to have Christ living in us. In particular, it helps us see the value and the danger of what has traditionally been called "the imitation of Christ."

Quite often, and at different times in the history of the church, Christians have sought to base their lives on the imitation of Christ. Probably the most famous instance is the late medieval book, attributed to Thomas à Kempis, that carries the title *Imitation of Christ*. But there have been many others. Paul called himself an imitator of Christ (1 Corinthians 11:1). Later, many martyrs were convinced that in their deaths they were imitating the sufferings of Christ. (For instance, early in the second century, Bishop Ignatius of Antioch wrote to some Christians in Rome, who apparently were plotting to free him from prison and martyrdom, "Allow me to be an imitator of the sufferings of my God.") In the Middle Ages, many argued that the highest form of Christian life was voluntary poverty in imitation of Jesus, who had been poor. Some went so far as to try to fashion their dress after what they imagined Jesus had worn. In more recent times, there was a popular book, *In His Steps*, by Charles M. Sheldon. Sheldon's basic premise was that at every turn in life we must ask, "What would Jesus have done in my place?" and guide our actions accordingly.

There is much value in all this, but there are also some real dangers. One danger is that we might overestimate our capacity to be imitators of Christ. Certainly, there is no better role model to imitate; but when measured by the standards of Jesus, we must all fall short. To imagine otherwise is to think either too highly of ourselves or too lowly of Jesus. An even greater danger is that we might substitute the form for the substance, imitating Christ in a number of things and yet not being truly transformed by him. Finally, there is the possibility that by imitating Christ, we reduce him to the level of a role model and forget that he is also Lord, Savior, Word of God incarnate.

The value of this imagery, on the other hand, lies in the fact that it is possible for practice to shape life and character. There are times, for instance, when I seem to be sad for no reason at all. At such times I simply do not feel like smiling; and if it were up to me, I would prefer to ignore everyone else. However, if at such times I force myself to smile, to continue smiling, and to greet people as if I were really happy to see them, quite often my inner attitude will slowly change. Eventually, I will find myself smiling and greeting people, no longer because I am forcing myself to do it, but rather because I am really enjoying it. Somehow, by acting differently, I have come to feel differently.

Likewise, there may be times when I do not feel like acting as a Christian should; sadly, there are many such times. If I were to act out of the depths of my heart at such moments, my actions would be most unchristian—and often they have been. Yet, I have also learned over the course of the years that if I force myself, even against my inner inclinations, to act as Christ would have me act and if I persist in it, there is a good chance my feelings and inclinations will change to fit my actions. And, as a result, I will find myself acting out of a heart that is beginning to be transformed.

If you have studied the life of John Wesley, you may remember that at a time when he was not sure he had found the saving grace of Christ, he was given the advice that, while he was still seeking, he should continue preaching *as if* he had found it; and that later, after having found it, he should preach *because* he had found it. Such advice, which may seem strange to us, worked in Wesley's case.

Obviously, there is always the possibility that, no matter how hard I smile, my expression of joy will be superficial. I may get to the point where I smile all the time almost automatically, even when my heart cries out in pain or in hatred. My smile becomes a permanent facade that I do not allow to touch my inner being, and I no longer feel the contradiction between my face and my heart. In that case, I have become a hypocrite. Likewise, the imitation of Christ, which can really help us to become more Christlike, can also be turned into a hypocritical religiosity, where form is substituted for substance and sham for truth. To be sure, Wesley did have his Aldersgate experience; his inner life and faith came to match his preaching and, eventually, to enliven it. But until then there was also the danger he might grow satisfied with preaching *as if* he had found what he was proclaiming and quit longing for what he did not yet have. Had the danger been realized, Wesley, instead of becoming a powerful and faithful preacher, would simply have become one more hypocrite.

It is for these reasons that, while affirming the positive value of imitating Christ, we must find other ways to express how he shapes our lives. And it is at this point that Paul's double metaphor of being "in Christ" and of Christ "being formed" in us is particularly valuable. Being in Christ means that he is the very ground on which we stand, the very air that we breathe. He is not just someone who goes ahead of us setting a good example so that it suffices to walk "in his steps." Christ certainly is that, but he is so much more! He is also the One who walks next to us, holding our hand when we stumble and pulling us back to our feet when we fall. He is the One who walks behind us, erasing the footprints of our wayward steps, watering and blessing the poor seeds we plant, pulling the weeds we leave behind.

Furthermore, having Christ "formed in us" means that he is not purely an exterior support or a model whom we imitate. Christ is also an inner reality, being shaped within us and in the process shaping us—again, much like a child being formed in the mother's womb shapes both her body and her life. When Christ lives in us, we are constantly being formed by his presence and influence.

The purpose of this book is to study the ministry of Jesus, to see how his ministry calls our ministry into being and how his ministry shapes ours. However, we are not seeking merely to learn how to imitate Jesus. It is much more a matter of probing the depths of what it means to be in Christ, to be transformed by Christ, and to have Christ formed in us and living in us.

It is crucial we understand that the process of being transformed by Christ is both individual and communal. Having Christ formed in us is a private matter that requires many of those hours in which we do as Jesus told his followers: "Go into your room and shut the door and pray to your Father who is in secret" (Matthew 6:6). We all need those hours, for without them our faith and commitment wither like flowers cut from the plant that gave them life. But being in Christ and having Christ formed in us is also a communal matter. The passage in Galatians in which Paul speaks of Christ being formed in the believers is in the plural; it is addressed to an entire church. Thus, one could say that the womb in which Christ is to be formed is not just the private womb of each one's inner being; it is also and above all the one womb of the community of faith—the body of Christ. Christ must be formed, not only *in me* but also *in us*; and both aspects are equally important.

Paul has a strong view on the bonds of this community of faith. In Galatians 4:19 he uses the image of pregnancy and childbirth in still another way: Not only must the Galatians have Christ formed in them, it is Paul who is in the pain of childbirth until that happens! He says he is in such pains "again." The first time apparently was when through his ministry the Galatians were born into the faith; this second time it is because they still have to be born as full Christians. The Galatians ought to know that Paul is not just telling them what to do and what to believe. He is also suffering as he sees them stray from their true course. Thus, as Christ is being formed in the Galatians, they are not the only ones going through the difficult adjustments of pregnancy. Paul is with them, suffering with them as in childbirth.

Likewise, as Christ is being formed in us, we must constantly remember that this is not a private enterprise and that our failures are not private failures. We are part of a single body to such a point that "if one member suffers, all suffer together with it" (1 Corinthians 12:26). Throughout my Christian life, I have been supported and have been brought back to obedience by many who suffered pains as of childbirth because I did not act as one in whom Christ was being formed. For them, I am most grateful; without them, my faith would most likely have been aborted. Again, we must constantly remember that having Christ formed is us is not a purely private matter; it is one that deeply affects those around us. We are all jointly in childbirth until Christ be formed in us. When Christ lives in us, he lives in us both as individuals—Christ in each of us—and as a community—Christ living in our common lives. Only when these two come together can we say that *Christ lives in us.*

****

This is a fairly short book, but it speaks of a long process. Do not read it all at once. Take the time to meditate on the Bible passages that are being studied. Take the time to allow Christ to be formed in you. Even if you read privately, do not read alone! This book is meant to be studied by those who are part of a community of faith. Therefore, if you study it privately, remember that for Christ to live in you requires that you live your faith in community. If, on the other hand, you read it as part of a group, take the time to consider privately some of the thoughts that your study might provoke.

If you are studying this book as part of a group, and especially if you are a group leader or teacher, you may wish to use the companion volume, *When Christ Lives in Us: Leader's Guide.*

CHRIST Us

CHAPTER 1
Calling

As he walked by the Sea of Galilee, he saw two brothers, Simon, who is called Peter, and Andrew his brother, casting a net into the sea—for they were fishermen. And he said to them, "Follow me, and I will make you fish for people." Immediately they left their nets and followed him. As he went from there, he saw two other brothers, James son of Zebedee and his brother John, in the boat with their father Zebedee, mending their nets, and he called them. Immediately they left the boat and their father, and followed him. (Matthew 4:18-22)

The Power of the Call

As we look at the life of Jesus, we see how much of his time was spent calling. In what is perhaps the best-known instance, he called the fishermen by the Sea of Galilee. But he also called Matthew from his tax booth (Matthew 9:9), the rich ruler away from his wealth (Luke 18:22), and an unnamed follower away from his father's funeral (Luke 9:59-60). Jesus repeatedly called his disciples to him in order to send them on a mission or to teach them (Mark 6:7; 9:35). He even called a young girl back from the dead (Luke 8:40-56) and Lazarus out of the tomb (John 11:1-44).

The variety of such instances—and many more that could be mentioned—is an indication that "calling" implies much more than we often think. In the modern world, we have come to undervalue the power of words and names; we seem to think that they do nothing but communicate ideas and describe reality. But in the Bible the power of speech and of naming is far greater than that. Look, for instance, at the first chapter of Genesis, where God creates all things through speech: "God said, 'Let there be . . .' and there was." God calls all things into being out of non-being; and precisely because God calls them, they come to be!

In the New Testament, the Fourth Gospel tells us something similar: "In the beginning was the Word. . . . All things came into being through him, and without him not one thing came into being" (John 1:1-3). One could say that, before coming into being, all things are pronounced by God and that it is because God pronounces them that they come into being.

But the Fourth Gospel goes one step further. It tells us that this Word that was in the beginning, this Word that is the creative power of God through which all things are made, "became flesh and lived among us, and we have seen his glory" (John 1:14). This is what we mean when we claim that Jesus is "the incarnate Word of God" or "the Word made flesh."

Therefore, when the fishermen by the Sea of Galilee were approached by Jesus, they were not being approached just by a teacher or even just by a miracle worker. They were being approached by the Word through whom all things are made. And when Jesus spoke to them and called them, the power in that calling was the same power that called light out of darkness and all being out of nothingness. Why can Jesus call the young girl from the land of the dead and Lazarus from beyond the tomb? Because the voice that is calling the girl and the man into life is the same voice that called them into being in the first place!

That is also the answer to a question that puzzled me when, as a young boy, I first heard this story. Matthew does not say a word about Simon, Andrew, and the rest having met Jesus before. The first time we meet them in the Gospel, Jesus tells them to follow. And they do! This always puzzled me because, among other things, I had repeatedly been warned not to follow strangers. And even after I grew up, it puzzled me; for Jesus gave them no reason to follow or to obey. He simply told them. Why, then, did they go with him?

The answer, at least in part, lies in the identity of the one who speaks. The one who speaks is the Word through whom all things were made. The one who speaks is the Word who says, "Let there be light"; and suddenly there is light! Therefore, when Jesus calls Simon and Andrew and James and John and us, he is not just issuing an invitation or even a commandment; he is creating a new reality!

That is also why, in calling Simon and his brother Andrew, Jesus has the power not only to persuade them to follow him but also to redefine and recreate their lives. Up to this point they have been fishing for fish; now they will become fishers of people. The same Word who calls the world from nothingness into being and Lazarus from death to life calls Simon and Andrew from fishing for fish to fishing for people. When God calls, God creates. When Jesus calls these four, he also makes them something they were not before. Eventually, he will even tell one of these, volatile and unstable

11

Simon, that he is to be called Peter, which in Greek means "rock"; for he is to become like a rock. And Peter the Rock he became!

Most of the time, when I call a friend on the telephone, I just want to kill time and chat for a while. At other times, I have some information to share or a favor to ask. But when Jesus calls, things happen! His very calling is also an act of creating. He not only calls us to be something, he also provides us with the power to be what we are called to be.

The Price of the Call

Still, that does not make it easy for those whom Jesus calls. The first thing that happens in the text we are studying is that these four follow him. But in order to follow him, they have to leave certain things behind. The first two, Peter and Andrew, leave their nets; and the other two, James and John, leave their father and their boat. Although these men have not yet been told where Jesus is going, it is clear that the call to follow means that he is going somewhere; and it is impossible to go somewhere and to stay put at the same time. These four have to make a decision, and every decision implies both a positive side—in this case, following Jesus—and a negative side— in this case, leaving nets, boat, and father. They cannot follow Jesus and remain by the Sea of Galilee. They cannot become fishers of people and remain fishers of fish. Not that there is anything intrinsically bad about the Sea of Galilee or about fishing as an occupation. But at that time and in those circumstances, to follow Jesus required abandoning accustomed place and occupation. In order to follow Jesus, they had to give up things that under other circumstances would be considered good and valuable.

A theme that appears repeatedly in the history of Christian devotion is that of renunciation—of giving up things and comforts in order to become a better follower of Jesus and his way. Much of the monastic tradition is built on the discipline of renunciation, to the point that eventually renunciation was seen as a virtue in and of itself. At times, this ideal of renunciation even led to cruelty both to oneself and to others. There was, for instance, the legend of Alexis, a moderately wealthy man who supposedly left his family to become a beggar. When he returned home, he had been so changed by his new style of life that even his relatives did not recognize him. According to the legend, he spent the rest of his days begging at the door of his own house. It was not until after his death that his family discovered who the old beggar at their door was. Clearly, the legend of Alexis, and many others like it, turned renunciation into what it is not supposed to be, as if there were something particularly Christlike in punishing oneself—and in the case of Alexis, those around him—with no other purpose than the punishment itself. For that reason, the language of renunciation has become unpopular in many Christian circles, to the point that we hardly use it today.

And yet, there is a sense in which renunciation is the necessary result of the call from Jesus. When Jesus called Peter and the other fishermen, they had to give up their nets, their boats, their family, and their way of life. There was a task to be done, there was a call to heed, and anything that could impede their following Jesus had to be left behind.

A more contemporary way of saying this is that those whom Jesus calls must be prepared to travel light. Inexperienced travelers often pack much more than they will need, or could even use, during their trip. One sees them at airports, train stations, and tourist spots with so much baggage that their luggage, instead of helping them and supporting them during their travel, becomes a hindrance. If their hotel is only a block away from the train station, they still must take a taxi. When they arrive at their hotel, they must spend hours unpacking; and they must spend hours packing when they prepare to leave.

A common consequence of not learning to travel light is that traveling becomes so cumbersome that many such travelers decide that they would rather stay at home. They do not want to spend a week packing suitcases and trunks and then cart them halfway across the world. It is much easier to stay home and read a book or watch a video about faraway places.

Quite often the reason for carrying such excessive luggage is that these travelers want to travel and stay home at the same time. They want to visit new places and have new experiences, but they also want things to be just as they are at home. It is almost as if they need to take with them as much of their customary environment as they can. But the result is that, precisely because they take so much of their home with them, they see and experience less of the places they visit. Some look for hotels that offer as much "comfort" as possible—which to them means hotels that are as much like home as possible.

In some cases, the less thoughtful travelers take with them things that are quite inappropriate for their destination. They are going to a tropical island, for instance; but they pack a suitcase with fur coats, simply because they like them and do not wish to leave them behind. Or they are going to a place where the voltage is different than at home; but they take with them hair driers, small TV sets, irons, and a host of other electrical appliances.

Most of the things in such travelers' luggage are not necessarily bad. On the contrary, their baggage probably contains many things that are good and that make life easier and more enjoyable at home. The problem is that what is a help at home may be a hindrance on the road.

That is the reason Simon, Andrew, James, and John must abandon their nets. In and of themselves, nets are good. They provide food and livelihood. But in this case these four men cannot follow Jesus unless they leave their nets behind. To carry their nets with them would make no sense. The nets would be a constant hindrance. And they would be completely useless along the roads of Galilee and Judea—like expensive fur coats on a tropical beach. And the boat! Can you imagine them trying to cart a fishing boat up and down the roads of Galilee?

This is what true renunciation is all about. It is not about punishing ourselves by depriving ourselves of this or that comfort. It is not about suffering for the sake of suffering. It is about traveling light on the road with Jesus. It is about leaving behind those things that will become a hindrance or that will be entirely inappropriate for the path we are taking.

Again, those things that must be left behind are not necessarily bad things. On the contrary, some of them may be quite good in their proper setting. Think of Dr. Albert Schweitzer, a renowned organist who in order to go to Africa as a medical missionary had to leave behind the organ on which he practiced, as well as his musical career. The organ was not bad. His music was not bad. But the climate in the place where he was going was such that an organ would not last. So, in order to follow his calling as a missionary, Schweitzer left behind his career as an organist—much as Simon and the rest left their nets, their boat, and even their family.

Obviously, it is quite possible to call oneself a Christian, even to become convinced that one is indeed a Christian, without having to relinquish much. All through the ages, there have been many such Christians. In fact, at one time or another, we have all been, or still are, such Christians. We wish to enter through the narrow gate while encumbered with all sorts of unnecessary baggage. We wish to take the narrow road but not the bumps that go with it. The problem is that when this is the nature of our Christian pilgrimage, we are like tourists who hope to see the world yet still make sure that everywhere they go is exactly like home. Or even worse, we are like travelers who are content with seeing the world through the slide shows of others.

Dietrich Bonhoeffer has put this matter quite clearly:

> If we would follow Jesus we must take certain definite steps. The first step, which follows the call, cuts the disciple off from his previous existence. The call to follow at once produces a new situation. To stay in the old situation makes discipleship impossible. Levi must leave the receipt of custom and Peter his nets in order to follow Jesus. One would have thought that nothing so drastic was necessary at such an early stage. . . . The call to follow implies that there is only one way of believing on Jesus Christ, and that is by leaving all and going with the incarnate Son of God.[1]

The Process of the Call

Bonhoeffer's words come from a passage in which he is arguing the double proposition that in order to obey, one has to believe; and in order to believe, one has to obey. The first proposition is often preached in our Protestant churches, for it matches the fundamental Protestant teaching that salvation is by faith rather than by works. Bonhoeffer has no objection to that. But he does object to the corollary often drawn from that premise, that it is possible to believe without obeying or that the relationship between faith and obedience is such that one must first believe and can obey only after believing. What Bonhoeffer argues, quite convincingly, is that the opposite is also true: Faith requires obedience just as much as obedience requires faith.

This sounds rather abstract, but it is in fact a quite practical consideration. Often, we find it difficult to believe because our own disobedience stands in the way. Furthermore, we use our genuine and sincere unbelief as an excuse for a disobedience that we find quite attractive or convenient. As long as we lack faith, we are exonerated; for there really is nothing we can do to have more faith. Thus, by blaming our poor relationship with God on our lack of faith and not on our lack of obedience, we in fact place the blame on God and feel quite justified in going on along our merry way.

Examples abound, even in our own lives. You suspect or even know that God wants you to do something for which you do not feel quite ready. Perhaps it is a new calling. Perhaps it is a financial sacrifice. Perhaps it requires risking some of your security. You tell yourself, *If I had enough faith, I would make that sacrifice*; or, *If I had enough faith, I would give up my career to do this other thing to which God is calling me. But,* you continue, *I just don't have the faith it takes. I must wait until God gives me enough faith to quit my job or to launch this new career or to make that costly sacrifice.* Naturally, what then happens is that we wait on God to give us faith; and meanwhile we are quite content to do nothing. In such situations the lack of obedience is a hindrance to faith, and we will not be able truly to believe until we obey. In my own experience my greatest shortcomings have not been related to faith but to obedience, and then I have seen my faith weaken and shrink because of my disobedience.

Look again at the call of Simon and the other fishermen. Jesus tells them to follow him. Because they have faith in him, they obey. But had they decided not to obey, that in itself would have hampered their faith. They obeyed because they believed, but it is also true that they believed because they obeyed. The two—faith and obedience—go together; and one cannot exist without the other. This is the point that the Letter of James makes: "So faith by itself, if it has no works, is dead" (James 2:17).

Thus, we would err were we to think that there is a necessary chronological sequence in which first comes belief and then comes obedience. Again, because this is belief in the Word who created all things, it is belief that by its very nature produces action. When Christ is formed in us, he is formed in the heart as much as in the mind, in attitudes as well as in ideas, in action as well as in belief.

Given this understanding of faith and works, there are at least two things we must say about the process of God's call. The first is that the call does not always come to us in private. In the passage we are studying, Jesus called Simon and Andrew together and then John and James, also together. Jesus calls not only individuals but also groups of people, couples, churches. And, even when the call refers specifically to individuals, it does not always come directly to them but may also come through the community of faith. Look, for instance, at Acts 13:1-3, where the call to Barnabas and Saul comes through a community of faith, which then acknowledges their call and commissions them.

The second is that the call does not come once and for all. Since we have just mentioned the apostle Paul, look at his story in the Book of Acts. What happens on the road to Damascus is dramatic indeed; but all that he is told at the time is that he is to go on to Damascus, where he will be told what to do. In Damascus, Ananias tells him something about the faith; and he is baptized. But it is much later, when Paul is in Antioch, that he is called to be a missionary. Still later, Paul receives the call to go on to Macedonia. And so on.

These two truths are important for us today as we seek to be obedient to our call. The first truth means that we must look not only to our own inner conviction but also to the guidance of our community of faith, the church, to help us determine what we are being called to do. The second truth means that the call does not end with conversion or even with a career choice. The call comes to us repeatedly, perhaps even daily, as we seek to discern and to do God's will for our lives.

The Promise of the Call

All the emphasis on obedience may make it seem that the call is a burdensome obligation, something we must do or else. But we must also remember that the One who calls is also the One who creates. When Jesus calls, he not only demands; he also gives. He does not tell Simon and Andrew that they must become fishers of humans; he tells them that he will make them such. Later, he does not tell Simon that he must be strong as a rock; he simply tells him, "You are Peter, and on this rock I will build my church" (Matthew 16:18); and, by the power of the Spirit, Jesus makes Peter what he has called him.

In another passage (John 15:15), Jesus tells his disciples that he has called them "friends." This is not just a change in the mode of address. It is a change in the nature of the relationship between Jesus and his disciples. And therefore it is also a change in who they are. All through the Bible and throughout the history of the church, we find instances in which God's call not only tells someone to do something new but also makes something new out of that person. Think, for instance, of the call to Abram (Genesis 12:1-3), a call that will eventually make him Abraham, the father of many nations. Or think of the call of Moses (Exodus 3:1-12), which will make him the liberator of an entire nation. In the New Testament and later in the history of the church, the number of those called is legion. Indeed, the number of those who have been transformed by God's call is exactly the same as the number of those who have heeded that call; for it is impossible to heed the call without being transformed by it.

17

To be called by Jesus is not a burden but a promise; not an obligation, but a gift; not just a challenge, but the beginning of a new reality. The call is a means whereby Jesus is being formed in us and we in him. Just as the eternal Word of God, pronouncing my name, called me from nothingness into being, so does the same Word, now incarnate in Jesus, make Jesus be born in me and I in him.

The Purpose of the Call

In the story of the calling of Simon and the rest, notice also that Jesus calls them in order that they may call others. They are to follow Jesus so that in turn they may call others to follow. In a sense, we can say that Jesus goes fishing for them so that they in turn will then go fishing for others. The story that begins with the calling of Peter and Andrew leads in the end to Luke 24:48: "You are witnesses of these things." In other words, these two—as well as the rest—are called in order to call.

Jesus summons us to summon others. Our calling others implies two things. It implies, first of all, inviting them to follow the One whom we follow. This is the obvious meaning of the words *to call*. We call others, as Jesus called Simon and Andrew, James and John; and we tell them, as Jesus also has told them, "Follow." Naturally, we do not tell them to follow us but rather to follow the Jesus whom we too follow. And thus the throng grows, as it has through the centuries, of "saints from every tribe and language and people and nation" (Revelation 5:9).

But there is a second dimension to our calling others. Our words are not nearly as powerful as the Word of God, but they too have power to create and to shape reality. Made after the divine image, we too have the power of word, the power of naming. That is the significance of the story in Genesis telling how all the animals were brought before Adam and he named them (Genesis 2:18-19). By naming them, he claimed power over them. (Note also that when the woman is brought before him, he does not give her a name. On the contrary, he recognizes her as bone of his bones and therefore shares his name with her, although in the feminine form [Genesis 2:20-22]. It is only after the Fall, and as a result of sin, that we are told that the man named his wife Eve [Genesis 3:20].) Even today, we still have the power to name; and by naming, we have the power to define and shape.

18

That is why in 1 Peter 3:9 there is a connection between blessing and calling: "Do not repay evil for evil or abuse for abuse; but, on the contrary, repay with a blessing. It is for this that you were called—that you might inherit a blessing." In order to understand this passage and the connection between calling and blessing, it is important to point out that the words translated here as "abuse" and "blessing" literally mean "speak evil" and "speak good"—much as in English "malediction" and "benediction" or in Spanish *maldecir* and *bendecir*. In other words, the contrast here is between speaking evil and speaking good, between pronouncing a word of evil over someone and pronouncing a word of good.

We often underestimate the power of our words. It is not true that although "sticks and stones can break my bones," words can do no real damage. That is one of the reasons why when a child is about to be born to us, we take so much care in deciding the name he or she will bear for his or her entire life. In my own case, my parents gave me a name that means "just," "fair," "righteous." It is also a name that was borne by my father and by my grandfather before him. I certainly have not lived up to that name; but still it has shaped my understanding of myself, and it has influenced the manner in which I have sought to live my life. This is so much the case that I can hardly conceive of myself with a different name; and if I had been given a different name, I am certain my life would have been different—whether better or worse, I do not know, but certainly different.

For similar reasons, we speak not only of physical abuse but also of verbal abuse. A parent who constantly says to a child that the child is no good may well be issuing a self-fulfilling prophecy. Words can certainly hurt as much as any stick or stone. And, just as a stick or a stone can produce a misshapen body, so can words produce a twisted soul. There are increasing tendencies in our day to use the power of words unwisely, to promote hatred and prejudice even over the airwaves, and then to plead surprise when such words result in violence and death.

Words can also heal. That is why Jesus often accompanied his miracles of healing with the even more miraculous words "Your sins are forgiven." That is also why there is so much power in words such as "I forgive you," "I love you," "It's all right," and "God loves you." That is why we are commanded to bless rather than to curse—to "speak good" rather than to "speak evil."

This does not mean that we must always be "nice" to everybody.

Jesus was not. When necessary, he was ready to speak harsh words. But he spoke them in love, seeking to create a new and better reality. Being nice just for the sake of avoiding conflict and difficulties is actually to ignore the significance and the reality of the other. To love means to take seriously, and taking seriously involves speaking truthfully.

If we are to call others, we must recover a sense of the power of words. Our capacity of speech is part of our being in the image of the One who spoke the light, and there was light. We have been given the power of words by the power of the Word. We must use this power wisely, as a great gift from the Giver of every good gift.

The first thing to be said about the ministry of Jesus is that it is a ministry of the Word. It is a ministry of the Word because he is the Word. It is also a ministry of the Word because it is a ministry of calling. Because Jesus has called us, we are called to call others. To call them to follow him and to call them with new names of blessing help create a new reality in them, in each one of us, and in the entire community; *for Christ lives in us and is being formed in us.*

---

[1] From *The Cost of Discipleship,* by Dietrich Bonhoeffer (Macmillan, 1963); pages 66-67.

20

CHAPTER 2
Praying

He was praying in a certain place, and after he had finished, one of his disciples said to him, "Lord, teach us to pray, as John taught his disciples." He said to them, "When you pray, say:

> Father, hallowed be your name.
>> Your kingdom come.
>> Give us each day our daily bread.
> And forgive us our sins,
>> for we ourselves forgive
>>> everyone indebted to us.
> And do not bring us to the time of trial."

And he said to them, "Suppose one of you has a friend, and you go to him at midnight and say to him, 'Friend, lend me three loaves of bread; for a friend of mine has arrived, and I have nothing to set before him.' And he answers from within, 'Do not bother me; the door has already been locked, and my children are with me in bed; I cannot get up and give you anything.' I tell you, even though he will not get up and give him anything because he is his friend, at least because of his persistence he will get up and give him whatever he needs.

"So I say to you, Ask, and it will be given you; search, and you will find; knock, and the door will be opened for you. For everyone who asks receives, and everyone who searches finds, and for everyone who knocks, the door will be opened. Is there anyone among you who, if your child asks for a fish, will give a snake instead of a fish? Or if the child asks for an egg, will give a scorpion? If you then, who are evil, know how to give good gifts to your children, how much more will the heavenly Father give the Holy Spirit to those who ask him!" (Luke 11:1-13)

Jesus at Prayer

Jesus prayed. And he urged his disciples to pray. This is a fitting subject to follow our discussion on the call; for when you stop to think of it, prayer is a form of call. It is a means whereby we call on God and a means by which God calls to us.

In this passage the eternal Word of God is praying to God. At first sight we say, "How strange!" But then we think again and say, "How beautiful!" Go back to the first few verses of the Gospel of John, which we mentioned in Chapter 1. In those verses we learn that "in the beginning was the Word" and also that "the Word was with God, and the Word was God." This means that from the very beginning, and eternally, God speaks, God pronounces the Word. And who is there to hear it, except God? To speak of the eternal Word of God means that the nature of God is such that there is an eternal conversation within the Godhead, that is, within the Trinity. I do not know all that this means and certainly will not try to explain it. But at the least it means that speaking and hearing—in other words, communicating and loving—is at the heart of God. To say that there is an eternal Word of God is to say that God can speak to God, that God can be love and loving, even apart from creation. And this in turn means that the ultimate reality beyond all transient realities is conversation, communication, love.

Thus the conversation begun before all ages continues now in Galilee; for Jesus is at prayer, speaking to God, listening to God. The Word that spoke and said, "Let there be light," the Word that called Simon and Andrew, is now calling on God.

What is surprising is that Jesus goes to "a certain place" (Luke 11:1) and apparently sets aside a certain time for prayer. We might imagine that, being who he was and having such unique communion with God, he did not need to set aside a time or a place for prayer. But he did set aside a time and place, thereby undermining the position of those who claim that we do not need to pray at specific times or places because, after all, our lives should be a constant prayer.

When we stop to think about it, Jesus's practice makes sense. If you really love someone, you set aside time to be with that person. That does not mean that the rest of the time you are not in love or that you forget your beloved. It means simply that, precisely out of love, you wish to spend time together. Likewise, the more you love God, the more you will want to set aside a time to be with God, not out of obligation or even out of a desire to foster your communion with God, but simply out of a sense of love and devotion.

* * * * * *

Teach Us to Pray

At any rate, the disciples see Jesus at prayer and ask him to teach them how to pray. (Or rather, one of them asks him to teach them; and he teaches all of them.)

Responding to the disciple's request, Jesus taught them an actual prayer (what we now call "The Lord's Prayer," or in some circles the "Our Father") and also taught them certain things about prayer. Let us look first at the Lord's Prayer.

What we have here is Luke's version of the Lord's Prayer—one of two versions that appear in the New Testament. As we compare it with Matthew's version (Matthew 6:9-13), it is clear that, although Matthew's version is slightly longer, it actually adds nothing new to Luke's; it simply expands the meaning of what is said in fewer words in Luke.

In Matthew's version God is to be addressed as "Our Father in heaven." This means that the prayer can never be purely and absolutely individual. (The same is true of Luke's version, although there the plural form of the pronouns is less clear in English.) Whenever we say these words, we are addressing, not only "my Father," but even more "our Father." Even if you are alone, you are addressing God as part of a larger community of God's children. That may be the congregation with whom you are praying. It may be the entire church. It may be all God's creatures, both living and inanimate. But it is never you alone, by yourself, as if the rest of the world did not exist.

Thus, the Lord's Prayer is not only petition, it is also intercession; and this should be the model for all our prayers. Note that throughout the entire prayer, we are not told even once to pray in the singular. It is not, "Give *me* this day"; it is, "Give *us* [italics added] this day." It is not, "Forgive *me* my debts"; it is, "Forgive *us* [italics added] our debts." When Jesus taught his disciples to pray, he taught them to pray not only for themselves individually but also for the entire community.

In sum, the Lord's Prayer can never be prayed in absolute isolation. It is always the prayer of the community and for the community—even when you say it in the privacy of your room as part of your personal devotions.

Note also that this One to whom prayer is to be addressed is "our Father" and is "in heaven." We often miss the contrast between these two phrases. To address God as "our Father" means that God is not

23

some distant despot, some capricious and unknown deity whom we must somehow placate. There were many religions in the first century whose gods were precisely such. They were distant, capricious, and conceited, demanding that humans accommodate them by means of worship and sacrifice. But Jesus taught his disciples that God is to be addressed as "our Father"—not as some tyrannical and feared taskmaster, but as a beloved parent. Later on in the passage we are studying, Jesus will explain more fully what that means. For the present, it suffices to underscore that this God is as approachable as our own parents—indeed, even more so!

But then there is the other side of the coin. This beloved Father is "in heaven." We should not read these words as a mere matter of location, as if saying that "heaven" is God's address. Rather, it is an affirmation of the divine majesty. "Heaven" is the highest place known. It is so high above us that it is unattainable. There is no way we could climb up to heaven. And those who try it will be confused and confounded—witness the story of the tower of Babel (Genesis 11). To say that God is "in heaven" is another way of saying that God's majesty is above our highest dream and reach. Both in Matthew and in Luke, this divine majesty is stressed in the phrase, "Hallowed be your name." God's name is to be hallowed or honored because it stands above every other name, high above earth and all our doings, as far above them as heaven is above earth.

Thus the phrase "our Father in heaven" involves a profoundly mysterious yet fundamental paradox: The God whom we can and must approach as "our Father" is also the God whom we must approach with fear and trembling, as the One in heaven, high and exalted above the furthest reaches of our imagination. Both aspects are equally important, and each becomes even more important because of the other. The beauty and the joy of being able to address God as Parent comes from the fact that the One above all is precisely the One whom we address with trust and familiarity. Conversely, this loving Parent is also God most high, creator and ruler of all, who dwells in highest heaven.

The significance of this paradox becomes clearer as we look at the next petition in the Lord's Prayer: "Your kingdom come." This has long been the prayer of Christians. Yet it is a prayer that we utter both with joy and with trepidation. Imagine that you are the heir of a great king, one who for whatever reason has not yet come into his own. As that king's heir you will eagerly await the day when he is crowned and all will obey him. Since you know him as your father, you are convinced that he will be a good king and that the realm will be happy under him. At the same time, however, you know that he is a just person, high above the narrow favoritism of lesser rulers. Therefore he will not look kindly on many of your own interests, which from the perspective of the total welfare of the realm look petty and selfish. When you hear that your father is about to gain the throne, you will rejoice; but when you remember that you have not always lived up to his high standards and that his reign will probably change much of your life, you will also shudder.

I can think of a similar example from my own experience as a young boy in school. My mother was the principal. She was a loving mother; my brother and I could approach her openly at any time with any concerns or needs we had. At school she also emphasized the need for discipline, order, professionalism, and hard work—to such a point that she turned the school into one of the best in the city. My brother and I understood the difference between those two roles, to the extent that my mother frequently remarked that not once had either of us ever called her "Mom" in school (or "Señora" out of school). Yet the two roles were together in a single person. As a result, this meant that when I was sent to the principal's office, I went with a curiously divided attitude. On the one hand, I probably feared her more than any of the other students did. For one thing, she knew me better than she knew the others. For another, it was certain that whatever the reason for my visit, it would impact my life well after the bell sounded at the end of the school day. And for a third, I knew that I could not fool her with a story about how the dog had eaten my homework or with any other such excuse. But at the same time, I went with a strange sense of confidence. After all, this was no stranger; this was my mother. I knew her. I knew that she was fair and that she loved me. Her judgment would probably be harsh, but under its harshness there would always be an underlying love that would not fail—a fact that made her judgment ever more painful. I remember that I would always hesitate at the door. She was my mother . . . ; but she was also the principal!

In a similar way, Christians throughout the centuries have been ambivalent about their prayer, "Your kingdom come." You probably have read about all kinds of groups that have prayed and hoped for the prompt return of Jesus. There are many such groups even in our time. In a way, we too pray for that when we say, "Your kingdom come." But it is also true that there has always been among Christians the tendency to hope that the end will be delayed—at least just a bit. In the second century there were churches praying "for the delay of the end" so they could put their own house in order and preach to as many people as possible. And even today, even while we pray, "Your kingdom come," most of us are hoping that it will not be right away.

We feel this way because we are calling for the reign of "our Father," but this is also the One who is "in heaven." God's reign, for which we yearn, is a reign of peace and justice. We all want that. But we also know that in the meantime, many of us benefit from the injustice in the world. Just to give one example, most of us are probably among the 40% of the world's population that receives 94.4% of the world's income, with the other 60% receiving 5.6%. That is certainly a condition contrary to what we call for when we pray, "Your kingdom come." Therefore, while we certainly yearn for the day when God will reign over all, we also know that such a day will require radical changes in our own lives; and we are not certain that we really want it just now.

The prayer that Jesus taught his disciples continues with a petition that is not for that day when God's reign will come but is rather for today, right now: "Give us each day our daily bread" (Luke 11:3). This is clearer in Matthew's version: "Give us *this day* [italics added] our daily bread" (Matthew 6:11). This is not, strictly speaking, a prayer about the coming reign of God. It is a prayer about today, about bread today, and about the possibility of hunger today.

But it is also a prayer about God's reign, for the phrase "our daily bread" strictly means the right measure that is necessary for life. A similar phrase appears in Proverbs 30:8b-9:

> Give me neither poverty nor riches;
> feed me with the food that I need,
> or I shall be full, and deny you,
> and say "Who is the LORD?"
> or I shall be poor, and steal,
> and profane the name of my God.

God's reign is one in which all will be fed, and each will have the just and necessary portion. Thus, when praying that God give us "our daily bread," we are also asking that at least in this regard God's reign may begin to be manifested and experienced among us.

In a way, the same is true of the petition about forgiveness. Here too the disciples are to ask for forgiveness but are also to commit

26

themselves to live as citizens and subjects of God's reign. God's reign is one of forgiveness, and on that basis we ask to be forgiven and commit ourselves to be forgiving.

The prayer (at least in Luke's version) ends with a request not to be brought to "the time of trial." This may mean several things; but most likely it is a petition not to be tempted or tested—perhaps even a recognition of our own frailty—for we fear we will be unable to withstand severe testing. In this regard, remember Peter's self-assured reply that he would never abandon Jesus and how he discovered that, in spite of his resolve, he was unable to stand at "the time of trial." Thus, the prayer that begins with the word of assurance, "Father," ends with a recognition that, like small children, those who pray still need the constant protection and support of the parent and are ultimately unable to stand on their own. Indeed, this last petition reminds us of children telling their parent that they are not ready to face the trial of walking alone and still need the parent to accompany them and hold their hand.

Finally, note once again that the entire prayer is in the plural. It is not "I" who prays; it is "we." Even when I pray, I come before God as a member of this great household of the family of God, as part of the vast "we" who can call God *our* parent. Again, this is both a prayer of petition and a prayer of intercession.

Beyond the Formula

This prayer, however, was not all that Jesus offered in response to the unnamed disciple's request for a lesson on prayer. Having given him or her, as well as the rest, what could be understood as a model prayer, or even as a formula to be repeated again and again, Jesus went on to teach them more about prayer. And he did this first of all by a parable and then by a series of everyday examples.

In order to understand the parable, we must note first of all that Jesus places the disciples at a specific place in the parable. Other parables give us the option of seeing ourselves, for instance, as the prodigal or as his brother, as the good Samaritan or as the man who was robbed. Here, however, Jesus places his hearers at a particular place in the story: "Suppose one of you has a friend, and you go to him at midnight and say to him, 'Friend, lend me three loaves of bread; for a friend of mine has arrived, and I have nothing to set before him.'" In other words, the disciple is caught between two friends. One is a traveler who has arrived, apparently unexpectedly, late at night. The other is a neighbor who is already asleep, with the door locked, in bed with his family. One has no bread and is counting on the disciple's hospitality. The other has bread, but the disciple must abuse his hospitality in order to get it for his visiting friend.

In other words, there is a sort of "chain of friendship" with three characters: A, B, and C. A is the visiting friend. C is the friend already in bed. And B is the disciple, caught between the two. Apparently, A does not know C. In any case, it is to the home of B that A comes; and therefore B (the disciple, you) finds himself in the difficult situation of having to find bread for A. The laws of hospitality require that he receive A in his home and feed him. But B has no bread. (It is probably not just, as we would imagine today, that the supermarket is closed. It is also that, among poor people such as the majority of Jesus' disciples, extra bread was difficult to come by. Remember the petition, "Give us each day our daily bread.") His only alternative is to go to C, who is already in bed, and ask him to get up and provide him the bread he needs for his other friend.

This point is followed by a series of words and examples, assuring the disciples that God does answer prayer. They are encouraged to ask, search, and knock, in the assurance that these activities lead to receiving, finding, and having the door opened. Then, in two more examples, Jesus talks about a child asking its parent for a fish or for an egg, certain that it will not receive a snake or a scorpion. And the parable ends with the ultimate assurance, based on the title for God with which the Lord's Prayer begins, "If you then, who are evil, know how to give good gifts to your children, how much more will the heavenly Father give the Holy Spirit to those who ask him!"

When we read the parable of the three friends and the words that follow, immediately after the Lord's Prayer, it is clear that these words do not mean that God will give us whatever we ask for if we simply insist on it. In the parable of the three friends, where Jesus tells the disciples that they are Friend B (the one who received unexpected company), it is equally clear that God is Friend C (the one who gets out of bed because Friend B brings his need to him). But note that Friend B does not go to C to ask for bread for himself, and he does not ask C to get out of bed because of a personal whim. He dares go to C, and even disturb him in the middle of the night, because he needs bread for Friend A.

When you look at it this way, the parable does not say, as we often think, that if we want something badly enough and keep asking God for it, God will give it to us. Nor do the words that follow urge us to "ask" for anything we please, with the promise that it will be given to us, or to "knock" at any door for whatever reason, with the expectation that it will be opened before us. The parable urges us rather, as disciples, as the "friend" who received an unexpected guest, to ask in behalf of the other, to knock for the other, so that the other might have bread and hospitality.

Today's disciples live in a world in which there are many who lack even their daily bread. Daily we pray, "Give us each day our daily bread." What the prayer and the parable mean is, not that if we ask for a Cadillac, God will give it to us, but that if we truly get up in the middle of the night (that is, make our every effort) out of concern for the needy guests and go to God with the pain of our inability to feed them, God will grant what we ask.

God granting this prayer is a greater miracle than God bestowing a Cadillac or a fur coat. This is the miracle of finding solutions and hope for a world in which there often seem to be no solutions and no hope. This is the miracle of seeing "your kingdom come" before our very eyes. This is the miracle of being able to forgive those who are indebted to us (including particularly the poor who cannot pay) in the knowledge that this is but a poor reflection of all we have been forgiven. It is for this that we pray when we say, "Our Father in heaven, hallowed be your name."

But note above all what it is that Jesus promises to those who ask (Luke 11:13): the Holy Spirit. God's greatest gift is the Holy Spirit. And what does the Spirit do but teach us what to do and what to ask for and give us the faith to continue doing it and asking for it? Jesus does not promise a rose garden, ease of life, success, or money. What Jesus promises is God's greatest gift: the Holy Spirit by which we may be attuned to the purposes of God, asking what God wants us to ask, which is what in fact is best for us.

Prayer is a significant aspect of the ministry of Jesus. It is also a significant aspect of our ministry as disciples of Jesus. If you try to be a true disciple, and therefore to be a friend to the world, you will often be caught in a difficult situation. Like the man who received unexpected guests, you will know that it is your obligation to do something for another; and yet you will not have the resources to do so. But you have a friend—or rather, a Parent—whose resources are much greater than you can imagine and who is never asleep with the door closed. What this parable tells us is that in such situations you can go to this friend and ask, with the full assurance that it will be given to you.

There is a famous story of a porter in one of the nation's major railroad stations. He had little education and no money. But, apparently, he had read this parable and taken it to heart. It is said that every time he was asked to carry someone's bags, he prayed that he would have the right word to say to that particular person. Over the years he received an enormous number of letters from people from all walks of life, all letting him know that the words he had said to them had become a turning point in their lives or had provided a word of wisdom or encouragement that they needed. This man knew that he had little to give of himself—much like the friend caught off guard by an unexpected guest. But he also knew where to go to ask for what he lacked. As a result, he was able to make a significant contribution to a vast number of people whose lives he briefly touched but touched deeply.

This porter's ministry is part of the ministry to which Jesus calls all his disciples. It is the ministry of asking for power, not for ourselves, but that we might empower others. It is the ministry of asking for daily bread, not only for ourselves, but for an entire famished world. It is the ministry of taking the needs of Friend A—a world in need of bread, justice, peace, and love—to the great and unequaled Friend C—our Parent who is in heaven!

But prayer is also asking for ourselves. We need to ask for ourselves because we must constantly remember that without God we can do nothing. No matter how wealthy you are, you must ask every day for your daily bread as a reminder not to trust in your wealth. No matter how healthy or how ill you are, you need to pray for your health as a reminder that your body and your life are a gift from God and are ultimately in God's hands. And no matter how devout you are, you must ask for God's greatest gift, the Holy Spirit.

In the last verse of our text, the matter of asking for the Holy Spirit leads us to another aspect of prayer, often forgotten in our modern activism. We moderns are so accustomed to doing, to being constantly active, that we tend to reduce even prayer to an activity. We think that we are praying only when we are talking to God, when we are expressing our needs, our gratitude, our hopes. But prayer also occurs when we are silent before the mystery and the power and the beauty of God, letting God speak to us. Being a good conversationalist is not only knowing what to say; it is also knowing when and how to listen. The discipline of prayer is not only talking to God. It is also letting God do the talking. It is even the discipline of developing such communion with God that, like two friends or two lovers, we can just sit quietly together in each other's company, allowing for the time when a word may be necessary, but also enjoying the mystery of silence. It is letting the Holy Spirit of God come and dwell in us so that when the time comes for asking, we will know what to ask for.

Finally, remember that the Lord's Prayer is in the plural form; that is, it is the whole church that prays "*Our* Father." It is the whole church that is called to be Friend B, bringing the world's needs to Friend C, who also happens to be the Most High. It is the whole church that must engage in the ministry of prayer as Jesus taught us to pray so that the world may have its daily bread and so that God's kingdom may come. This is what is meant by "the priesthood of all believers." It is each of us, and all of us together, that must pray the same prayer, not only for the world but also for the church, that it may be more faithful to its vocation and may more truly pray the Lord's Prayer.

Meanwhile, there is one thing you and I can and must do. We can pray as Jesus taught us to pray. We can say *our* Father even in the name of those who do not pray. We can forgive debts. We can share bread. We can pray over and over again, "Your kingdom come"; and we can insist on and persist in it *because it is Christ who lives in us.*

31

CHAPTER 3
Feeding

After this Jesus went to the other side of the Sea of Galilee, also called the Sea of Tiberias. A large crowd kept following him, because they saw the signs that he was doing for the sick. Jesus went up the mountain and sat down there with his disciples. Now the Passover, the festival of the Jews, was near. When he looked up and saw a large crowd coming toward him, Jesus said to Philip, "Where are we to buy bread for these people to eat?" He said this to test him, for he himself knew what he was going to do. Philip answered him, "Six months' wages would not buy enough bread for each of them to get a little." One of his disciples, Andrew, Simon Peter's brother, said to him, "There is a boy here who has five barley loaves and two fish. But what are they among so many people?" Jesus said, "Make the people sit down." Now there was a great deal of grass in the place; so they sat down, about five thousand in all. Then Jesus took the loaves, and when he had given thanks, he distributed them to those who were seated; so also the fish, as much as they wanted. When they were satisfied, he told his disciples, "Gather up the fragments left over, so that nothing may be lost." So they gathered them up, and from the fragments of the five barley loaves, left by those who had eaten, they filled twelve baskets. When the people saw the sign that he had done, they began to say, "This is indeed the prophet who is to come into the world." (John 6:1-14)

Jesus Practices What He Preaches

The story is well-known, particularly since there are parallel passages in every one of the other three Gospels. However, reading this passage immediately after the one from Luke 11 (see Chapter 2) makes some interesting connections stand out. For one thing, Jesus finds himself in a similar position to the man in the parable of the three friends who suddenly had to provide for an unexpected guest. In that parable (Luke 11:5-8) Jesus told his disciples that they were like a man who, when an unexpected guest arrives, has to run to a friend and ask for bread to feed the visitor. Here, he looks at the horizon and sees many unexpected guests—five thousand of them!

Like the man in his own parable, Jesus has nothing with which to feed them. Yet he acknowledges the law of hospitality: These people must be fed; and, since they came to see him, it is his responsibility to feed them. That is what he indirectly tells Philip, who is quick to point out the difficulty: Even if there were a place to buy food for that many people, it would take an enormous sum to do so. Thus it is not only Jesus but also his disciples who now find themselves in the situation of the Lukan parable.

The other element that comes to mind from the passage we studied in Chapter 2 is the prayer that Jesus commended to his disciples: "Give us this day our daily bread." Studying that prayer as well as its context, we saw that the "us" is much wider than the one or two who may be praying. In praying that prayer, the disciples are to pray not only for themselves but also for all those others who call God "our Father"—and even for those others who do not acknowledge God as Parent. Now, in the passage in John, the "us" has become unexpectedly large and concrete: five thousand persons, all needing to be fed!

Jesus had an easy way out. He could have told the five thousand that he had come to offer spiritual teaching and eternal life and that therefore when it came to their material needs, they must fend for themselves. He could have preached a stirring sermon on how the soul is more important than the body, and therefore people ought not to be too concerned about food. Or he could have sent his disciples to tell the crowd to stay away because he needed to pray and should not be disturbed. Any of these excuses they would have understood; for there were at the time, just as there are now, plenty of religious teachers claiming that God is concerned only about spiritual well-being and that physical matters are secondary. Jesus could also have used the laws of purity as an excuse to stay away from the crowds. After all, as a good religious leader he was supposed to keep himself free of all uncleanness or defilement; and there were sure to be among such a crowd quite a few people who were unclean. The disciples as well as the crowd would have understood this too.

But as John's Gospel reports, Jesus did not take any of those courses of action. Instead, he took upon himself the responsibility of feeding all these people, even if they had put themselves in this predicament by coming out to see him without making provision for their needs. He did not take the easy route of establishing a sharp distinction between the spiritual and the material because that would have been untrue to the nature of God and to all that God had revealed to Israel. The God of the Bible is a God who creates "heaven and earth"—that is, the material as well as the spiritual—and sees that both are good. The God of the Bible is the God who provides a garden for Adam and Eve, the God who, when they must be expelled from the garden, furnishes them with animal skins as protection for their bodies; who feeds Israel in the wilderness; who provides rain and sun at their allotted times so that there may be harvests and creation may be fed. It would have been easy for Jesus to claim that he was only a teacher of spiritual matters and that he therefore had nothing to do with the need to feed this hungry crowd. It would have been easy, but it would have been a betrayal of his mission and his truth. So he issued instructions that the five thousand were to sit down—in other words, he welcomed them into his space, just as the man in the parable welcomed his unexpected guest and then went to look for bread.

As Christians, when we are put in a similar predicament, we are often tempted to offer the "spiritual excuse." Think, for instance, of the way many of us react when told of the problem of hunger in our own cities and throughout the world. It is obviously a problem so enormous as to be overwhelming—much like being in the middle of a field, far away from any city and with little money, and suddenly being told that five thousand unexpected guests have just arrived for dinner. If we look in our pantries and freezers, we see a few canned and frozen goods, far too little to make a dent in the hunger of such an enormous multitude of hungry people in our time—in proportion, even less than the five barley loaves and two fish that the boy had long ago. Like Jesus in that field, the church finds that its prestige as a community of love and service is at stake. What are we to do?

Too often, we do take the easy way out, pleading the "spiritual excuse." After all, we say, spiritual matters are·more important than food or shelter; therefore our real task is to preach the gospel, to save souls by bringing them to Jesus. Yes, we shall feed a few, send a bit of money to the hungry as a sign of Christian compassion; but our real task is spiritual, and we must not allow ourselves to be led astray by purely material concerns such as physical hunger.

The problem with that excuse is that Jesus himself will not allow us to get away with it. Under similar circumstances, he simply fed the five thousand—and the text does not even say that he preached to them. He did it out of compassion. But he did it also because he is the Word through whom all things are made—soul, mind, and body; sun, rain, and harvest; inquiring mind, restless spirit, and even hungry stomach. Being who he was, he could not simply plead the "spiritual excuse" and go about his business.

And the church also, being what it is and following the one whom it follows, cannot plead the "spiritual excuse" and remain faithful to its calling and its Caller. Hunger and feeding must be our concern because they are also our Lord's concern.

At other times we plead the "purity excuse." The church, so the argument goes, is the body of Christ and therefore ought to keep itself free of all impurity and contamination. It is true that there are many homeless in our town and that as Christians we should show compassion for them and do something about their predicament. But look at these homeless people. You will see that many of them are alcoholics and drug addicts; that some are violent; that when they get into an argument, they use words unfit for Christian ears and even curse God. Think of our children. We must guard them against such pollution. And think of our church. We must not allow it to be tarnished by such people. Why, in that other church they began providing shelter for the homeless; and their toilets clogged up, and they even have found needles and condoms in the bushes by the parking lot! The church must remain pure. It cannot allow itself to be befouled by such people and their dirty and unholy customs. Yes, let us show compassion. But let us not allow our compassion to render us unclean or unworthy of our good name and social prestige.

Jesus could easily have pled that excuse, for he lived in a society in which the laws of purity were considered quite important—much more important than in our day. There were laws as to what one could eat, since certain foods were considered unclean. There were laws that rendered women unclean after childbirth or at certain times during the month. There were laws that said that if one touched an unclean person or an unclean thing, one became unclean. Actually, that was one of the reasons many Jews in Jerusalem looked askance at Galileans: In Galilee there were too many Gentiles and too many opportunities to be defiled. Thus, if Jesus had pled the "purity excuse," his disciples would have understood. Even the five thousand would have understood. He could easily have kept them at a distance and still retained his standing as a prestigious religious teacher.

But that is not who Jesus is. Actually, more than once he risked and even sacrificed his religious standing and his own personal purity in order to reach out to those whom society considered unclean and even damned. Jesus saw a woman whose physical illness kept her bent down; and even though it was the sabbath and he was in the synagogue, he cured her (Luke 13:10-14). Jesus saw a dead girl; and even though touching a corpse would render him unclean, he took her hand and bid her rise from the dead (Mark 5:21-43). Jesus saw a publican collecting taxes; and even though publicans were among the most despised in that society, Jesus bid him follow (Mark 2:13-17). Jesus ate with publicans and with sinners (Matthew 9:10-13). When a woman with a hemorrhage—and therefore supposedly unclean—touched him and was healed, Jesus commended her for what she had done (Matthew 9:20-22). Jesus saw a leper and—horror of horrors—he touched him in order to heal him (Matthew 8:1-3). Not once in all his ministry did Jesus adduce the laws of purity to stay away from those in need.

So, when we as Christians plead the "purity excuse," we find ourselves in rather strange company: not with Jesus who healed the woman on the sabbath, but with the Pharisees who objected; not with Jesus who ate and drank with sinners, but with those who stayed away from such meals and then made negative comments.

In the feeding of the five thousand, Jesus passed the test of his own parable of the three friends. The one whom we have called "Friend B" would normally be tempted to tell his unexpected guest that he had nothing to give him—which was true—and leave it at that. The disciples of Jesus were constantly tempted in the same manner. But Jesus shows them, and us, another way—a way that begins by facing up to the needs of the unexpected and needy guest.

The Unworthy Poor

There are all sorts of reasons for following Jesus. In Chapter 1 we saw the story of four people who followed Jesus simply because he called them and because in his calling there was power to convince. Here we see a huge crowd following him for other reasons. "A large crowd kept following him, because they saw the signs that he was doing for the sick." It is not clear whether they followed him because they wanted him to do miracles for them, because they were curious and eager to see some more miracles, or for some other reason. What is clear is that, although they followed Jesus, they were not really his followers. They were not there to learn from Jesus, much less to allow him to transform them. Nor are we told that they had left anything in order to follow. Actually, if we go back for a moment to the subject of Chapter 1, "Calling," Jesus had not called them at all! Most likely, they simply represented one of those phenomena, so common even in our day, in which a crowd develops a passing interest in something or someone. Jesus and his miracles were the attraction of the moment, so the crowd went to see him.

Since they are not real followers of Jesus, they are not with him most of the time, like the actual disciples. They come and go; or they show up wherever they hear that Jesus is, hoping to see a miracle or some other sort of entertainment.

We are all familiar with this sort of follower, who goes along with the crowd and does not follow out of commitment. Indeed, throughout the history of the church, there have been many such followers of Jesus. And there have been many others who have felt that it was their duty to identify such lukewarm Christians, to tell them that they are not real believers, and in general to chastise them for their lack of commitment. In our day there are some who use the phrase "born again," not so much as a sign of joy for what God has done for them, but rather as a way to distinguish themselves from others who in their judgment do not have the same commitment. Over and over again, particularly on radio and television, we hear sermons casting such crowds of "lukewarm Christians" into outer darkness.

In the passage we are studying, Jesus sees a crowd coming. He knows why they are there. He is not deluded into thinking that they have come because they want to follow him or his way. Most of them are thrill seekers—actually, the same sort of person who would later go to see his crucifixion for the excitement. They are there because they have heard of Jesus' miracles, and they are curious. Jesus, however, does not ask them why they are there; he does not chastise them for trivializing him and his message. On the contrary, he immediately realizes that they will be hungry and that there is no food for them.

Thus, perhaps the most astounding thing about this story is not that Jesus fed five thousand people but who the five thousand he fed were! He did not ask whether they were worthy or really needy or just lazy people out for a holiday. He simply saw them coming and knew that they would be hungry and must be fed. And feed them he did.

In this, Jesus was quite different from some of his followers. Many of us Christians are so concerned with making sure that others are true followers of Jesus that we spend more time judging them than we do giving them signs of God's love. Specifically, when it comes to helping the needy, quite often the first question we ask is not, "What do they need?" but rather, "Are they worthy?" Typically, we distinguish between "the poor" in general and "the worthy poor." What this distinction means is that there are two kinds of poor people, some who deserve to be poor and some who do not. According to this view, those people who are poor because they do not work or because they repeatedly make bad decisions or because they are addicted to alcohol or some other drug or because they had their chance and did not make good use of it are not worthy of further help. In contrast to them are other poor people who are "worthy," and these are the ones we should help.

There are three problems with this view. The first is the minor but revealing point that the poor seem to become worthier in direct proportion to their distance from us and in reverse proportion to how much we can actually do for them. For some strange reason, the homeless in our own town do not seem to be as worthy as the homeless halfway around the world. It is almost as if salt water made the poor worthier! Yet when we stop to think about it, we must recognize the possibility that we do this, albeit unwittingly, in order not to have to deal with the poor firsthand—with the poor who, like the man in the parable, may demand our hospitality or who, like the crowd of five thousand, may bring uncleanness into our lives.

The second and most important problem with this view is that Jesus never distinguished between the poor in general and the worthy poor. He never asked the hungry why they were not working. He actively contradicted those who tried to blame a blind man for his blindness (John 9:1-3). Jesus simply saw hungry people and fed them; he saw sick people and healed them; he saw lost people and offered them salvation. If he, being who he is, did not limit his love and service to the "worthy," how dare we do otherwise?

Jerome, a Christian writer of the fourth century, pointed out the third and perhaps most compelling problem with this view. Jerome's argument, briefly stated, is that by making this distinction, we take a serious risk. Suppose, just for the sake of argument, that there are some people who are needy out of their own fault and do not "deserve" our help and compassion and some people who are needy due to circumstances beyond their control and therefore do "deserve" our help. In that case I have two options: Option A is to go about my life trying to help only those who are worthy. Option B is to try to help as many people as possible, not worrying about how worthy they are. The problem is that by following Option A, I take the serious risk of refusing to help someone I should have helped and thus risk hearing Jesus say to me at the time of the Final Judgment, "I was hungry and you did not feed me." In other words, the distinction between the worthy poor and the unworthy may well make *me* unworthy!

What Then Shall We Do?

As we look at the world today and at our place in it, we can well see ourselves in a situation similar to that of "Friend B" in the parable of the three friends or to that of Jesus when he saw the crowd approaching. There are so many hungry, so many poor, so many wretched! It is no longer a crowd of a mere five thousand but a crowd of teeming millions and more millions being born after them and still more millions. . . . No wonder, then, that we despair and sympathize with Philip's comment that even six months' wages would not begin to feed the five thousand. Today, it would take billions to feed the millions who are hungry! What can we do? What *must* we do as disciples and followers of Jesus?

The first thing Jesus did was to bid the crowd sit down. That was a gesture of welcome; and by welcoming them, it was also an act of taking responsibility. Before he had them sit down, he still had the option of sending them away. But once he welcomed them, they were his responsibility. In the same manner, the first thing that we as Christians must do is to welcome the needy and in welcoming them to claim responsibility for them. We must not send them away, pleading any of the excuses discussed above. The message we proclaim and the Lord whom we follow will not allow us to do that.

The next thing we must do is to take stock of our resources. Andrew found a boy who had five barley loaves and two fish. What do we find when we look at our resources? Obviously, we have some money, food, and other material resources. We also have among our number some whose expertise could help alleviate hunger in various ways—through better land and water management, better nutrition, better distribution of goods, and so forth. Thirdly, as people living in a democracy, we have a measure of political power; and since our democracy is probably the most powerful nation in the world, that too is a considerable asset.

When we look at all these resources, it soon becomes obvious that the problem of world hunger is not a matter of real lack of food but of poor distribution and management of resources. Indeed, some experts tell us that the world is quite capable of feeding much more than its present population—and of doing so without further damage to the environment. What we must do is prevent waste, overconsumption, mismanagement, and unequal distribution. As it has often been put, what we lack is not the resources but the political and moral will to see these resources made available to those who most urgently need them.

Even so, that is a tall order. I do not have the power to change the world economic order, which ends up funneling resources from the poor countries in the South to the richer lands in the North. I do not have the power to prevent large tracts of land in some of the poorest countries in the world from being devoted to drugs or to flowers intended for sale to the richer nations rather than to food for the people of those poorest countries. I do not have the power to order the military in a Central American nation to stop evicting peasants so that the rich can take over their lands and raise beef for export.

When I look at it this way, I become frustrated. Again, Philip's response becomes my model: It would take enormous resources, which neither I nor the church around me have.

But there is another way to look at it. I cannot be held accountable for not using power I do not have. I can only be accountable for what I do have. But for that I *must* be accountable. It may seem little, but I cannot use the excuse that what I have is not enough and therefore I am not responsible. At this point I begin feeling a little bit like Andrew, with a glimmer of hope and yet bewildered at the task before me: "There is a boy here who has five barley loaves and two fish. But what are they among so many people?" (John 6:9). I have a bit of time and money, but what are they among so many people? I have some connections through the church, and some of them can help provide better agriculture and nutrition in a few villages; but what are they in the entire world? I have some political power, and I could perhaps write a few letters and change a few laws; but what are they in a world so guided by greed?

To the question, "What are they?" there is only one possible answer: They are what I have received in order to be responsible. They are all that I have received. Therefore either I use this little that I have responsibly, or I am not responsible at all. I cannot eschew my responsibility on the grounds that I have little. What little I have, I must use to feed the hungry, clothe the naked, support the weak.

40

In concrete terms, this means I can give; I can be informed; I can vote; I can express an opinion. I must give, as John Wesley correctly said, all I can. I must be informed so that my giving may be more responsible and so that my voting and my opinions may be more faithful. I must vote, not for whatever favors my interests and my inclinations, but for whatever and whomever will best feed the hungry, clothe the naked, and provide shelter for the homeless. It is true that this is about all I *can* do, but it is also true that all this I *must* do.

In the parable of the three friends, there is a strange word (in Luke 11:8) that the New Revised Standard Version translates as "persistence" and the King James Version as "importunity." It can also be understood as "shamelessness" or "daring." The most common interpretation is that the man was rewarded because he knocked and knocked; therefore, we must keep on praying and praying until we get an answer. That may well be true, but there is another possible interpretation of that word. The man (the one whom we have called "Friend B") was daring and even shameless in that he welcomed his unexpected and uninvited guest even though he knew he could not feed him. What Friend B did that was persistent was not just going to his neighbor (actually, the text does not say that he knocked) but maintaining an attitude of welcoming Friend A, getting up for his sake, and then going and asking Friend C to provide the bread that his friend A needed.

That is the sort of persistence demanded of us Christians in the face of world hunger. First, we must have the gall to "welcome" the hungry, to ask the crowd to sit on the grass, to claim them as our responsibility. Then we must offer what we have: the bed for the unexpected guest, the few barley loaves and fish, the money in the offering plate, the vote at the polls, the letter to our U.S. Senator. Finally, we must go to Friend C; or, like Jesus, we must give thanks to God for the loaves and the fish and let God do what God wills.

We may be surprised. Our small loaves may multiply. The church's program against hunger may flourish. Our representatives in Congress may even vote to save the lives of people far away who will never have a chance to vote for them.

Meanwhile

Meanwhile, let us remember that the One who broke the barley loaves by the Sea of Galilee is also the "bread of life" (John 6:35). By the sea, he broke and offered the barley loaves and the fish. Later, on

41

Calvary, he would offer himself to be broken. At a meal on the night he was betrayed, he broke bread and gave it to his disciples, saying, "This is my body, which is given for you. Do this in remembrance of me" (Luke 22:19). Ever since, and to this day, his disciples have gathered to break bread in remembrance of him, of his death, and of his resurrection. Ever since, and to this day, his disciples have heard the calling to break bread with a world in need and, if need be, to be broken for the sake of the world.

When we gather to break bread, as Christians have done regularly through the ages, we do this in remembrance of him, inviting him to come into our lives and be our food and our salvation.

When we offer the bread and the resources we have to be broken with the world in need, feeding the hungry who have no bread, we do this in remembrance of him, proclaiming his love and his salvation to a desperate and lost world.

When we offer ourselves to be broken so that others may be fed, this too we do in remembrance of him, praying that in our giving and in their eating they might come to know the One who by giving of himself has become the Bread of Life.

This we have done. This we must continue doing *because Christ lives in us!*

CHAPTER 4
Healing

They came to Jericho. As he and his disciples and a large crowd were leaving Jericho, Bartimaeus son of Timaeus, a blind beggar, was sitting by the roadside. When he heard that it was Jesus of Nazareth, he began to shout out and say, "Jesus, Son of David, have mercy on me!" Many sternly ordered him to be quiet, but he cried out even more loudly, "Son of David, have mercy on me!" Jesus stood still and said, "Call him here." And they called the blind man, saying to him, "Take heart; get up, he is calling you." So throwing off his cloak, he sprang up and came to Jesus. Then Jesus said to him, "What do you want me to do for you?" The blind man said to him, "My teacher, let me see again." Jesus said to him, "Go; your faith has made you well." Immediately he regained his sight and followed him on the way. (Mark 10:46-52)

The Main Actors

Here again the story involves a large crowd. And here again, as in the story we considered in Chapter 3, the crowd is not particularly committed to Jesus. This time, however, they are apparently following him, at least to see what will happen next. Jesus is leaving Jericho on his way to Jerusalem, which is only fifteen miles away. Although Mark does not mention it, we can well imagine the excitement among the crowd. Jesus is headed straight for the center of religious power, which is also the ancient capital of David. What will happen there? Will he be proclaimed king of the Jews and begin the restoration of the throne of David? Will he clash with the religious and political leaders of Jerusalem? If so, will he overcome or will they? One may well picture the mixed emotions of the crowd, hoping against hope that this man will indeed prove to be the liberator of Israel and at the same time knowing that if he does not, there will still be a show worth watching.

In the midst of that crowd go also the disciples. They are the longtime followers of Jesus, who have left their nets and their boats and their tax-collecting benches in order to follow him. But they too are rather confused as to what Jesus intends and what it all will mean for them. In the verses just before this story in the Gospel of

Mark (Mark 10:35-45), there is another story, which does not show disciples James and John in a good light. They came and told Jesus that they wanted something from him. Jesus asked them what it was. They said that when Jesus came into his glory, they wanted him to give the two of them the positions of honor, one at his right and one at his left. These two men were no raw recruits; Jesus had called them immediately after calling Simon and Andrew (see Chapter 1). By this time, they should have known better!

When the other disciples heard this, they were indignant at the two brothers. Yet they too should have known better. Such serious misunderstanding on the part of their companions James and John should have been the cause of sadness, not anger. So Jesus told all of them that his disciples were to live by a different order than the Gentiles. He said, "You know that among the Gentiles those whom they recognize as their rulers lord it over them, and their great ones are tyrants over them. But it is not so among you; but whoever wishes to become great among you must be your servant, and whoever wishes to be first among you must be slave of all" (Mark 10:42-44).

One could say that the entire episode showed how blind even the disciples were. After following Jesus and hearing his teachings for so long, they still seemed to have little idea what he was all about.

Then, there is someone else amid the crowd. Strictly speaking, he is not part of the crowd; for they are moving along with Jesus, and he is just sitting there—probably sitting where he has sat for many years, day in and day out, begging. On the social ladder of his time, he is practically on the bottom rung. He is blind. He is poor. Mark, who seldom tells us the names of those whom Jesus healed, says that he is "Bartimaeus son of Timaeus." Even that name is a sign of how low he is. First, it is not a real name. Notice that "son of Timaeus" is just a translation of "Bartimaeus." In other words, he does not have his own, personal name (as, for instance, Simon son of Jonah or James son of Zebedee). We are simply told twice, once in Greek and once in Aramaic, that he is the son of Timaeus. Second, to make matters worse, "Timaeus" means unclean. It is impossible to tell whether this was the actual name of his father or just a sort of uncomplimentary nickname given to Bartimaeus or to his father. If it was his father's real name, there must have been a family history of exclusion and perhaps of disease. If it was just a sobriquet given to Bartimaeus or to his father, it represented the terrible judgment of others that his blindness and misery were somehow a curse from God due to impurity and sin.

Bartimaeus is not there, as are the rest, because Jesus is there. He is simply sitting, most likely at his customary place, begging. He wonders what the noise is all about, and so he inquires and receives the explanation that Jesus of Nazareth is passing by. So, perceiving that his chance is passing by as well, Bartimaeus begins to shout, "Jesus, Son of David, have mercy on me!" (Mark 10:47).

A Strange Son of David

This is the first time that anyone in the Gospel of Mark refers to Jesus as the "Son of David." Having a blind man call to the "Son of David" on his way to Jerusalem would immediately make devout Jews think of the story told in 2 Samuel 5, the story of David marching on Jerusalem. The Jebusites, defenders of Jerusalem, told David that the blind and the lame would stop him—apparently meaning that David's army was not strong enough to fight even against people with these conditions and therefore would be easy prey for the well-armed and able-bodied Jebusite army. But David would not be stopped. He entered the city and, in apparent response to the Jebusite boast, had the lame and the blind killed (2 Samuel 5:8).

Now there is another march on Jerusalem. Jesus and his companions are less than twenty miles from the city of David when for the first time someone calls him "Son of David"—son of the man who would not be stopped by the lame and the blind and who ordered them destroyed.

The parallelism is obvious. But so is the contrast. Jesus, son of the David whose march on Jerusalem neither the blind nor the Jebusites could stop, stops for this blind man. Mark makes the contrast clear by stating the obvious, that Jesus, in order to speak to the blind man, had to stop: "Jesus stood still and said . . ." (Mark 10:49).

A commentator was quite right when he stated, "Jesus never healed anybody on the run. 'Stopping' is a necessary part of any genuine ministry to life."[1] Thus, while the original David would not be stopped by anything or anybody, this Son of David is quite willing to stop for a blind beggar, for someone who from the point of view of those around him is less than a nobody. In this Jesus followed what he himself had taught in the parable of the good Samaritan, who stopped—incidentally, along the same road between Jerusalem and Jericho—to help the one in need while others continued on their way without stopping. To quote again from the same commentator, "Compared to the panorama of events which was to unfold in Jerusalem, it was—nothing. Nothing but a person and a need. Nothing but a work of love and mercy to be done. And he did it."[2]

Had it been the original David, bent on military conquest, he would not have stopped. Nor would he have wished to be associated with a blind man whom others called "son of the unclean." But this Son of David is about the task of establishing a different sort of kingdom by a different sort of means. So, he stops.

Healing begins by stopping: Stopping to hear the cries of those in need of healing, stopping to get beyond the enthusiasm of the multitude or the flowing stream that would carry us onward. One wonders how many people had stopped for an instant to drop a coin in Bartimaeus's begging cup. But that is not real stopping. Stopping is putting aside the plan we have made, the goals we have set, in order to meet a need that unexpectedly confronts us. Sometimes the greatest problem we have as we attempt to be a healing influence is that our plans—our good plans, even our plans for healing—stand in the way of our stopping. They push us onward because we have already set a goal, and we must meet it. Jesus had set his face to go to Jerusalem. That was a good plan. Indeed, one could even say that it was the Plan of the Ages. Yet even that good and great plan was postponed while Jesus stopped to pay attention to this one, shouting beggar.

The same is true of our plans. We need them, for otherwise we would simply wander aimlessly; but our ultimate aim must not be to fulfill the plan, whatever that might be. Our ultimate aim must be to serve and follow the One who interrupted his plan in order to pay attention to a blind beggar by the wayside. To be healers after the fashion of Jesus, we must begin by allowing the voices of those who hurt—mentally and spiritually as well as physically—to stop us in our tracks.

Response to the Call

In Chapter 1, we saw that the call of Jesus to follow him implies leaving some things behind. Here again, the one whom Jesus calls leaves something behind: "Throwing off his cloak, he sprang up and came to Jesus" (Mark 10:50). One can well imagine what this cloak meant to the beggar. The price of a cloak at that time was quite high; therefore, that cloak may well have been the beggar's only possession. One wonders how he had come by it. In any case, this was the cloak that protected him from rain and sun. This was the cloak that defined his space when, wrapped in it, he sat begging for alms. Most likely, this was also the cloak that provided him shelter at night.

But now, hearing that Jesus is calling him, the man throws off his cloak and springs to where Jesus is. The blind man who probably sat amid the milling crowd in order to avoid stumbling now jumps up and runs to Jesus. And Bartimaeus leaves his cloak behind—much as Simon and Andrew left their nets.

This is one of the dramatic highlights of the incident. The blind man who usually sits begging now runs to Jesus. Part of the drama is in the image of a blind man running, almost as if he could see. And perhaps what Mark wishes to underline by giving us this detail is that in a sense the man can already see. As a commentary on Mark puts it, "Bartimaeus, with his trustful attitude and movement toward faith, stands in sharp contrast to the disciples. They ask about positions of rank and preference in the Kingdom; he only asks for mercy from Jesus. He is blind but sees; they see but are blind."[3]

Because Jesus has called him, Bartimaeus sees an entirely new future. And he dashes forward to meet it.

Giving Voice to the Silenced

When Bartimaeus first began shouting, there were those who sought to silence him. They "sternly ordered him to be quiet" (Mark 10:48)—although, fortunately, to no avail; for the more they tried to silence him, the more loudly he cried. Perhaps they thought it unseemly to interrupt this march on Jerusalem with the cries of an unclean beggar. Propriety must be kept at all costs! Or perhaps they worried that, at the time when Jesus was going to Jerusalem, the last thing he needed was to have someone shouting that he was "Son of David"—a messianic title that would immediately arouse the suspicion of Jewish and Roman leaders alike. Jesus must be protected from this man who might well end up making trouble for him.

This is not an unusual situation in the Gospels. A clear parallel is what happens when people begin bringing children to Jesus and the disciples speak sternly against those who are doing so (Matthew 19:13; Mark 10:13; Luke 18:15). The disciples are trying to protect their Master; they think he has more important things to do.

But Jesus rebukes the rebukers, telling them that the little children are to be allowed to come to him; for the reign of heaven belongs to them!

In the case of Bartimaeus, the reprimand of the rebukers is not as explicit as in the case of the children; but it is there nevertheless. The rebukers are telling Bartimaeus to be quiet. Jesus orders that Bartimaeus be brought to him; and by asking him a question, Jesus clearly tells him not to be quiet.

That is part of the miracle of healing. Giving Bartimaeus his sight back is such a bright event that we are blinded by its light and do not see that the miracle begins even before the physical healing. Jesus stops for the blind, unclean beggar. Healing begins at that point. Jesus asks him a question. In so doing, he gives Bartimaeus back his dignity. And that is the next step in true, profound healing.

This moment in the narrative reminds me of a story I heard from a friend of mine who is a priest serving in Latin America. He says that he was leading a study group sitting in a circle under the shade of a tree in a poverty-stricken village. People were discussing some point or another when he noticed that there was an old man, clearly poor and uneducated, sitting quietly to one side, as if he did not dare enter the circle. The priest turned to the man and asked, "What do you think about this?" The man was quiet for a long time, and then my friend noticed that there were tears running down the man's cheeks. Afraid that he had somehow said something inappropriate, my friend said, "Forgive me. Have I offended you?" "Oh no!" said the man. "It is just that this is the first time anyone has asked me for my opinion." The man was crying because for the first time in his long life, someone had thought that he was really somebody, capable of having an opinion of his own.

And so with Jesus: After first stopping for the blind man's sake, then calling the man to him, Jesus asked him what his wishes were. Jesus did not tell Bartimaeus that he had great words of salvation for him. Jesus did not even tell him that he was about to make him see. Jesus asked him—he asked poor, unclean, apparently worthless Bartimaeus—what *he* wanted. And in the asking, Jesus may well have given him what he needed most: dignity!

Jesus did not always give people what they wanted. In the passage immediately preceding this story, where we are told that James and John came to Jesus seeking special privileges, the same question appears: "What is it you want me to do for you?" (Mark 10:36). Yet when James and John told Jesus what they wanted, he told them that he could not give it to them and suggested that their asking showed they did not really understand his teachings.

In both cases, Jesus asks what the others want. In the one case, he tells them that he cannot grant what they request and then asks them whether they are able to drink of his cup and be washed in his baptism. They say they are; and Jesus grants them this, although they hardly know what it really means: that they will suffer as he is to suffer. In the latter case, he does not tell Bartimaeus that he is about to regain his sight. First, Jesus asks him what he wants. Then he grants the man's wishes.

Real, full, profound healing requires listening. Too often, we decide what it is that people need; and then we are surprised that they do not appreciate it when we give it to them. What we are offering is probably quite valuable and helpful. But in the act of giving without listening, there is a dimension of dehumanization that is contrary to the notion of healing. We study a community, decide what it needs, and establish a program to meet that need; but we never bother to ask the people of the community what their needs are. We think that we know better than they do. And because we think that we know better, all our good intentions produce little healing. Healing is above all a restoration of dignity—by stopping, by listening, by asking.

As Christians, that is also our experience of how it is that Jesus has healed us. He asks us what we want from him. He will not force himself upon us. Sometimes, as in the case of James and John, he corrects us and offers something we had not asked for. At other times, as in the case of Bartimaeus, he gives us exactly what we request. Patiently and insistently, he asks of us, "What is it that you want from me?" He asks us because he loves us. And that means that he takes us seriously.

What, then, is the meaning of discipleship in a society such as ours, a society so much in need of healing? Being Jesus' disciples clearly means that we must both stop and listen. It also means that we must find ways for the voice of the voiceless to be heard. Nobody was listening to the cries of the beggar. He was just a nuisance, and as such he was told to be quiet. But Jesus heard him, even over the tumult of the crowd. And, having heard him from a distance, Jesus gave him a chance to speak when he came near.

There are many in today's world who are forced to remain practically voiceless while the world passes by. There are the poor and the hungry in so many of the impoverished countries of the world. There are ethnic minorities—some of them native tribes whose ancestors have been on this land for thousands of years. There are the mistreated and abandoned children. There are the millions of women abused both physically and mentally. There are the poor, the homeless, the elderly. There are, in short, the vast numbers of "Bartimaeuses" whom the world chooses to ignore as it goes about its business.

To be followers of the Jesus who stopped and called Bartimaeus means that we too must stop and speak to those who have been made voiceless, so that at least in our conversation their voice may be heard. We must not allow our plans and agendas for the poor and the homeless to override what the poor and the homeless themselves tell us. Above all, we must remember that we too are but blind beggars whom Jesus has healed—and not hotshot disciples worthy of sitting at a special place in his glory. As the hymn "Amazing Grace" says,

> I once was lost, but now am found;
> was blind, but now I see.[4]

Go; Your Faith Has Made You Well

Jesus responded to the man's request with a concrete action: He healed him. Jesus did not set conditions. Jesus did not even ask the man if he would follow him if he was healed. Jesus simply healed Bartimaeus. Furthermore, even in the act of healing him, Jesus released Bartimaeus from any obligation to his benefactor. Jesus did not say, "I will heal you so that you can follow me." Quite the contrary, Jesus healed him and gave him leave to "go; your faith has made you well" (Mark 10:52).

Not surprisingly, the story ends by telling us that Bartimaeus followed Jesus. And Bartimaeus followed freely. One may surmise that he followed because someone who would grant such a boon without asking anything in return—not even gratitude—was certainly worth following. Thus, by stopping, listening, and healing with no strings attached, Jesus gained a follower.

While stopping and listening are essential, that is not all that Jesus does. He actually heals the man. In fact, the act of stopping is in itself a promise that he will listen to the man; and the act of listening is an implicit promise that, if what Bartimaeus asks can be done, it will be. That is why, when he learns that Jesus has stopped, Bartimaeus leaps and leaves his cloak behind. That is also why, when Jesus asks him what he can do for him, the man bears his soul and tells Jesus of his deepest wish: that he may see.

To stop and then not to listen or to listen and then not to respond was not Jesus' way. His act of stopping committed him to listening, and his listening committed him to responding.

As we study this healing act of Jesus and ponder what it might mean for us and for our ministry both as individual disciples and as a church, we see that there are three courses of action that are *not* open to us.

The first course of action we cannot follow is to respond to people's needs and hurts without letting them know that we do this in the name of Jesus. There are Christians who seem to think that it is wrong, when they serve or help someone, to say that they do it because they are followers of Jesus. Thus they insist, for instance, that the social services that the church offers in impoverished communities must be offered without any attempt to make clear the faith that impels us. Such an attitude tends to forget that, as Christians, we believe that full healing includes faith in Jesus and communion with him and with the community of his followers. To withhold that possibility from others, for no matter what reason, is to withhold full healing.

The second course of action we cannot follow is to limit ourselves to listening without doing all we can by way of healing. We hear so much these days about the necessity of paying attention to those around us that we may be tempted to substitute listening for responding. Yet when we do that, we betray the promise implicit in the act of stopping and listening. Actually, that may be one of the reasons why, when we ask others to tell of their deepest hurts and hopes, they sometimes refuse to answer—or they do not answer with full trust. That certainly is one of the reasons why so many in our impoverished communities distrust those who come to "study" them. They have been studied again and again, always with the implicit promise that something would come out of it; and in the end they feel betrayed.

If we are to be disciples of Jesus who healed, we must heal. We cannot substitute fine words or understanding nods for the actual attempt to heal, to respond to the hurt. If the church is to have the right to call itself the church of Jesus Christ, it must practice healing. It must practice healing among its members; and it must practice healing among those who sit by the roadsides of life, like so many blind beggars, regularly ignored except perhaps for a coin tossed at them by a passerby.

The third course of action we cannot follow is to limit our healing to prospective believers or to heal only for the purpose of having people become believers. Before healing Bartimaeus, Jesus did not ask him if he would follow him. And after healing Bartimaeus, Jesus did not ask him to follow.

The healing ministries of the church are not optional. Social services to the community are not optional. They are part of who we are called to be, *when Christ lives in us.*

[1] From "Mark," by Halford E. Luccock, in *The Interpreter's Bible,* Volume 7 (Abingdon-Cokesbury Press, 1951); page 821.

[2] From "Mark," by Halford E. Luccock, in *The Interpreter's Bible,* Volume 7 (Abingdon-Cokesbury Press, 1951); page 822.

[3] From *Mark,* by Walter P. Weaver, in the **Basic Bible Commentary**, Volume 18 (Abingdon, 1994); page 102.

[4] From "Amazing Grace," in *The United Methodist Hymnal* (Copyright © 1989 The United Methodist Publishing House); 378. Used by permission.

CHAPTER 5
Commissioning

Now the eleven disciples went to Galilee, to the mountain to which Jesus had directed them. When they saw him, they worshiped him; but some doubted. And Jesus came and said to them, "All authority in heaven and on earth has been given to me. Go therefore and make disciples of all nations, baptizing them in the name of the Father and of the Son and of the Holy Spirit, and teaching them to obey everything that I have commanded you. And remember, I am with you always, to the end of the age." (Matthew 28:16-20)

The Great Commission

This passage ends with one of the most frequently quoted sections of the Bible, the Great Commission, which has long been seen as the basis for the Christian missionary and evangelizing enterprise: "Go therefore and make disciples of all nations."

Here, the word *therefore* tells us that the Great Commission must not be read as standing alone. There is a foundation for it, something prior to it on whose basis Jesus says, "Go therefore." That something prior is the statement that immediately precedes the Great Commission: "All authority in heaven and on earth has been given to me."

The phrase "in heaven and on earth" is a bold assertion that nothing is to be excluded from Jesus' authority. The "all" is absolute. Similarly, when at the beginning the Bible says that God made "the heavens and the earth," that is another way of saying that all that exists is God's creation. Likewise this is the case when we affirm in the Apostles' Creed that God is "maker of heaven and earth." Just as it would be impossible to find anything in heaven or on earth that is not God's creation, so would it be impossible to find anything or anyplace in heaven or on earth over which Jesus has not been given authority.

This is a bold statement indeed! He who a few days before had refused to claim that he was king of the Jews, now claims that he has authority, not only over all the Jews but also over all the Romans, Greeks, Scythians, and whomever else the world might contain. He has authority over the high priest in Jerusalem and over the emperor in Rome. He has authority over believer and nonbeliever. He has authority over sea and wind, over mountain and glade. He has authority over all the angels in heaven and over all the demons in hell. "All" means precisely that: *all*.

But Some Doubted

Yet this statement appears sandwiched between two others that show that Jesus' authority, though real, is not yet accepted by all. Just before quoting these words of Jesus, Matthew tells us that when the disciples saw Jesus, "they worshiped him; but some doubted." And, immediately after claiming universal authority over all things, Jesus tells his followers that they must go and make disciples—which is a clear recognition that this universal authority is not recognized by many.

At one side of the sandwich, we are told that some among the disciples doubted. These were among the eleven who had followed Jesus during most of his ministry, had heard his teachings, and had witnessed his miracles. Now he appeared to them after his death, and yet they had misgivings! The text does not spell out what it was that they doubted. Probably, it was the resurrection of Jesus. Apparently, they thought that they were seeing a ghost. But whatever it was they doubted, the fact remains that while some worshiped, others doubted.

This should serve as a reminder that no amount of proof can produce faith. Faith is not the result of either a mathematical calculation or a physical experiment. An experiment can prove that water boils when heated. By repeating the experiment a few times, I can become thoroughly convinced. But no number of miracles will ever suffice to produce faith. Witness these disciples. They had seen Jesus heal the blind and the lame and even raise the dead, yet they still doubted.

As many medieval theologians said, faith is "an act of the will." This did not mean that faith is something we can simply decide to have by willing it. What they meant is that faith cannot be forced—not even by supposedly undeniable proofs. The Gospels record many instances in which, in the face of the same miracle, some believed and others simply became more vigorous opponents of Jesus. Part of the reason is that, as we pointed out earlier in quoting Dietrich Bonhoeffer (page 15), faith and obedience go hand in hand.

Doubting, therefore, is not just a matter of suspending judgment; it is also a matter of suspending obedience. When I am not ready to obey, I am not ready to believe, no matter how many proofs are given or how powerful they are. On the other hand, when I am ready to obey, belief does not require absolute and unassailable argument. As Soren Kierkegaard would say, faith always involves a leap. There is no easy way to cross the gulf between lack of faith and faith by going over a bridge of proofs and arguments. Faith is the decision to entrust our lives to God, and that decision does not flow naturally and irresistibly out of miracles and other proofs. These disciples, who had seen Jesus perform so many miracles and wonders, still doubted.

We are not told why they doubted or even what they doubted. But we can sympathize with them because we too are doubters. Perhaps not all the time, but at least some of the time or on some matters, we are doubters. We have decided to follow Jesus, but we do not really entrust our all to him. We believe that it is in following him that life becomes joyful and significant, yet we hedge our bets. We may be willing to leave some of our nets, but we are not willing to leave them all. And, in order to justify our doubts, we say, "If only God would show me the way by some clear, unmistakable sign, by some undeniable miracle, I would do this and that." But if we are determined to disobey, then even if God provided a thousand miracles, we would always be able to interpret them in such a way as to avoid obedience. And if we are determined to obey, we will not need any more signs than God has already given us. If we do not believe, it is not because we lack sufficient proof. And if we do believe, it is not because we have been forced to do so by undeniable proof. As Bonhoeffer so starkly put it, only one who truly believes obeys; and only one who truly obeys believes.

And yet, even though some among his closest disciples still doubted, Jesus could make the astonishing and absolute statement, "All authority in heaven and on earth has been given to me." His authority is such that it is not diminished in the least when some among those who have had the most abundant proofs still doubt.

And Others Had Not Heard

Then there is the other side of the sandwich: "Go therefore and make disciples." It is not only some among the eleven who doubt. There is still the vast majority of the human race who do not believe—who have not even heard of him. And this too does not diminish his authority!

What both sides of this sandwich show is that the authority of Jesus does not ultimately depend on its being accepted by others. Obviously, he wishes people to know him and to accept his authority. That is the reason he tells his followers to go and make disciples. But even if they do not accept him—and certainly while they do not—he still has all authority in heaven and on earth. In other words, the lordship of Jesus does not depend on our accepting it. We do not make Jesus Lord over our lives by deciding to follow him; he was Lord even while we were disobedient. Nor do we make Jesus Lord over others when we witness to them and they are converted; he was already Lord over them. What happens in both cases is that his lordship, which was already there, is now heeded—for our and their salvation.

Think of it this way: The lordship of Christ is as certain and immovable as a rock in the sea. The rock is there both for those who acknowledge it and for those who choose to ignore it. We do not place it there by acknowledging it. Yet, we ignore it at our own peril. Likewise, the lordship of Jesus is there. We make it no greater by obeying it and no less by ignoring it. But we do the former for our salvation, and we do the latter at our peril.

Therefore, what the disciples are commanded is not, as we often think, to extend Jesus' authority. What they are commanded is to call others to accept that authority, which already extends everywhere.

The Doubters Are Sent Too!

Note now who it is that Jesus sends on this errand: his disciples—*all* of them. He sends those who doubt as well as those who worship him. The Great Commission makes no distinction between the two groups.

This is a strange procedure. One would think that Jesus would tell the ones who were ready to worship him that they were therefore ready to go out and make disciples and that he would tell the others that they needed to strengthen their faith before they would be ready to go. How could this latter group, imperfect and doubting disciples that they were, go out and make disciples among the nations? Yet Jesus gives them the same commission he gives those who fully believe.

There are two reasons for this strange behavior. The first is the consequence of what we have just been saying. If it is true that only one who obeys is a true believer and that the greatest obstacle to belief is disobedience, then by sending these doubting disciples, Jesus is prescribing the medicine they need. The beginning of the prescription is in the sending itself; for when Jesus gives them the commission, those words are already empowering and faith producing. Further, it is as these disciples obey him in mission, witnessing to others, that they will come to fuller faith. As any teacher knows, people learn by doing. And what is true for general skills is true also in this case for matters of faith. Faith is nourished and strengthened by witnessing. Those who set out to witness, even though their faith may not be all they wish, will see that faith develop, flourish, and mature. Likewise, the contrary is also true: Those who wait to begin witnessing until they have what they or others consider "sufficient faith" will see what little faith they have wither and die.

I know of this by personal experience. I grew up in The Methodist Church in Cuba, attending Sunday school and services every week. In my late teens, I was a regular attendant at church and occasionally at the Methodist Youth Fellowship. Although I had never thought much about the matter, I was a believer. I knew and accepted the basic doctrines of the church; and if anyone had asked me, I would have said that Christ was indeed my Savior.

One day, someone did ask. The school I attended at that time was a large government school where it was impossible to know all our classmates. It seemed even larger to me, since I had transferred recently and all my classmates were already part of the various little groups that usually form in such situations. On this particular day, one of my classmates whom I hardly knew asked me if it was true that I was a Protestant. It was a question to which I had grown accustomed, for in those days in my country Protestants were a small minority and little known by the community at large. Most often, it was a question asked in curiosity or even in horror by my traditional Roman Catholic classmates, who often crossed themselves when they learned that what they had heard was true: I was in fact a Protestant heretic (this was in the days before Vatican II brought much welcome change in the Roman Catholic Church).

I had always responded to that question with firmness and openness, saying that I was indeed a Protestant and then insisting that much of what was said about us Protestants was not true. But this time the question had a different tenor. This time my classmate, who did not belong to any church and would not even call himself a Christian of any sort, really wanted to know about my faith. So I told him what was essentially the outline of the standard evangelistic sermon I had heard over and over again for as long as I could remember. All that I told him, I believed; but I believed it with a familiarity that took it for granted, that had little or no excitement about it.

Then the unexpected happened. My classmate asked if I could bring him to my church. I did. He asked about a Bible study that he heard advertised in the Sunday service. We started attending together. I could see his life change before my eyes. He was baptized, joined the church, and eventually went to seminary to become an ordained minister. And, as his life changed, so did my life and my faith. To this day, I do not know which is truer, that I brought him to faith or that he brought me to faith; for it was in communicating my faith to another that my faith grew and flourished.

Thus, when I read in the Gospel of Matthew that Jesus told some disciples who still doubted that they must go out and make more disciples, I fully understand. The commission itself was the beginning of the cure for doubt. It was in communicating their faith and their experiences with Jesus that those experiences would gain new significance, and their faith would be strengthened. The defective disciples would come to fuller discipleship by sharing their faith.

Further, I imagine that Jesus told these disciples to go and make disciples of others, even though their own discipleship was still defective, because they would meet him again as they went to "the nations." If it is true, as Jesus says, that all authority has been given to him in heaven and on earth, there is no place on earth where the disciples can go where the authority of Jesus is absent. We often think that the disciples and other preachers and missionaries take Jesus to new lands and places; but, in truth, Jesus is there long before they get there. "All authority in heaven and on earth has been given to me. Go therefore and make disciples."

We see this at work in Acts 10—the story that we usually call "the conversion of Cornelius." As we read that story carefully, we come to realize that the pagan centurion Cornelius has a clearer vision than Peter. Actually, the text says that Cornelius "clearly saw" (Acts 10:3); in contrast, what Peter saw was "something" (Acts 10:11) that he did not understand at all. It is in going to Cornelius that Peter discovers the breadth of the gospel, which is intended also for the Gentiles.

Thus, in going to "make disciples" of another nation, Peter discovers more of what Jesus meant in commanding him and the others to go. Long before Peter arrived at Caesarea and spoke to Cornelius, Jesus had been there and, through the Spirit, had already spoken to Cornelius. Thus, in going to the pagan centurion, Peter both takes Jesus to Caesarea and goes to meet him there. Unfortunately, in much of the history of the church, we have understood our mission as simply taking Jesus someplace and not also as going to meet him where he is and from where he calls.

Calling and Sending

It is also important to note that there is a close relationship between calling and commissioning. As we saw in Chapter 1, when Jesus called his first disciples, he told them that they would become fishers of people. In other words, in the act of calling them to follow, he was already calling them for an act of going. Those whom Jesus calls, he makes anew—he gives them a new reality, a new name, a new definition. And those whom he makes anew, he commissions to join in his ministry. Thus, the Great Commission in Matthew 28 is not only a sending; it is also a calling that redefines even those who still doubt.

That is why in recent years there has been a renewed emphasis on baptism as a form of commissioning. Baptism marks both our calling to discipleship and our being commissioned to witness. That was the understanding of the early church, but it was lost later when the emphasis on baptism fell on the forgiveness of sins. In its fuller sense, baptism is, among other things, an anointing whereby we are made ministers with Christ and are commissioned by him to do his work on earth. In that sense, all of us who are Christians are also commissioned, sent by Christ to carry on his ministry.

In baptism, then, we are made ministers of Christ. But such ministry takes many forms, and we must discover to what particular form of ministry Christ wishes to send us. It is at this point that commissioning by the church becomes important. The word *commission* implies that someone is sending us. One cannot commission oneself. We all must be commissioned by others.

Suppose, for instance, that I believe that I may be called to the ordained ministry, and particularly to preach and to serve as pastor of a church. One of the ways—one of the most important ways—in which I can confirm that calling is by putting it to the test of the community of faith. If my church and its appropriate committees believe that I am indeed called to ministry, that is a positive indication reinforcing my own belief. Then, in most denominations we have means by which a larger body—in the case of The United Methodist Church, it is the annual conference—confirms that calling and commissions me to fulfill it. This is a procedure with which most of us are familiar.

What we often miss, however, is the fact that a similar—though less formal—process of commissioning takes place in many other ministries. If my ministry, for instance, is to visit people in the community in order to evangelize them, most probably this ministry will be acknowledged, perhaps quite informally, by whatever committee or group is planning such visitation. That acknowledgement is a form of commissioning. The same is true when some are sent to participate in an every-member financial canvas or to visit a home for older adults or to lobby city hall against some regulation that we perceive as unjust. In all these cases, we are commissioned by a community of faith that recognizes our gifts and tries to figure out the best way for us to use those gifts.

The Task of Commissioning

A clear example of how this process works appears in Acts 13:1-3, to which passage we referred in Chapter 1. In Acts 13, the community—or its leaders jointly—discovers in the midst of worship that the Spirit wishes Barnabas and Saul to be set aside for a particular task; and in acknowledgement of that they (1) fast and pray, (2) lay their hands on the two men, and (3) send them off. Commissioning normally involves these three steps.

The first step is the communal search for the guidance of God. The leaders in Antioch were worshiping and fasting when they received the direction of the Spirit. Yet, we are told that before actually commissioning Barnabas and Saul, they again fasted and prayed.

Fasting is a way of suspending the common activity of eating and with it all our other common activities and wishes. Fasting is a reminder that there are other values besides self-gratification and meeting our own needs. In recent times, fasting for religious reasons has become rather uncommon in many of our churches. Significantly, it has also become rather uncommon for us to realize that in order to seek the will of God, we need to set aside our own self-interests and desires. It is time we restore the notion of fasting, both in the literal sense and in the figurative. In the figurative sense, fasting may be turning off the baseball game or staying home instead of going to the mall or skipping our favorite soap opera or canceling a trip to the beach. Why? In order to remind ourselves that we must seek God's will above all and in order to spend time in prayer. We need fasting and praying to help us discern the will of God before we set about commissioning anyone—or before we take on a commission for ourselves.

Secondly, the leaders in Antioch laid their hands on Barnabas and Saul. This was an act of blessing and recognition. Commissioning is not only discovering God's will for someone. It is also announcing to that person and to any who might be interested that the community of faith, after seeking to discern God's will, has decided that this particular person is called by God to this particular ministry. We do that in the ordination of ministers. We must learn to do it also in the case of various lay ministries.

Consider some of these lay ministries. A member of our church is called to visit the sick in hospitals. Another is called to visit those who for health reasons are confined to their homes. A third is called to work at a shelter for the homeless. Still another is called to teach children. These are not individual ministries that people undertake simply because they personally feel called to them. These are ministries of the church; and the church has the obligation, after seeking God's will in prayer and fasting, to acknowledge these people and their callings in an official manner. As a community of disciples whom Jesus has commissioned, it is our task to commission others, to give outward and clear signs that these people are where they are as a result of a call from God—a call that is acknowledged both by them and by the church. Naturally, in some cases such commissioning will be more formal—for instance, in the ordination of pastors—while in others it will be less so—as when the congregation prays for its choir or when the bulletin acknowledges someone's particular gifts and ministry.

Finally, the leaders in Antioch sent Barnabas and Saul on their way. The two went with the blessing and support of their community.

When we are gathered, we acknowledge God's calling of the various members/ministers in the church. But then, when we are dispersed in our various areas of service—even to the ends of the earth if need be—we are still united because we have been sent, because we have the support and the continuing prayers of the community of faith.

Remember that when Jesus commissioned his disciples, he promised that he would be with them "to the end of the age." He was not sending them out on their own. Then, in another passage (Acts 1:8), we read how he promised the Holy Spirit would be with them "in Jerusalem, in all Judea and Samaria, and to the ends of the earth." Commissioning is not sending away; it is sending with blessing, support, and accompaniment. It is in this way we have been sent, and it is in this way we must send others.

Notice that in the passage from Matthew (the Great Commission), the disciples are told to make disciples. Those whom Jesus has taught are told to teach. Those whom Jesus has called to obedience are told that they must call others to obedience. Commissioning is a continuing chain in which each link fulfills its purpose by connecting to other links both before and after it. The original disciples are not fully disciples until they help others become disciples. The original learners have not really learned until they teach. Those who have been told to obey do not really obey until they call others to obedience. This continuing chain of being commissioned and commissioning in turn binds the generations together. It goes back to the original Great Commission, "Go therefore," and forward "to the end of the age."

There is another passage that is particularly significant as we consider the matter of commissioning: John 20:21-22. This passage tells how the disciples were meeting behind closed doors because they were afraid. Jesus came to them and said, "Peace be with you. As the Father has sent me, so I send you." And then he breathed on them and said, "Receive the Holy Spirit." The first point to be noted in this story is that the Holy Spirit is given to the disciples for the sake of their mission. Jesus sends them and at that point grants them the Holy Spirit, presumably so they may be faithful in the mission.

The second point to be noted is that the disciples are sent as Jesus is sent. Jesus gives them a commission that is somehow a reflection of his own commission: "As the Father has sent me, so I send you." Just as Jesus himself was sent into the world to save the world, now he sends his disciples out of a closed room—closed out of fear—and into the world to proclaim and make manifest his work of salvation. As with the Great Commission, the basis for our being sent is Jesus himself. In the Great Commission, it is the authority that has been given to Jesus in heaven and on earth. Here in John, it is the nature of Jesus' own commission from the Father.

This means that if we are to be "conformed to the image" of Jesus (Romans 8:29) or if Christ is to be formed in us (Galatians 4:19), we must be sent just as he was sent. All the things we have studied so far—calling, praying, feeding, healing—that are things Jesus was sent to do, are also things we are sent to do.

To have Christ living in us is to be defined by a mission similar to his. This is not to say that we are to become little messiahs or that we are to set out to save the world. That is who he is and what he has done, both for us and for the world. But we are to go into the world, as he did, to give of ourselves for the sake of others, to proclaim good news, to call others to salvation, to heal the sick, and to feed the hungry.

The same is true of the more specific matter of commissioning. Just as Jesus was commissioned, we are commissioned—commissioned by him through the church. We are all to be commissioned to something. It is a matter of discovering—and the community helping us discover—what that is and making our commission effective. But no matter what our commission, one thing is certain: We have been commissioned to be part of a commissioning community!

What is a commissioning community? It is a community that is in prayer and fasting, asking God to help it discern each member's calling and ministry. It is a community that, having begun to discern such callings and ministries, affirms them, both by formal acts of commissioning and sending and by celebrating those gifts in various ways. Finally, it is a community that supports those whom it has commissioned to minister in its name and in the name of Jesus.

This is not the way we usually think in many churches. Quite often, we imagine that it is up to each person to discern his or her own calling. Or we imagine that the only commissioning for which we are responsible is supporting those who are to be engaged in ordained ministry. Or we are afraid of sending people out into the world for fear of losing them or because we think that the only valid Christian calling is service within the church.

These ideas and attitudes are wrong, for they reflect neither the way Jesus was sent nor the way he sends us. We must not forget that the church was born out of a commission and lives by being faithful to that commission and by commissioning others.

Jesus said, "As the Father has sent me, so I send you" (John 20:21).

We are sent to send, commissioned to commission, just as Jesus was sent to send and commissioned to commission. We must follow his example and his command by sending others to do his work, *because Christ lives in us.*

CHAPTER 6
Teaching

When he entered the temple, the chief priests and the elders of the people came to him as he was teaching, and said, "By what authority are you doing these things, and who gave you this authority?" Jesus said to them, "I will also ask you one question; if you tell me the answer, then I will also tell you by what authority I do these things. Did the baptism of John come from heaven, or was it of human origin?" And they argued with one another, "If we say, 'From heaven,' he will say to us, 'Why then did you not believe him?' But if we say, 'Of human origin,' we are afraid of the crowd; for all regard John as a prophet." So they answered Jesus, "We do not know." And he said to them, "Neither will I tell you by what authority I am doing these things." (Matthew 21:23-27)

A Trap That Backfires

This is a fascinating passage, for in it Jesus turns the tables quite nicely on those who would entrap him. At other places in the Gospels, we have accounts of how Jesus' enemies try to trick him into making statements that would compromise him or his mission. Thus, for instance, they come and ask him whether devout Jews should pay taxes to the Roman Empire (Matthew 22:15-22; Mark 12:13-17; Luke 20:20-26). If he says yes, he will be perceived as a pro-Roman sycophant who has no sympathy for the plight of the people of Israel. For they have to pay exorbitant taxes to a foreign power; and many of them believe that to pay taxes to Caesar is to accept him, rather than God, as Lord. If Jesus says no, he will immediately find himself in trouble with the Roman authorities, who will classify him as a troublemaker and a rabble-rouser. So Jesus sidesteps the trap by pointing out that the coin bears the image of Caesar and that therefore there is a contradiction in withholding it from the Romans and at the same time claiming to do so in order to be faithful to the God of Israel. The religious leaders made use of the political situation in an attempt to try to entangle Jesus in it. He escapes their trap by showing the contradiction in the attitude of the super-religious who would argue against paying taxes to Caesar but are quite content keeping coins that bear his image.

Here, however, the shoe is on the other foot. The chief priests and the elders have what appears at first to be an entirely legitimate question: By what authority is Jesus teaching? As guardians of the faith of Israel, it is indeed their responsibility and their prerogative to ask such a question. Otherwise, all kinds of charlatans could teach in the Temple; and their teachings could be entirely contrary to the faith of Israel. But knowing the attitude of these leaders toward Jesus, we know also that the question is a veiled trap. If he says that he is teaching on God's authority, they will accuse him of blasphemy. If he says that he is teaching on his own authority, they will have the right to order him silenced and expelled from the Temple. And if he insists that he is teaching on his own authority and that this is equal to God's, he will really be in trouble!

Jesus, however, turns the tables on the leaders by asking them a question that puts them in a similar quandary: By what authority did John baptize? If they say that John's baptism was of God, they will be condemning themselves; for they opposed John. They will also find themselves in trouble with the authorities who had John imprisoned and eventually beheaded. If, on the other hand, they say that John had no divine commission to baptize, they will alienate the crowd, among whom sympathy for John runs high. Thus, because of fear of the same sort of political entanglement in which they would like to place Jesus, they are forced to declare that they do not know the source of John's authority. But the answer is also an admission that they are not as authoritative as they claim. They are supposed to guard the teaching of the faith, yet they cannot answer as direct a question as that. If they cannot tell whether John's baptism was from God or not, what business is it of theirs by what authority Jesus is teaching? If they cannot answer the question with regard to John, why do they want Jesus to answer the question with regard to himself?

A Question of Authority

Still, the question of the priests and elders is a legitimate one; teaching requires authority. That is why we have means by which we certify teachers for various fields and levels. We want those who teach our children to know their subject matter. We also want them to know how to teach and how to provide a good example for our children. In other words, we want them to be authorized. That is why as parents we demand a process of teacher evaluation and certification. Likewise, if we are thinking about taking an evening course on investing, we want to know who the teacher is, what position she holds in what company, where she has learned about investments, what have been the actual results of her own investments, and so forth. Or, if we are considering purchasing a cookbook about Turkish cooking, we look at the back cover in order to find out where the author has learned about the subject matter, how long he has lived in Turkey, where he practiced his cooking, and so forth. In short, a teacher must have authority.

When speaking of Jesus as a teacher, we often emphasize his methods so much—for instance, his teaching in parables—that we forget his first and foremost qualification: his authority. At the end of the Sermon on the Mount, Matthew tells us that "when Jesus had finished saying these things, the crowds were astounded at his teaching, for he taught them as one having authority, and not as their scribes" (Matthew 7:28-29). And at the beginning of that sermon, Matthew has given us a more subtle but, in a sense, more powerful indication of Jesus' authority. When Matthew says that Jesus "went up the mountain" (Matthew 5:1) to teach, it is a veiled reference to Moses, who also went up the mountain and there received the commandments of God. Throughout his Gospel, Matthew presents Jesus as the new Moses; and in the Sermon on the Mount, Matthew presents Jesus as one who spoke with an authority at least the equal of Moses'. This becomes abundantly clear in the very heart of the Sermon on the Mount, where Jesus refers repeatedly to the law of Moses and then adds, "But I say to you . . ."

What does *authority* mean? The word comes from the same root as "author." This makes sense, for no one knows better how a thing is to be handled or understood than the one who made it; that is, no one is a better *authority* about something than its *author*.

Let me illustrate. There is an old story about a church where someone built a magnificent organ. For some time, the man who had built the organ remained in the community and played the organ. Its music became so famous that people came from far away to hear it. One day the man left town, and others continued the tradition of magnificent organ recitals. But little by little the organ deteriorated, to the point that it no longer played. Many people came and tried to fix it, but no one could make it work. One day, when all had given up hope of fixing the organ, an old man came by and asked to see it. He worked with it for some time. Then the organ suddenly broke forth with beautiful music. The people in the town rushed to witness the apparent miracle and were dumbfounded by it until someone asked the old man at the keyboard how it was that he was able to fix the organ when everyone else had failed. "Simple," said the old man, "I am the one who built it!" Because he was the "author" of the organ, he had unequaled "authority" over it.

And so with Jesus. He teaches with authority, not because someone has certified him, but because he is the author of the life about which he is teaching. No one knew how the organ should work as well as the man who made it. When we buy a new product, we read the manufacturer's instructions because no one knows better than the manufacturer how the product is to be used. Jesus teaches with an authority that is unlike that of the scribes because they are basically repeating what others have told them. In contrast, he is giving, so to speak, the Manufacturer's instructions for life. If the first thing that qualifies a teacher is knowing the subject matter, Jesus is an unequaled teacher.

A Strange Pedagogy

Most of us have probably heard someone say that Jesus was a great teacher and that this can be seen in his parables. After all, she or he insists, Jesus' parables were attempts to express difficult matters through examples taken from daily life so people could understand what he was saying.

That sounds nice, but it is not true. In the Gospels we are repeatedly told that Jesus used many of his parables to hide his meaning from others rather than to communicate it more clearly. In the Gospel of Matthew, from which our main reading for this chapter comes, it is quite clear that Jesus taught in parables to the crowds, and sometimes to his enemies, precisely so that they would not understand fully what he was telling them. Look, for instance, at Matthew 13:1-13. There we are told that, since the crowd was quite large, Jesus sat in a boat; his listeners stood on the beach, "and he told them many things in parables" (Matthew 13:3). Then, after the end of his speech to the crowd, his disciples ask him why it is that he speaks in parables. His response is, "To you it has been given to know the secrets of the kingdom of heaven, but to them it has not been given. . . . The reason I speak to them in parables is that 'seeing they do not perceive, and hearing they do not listen, nor do they understand' " (Matthew 13:11-13). A little later Matthew comments,

"Jesus told the crowds all these things in parables; without a parable he told them nothing" (Matthew 13:34) and declares that in so doing, Jesus was fulfilling prophecy.

The parables, however, do not lead to complete obfuscation. On the contrary, they have a cutting dimension that is quite understandable to those they criticize. Thus, in Matthew 21:45 we read, "When the chief priests and the Pharisees heard his parables, they realized that he was speaking about them." The result is not, as we would expect from a bland parable, that the Pharisees are edified but rather that they want to arrest him. They are only held back by fear of the crowds, who believe that Jesus is a prophet.

Most parables are much more than an illustration taken from everyday life. They are words of both grace and judgment requiring the reader to take a stance, not as an observer, but as a participant. Take, for instance, the well-known parable that we call the parable of the prodigal son. Jesus did not tell that parable in an evangelistic setting. The point was not simply that if we are prodigals who have gone away to a strange land, God is waiting to receive us with open arms, like the father in the story. Rather, Jesus told the parable in a setting in which many of his hearers considered themselves faithful. Indeed, Luke introduces the parable—and two others that stand together with it—in a context of hostility in which the scribes and the Pharisees were grumbling because Jesus welcomed sinners and ate with them (Luke 15:1-2).

In that context, Jesus tells "them"—that is, the scribes and Pharisees—three parables: one about a shepherd who loses a sheep; another about a woman who loses a coin; and, finally, a longer one about a father who loses a son. In all three parables, however, the point is that in a strange way being lost makes a thing, not less valuable, but more valuable. The shepherd leaves the ninety-nine sheep in the wilderness. The woman who has lost a coin does not worry about the remaining nine and rejoices more about having found the tenth than about having kept the others. The father has two sons and gives a banquet to celebrate the return of the prodigal while the more faithful one complains that he has never had even a small party in his honor. In the setting in which these parables are placed, their meaning is clear: The scribes and Pharisees who complain about Jesus welcoming sinners and eating with them are like the ninety-nine sheep abandoned in the wilderness or like the older son who boasts of his faithfulness and resents his father's liberality with his brother.

69

As we look at these parables, we realize that they constitute a strange sort of teaching. They are a teaching that requires response, not in the sense of taking an exam or giving the right answer, but in the sense that one has to place oneself within the story. If I were a scribe hearing the parable of the father and the two sons and resenting the manner in which Jesus was welcoming sinners, I would be put in the position of having to decide: Was I to insist on my rights as the faithful child that has never strayed? Was I to change the story and become a faithful child who welcomes the prodigal? Was I to acknowledge that in spite of all my supposed faithfulness, I too had strayed and needed to be received as a prodigal? There are all sorts of possible answers. What is *not* possible is to take the story as a simple lesson in general morality or as an example that people ought to follow. The parable demands response; it demands that the hearers become actors in the story.

When we look at them in this light, the parables of Jesus, far from being a bland appeal to common sense, are the direct result of his authority—or, as suggested above, of his "authorship." In the parables, as well as in all his teachings, Jesus confronts his hearers as one who has authority. As we say in common speech, he is "telling it like it is"; and, because of who he is, he knows how it is. He teaches in parables, not to illustrate difficult points or to make his teaching appealing, but to force his hearers to a decision. And those who are not ready or willing to make a decision will see and not perceive, hear and not listen.

The Scope of His Teaching

The parables also point us in another direction that we often miss. It is frequently noted that Jesus chose his parables from situations and issues in everyday life. What we seldom notice is that few of the parables of Jesus deal directly with matters of religion. There is certainly a parable about a Pharisee and a publican praying. But most parables are about sheep, coins, kings, slaves, farmers, plants, and so forth. This is not just a sign of Jesus' ingenuity as a teacher; it is also a sign of the manner in which he understood and proclaimed faith. Faith is, among other things, the ability to place all things under the perspective of God's will. Therefore, there is nothing that by its nature is alien to faith. That is part of what we mean when we declare in the Apostles' Creed that God is "maker of heaven and earth."

70

Jesus taught people the will of God and called them to obedience to God while saying fairly little about religion per se. Sometimes he spoke of common, everyday things that his hearers would know by direct experience: mustard seeds, sheep, leaven in a mass of dough, tares growing amid the wheat. At other times he spoke of the "lifestyles of the rich and famous" and of the greed that reigns in high places: a man whose king forgave him an astronomical debt of ten thousand talents but who himself would not forgive another who owed him the pittance of a hundred denarii (Matthew 18:23-35). On still other occasions Jesus spoke of corruption in administration; for example, the case of a manager who used his master's wealth to feather his own nest (Luke 16:1-8). Or Jesus spoke to people's fantasy of discovering hidden treasure in the midst of burdensome toil (Matthew 13:44).

What is significant in this list is that there is no stark line of demarcation between the religious and the secular. Perhaps that is one of the reasons the religious leaders of Jesus' time did not like him: He took religion out of the Temple and the synagogues and into the fields and the kitchens. Many religious folk want to talk about religion, about the sacred, and to leave the profane to others. But when Jesus taught, such distinctions were blurred. The profane had become sacred. What place was left for specialists on the sacred?

Thus we come back once more to the matter of authority and authorship. To the Word through whom all things were made, all things are equally sacred. They are all equally made by the Word. They are all equally capable of being placed under the judgment of the Word. They are all equally capable of being used to proclaim and communicate the Word.

To Teach as He Taught

In giving them the Great Commission, which we studied in Chapter 5, Jesus commanded his disciples to make disciples, "teaching them to obey everything that I have commanded you" (Matthew 28:20). Thus the Great Commission is also a commission to teach; and in a sense it is a commission to teach as Jesus taught, for we are to teach others to obey that which we have also been commanded to obey.

The first thing to be noted here is that Christian teaching is teaching for obedience. Certainly, all teaching involves information; but the teaching for which Jesus commissioned his disciples and us

71

is not limited to information. We may tell people all about Jesus and give them such detailed information that there is nothing more for them to learn in that respect and yet not have fulfilled our task as Christian teachers. Information is certainly part of the equation, but it is not enough. Our teaching must also call people to obedience, just as we have been called to obedience.

What this means is that the teaching we are called to do goes beyond *information* and into *formation*. It is to be a teaching that forms all of us, individually and as a community, in such a way that we obey the things that Jesus has commanded. It must be a teaching of such a nature that Christ will be formed in us (Galatians 4:19). Expressing a similar concern, a Latin American educator once put the matter thus: "Anyone can instruct; but to educate, you must be a living gospel."

That is a tall order. It means that we must, quite literally, teach as Jesus taught. Yet how can we do such a thing, for he taught with an authority that we can never attain? Obviously, the only possible way is somehow to be able to claim his authority. Now that sounds simple, and there are people who are quite content with claiming the authority of Jesus because they repeat his words. They say, "It was good enough for Jesus, and it's good enough for me." On that basis they refuse to say or to teach anything that they do not find quite literally in the Gospels. Obviously, that would suffice if our only task were to convey information. In that case it would be enough to parrot the Sermon on the Mount and to insist that people memorize it. But since teaching is much more than providing information, that is not what is meant by claiming the authority of Jesus.

Nor does claiming the authority of Jesus mean that we must have the moral and ethical authority to speak in the name of Jesus. Often, we think that in order to be able to claim the authority of Jesus, we must be as ethically faultless as he was. In my own experience, it is this view that has most undermined my own readiness to teach others about Jesus' demands. Most of the time, I know full well what I am to teach. My problem is that I doubt that I have the authority to teach it. And this has little to do with what people might think or know about me; it has much more to do with what I myself know are my own shortcomings in obedience. Likewise, I use the same view as an excuse for my unwillingness to obey. When someone—be it an individual or the community of faith—points me in the direction of greater obedience and I do not wish to listen, all I have to do is question the moral authority of the person or the community speaking to me. (Interestingly enough, in such circumstances I find myself asking the same question of my teacher that the chief priests and the elders asked of Jesus: "By what authority are you doing these things?" Therefore, when I see the chief priests and the elders asking that question, I must not be too harsh on them; for I see myself in them.)

It is true that in order to claim the authority of Jesus, we must subject ourselves to his authority. Even in matters of mere information, teachers can only teach what they have learned. In matters of formation, Christian teachers can only teach what they have appropriated by themselves being formed by Jesus. But this does not mean that we must have achieved sinless perfection. It means rather that we must accept the authority of Jesus and his commandments over us and be convinced that following those commandments is the best way to live. And it means above all that we must have Christ living in us. When Christ lives in us, that does not eliminate the possibility that we may be rebellious sinners. But it does open up the possibility that our teaching may be done by his authority—not because we are good or pure or wise or committed, but because in a sense it may be Christ who is teaching through us.

Having said that, it is important to assert that we only teach by that authority when we ourselves are taught by others in the community, others who also share in the life of Jesus. I cannot claim that I have Christ in me, and therefore all the rest of the Christian community must do what I say. I can only claim to have Christ living in me—being formed in me—when I so listen to the church that I too am being taught by the same authority on which I am attempting to teach. Otherwise, rather than a Christian teacher, I risk becoming a tyrant and a hypocrite.

Teaching begins with being taught. Those who have never been learners cannot be teachers. In the case of Christian teaching, we can only claim to teach in the measure that we are learners. And this is true not only of us as individuals but also of the community of faith as a whole. Individuals who claim to teach others must in turn be taught by the entire community of faith. And the community itself must also in turn be taught by the insights of individuals within it. In order to teach, all of us, both as individuals and as a community of faith, must constantly be taught by the Christ who is being formed in us—or, using a similar Pauline metaphor, *by the Christ who lives in us.*

CHAPTER 7
Witnessing

So when they had come together, they asked him, "Lord, is this the time when you will restore the kingdom to Israel?" He replied, "It is not for you to know the times or periods that the Father has set by his own authority. But you will receive power when the Holy Spirit has come upon you; and you will be my witnesses in Jerusalem, in all Judea and Samaria, and to the ends of the earth." (Acts 1:6-8)

False Expectations

Reading this passage, it becomes clear that the disciples have false expectations of Jesus. Jesus is about to leave them. Yet instead of asking him about where he is going or what they are to do, they simply take for granted that he is to remain with them; and they wonder if the time has come for the kingdom of David to be restored. Thus their first false expectation is that things will continue as they are or that they will continue improving.

Jesus is with them, and the disciples expect him not only to remain but also to claim political power over David's ancient kingdom: "Lord, is this the time when you will restore the kingdom to Israel?" Jesus' response shows that in this too they have false expectations— but not for the reasons we usually think. Most often when we read this passage, we imagine that what is wrong with the disciples' question is that they are talking about a restoration of the Kingdom—about a kingdom, a political reality—when in fact Jesus is talking about something else. But when we look at the entire Gospel of Luke—the first volume of the two-volume series Luke/Acts—we see that Jesus himself repeatedly spoke about the kingdom of God. And in Acts 1:3, when summarizing what Jesus taught his disciples during the time between his resurrection and his ascension, Luke says that he spent that time "speaking about the kingdom of God."

Thus, although it is clear that in many ways Jesus attempted to correct his disciples' view of the Kingdom, it is also true that the Kingdom was always a central feature in his teaching. The reign of God about which Jesus taught both before and after the events of Easter is political in the sense that it is a new order—an order that is

74

ultimately incompatible with the political arrangements of society at large, for "the kings of the Gentiles lord it over them; and those in authority over them are called benefactors. But not so with you; rather the greatest among you must become like the youngest, and the leader like one who serves" (Luke 22:25-26). The main difference between Jesus' message and the ways of "the kings of the Gentiles" is not that his message is spiritual while the concerns of the kings are political. What is different is that in one sort of kingdom the powerful lord it over the rest, and in the other it is the servants who are most important. To say that the message of Jesus is not political is true only if by that we mean that it is not a wholesale endorsement of any political system or that it is not about overthrowing one secular regime in order to install another. The message of a reign in which the last are first and the most important are those who serve would have been seen by the authorities of the Roman Empire as highly political and even subversive. Rather than not being political, the message of Jesus is a strong indictment of any political order in which "the kings" who have authority lord it over the rest.

The Message of the Reign of God

What Jesus actually says is, "It is not for you to know the times or periods that the Father has set by his own authority. But you will receive power when the Holy Spirit has come upon you." In other words, the disciples' mistake is not in expecting the restoration of the Kingdom. Their error is in trying to find out when and how this is to take place. The restoration of the reign of God is in the hands of God, and it is not the disciples' place to know God's hidden designs.

Instead of telling them when the reign is to be restored, Jesus promises the disciples something for which they have not asked: "But you will receive power when the Holy Spirit has come upon you; and you will be my witnesses." Here again, at first it looks as if Jesus is about to promise them precisely what they wanted when they were asking about the restoration of the Kingdom. They will receive power. Remember that earlier there had been a dispute among the disciples because two of them wanted special power in the reign of God, one to sit at the right of Jesus and the other at his left. Now Jesus promises them power. Perhaps they are not to know when the Kingdom is to be restored, but they will still have their place of honor and power! Then Jesus deflates their expectations once again: This power is not so they may lord it over others or even so they may have all their wishes fulfilled. It is so they may be witnesses.

Then Jesus corrects their expectations on another crucial point. The disciples are asking about the restoration of the Kingdom "to Israel." In other words, they have a rather provincial view of what God is accomplishing in Jesus and his resurrection. But Jesus tells them that having such limited horizons is a mistake. They are to be his witnesses "in Jerusalem, in all Judea and Samaria, and to the ends of the earth." To be Jesus' witnesses is to proclaim the reign of God that he has inaugurated. Thus the questioners could easily understand that they were to be Jesus' witnesses in Jerusalem, which after all was the capital of David's kingdom. To go to "all Judea" would also be readily understood, since Judea was the area whose traditional capital was Jerusalem. Even the addition of Samaria made sense, for this too was part of the kingdom of David and Solomon. It was now populated by people whom devout Jews despised as having abandoned the true faith; still, it was part of the old kingdom of Israel. Therefore, to witness to Jesus in Samaria would be a sign that the old kingdom was being restored to its ancient borders. But then comes the clincher: Jesus tells them that they are to be his witnesses "to the ends of the earth." The Kingdom is not to be restored just to Israel. The reign of God, which it will be their task to announce as witnesses of Jesus, is to extend far beyond the borders of Israel, to the very ends of the earth.

Wrong Question, Right Answer

We will return to the matter of witnessing in the next section. Before we do that, however, it is important to note how what is reported in Acts 1:6-8 speaks to our modern religiosity. For just as those who questioned Jesus had mistaken assumptions, so are there now many who have assumptions that these words of Jesus contradict.

First, there are many people, even to this day, who insist on asking the question that these disciples posed to Jesus: Is this the time? Is the end about to arrive? When will Jesus return? Furthermore, there are people who claim that the Holy Spirit has revealed to them the answers to those questions.

But as we read this text, it is clear that seeking answers to such questions is not at all what true disciples of Jesus are supposed to do. On the contrary, Jesus himself told his first disciples that it was not for them to know the times or the seasons, which are solely in the hand of God. Thus, to claim to know the answers to such questions is to contradict Jesus himself. Moreover, when such people claim that the answers have been given to them by the Holy Spirit, they are also misunderstanding and misrepresenting the role of the Spirit, who is not given to the disciples so that they may know the times or the seasons but rather so that they may have the power to be witnesses.

A second lesson to be drawn from this dialogue between Jesus and his disciples concerns the breadth of the Kingdom. The disciples are interested in the restoration of the Kingdom to Israel; Jesus sends them out "to the ends of the earth." They believe that the message is only for them and people like them; Jesus sends them to the Samaritans and then even farther, to faraway places with strange customs, languages, and religions.

We are so used to hearing about the gospel being a message to all nations that we do not realize how shocking that idea would have been to the early followers of Jesus. They were all Jews, brought up in the traditions of Israel. That is why they asked about the restoration of the Kingdom *to Israel*. To them, that was what Jesus' message and work were all about. All others, the Gentiles and even the Samaritans, were unclean; and devout Jews ought to have nothing to do with the unclean. But now Jesus tells the disciples that the message is for *all* people, not only those in Jerusalem and Judea but also those in Samaria and even at the very ends of the earth— that is, those as far away from Jerusalem as was physically possible.

Time has passed, and Christians often remark on the narrow mindset of those early disciples who apparently could not see beyond their noses. How could it be, we ask, that after three years with Jesus, listening to his teaching and seeing his example, they still were so confused?

To such a question, probably the best answer is another question: How can it be that after twenty centuries of Christian preaching, we Christians act and think as we do? We know that the gospel is for all people equally and that God shows no partiality (Acts 10:34, or as the King James Versions says, God "is no respecter of persons"). And yet, throughout the history of the church and even to this day, we in the church have erected barriers against others who are not like us. We have had, and still have, churches segregated by race. We have had, and still have, churches segregated by class and income. We have had, and still have, churches segregated by levels of education. We have had, and still have, churches segregated by ethnic backgrounds and countries of origin. And—being the tribal animals that we are—we each convince ourselves that our group is the best group and even that it is somehow God's favorite.

But to us the words are addressed, "You will be my witnesses . . . to the ends of the earth." If we are to be true and faithful witnesses to Jesus, we too are sent, like those early disciples, to transcend and cross every border and barrier that humans have erected between themselves. All people—even those who from our point of view are at "the ends of the earth"—are called to join our Lord and us in God's reign. To pretend that we are true Christian witnesses and then to limit our outreach to a particular group or to close our fellowship to any others is tantamount to those early disciples having responded, "Well, Lord, you know, Judea we understand. Even Samaria might do. But beyond that we will not go. It is just not fitting for good and faithful believers to be mixing with all sorts of people."

The Spirit was promised to those early disciples—and then given to them—so that they might have the power to be witnesses. The Spirit was not given to them so that they could rejoice in their holiness. The Spirit was not given to them so that they could boast of having spiritual gifts. The Spirit was given to them so that they might have power—power to witness in Jerusalem, in all Judea and Samaria, and to the ends of the earth. Likewise, the Spirit is given to us today, not so that we may boast of how lively and active our church is and not so that we may feel superior to others and therefore feel free to ignore them, but so that we too may be witnesses: at home, in our churches, in our communities, in the worst sections of our towns, and to the ends of the earth.

The corollary to that is ominous: If we do not have the power to be such witnesses, then let us simply confess that we do not have the Spirit of God; and let us pray that we be forgiven and that the power of the Spirit may indeed come to us. And that is true not only of each one of us as individuals; it is equally true of the community of faith as a whole. A church that does not have the power to witness to the length and breadth of human society today lacks the power of the Spirit. There are no "ifs" or "buts" about it!

Teaching and Witnessing

In Chapter 6 we saw that Jesus sent his disciples to teach. Now we are studying a text in which they are sent to be witnesses. These two tasks are quite similar. And yet, to teach is not the same as to witness. Teachers communicate what they have learned, either from study or from experience. Thus, for instance, someone who went to school and studied mathematics teaches mathematics to others; or someone who has learned how to fix cars by practice can in turn teach others who do not have the same experience. A witness, in contrast, points to an event he or she has seen. From a teacher I can learn that the angles in a triangle add up to 180 degrees or how to clean a carburetor. From a witness I can learn who stole the cookies from the cookie jar or what the President said in his last speech. In general, teachers communicate fixed principles—that the angles of a triangle add up to 180 degrees or that carburetors have to be cleaned—whereas witnesses communicate events—that Joey took the cookies from the cookie jar or that the President said he would veto the bill. Teaching has to do with facts; witnessing has to do with news—hence the popular title for local television news shows, *Eyewitness News.*

Note then that historical facts stand somewhere between mere facts and news. At some point, they were news. Some people had heard of them, and whoever first spoke of them told of something that others had not yet heard. Imagine, for instance, the first runner arriving at a city in southern Italy in the year 410 and shouting, "Rome has fallen to the Goths! Rome has fallen!" That was news! Today, however, a teacher stands up in class and writes on the chalkboard "Rome fell to the Goths in the year 410." That is hardly news now; it is just historical fact. At first it required a witness to tell it; now it is a teacher who communicates it. Still, when you stop to think about it, you realize that even this teacher who is stating a fact is actually communicating what has come to her or him through a long chain of witnesses: from that first runner who told of the event, to others who heard it, to others who eventually wrote it down. Without original witnesses, it would be difficult if not impossible for this teacher to state even so simple a fact as this one, that Rome fell to the Goths in the year 410.

Now look at the case of Jesus and what he told his disciples. Jesus taught certain things and gave certain commandments that it is possible for others to teach. We can, for instance, teach that people should do to others what they would like to have done to them or that they ought to love their enemies or that they should be like God, who makes rain to fall on the good and the bad with loving impartiality. As we saw in Chapter 5, Jesus commanded his disciples—and commands us—to go and teach the nations to obey the commandments that he had taught them. Thus, when Christ lives in us, we teach as he has taught us.

But in the text that we are now studying, Jesus tells his disciples that they will be his witnesses. That is because Jesus is more than a series of teachings and commandments. Jesus is a person, a person the events of whose life are of great importance for us and for the rest of the world. As a person and as an event Jesus needs not only teachers but witnesses as well. We are commanded not just to teach what Jesus taught but also to witness to him, to the mystery of his death and to the power of his resurrection.

Just as there are two steps in teaching—first one learns, and then one communicates what one has learned—so are there two steps in witnessing: One has to have seen, and one has to speak. Think for instance of a murder trial. Someone who comes to court and says, "I saw the butler do it," but in fact did not see anything is not a true witness. On the other hand, someone who in fact saw the butler do it but does not come forth in court is not a witness either. It is the combination of the two that makes a witness. Likewise, in order to be witnesses of Jesus, two things must be true of us. First, we must have "seen"—experienced, lived, felt. Second, we must be willing to speak. If the first is lacking, we are nothing but false witnesses. If the second is lacking, we are like cowardly bystanders who choose to stand as observers when the trial of the ages is taking place and we have privileged information.

The Power of the Spirit

What links these two poles of the act of witnessing is the power of the Spirit. It is by the power of the Spirit that we are able to stand as witnesses of events that took place almost two thousand years ago. The Spirit brings those events to our day and makes Jesus our contemporary so that we can stand at the cross with him and see him raised for us. How that can be, I know not—in truth, nobody knows, nor can anybody know. But the fact is that we see this miracle of the Spirit happen again and again as thousands upon thousands of Christians in every generation come to call on Jesus as their Savior and to follow him as their Lord—him whom they have not seen but who stands closer to them than their own souls. In a way, that is what we mean when we say that Christ lives in us: By the power of the Spirit we see him as clearly as if we had been standing on that mountain on Ascension Day.

Then, it is also by the power of the Spirit that the second phase of witnessing takes place. The disciples were not told to brave it out as they went to Jerusalem and Judea and Samaria and to the ends of the earth. Nor were they told that it would be easy and that there was nothing to worry about. They were told that they would have the power of the Spirit and that it would be in virtue of that power that they would do what they were being told to do. The commandment to go was thus joined to the promise that the Spirit would be given to them. It was by the power of the Spirit that they were able to bear witness, as the rest of the Book of Acts amply shows.

Have you ever noticed that the Book of Acts does not really end? Look at Acts 28: After following the life of Paul for some time, we are left wondering whatever became of the apostle after his imprisonment in Rome. There are many possible explanations for the abrupt ending of Acts. However, I prefer the following: The Book of Acts does not end because the story it is telling has not ended. The story in Acts is not about the apostles but about the Spirit of God and about how the Spirit moved the church to witness to Jesus in ever widening circles and varying circumstances. If the story had continued to the death of Paul, we could have thought that it was already ended. But the story does not end, precisely to let us know that we are still living in it. Acts leaves off in Chapter 28. Imagine Theophilus and his contemporaries reading it and realizing that, because the book did not end, they were living in Chapter 29 or 30. Imagine the martyrs of the second century, living at a time when the word *witness—martyr*—had come to imply suffering in testimony of Jesus and realizing that they were living in Acts 40 or 50. And what about us? We too are living in the time of Acts, in the age when the Spirit gives us power to be witnesses to Jesus, even to the ends of the earth. After such a long chain of witnesses and martyrs, ours may well be Chapter 578. But it is still another chapter in the long and glorious story that Jesus promised his disciples when he said to them—and to us—"You will receive power when the Holy Spirit has come upon you; and you will be my witnesses in Jerusalem, in all Judea and Samaria, and to the ends of the earth."

Ever since the time of Jesus, through all generations and in ever more lands, there has been an uninterrupted chain of witnesses giving testimony by the power of the Spirit. Sometimes witnessing has required confrontation with political authorities to the point of suffering and death. Sometimes it has required great initiative and creativity in relating to different cultures. Sometimes it requires simply that we speak to our neighbors and business associates. But in every case it requires also the power of the Spirit. When you speak of Jesus and what he means to you to a friend, a colleague, or a stranger and your witness is received, you do not do this on your own. You are experiencing the power of the Spirit working in and through you.

Witnessing Requires Declaration

Why have I just said "when you speak"? Aren't there other forms of witnessing? For instance, does the church not witness to Jesus Christ by feeding the hungry, clothing the naked, visiting the sick, and so forth? Yes, and no. Yes, in that all these things are necessary to our witness. No, in that they do not suffice. Let us look at each of those two in order.

First, all these things—feeding, clothing, visiting—are necessary elements of our witnessing. Without them our witness is neither credible nor authentic. Think again about a witness in a court of law. The witness declares that he saw the butler do it. The witness was standing about a hundred yards away, waiting for a bus, when he saw it all. But upon cross examination it turns out, first, that the supposed witness has been behaving for some time as a pathological liar. Second, he had no idea where the bus that stops at that particular corner goes. Finally, he is so shortsighted that he can hardly distinguish objects twenty yards away; and he has no glasses. No matter how much such a witness insists and even swears that he actually saw the butler do it, he is not a credible witness; and most likely he is not authentic.

The same is true of the Christian witness. If the church says that it knows Jesus and that Jesus is the Lord of all but at the same time promotes hatred, prejudice, division, and greed, its witness is hardly credible; and people will quite rightly question its authenticity. If a particular Christian speaks of Jesus to others but cheats at work, is a tyrant at home, and shows no mercy to the needy, how can such a person's witness be credible? Thus, it is certainly true that all these things—loving, feeding, clothing, visiting—are necessary for a true and credible Christian witness.

On the other hand, however, these things are not in themselves sufficient. Think again of a court of law in which the butler stands accused of murder. If a respectable and loving person comes in as a witness for the defense and refuses to say anything, insisting on only smiling at the butler and in general treating him as innocent, the supposed "witness" will hardly be such. Some particularly perceptive jurors may conclude that the "witness" who refuses to witness likes the butler or even that he thinks the butler did not do it. But even such jurors will hardly be justified in accepting such wordless "testimony" as a basis for acquittal. Likewise, if Christians go through life—as they should—feeding the hungry and clothing the naked but never say why they do these things or what sort of faith inspires them, they will probably be considered good and loving people; but they will not be witnesses for Jesus Christ. And when the church feeds people, builds schools and hospitals, creates community centers, and so forth but refuses to tell the people receiving these services why it is doing all this, it may well gain respect in the community—it may even avoid alienating those who do not wish to hear anything about faith—but it is not giving a faithful witness to Jesus Christ.

In recent decades this point has often been forgotten. Part of the reason for this forgetfulness is a backlash against the obviously mistaken notion that the only reason we must help the needy is to bring them to Christ. In reaction to such a grave error and to the negative image of Christianity it fostered, many have simply decided that the church ought to serve people without ever inviting them to become disciples of Jesus. This too is a mistake. We are called to be witnesses, and there is no way we can be witnesses without somehow speaking the name of Jesus and inviting others to follow.

In a court of law, witnessing is a fairly formal act. One takes the stand; one takes an oath; one answers questions as precisely as possible. We must not make the mistake of thinking that Christian witness is any less important. It is true that most of us will never be put in a formal setting such as a witness stand and asked to speak about our faith. But it is also true that witnessing for Christ is a deliberate, conscious act. Although sometimes it "just happens," we are not supposed to sit around waiting for it to happen. We are to take, if not the stand, certainly a stance. We must deliberately and consciously act as witnesses—which does not deny the fact that Christians also witness by their every action, including unconscious actions. There are times and situations in which we must speak; to refuse to speak is to reject and contradict the power of the Spirit that is promised us.

If it is true that Christ came to the world to save the world and if it is also true that he lives in us, then the Christ who lives in us will do just as he did when he walked the roads of Galilee. He will seek to heal the sick, not in order to convert them, but because they are sick and should be whole. He will clothe the naked, not as a way of turning them into his disciples, but because they should not be cold. He will speak to those who do not believe in him, not with apologies, as if he had no right to speak, but with the assurance that what he has to say is good news—good news to the poor, who shall be fed, and good news to the lost, who shall be found. All these things, and much more, will Christ do through us *when he lives in us!*

CHAPTER 8
Giving

For this reason the Father loves me, because I lay down my life in order to take it up again. No one takes it from me, but I lay it down of my own accord. (John 10:17-18)

Let the same mind be in you that was in Christ Jesus,
      who, though he was in the form of God,
         did not regard equality with God
         as something to be exploited,
      but emptied himself,
         taking the form of a slave,
         being born in human likeness.
      And being found in human form,
         he humbled himself
         and became obedient to the point of death—
         even death on a cross.
      Therefore God also highly exalted him
         and gave him the name
         that is above every name,
      so that at the name of Jesus
         every knee should bend,
         in heaven and on earth and under the earth,
      and every tongue should confess
         that Jesus Christ is Lord,
         to the glory of God the Father.
                          (Philippians 2:5-11)

Jesus the Giver and the Gift

Throughout this book we have been studying several things that Jesus did during his ministry and things that he does when he lives in us. We have seen Jesus calling, healing, and so forth. However, if we had to summarize all these things in a single word, an excellent choice would be *giving*. When he called others, Jesus gave them new direction and meaning in life. When he healed others, he gave them health and dignity. He gave of himself when he prayed, when he taught, and when he fed. He gave, and then he gave again, and then he gave some more. And when he seemed to have given as much as any could expect, he gave his life.

Jesus' self-definition is in terms of giving. Think for instance of the several images by which he describes himself in the Gospel of John—the "I am" sayings: He is "the bread of life" (John 6:35, 48), which implies being broken so that others may live. He is "the light of the world" (John 8:12; 9:5), which implies being dispersed so that others may see. He is "the gate for the sheep" (John 10:7, 9), standing there so that through him others may come to the knowledge of God. He is "the good shepherd" (John 10:11, 14), who gives his life for the sheep. He is "the resurrection and the life" (John 11:25), who gives life to Lazarus and to any who believe in him. He is "the way, and the truth, and the life" (John 14:6) so that by following him, others may come to truth and life. He is "the true vine" (John 15:1) that provides nurture to the branches and without which the branches can bear no fruit.

Yet in order to see how much he is the Giver, we have to go back to the beginning of the Gospel of John where we are told that "all things came into being through him, and without him not one thing came into being" (John 1:3). You admire that beautiful sunset with its shining reds and golds? That is his gift. You enjoy the singing of the birds in the early morning hours? That is his gift. You delight in the feel of life rushing through your body? That too is his gift. You cultivate the life of the mind and the soul through reading and praying? Even that is his gift. The most distant star that shines upon the night and the invisible atom where electrons swirl—they too come from him. Again, "All things came into being through him, and without him not one thing came into being" (John 1:3).

Yet that is not the most surprising fact about this one who can say, "Before Abraham was, I am" (John 8:58). The most surprising fact is that in him the Giver became also the Gift. In John's famous words, "God so loved the world that he *gave* [italics added] his only Son" (3:16). Jesus is not only giver; he is also gift!

A Sometimes Unwelcome Gift

Significantly, in this culture the traditional time for giving gifts is Christmas. This is so much the case that most of us join the frenzy of buying and wrapping gifts without even giving much thought to the reason we are doing so. For many people, this gift giving has become almost an obligation. We make a list of all the people to whom we have to give something, and then we rack our brains to see what we can give them. "Christmas shopping" has become one more chore, which some of us do early in the year and others postpone until the last minute—but in any case, it is still a chore.

In all this gift buying and gift wrapping, the real gift that we are supposed to celebrate in Christmas is often forgotten. Santa Claus has become more important than Jesus because he is the one who brings the goodies—and because the picture of Jesus lying in a manger amid cows and horses does not contribute to the level of unbridled spending that the economy expects and requires of us at Christmas.

Perhaps, however, there is a deeper reason why we have obscured the centrality of Jesus in Christmas. Jesus himself said that "it is more blessed to give than to receive" (Acts 20:35). This is true, and we will return to the point later on in this chapter. But the saying could also be translated as, "It is happier to give than to receive." In the case of Christmas, it certainly is *merrier* to give than to receive. But in our frenzied Christmas shopping and wrapping, we often manage to forget the Gift of Christmas. And in a sense we prefer it that way because it is *easier* to give gifts than to receive the Gift. When we buy and give gifts, all that is challenged is our imagination and our pocketbook. When we receive the Gift, our very being is challenged to its core. Thus, as Christmas approaches, we avoid the threat of the Gift by hiding behind the noise of jingling bells and ho-ho-hos.

How does the Gift threaten us? First of all, the Gift threatens us by the implication that we actually need it. We like to think that we are self-sufficient; that we can manage our own affairs; and that if we have any problems, all that we need is a bit of effort and ingenuity and we will solve them. But the gift of Jesus tells us otherwise. We are not as self-sufficient as we would like to think we are. By managing our own affairs, we have actually botched them—both as individuals and as an entire human race. Even our efforts to solve our own problems often lead to even greater problems. In a word, we are sinners. We would rather define ourselves otherwise—to say, for instance, that I am a lawyer or a carpenter or a student. But the Gift means that a significant and unavoidable part of our reality is this element that we would much rather forget: We are sinners; we are lost; we are not even in control of our own lives. In this sense, the words of Jesus in Revelation, addressed to the Christians in Laodicea, apply to us quite well: "For you say, 'I am rich, I have prospered, and I need nothing.' You do not realize that you are wretched, pitiable, poor, blind, and naked" (Revelation 3:17).

Then the Gift also threatens us by demanding that we too become givers and gifts. Receiving usually requires the reciprocity of giving. This is true even in the gift giving that takes place around Christmas, birthdays, and other celebrations. One of the social conventions of our culture is that favors are to be returned. Many people would rather not ask another person for a favor because then they would be obligated to return the favor at a later point. For example, if someone invites us to dinner, we feel that in the near future we must return the invitation. Likewise, sometimes we put someone on our list for Christmas gifts simply because he or she gave us something last year. The result is that a gift received is in a sense an obligation acquired; so the more gifts we receive, the more our Christmas list grows.

In this case, what is true in our common practices of giving is also true in matters of faith. Paradoxically, receiving the Gift also means belonging to the Giver. He is ours, and we are his. These are two sides of the same coin; one cannot exist without the other. To claim the Gift, we have to give ourselves to him. There is no other way. And it is precisely because there is no other way that we are so tempted to obscure the offer of the Gift with all sorts of glittery decorations and with feverish gift giving and gift wrapping.

That is why in a sense Jesus is an unwelcome gift. As the Gospel of John put it, "He came to what was his own, and his own people did not accept him. But to all who received him, who believed in his name, he gave power to become children of God" (John 1:11-12). He came to offer himself; he did offer himself—and we insist on cheapening his gift with glittery celebrations, ritual gift giving, and religious banalities.

The Gift Above Every Other Gift

And yet, this is the Gift above every other gift. It is above every other because it is the gift of life itself. As Jesus told his disciples, no one was actually taking his life from him. Had he wished to do so, he could have avoided the cross. He was even tempted to do so. But Jesus stayed the course, with his face set toward Jerusalem (Luke 9:53) and the cross.

This is the Gift above every other gift because it is the gift of divinity itself, which he gave up in order to be one of us. It is the gift above every other gift because he

did not regard equality with God
as something to be exploited,
but emptied himself,
taking the form of a slave,
being born in human likeness.
And being found in human form,
he humbled himself
and became obedient to the point of death—
even death on a cross.

Or as the traditional hymn "Thou Didst Leave Thy Throne" says,

Thou didst leave Thy throne and Thy kingly crown
When Thou camest to earth for me.[1]

And, finally, this is the Gift above every gift because it is the gift by which alone we live. It is the gift of life itself, not only in the sense that Jesus' life was given up for us but also in the sense that his gift gives us life. As Jesus himself put it, "I came that they may have life, and have it abundantly" (John 10:10). It is by his being born among us, by his death and resurrection, and by his indwelling presence— in other words, by his gift—that we live. Thanks to his gift, we live, not in the mere sense of breathing and walking and eating, but in the deeper sense of knowing whose we are and trusting him in life and in death. As Paul expressed it, for us "living is Christ and dying is gain" (Philippians 1:21). Or, as the title of this entire book suggests, it is when Christ lives in us—in other words, when we receive his gift that is above every other gift—that we truly live.

The Gift of Giving

In previous chapters we have seen that Jesus' call to us leads us to call others and that his having healed us calls us to the ministry of healing. The same is true when we look at Jesus' giving. His gift to us brings many things—joy, peace, meaning, power—but perhaps most noteworthy among them is the capacity to give. That is why the hymn Paul quotes in Philippians is preceded by the introduction, "Let the same mind be in you that was in Christ Jesus" (Philippians 2:5). In other words, just as Jesus did not insist on keeping his prerogatives and his status but humbled himself and gave of himself, so are we not to insist on our prerogatives and our status but must humble ourselves and give of ourselves.

This is easy to say but hard to do. There are two apparently opposite attitudes that make it difficult. The first, and the most prevalent in the dominant circles of our society, is the attitude that claims we have somehow earned all that we are, have, and own and that these are ours to use as we please. Such an attitude is typical of what in our society we call the "self-made man"—a self-contradictory phrase if there ever was one, for to be human is by definition to be made by another and to be dependent on countless others. It is the attitude of those who think that the only purpose in life is to enjoy as many pleasures and as much ease as possible.

On the other hand, there is the apparently opposite attitude of those who employ giving as a way of gaining. This is the temptation most typical of those in our society who are often denied direct access to power—and is therefore more prevalent among women, the poor, and ethnic minorities. This is the attitude of the mother who is constantly making sacrifices for her children and who in subtle ways reminds them that they owe her so much that they ought to treat her with particular respect and devotion. And this is the attitude of all who abase themselves and hurry to do their various superiors' bidding in order to gain emotional control over them.

These two attitudes are understandable and in some cases are even to be expected. But when Christ lives in us, both attitudes are left behind.

The first attitude—that of the assured "self-made man"—is left behind because when we accept the gift of Christ, the first thing we come to acknowledge is that the message to the Laodiceans in the Book of Revelation is indeed right and that no matter how rich, powerful, and self-sufficient we might appear to be, the truth is that we are poor, weak, and wretched. It is impossible to accept the Gift without acknowledging our need of it. Therefore, when we accept the Gift, we come to see that, not only this particular aspect of our lives, but all aspects—money, career, health, and life itself—are given to us by the same one who now grants us this greatest of all gifts. As a result, the moment we open our hearts to the Gift, we open our hand for giving because Christ lives in us.

Likewise, the second attitude—that of "sacrificial self-denial" so that others may become our debtors—is also left behind. We now come to recognize that there is a difference between manipulation and love and that manipulating others is a way of dehumanizing people. But even more, we come to recognize that the Christ who lives in us merits the highest respect. Humiliating ourselves beyond measure for the sake of attaining some ulterior goal is to debase the Christ who lives in us. Acting as if we were really giving freely, as Christ has given himself to us, when in truth our giving has emotional and psychological strings attached, is to deny and insult the Christ who lives in us.

What all of this means is that the kind of giving Jesus expects of us is not something we can do in and of ourselves but is itself a gift. It is when the Christ who gave himself for us lives in us that we begin to be able to give as he gave and as he calls us to give.

Exercising the Gift of Giving

Although giving is a gift, it is also something we can cultivate. Remember the parable of the talents (Matthew 25:14-30; Luke 19:11-27). The talents that each of the servants received were not their own. Yet they could invest them so as to increase them and thus be able to render to their master more than they had received. Likewise, real, selfless giving is a gift from Christ—it is not something we can attain on our own. But it is a gift we are expected to use in a certain way. We must invest it, we must use it, in order to see it grow. If not, we are like the steward who buried his talent for fear of losing it, with the ironic result that he was the only one who actually lost what had been entrusted to him! Just as we have received every other gift from God, we have received the gift of giving. And, just as the gift of the body needs exercise in order to develop as intended, so does the gift of giving need exercise in order to develop. The gift of giving, if not employed and exercised, may well be lost, with the sad result that we lose some of the joy that should be ours when Christ lives in us.

How do we exercise the gift of giving? Quite simply, by giving! Or, in the United Methodist tradition, by following John Wesley's famous suggestion that we (1) make all we can, (2) save all we can, and (3) give all we can. Unfortunately, the way this dictum has been interpreted is in the sense that we should make as much money as we can, stash away as much as possible, and then give whatever is left over. But that is not what Wesley meant. What he meant was that his followers should work hard and be responsible so as to make all they could. Then they should avoid unnecessary expenditure—the "save all you can" did not mean "stash away all you can" but rather "use as little as possible." The final point of the triad did not refer to giving leftovers but to giving whatever one did not actually have to spend on oneself. But above all, Wesley did not conceive of these three as parallel activities that one performs independently of each other—like a person building three stacks of bricks and keeping all three at the same height. He was not speaking of three tasks to be kept in balance with each other, as one should keep in balance, for instance, mental and physical activity. On the contrary, he envisioned the three as a series of steps leading to the highest, the third, which is the goal of the whole. One was to make all one could, not in order to be wealthier, but in order to be able to give more. One was to save all one could, not in order to increase one's savings, but in order to be able to give more.

Giving, however, involves more than money. The most effective giving—the giving that most helps both the recipient and the giver—is the giving of oneself. We have much more than money to give. To name just a few examples, we have time; we have words; and we have gestures.

Think first about words and gestures. Here you can easily apply the third of Wesley's three suggestions without having to worry about how many words or gestures you have or how you can save them. In many sorts of situations, a word or a gesture of support can be more meaningful than a bagful of money. Yet here again you must make certain that your gift is sincere. As we all know, "words are cheap" and can be substituted for needed actions. Thus, when people do not really wish to help someone, they can say something like, "I am really pulling for you," and then do no actual pulling at all! Still, when words and gestures are genuine expressions of love—when they flow from the Christ who lives in us—they are an invaluable gift.

Now think about time. In this case you can apply only two of Wesley's suggestions. You can save time. You can give time. But you cannot make more time. That is because, in spite of what common wisdom says, time is not money. Time is life. Just as you cannot make more time, for every day has twenty-four hours and every hour sixty minutes, the possibilities of extending your life are rather limited. You may be able to live longer through exercise and a healthy diet or by medical intervention. But those possibilities are fairly limited; and, in any case, there is no certainty that they will produce positive results. There is always the possibility that any minute will be the last of your life. That is why one can say quite accurately that time is life and also that time—precisely because it is life—is the most valuable gift anyone can give.

To develop the gift of giving, we have to exercise it. To do so, continuously, is not easy. There is so much need out there that we are always threatened by what has been called "compassion fatigue"—a feeling that, since the needs are so various and so overwhelming and since we cannot really solve every problem or assuage every suffering, it is better simply to ignore suffering in the world and carry on with our own lives. As we look around, we see a fractured and pained society in which many are in need of physical, emotional, and spiritual support. We know that there is just so much we can do with our money; we cannot give to every worthy cause. Nor can we be present at every place where there is need for love and personal warmth. Therefore, we simply get tired of giving and turn to something else.

That is similar to what happens to many of the physical fitness programs on which we embark. They are hard work. The first few days are relatively easy, for the program still has the allure of novelty. Then comes a time when we begin to wonder whether it is worth all the effort. Our muscles ache, we see little difference in our fitness, and we have too many other things to do. It is at this stage that most physical fitness programs are abandoned. Yet, if at that point we give up, whatever gain we have made in the earlier period will be lost. In a similar manner, when we become aware of a significant need and feel called to help meet it, the first stages are relatively easy. But eventually compassion fatigue sets in. We tire of hearing sad stories about people in need. At that point we are tempted to direct our energies in another direction—perhaps to our own individual spiritual life or to our family or to our church. Clearly, these other areas are worthy and should be tended to. But if we allow them to distract us from exercising the gift of giving, the consequences will be similar to those we suffer when we abandon a physical fitness program: Our gains will be lost, and we will find that we have to begin all over again.

Then, when it comes to exercise, there is always the temptation of "substitute exercise." Going out on a field and running requires too much effort. If it is hot and muggy, we will perspire and grow thirsty. If it is cold and dry, we will freeze. Therefore, we turn on the television set and watch a game in which others do the exercise for us. We enjoy much of the excitement of a real game—but without the sweat and the pain. We can easily become "couch potatoes" while at the same time we claim expertise in a dozen sports we never practice. Along similar lines, we are also tempted to use money as a means of "substitute presence"—to pay for someone to deal directly with the suffering and the needy while we remain physically and emotionally absent. By writing a check, we clear our conscience; and then we can go on with the business of life without having to deal directly with the pain in the world—just as our sense that we ought to exercise is cleared by watching a good baseball game.

The gift of giving must be exercised in order to develop. Just as a good physical fitness program exercises the whole body, so does the gift of giving need to be exercised simultaneously with all the things we have received in order to give—with money, other resources, words, and time. At some points, like any fitness program, it will be painful or unexciting; and we may be tempted to interrupt the exercise regime. And yet, as we continue exercising the gift of giving, we will see it develop, just as we see our muscles developing with physical exercise. Slowly, but undeniably, our joy in giving will increase—and this, not just because we will be more accustomed to giving, but even more so because the Christ who lives in us will find expression in our deeds.

The Gift Returned

As was mentioned above, in much of our daily life we expect gifts to be reciprocated—even though we seldom say so. Much that today goes by the name of giving is in fact an investment of a different sort. We give someone a hand at a particular task, expecting that when we in turn need help, that person will return the gift. Parents make enormous sacrifices for their children, expecting that their children will care for them in their old age. Churches sponsor refugee families, expecting that they will become active church members. There is nothing wrong with this expectation as long as it does not become the motivation for our giving. When it does and the person whom we helped fails to return the gift, we become angry at that person—and at ourselves for being duped. The result is that we cease helping, and the church that began enthusiastically sponsoring a refugee family refuses to sponsor others. Thus, our giving is no longer governed by the love of Christ but by the positive or negative responses of the recipients.

In both passages quoted at the beginning of this chapter, there is a final movement in which the gift is received back. In the passage from John, Jesus says that he lays down his life; but he says also that he will take it back. In the passage from Philippians, the humiliation and death of Jesus are followed by his exaltation and eventually by the worship of every creature. Thus, the gift that Jesus made of his own status and life was returned to him. He lay down his life, and he rose again. He emptied himself of his glory, and he is full of glory.

Jesus himself told his disciples that their giving their lives and possessions for him would not go unrewarded: "Everyone who has left houses or brothers or sisters or father and mother or children or fields, for my name's sake, will receive a hundredfold, and will inherit eternal life" (Matthew 19:29). And he said also that "those who lose their life for my sake will find it" (Matthew 10:39).

It is at this point that the saying of Jesus becomes clear: "It is more blessed to give than to receive" (Acts 20:35). In true Christian giving, the blessedness—the joy—does not come primarily from the receiving but from the giving itself. When we give only for the joy of receiving a reward, we have not really given; we have invested. Investments can prove to be quite fortunate; or they can go sour, depending on the return. When our giving is for the sake of receiving, the response of the recipients will ultimately govern our giving. When, on the other hand, our giving is truly a gift, the joy and the blessedness are in the giving itself rather than in the eventual receiving. This is true Christian giving. This is the sort of giving that comes from the same mind being in us that was in Jesus Christ,

> who, though he was in the form of God,
>> did not regard equality with God
>> as something to be exploited,
> but emptied himself,
>> taking the form of a slave,
>> being born in human likeness.
> And being found in human form,
>> he humbled himself
>> and became obedient to the point of death—
>> even death on a cross.

This is the giving that takes place in us when we have truly received the Gift that is Jesus Christ—or, in other words, *when Christ lives in us!*

---

[1] From "Thou Didst Leave Thy Throne," in *AMEC Bicentennial Hymnal* (The African Methodist Episcopal Church, 1984); 105.

Unconclusion

It is customary to end a book with a "conclusion." Doing so, however, gives the impression that, having reached that point, one comes to the end of the matter. For that reason, I have called this last chapter "Unconclusion," hoping to stress the fact that the life of discipleship is always unconcluded. As Soren Kierkegaard put it,

Faith means just that: that what I seek is not here, which is precisely the reason I believe it. Faith signifies precisely the deep, strong, blessed unrest which urges on the believer, so that he cannot find rest in this world, so the one who does find complete rest here, would also cease to be a believer; for a believer cannot sit still, as one sits with a walking-staff in his hand; a believer pushes forward.[1]

You have now finished reading this book, and I have finished writing it. But our common pilgrimage may be just beginning. What I have written, and what you have studied, barely touches the surface of what it means to live in Christ and to have Christ living in us.

What now lies ahead is a continuous pilgrimage, where every turn in the road will bring unexpected vistas and new challenges, where every mountain climbed will reveal loftier peaks to ascend, and where every valley visited will open new fields of service.

Thus, dear reader, as we each alone and all together continue along our pilgrimage, I bid you farewell, with the certainty that, since we travel on the same Way, we will meet again—if not along the road, certainly at the End!

---

[1] From *The Gospel of Our Suffering and the Lilies of the Field*, by Soren Kierkegaard (Augsburg, 1948); pages 5-6.

ILLEGAL PEOPLE

How Globalization Creates Migration
and Criminalizes Immigrants

David Bacon

BEACON PRESS, BOSTON

Beacon Press
25 Beacon Street
Boston, Massachusetts 02108-2892
www.beacon.org

Beacon Press books
are published under the auspices of
the Unitarian Universalist Association of Congregations.

14 13 12 11   8 7 6 5 4 3

This book is printed on acid-free paper that meets the uncoated paper
ANSI/NISO specifications for permanence as revised in 1992.

Text design by Susan E. Kelly
at Wilsted & Taylor Publishing Services

Library of Congress Cataloging-in-Publication Data

Bacon, David
  Illegal people : how globalization creates migration and criminalizes immigrants /
David Bacon.
    p. cm.
  ISBN-13: 978-0-8070-4230-4 (pbk : alk. paper)
    1. Alien labor—United States. 2. Alien labor—Developing countries. 3. Globalization
—Economic aspects. 4. Globalization—Social aspects. 5. Labor policy—United States.
6. Labor movement—United States. 7. Labor unions—United States. 8. Illegal aliens—
United States. I. Title.

  HD8081.A5B33 2008
  331.6'20973—dc22   2008015394

"Huelga en General" was adapted from a Mexican *corrido* by Luis Valdez. It is
excerpted here by permission of El Teatro Campesino.

"El Corrido de Industry" by Omar Sierra and "La Frasesita" are excerpted
here by permission of Los Jornaleros del Norte and the National Day Laborer
Organizing Network, Los Angeles, California.

Contents

Preface

The word "illegal" has become a one-word mantra in the U.S. political debate. For many years, immigrant-rights activists have sought to encourage people to use the word "undocumented" instead, which describes more accurately the predicament of people living in the United States without immigration papers. Activists have especially opposed using "illegal" as a noun, to describe people rather than their actions. One of the most heartfelt slogans shouted in the huge immigrant marches of the last few years, printed on millions of signs and buttons, is "No human being is illegal!" This is an eloquent demand for rights and equality, and a protest against deportations and injustice.

What accounts, then, for the almost universal use of "illegal"? Without a doubt, this has been a victory for a small but vocal nativist movement, with deep racist roots. Using the word to demonize undocumented people is part of this movement's campaign to oppose all immigration. It feeds an anti-immigrant hysteria promoted by some politicians and feared by others. It has important economic payoffs for many employers. It is used incessantly in the media by people who don't think about what the word really means, or what happens to those so labeled.

But "illegal" also describes a social reality—inequality. Applied to immigrants, it has very little to do with the violation of a law or crossing a border. For centuries there were no visas or "papers" needed in order to enter the United States, and anyone could walk across the border. It's still only a minor civil violation to be in the country without documents. "Illegal" is all about social and political status. "Illegal" says society is divided into those who have rights and those who don't, those whose status and presence in the United States is legitimate and those whose status is illegitimate, those who are part of the community and those who are not. Yet those branded as illegal are part of the economic engine of this country.

In the United States the ideas and practice of social inequality, of inclusion and exclusion, are very old. They developed in the first settlements of Europeans in a land belonging to others, and in the importation of chattel slaves to labor and create wealth. These ideas became codified in the "legal" justification for these injustices. Today inequality is being re-created and reproduced by a global economic system. "Illegal," or "bracero," the word used by Rigoberto Garcia, or *clandestino,* the word sung by Manu Chao, all describe the same unequal status of a huge number of people, forced into migration around the world.

This book is titled *Illegal People* in recognition of this reality. A globalized political and economic system creates illegality by displacing people and then denying them rights and equality as they do what they have to do to survive—move to find work. This book tells the story of that process, from their point of view.

In its first chapter, the book begins by looking at what it means to be illegal—how the lack of legal status is used to keep people vulnerable, to criminalize and punish them when they try to improve their conditions. At the Woodfin Suites Hotel in California and the Smithfield meatpacking plant in North Carolina, immigration enforcement didn't just affect those who had no status—it hurt the other workers around them. In Chapter 2 the narrative then travels back to Mexico, the country of origin of many Woodfin and Smithfield workers, and examines the process of displacement that forced people to migrate to survive. It tells the stories of two recent events—the uprising in Oaxaca and the miners' strike in Cananea—to uncover the social forces uprooting communities.

Chapter 3 puts the two pieces together. It contends that the same economic system benefiting from the changes causing displacement in Mexico also benefits from the labor displacement produces, especially undocumented labor. It focuses on the role that the North American Free Trade Agreement and economic reforms play in this process.

Chapters 4, 5, and 6 explore the politics of the debate over immigration and trade policy in the United States. Chapter 4 analyzes guest-worker programs, and recounts the personal experiences of the workers involved. It then traces the development of the employer lobby set up to win expansion of those programs. Chapter 5 tells the story of the Los Angeles upsurge among immigrant workers (the "rising of the million," union organizer Peter Olney calls it). Those events reshaped the way U.S. unions look at immigrants, and won labor as a sometimes-uncertain ally instead of an obstacle. Chapter 6 proposes that alliances between immigrants, African Americans, and unions can win immigration reform, by making it part of a larger political program.

In the last two chapters, the book returns to the historical development of the concept of illegality. It examines its function in a modern world of high-tech guest workers and countries increasingly dependent on exporting people to labor in the global North. And finally the book suggests some alternatives, always the hardest part of the immigration debate. It concentrates on some of the most progressive ideas, which have been put forward by immigrant-rights activists and by migrants themselves.

For the last two decades I've worked as a journalist and photographer, writing stories and photographing many of the events described here. The book combines interviews and personal histories documented over a long period of time, with political analysis that puts these experiences into context. The sources for the facts and conclusions presented are usually identified in the text, and are very often those of the people directly quoted. These voices and that context are very necessary in today's debates over "free trade" and "immigration" policy. Both words are actually misnomers, as the book will argue, and create illusions about the nature of a globalized economic system.

In the United States, the political problems of trade and immigration are discussed in isolation from each other, as though Congress, in passing a trade bill, will not have to deal with the displaced people created by the legislation the next time it takes up immigration reform. It's not surprising, therefore, that these problems seem so insoluble. Further, the complex process of displacement and migration is usually discussed in a vacuum. Those who live with globalization's consequences are not at the table, and their voices are generally excluded along with those who propose progressive alternatives. This doesn't help anyone understand its true cost or who pays it. Yet people enduring those consequences often have a truer understanding of that cost, and their experiences present a much more realistic picture of the way the system really functions.

This book takes their side. Faced with poverty, migration, and deportation, neutrality is not really possible. One either tries to understand and change social reality or one doesn't. The book doesn't offer a fix-all solution, but presents instead some of the political and economic alternatives proposed by those often shut out of the debate.

There are important resources for readers who want to explore these issues further, which have also been useful to me in more than a decade of reporting. A network of immigrant-rights organizations collects and distributes data about the impact of immigration laws and policies, many with listserves. There are probably more newspaper and magazine articles about immigration published today than most other issues, and it's often hard to keep up. One of the many listserves is Immigration News Briefs, sent out by members of the former Committee for the Human Rights of Immigrants in New York (to get on the list, send a note to immigrationnewsbriefs@gmail.com). One of the best sources of independent analysis and passionate advocacy is the National Network for Immigrant and Refugee Rights, in Oakland, California (www.nnirr.org). In addition, the network brings together a host of community-based immigrant-rights organizations around the country, and each of them is a great source of information and inspiration.

Other sources of information, particularly on trade issues, include the Red Mexicana de Acción Frente al Libre Comercio (the Mexican Action Network on Free Trade—www.rmalc.org.mx/index.shtml),

the American Friends Service Committee (www.afsc.org), and the
Alliance for Responsible Trade (www.art-us.org/). The IBON Foundation in Manila has important information and analysis about Philippines overseas workers and the country's labor-export policy (www
.ibon.org/). The National Immigration Law Center (www.nilc.org)
has up-to-date news and analysis of current immigration law.

I've had the help of many people who provided material and im-
portant feedback for this book. They include John Womack, Jeff Faux,
Sarah Anderson, Juan Manuel Sandoval, Enrique Davila, Mary Bauer,
Victor Narro, Bill Chandler, Bill Fletcher, my wife Lillian Galedo,
Maria Blanco, Susan Alva, Edgar Ayala, Sergio Sosa, Colin Rajah, Ben
Davis, Rufino Dominguez, Eduardo Stanley, Bob Bach, Cathi Tac-
taquin, Arnoldo Garcia, Frank Martin del Campo, Frank Curiel, Renee
Saucedo, Peter Olney, Nativo Lopez, Ramon Ramirez, Bruce Gold-
stein, Ernesto Medrano, Martha Ojeda, Isabel Garcia, Mike Davis,
Mike Eisenscher, Karl Kramer, Sarah Norr, Brooke Anderson, Jona-
than Fox, Gaspar Rivera-Salgado, Alejandro Alvarez, Maria Estela Rios,
Steve Pitts, Phil Hutchings, Centolia Maldonado, Dolores Huerta,
Katie Quan, Agustin Ramirez, Jean Damu, Jim Evans, Harold Meyer-
son, Mike Casey, and Dean Alegado. I thank them all. Any errors I've
made here belong to me, however, not to them. I also thank the
magazines and foundations that have supported the work that led
to this book, including the *Nation,* the *American Prospect,* Pacific News
Service/New American Media, and the Rockefeller Foundation.

I was a union organizer for two decades before I began writing and
taking pictures. The working perspective formed in those years has
been a great advantage in trying to understand the problems of migrants and displaced communities. People don't exist just to fulfill an
economic function, and the book argues strenuously against that idea.
But the mainstream media and policy discussions suffer from the lack
of a class perspective.

As a union organizer and writer, I've also been active in the
immigrant-rights movement. I was a board member of the Northern
California Coalition for Immigrant Rights. I helped organize the Labor

Immigrant Organizers Network and People United for Human Rights. Together we've helped many people fight for their rights as immigrants and workers. I'm still doing that, as a journalist and photographer. I believe good journalism stands on the side of social justice, and that journalists should be involved in the world and unafraid to try to change it.

One

MAKING WORK A CRIME

Merry Christmas. You're fired.
On a rainy December day in Emeryville, California, a small city on
the eastern shore of San Francisco Bay, organizers handed out um-
brellas to a small group chanting and yelling in front of the Woodfin
Suites Hotel. Half the picketers were church and union folks—people
who turn out for demonstrations rain or shine. The other half of the
crowd had just come off work in the towering hotel looming above
them. Some held animated discussions as they walked up and down
the wet sidewalk in their uniforms, but most just looked tired.

Under one umbrella, Luz Dominguez, a Mexican woman in her
forties, huddled against another housekeeper. Dominguez and her colleague were already dreading the next day, when they'd once again
put on their gray work clothes and make the trek back to Emeryville
to clean hotel rooms. "I feel really exhausted at the end of my shift,"
she said with a sigh. "When I get home, I have no energy for my family. All I do is worry about what tomorrow will be like—if the rooms
will be the same, or even dirtier."

You wouldn't think that anyone would try to keep such a draining
job, but Dominguez and twenty coworkers had been fighting all fall
and into the winter to stop the hotel from firing them. Their 2006 pre-
Christmas picket line was one more effort. Woodfin hotel jobs were
suddenly worth a lot more to housekeepers, because a new ordinance
promised to lighten the workload that left them exhausted every day.
But just as the law seemed about to give the workers more time and

I

money for their families, the women found themselves at the center of the national firestorm over immigration.

On December 15, hotel managers sent Dominguez and her friends home. The workers were just twenty-one of thousands fired, and in some cases deported, in the Bush administration's offensive to root undocumented immigrants out of workplaces. An action a month earlier targeted workers at Cintas, the largest industrial laundry in the United States. And just days later, in raids at six Swift & Co. meatpacking plants, more than thirteen hundred laborers were detained and deported.

The firings and deportations of 2006 did not directly affect most of the estimated 12 million people then living in the United States without immigration papers. But they did make a political point. In a Washington press conference, Homeland Security secretary Michael Chertoff told reporters that his enforcement efforts highlighted the need for "stronger border security, effective interior enforcement, and a temporary-worker program." He took the opportunity to promote the president's proposed guest-worker program, which failed in Congress a few months later.

Labor and immigrant-rights activists saw an additional motive for the firings. Terminations, they said, targeted workplaces where people were organizing unions, trying to enforce labor-protection laws, fighting to improve wages and benefits, or otherwise standing up for their rights.

Emeryville's Woodfin Suites was a prime example for their accusations.

In November 2005 Emeryville voters had passed a worker-protection ordinance—Measure C. The initiative was the brainchild of the East Bay Alliance for a Sustainable Economy (EBASE), a worker advocacy group that embodies some new thinking in the labor movement. EBASE brings together union and community activists in a permanent coalition. Its young organizers are labor's shock troops, turning out for demonstrations exposing worker abuse and campaigning for living wages throughout the East Bay.

It was no accident that the group set its sights on Emeryville, a small town originally carved out a century ago as a tax-free haven for big factory owners at the foot of the Bay Bridge. The city's old industrial plants are long gone, and in their wake Emeryville reinvented itself as a home for hotels, malls, and loft apartments—businesses that all rely on immigrant labor. "The old guard was very business-friendly and gave the developers whatever they wanted," said city council member and lawyer John Fricke. "But the people who came to live in the new lofts and apartments are young people priced out of San Francisco. They have a pretty supportive attitude toward workers and immigrants."

EBASE organizers looked at the changed demographics and predicted that Emeryville would take to heart the plight of its primarily immigrant hotel workers. They collected signatures for a living-wage ordinance that mandated a nine-dollar hourly minimum, and an eleven-dollar average, in each of Emeryville's four hotels. Any housekeeper required to clean more than five thousand square feet in an eight-hour shift would earn time and a half.

The city's hotels—Holiday Inn, Marriott Courtyard, Sheraton Four Points, and Woodfin Suites—all opposed the ordinance. Under the name of the Committee to Keep Tax Dollars in Emeryville, they spent $115,610 for an election in which only 2,296 people voted, or $110 for each "no" vote cast. Despite their efforts, the ordinance prevailed 1,245 to 1,051. Afterward, the hotels tried but failed to prevent the measure's implementation with a court challenge.

Over the following spring and summer, EBASE organizers met with workers at the four hotels and explained the law's new requirements. Marcela Melquiades had been cleaning rooms at Woodfin Suites for two years. "The workload was very heavy," she recalled. "I'd be really tired at the end of the shift. I'd go to the bathroom right away and pour hot water on my hands. I still had to go home, make dinner for the kids, clean the house, get my uniform ready for the next day, get up early in the morning. It was exhausting."

Melquiades and her friend Dominguez became believers that Measure C could make things better. "Before it was approved, we cleaned sixteen suites a day, sometimes seventeen," Dominguez said. "A suite is made up of a bedroom, a hall, and a kitchen. We'd clean the whole thing in thirty minutes. When people would party and leave it dirty, we'd still have to clean it in that time."

Following the passage of Measure C, Woodfin Suites general manager Hugh McIntosh said the hotel changed its cleaning regimen to comply with the ordinance. "We reduced the rooms cleaned per day from seventeen to ten and a half, which is within the five-thousand-square-foot limit," he said. EBASE organizers say the correct number of rooms should be eight or nine. Still, there was no question that Measure C had transformed the housekeepers' jobs.

Then, in September, the hotel began accusing longtime workers like Dominguez and Melquiades of not having valid Social Security cards.

To get a job, everyone living in the United States must complete an I-9 form, which has to be accompanied by two pieces of identification, including a Social Security number. The form asks applicants to state whether they are citizens or legal residents. All the hotel's workers had long ago completed such paperwork and gone to work without objection. But on September 27, Dominguez, Melquiades, and nineteen others were given a letter by Mary Beth Smith, at the time the hotel's director of human relations. The letter gave them twenty-four hours to provide valid Social Security numbers. If they failed, they'd be fired.

The Social Security Administration writes to thousands of businesses every year, listing the names of millions of people whose numbers don't jibe with those on file. In 2001 the agency sent out 110,000 such letters, and the number increases every year. In 2007 SSA announced it would send out letters to 160,000 employers, listing the names and numbers of an estimated 8 million people.

There are many reasons a worker's Social Security number might not match government records. Some are undoubtedly clerical mistakes—the government's database is notoriously full of errors. But other workers, including the millions who are in the United States without proper documentation, make the list because they've used a nonexistent number, or one that belongs to another person. If they don't provide a number to their employer, they can't get hired. And because they have no immigration papers, they can't apply for a number of their own.

The Bureau of Immigration and Customs Enforcement (ICE), a division of the Department of Homeland Security, calls such use identity fraud. But using someone else's Social Security number to get a job is hardly the same as using someone else's credit card to purchase expensive stereo equipment. There is no evidence to suggest that the genuine holder of a Social Security number is harmed when someone else uses that number on the job. After all, an employer will be depositing extra money into the true cardholder's account, and the worker using the incorrect number will never be able to collect the benefits those earnings will accrue.

Social Security has issued no-match letters for many years, and they originally had a benign aim—ensuring that workers were properly credited with the money deducted by their employers. That, in turn, protected their disability and pension income. In other words, Social Security was meant to benefit workers, and the no-match letter was simply a clerical means to keep accounts in order. Further, the Social Security card is not a national identification card. In the United States, unlike many other countries, there is no national ID card, nor any obligation requiring residents to possess one. Every bill to create a national ID has failed in Congress.

Things began to change, however, after the Immigration Reform and Control Act was adopted in 1986. One provision of the law, employer sanctions, for the first time prohibited the employment of people without an immigration visa allowing them to work. But in making it illegal for the employer to hire them, the law also made it a crime for those workers to hold a job.

In the administrations that followed—Reagan, Bush senior, Clinton, and Bush junior—the Social Security database began to acquire a new character. Since it could be assumed that the Social Security numbers provided by undocumented workers wouldn't match the names attached to them in the database, these no-matches could be used to identify workers without immigration papers. Successive administrations then began pressuring Social Security to use its database in various ways to identify the undocumented.

No-match letters could also be used to pressure employers directly. Since workers listed might be assumed to be undocumented, their employers were in violation of the law if they continued to employ them. Many fearful employers simply fired workers on receiving the letter. No one keeps track of how many people have lost their jobs this way. In the debates over immigration reform, many lobbyists on both sides have claimed that employer sanctions were never enforced, and cite the low numbers of employers actually fined for violations. But they never count, or even consider, the thousands (at least) of workers driven from their jobs. Workers have paid the price for the enforcement of employer sanctions, not employers.

The letters also proved convenient to many unscrupulous companies, who used them as a pretext to fire workers active in organizing unions or, as in the case at Woodfin Suites, enforcing labor-protection laws. In the late 1990s, protests by labor and immigrant-rights activists over this practice forced the Social Security Administration to include a crucial paragraph in the no-match letters, cautioning employers not to construe a discrepancy in numbers as evidence of lack of immigration status. Employers are asked only to advise workers that they've received such a notice.

At Woodfin Suites, when pressed to justify firing workers when the letter specifically tells employers not to, hotel manager McIntosh alleged: "The law requires that, for an individual to work, they have to complete the I-9. That requires the workers to provide a valid Social Security number. We've simply asked them to get a document from SSA saying they've completed the I-9 requirements."

That didn't quite make sense. Under the immigration regulations then in force, once an employer accepted an I-9 form and an employee went to work, the employer couldn't later ask the worker to re-verify that information. Such re-verification has been viewed by the Department of Justice as discrimination, which is prohibited by the Immigration Reform and Control Act. EBASE didn't challenge the firings on that basis, but Marielena Hincapié, staff attorney for the National Im-

migration Law Center, says re-verification as a result of a no-match
check is a violation of section 274-B of the Immigration and Nationality Act. Congress expressly included this prohibition out of concern
that re-verification would lead to discriminatory worker dismissals.

Labor advocates saw another motivation for the Woodfin terminations. In court proceedings surrounding the firings, Woodfin Suites
revealed that it had received a letter about its workers' Social Security
numbers in May 2006. But managers took no action until September,
after employees had complained to the city council that the hotel
wasn't abiding by Measure C. Dominguez believes she knows why she
and her coworkers were dismissed: "The reason the hotel was saying
this was because we were demanding our rights."

Within a week of the firings in December, EBASE and the Emeryville city attorney went to court seeking an injunction returning the
housekeepers to their jobs. The city argued that it needed their presence until it could investigate whether the firings were retaliatory.
"It is very important for the city to keep the workers employed until
it can determine whether their allegations of retaliation are bona fide,"
said city council member Fricke. The councilman added that he asked
the hotel's manager if federal authorities were demanding that it terminate the workers. "He said no. Our problem is that if the city council allows an employer to threaten workers—although the hotel says
it's acting for some other reason—this has a strong, chilling effect on
the willingness of others to come forward and report violations."

McIntosh denied that the hotel was retaliating for the workers'
efforts to enforce Measure C. "We'd like to see them come back," he
said. But after the city council went to court, Congressman Brian Bilbray (R-San Diego), chair of the House Immigration Caucus, called
Homeland Security on behalf of company president Samuel Hardage.
Woodfin's headquarters and Hardage's office are in San Diego. Bilbray
got the Bureau of Immigration and Customs Enforcement to jump-
start an investigation of the immigration status of the workers.

Shortly after New Year's Day, once Alameda County Superior Court
judge Ronald Sabraw ordered the hotel to reinstate them, Dominguez,
Melquiades, and nineteen other housekeepers returned to the hotel.

They worked for a few weeks more, but eventually all those who had been listed in the no-match letters were looking for jobs elsewhere, caught between their need for employment and their growing unease about the immigration climate. And once the grace period had expired, all were eventually terminated.

EBASE and the twenty-one women had prevented the firings for at least six months, and kept noisy picket lines going for a year. In August of 2007 the city held a hearing on the hotel's compliance with Measure C, and told Woodfin to pay the women $250,000 in back wages owed during the time the hotel wasn't in compliance. The hotel announced it would not pay and intended to appeal the ruling. Its lawyer, Bruno Katz, was ejected from the council chambers for his constant interruptions during the council's discussion of the issue.

How the Housekeepers Saw It

Emeryville's housekeepers don't actually live in Emeryville. Many live in Oakland's Fruitvale district, the largest Latino barrio in the East Bay. For Dominguez and Melquiades, home is a gray, two-story apartment complex. Outside, along International Boulevard, signs in market windows list groceries in Spanish—chiles, tortillas, mangoes, and the other comfort foods of Mexico and Central America.

Dominguez's small two-bedroom unit isn't stuffed with furniture. A couch and foldout futon in the living room face a console with a TV and boom box. A huge stuffed floppy dog lies on the futon; atop the television, a big white stuffed bear with red satin hearts instead of paws holds two more red hearts stitched with the word *amor*—Spanish for *love*. Christmas lights around the front window light up the room.

The Fruitvale isn't really like Mexico, but there are enough Mexicans living there for it to feel like home. "You feel good here, but there's no work," Dominguez said. "You have to leave to find a job. That's why we go to Emeryville."

When Luz Dominguez first came to Oakland in 1995, she didn't know anything about any of the cities of the East Bay—not even the one where she was living. "It was very hard to find work," she remembered. "I would just walk up one street and down another, asking any-one I saw, people I'd never met before. If I didn't have any luck on one street, I'd just go on to the next. It hurt, and I was ashamed. But you always have to think, 'I'm going to find a way.' If you get negative, it paralyzes you."

As time went on she learned enough about her new home to begin finding cleaning jobs, which eventually led her to the Woodfin. That's where she met Marcela Melquiades, who grew up in a neighboring town on the fringe of Mexico City. Neither knew many people in Oakland or had an extended family in the United States. Melquiades came here at nineteen with her husband. They later separated, leaving her a single mother of three children, aged eleven, eight, and seven. Now she lives next door to Dominguez.

"We share memories of the food and the places we both remember, and forget our problems for a little while," Dominguez explained. "We've become good friends." The two women are fifteen years apart in age, but they laugh and put their heads together and their arms around each other as though they were classmates in high school.

When she arrived in Oakland eleven years ago, Melquiades didn't intend to stay long. "For a while, we came and went," she recalled. "Like every immigrant, you always think at first that you're going to make life better at home—build a house or start a business. But time passes. You realize you can live better here, and you forget about your old goals. And you stay."

But she also had difficulty finding a good job, and having young children didn't make it easier. "Everything was new and strange," she recalled. "You don't know how things work. You don't know anyone. You have to ask about everything: doctors, school, whatever." She worked one Christmas in a factory, making tree ornaments. Other years she was a domestic. Eventually she, too, got work in hotels. "I don't like kitchens or restaurants," she said with a laugh, thinking about the places where most immigrants in the Fruitvale enter the workforce. "I like cleaning."

Eventually, Dominguez and Melquiades came to feel comfortable working at Woodfin Suites. For years Mary Beth Smith and other managers had been watching the housekeepers make beds, wash toilets, vacuum carpets, and clean up after messy guests. "I thought I had a place where people knew my work and respected me," Dominguez said. "When I first started working they didn't give me gloves, and I still cleaned the sinks and the toilets. I pulled garbage from the trashcans with my bare hands. I never said, 'If you don't give me gloves, I won't do it.' I needed a job, and I wanted to work.

"I felt appreciated," she continued. "Guests would say, 'Doña Luz, you're doing a great job.' I didn't care if they left me tips. In 2005 the hotel even gave me their Employee of the Year Award. So when they began demanding the card, I felt destroyed inside. I cried. I said to myself, 'How can you ignore all the good things I've done?'" When Dominguez describes what happened at the hotel, she is still so angry that her voice trembles. "She [Smith] told us we'd have to show her our Social Security cards so they could check the numbers," she recalled bitterly. "Before, they'd tell us sometimes they'd received a notice about our numbers not matching, but they never required us to take any action, or told us we couldn't continue working."

Emeryville is still a beautiful city to her, but at the hotel everything changed. "People in the office used to greet me," she said. "Afterwards, they turned their backs, like we were criminals."

After work one December night, with her family fed, Dominguez and her friend Marcela sat at the Formica table in Dominguez's kitchen. Cups of cinnamon tea rested on little white doilies alongside a plate of tiny white guava-jam sandwiches with their crusts cut off, like an English tea party with Mexican flavors. Drinking tea, the two mothers remembered home.

"My father taught us to work," Dominguez recalled. "'We are working people,' he told us, 'and nothing is given to us.' He always had his sayings. One of them was, 'We help people without expecting to receive something in return. What matters is what you're like inside—that is what God will see. So maybe we won't be rich, but we will have peace inside us.'"

It's hard for her to feel that peace now. "I don't feel comfortable," she said of the world beyond the workplace. "We live in a Latino community, and we bring our customs here, but we're looked down on, judged, and criticized. People have the right to say we have to adapt to life here. It's their country. We're the foreigners. But I want us to be taken into account."

Dominguez also made another type of sacrifice common to immigrant families—separation. Her oldest daughter is twenty-four and attending college in Mexico City, for which her mother sends back money every month. She is unlikely to settle in the United States with the rest of her family. "You have to make a lot of sacrifices, and one is that some children will live here, and some will live there," she mourned. "We won't be together. You can't have everything."

Melquiades also learned survival skills from her father. After a lifetime as a construction worker, he came to live with her, saying how proud he was of her accomplishments in the United States. "When I was a girl, he worked in factories in Mexico," she remembered. "He was always fighting for the rights of the people around him, always getting fired for it." His daughter's predicament sounded familiar. But now she also feels insecure about whether she's really found a home here. She wakes up in the middle of the night tormented by bills and problems. "I'm just living from one day to the next on what I make," she said. "I don't know what I'm going to do without a job. I'm always worried about the next day. I'm just living with anxiety, all the time."

Dominguez grew bitter about the lack of value given to her work. "A Social Security number can't wash toilets or vacuum floors or make beds," she declared angrily. "Only human beings can do that. Legal documents are very important, but real, physical work is what counts." Recognition of their labor is the yardstick both women fall back on to measure their acceptance in the United States. "All we want is to work," Melquiades pleaded. "We're just fighting for the right to work."

As a result of Congressman Bilbray's intervention, however, immigration agents began to visit the homes of the protesting workers, asking them questions, not only about their immigration status but about the campaign to enforce Measure C. After Luz and Marcela were visited, they both moved out of their apartments.

The Smithfield Raids: Overt Union-Busting

As workers were battling hotel managers at Woodfin Suites, others found themselves in a similar predicament. In November 2006 nearly four hundred workers in laundry plants across the country were pulled off their jobs after their employer, Cintas Corporation, the largest industrial laundry in the United States, advised them they'd been named in a no-match check.

UNITE HERE, the union for hotel, garment, restaurant, and laundry workers, had been trying to organize Cintas since 2004, in a campaign marked by firings and unfair-labor-practice charges. The company claimed it was merely complying with Bush administration requirements. "All employers have a legal obligation to make sure that all employees are legally authorized to work in the U.S.," Cintas spokesman Wade Gates told the *San Jose (California) Mercury News*. Elena, an immigrant working in the San Jose facility, told the *Mercury News*, "This is discrimination, because we were helping with union organizing."

The most celebrated use of immigration enforcement against a union came at the Smithfield Foods pork slaughterhouse in Tar Heel, North Carolina, on January 24, 2007. To organizer Eduardo Peña, "the raid was like a nuclear bomb." Actually, like a neutron bomb, the ingenious cold war weapon whose radiation would kill a city's residents but leave its buildings standing. After the workers were picked up, the factory was still intact, the machinery of the production lines ready to clank and clatter into its normal motion. But most of the plant lay still.

Twenty-one people were detained that day by ICE agents, who workers call *la migra*. Agents took care not to alert the rest of the plant's laborers. One by one, supervisors went to Mexicans on the line, saying they were needed in the front office. The workers would put down their knives, take off their gloves, and walk through the cavernous building to the human resources department. There, agents took them into custody, put them in handcuffs, and locked them up in a temporary detention area. Later, they were taken out in vans and sent to immigration jails as far away as Georgia.

"To keep people from guessing what was up," said Keith Ludlum, one of the few white workers on the production floor, "they also called up African Americans and whites, and told them they had to take drug tests. If they'd only called Latinos, people would have known what was happening." If word had gotten out, hundreds of workers would undoubtedly have run from the lines. Valuable meat would have been left to spoil—a day's production lost. At Smithfield, fifty-five hundred people slaughter and cut apart thirty-two thousand hogs a day. Keeping the raid secret meant workers worked to the end of their shift and the company got its product out.

Eventually the truth came out, however. Parents didn't show up to collect their kids from school or daycare. "A friend called me at nine or ten that night and told me someone from my town hadn't come home," recalled Pedro Mendez, a worker whose name has been changed to protect him. "That's when we knew what had happened. I couldn't sleep that night, knowing my friends had been picked up. I worried about my own family."

While Mendez lay awake, word spread to employees of QSI, the company Smithfield contracts to clean the blood and gore off the machinery after midnight. Afraid *la migra* might still be in the plant, the cleaning crew didn't show up for their shift. U.S. Department of Agriculture inspectors won't allow the lines to start in the morning if they haven't been hosed down the night before, so the few production workers who came to work the next day found the kill floor taped off with yellow plastic barriers. With no freshly killed hogs on the hooks, the rest of the plant had nothing to do.

The raid's shock waves swept outward from the factory through the barrios of the small southern towns around it, leaving behind children missing mothers or fathers. Parents were afraid to go to work or send their kids to school. The terror it inspired dealt a body blow to the plant's union-organizing drive as well, just when it was making real progress: Overcoming ten years of lost elections and Smithfield's hardball antiunion campaigns, workers were just beginning to lose their fear. Fired employees had been rehired after years of court appeals. Union supporters were discovering that collective action on the line could actually make conditions better. That rising consciousness was the raid's biggest casualty.

According to many workers, those organizing efforts, and not the twenty-one detained immigrants, were the raid's real target. Mark Lauritsen, packinghouse director for the United Food and Commercial Workers (UFCW), said the Department of Homeland Security and the company "were worried about people organizing a union, and the government said, 'here are the tools to take care of them.'"

Smithfield has been trying to block union organizing in Tar Heel for over a decade. In 1994 and 1997, its workers voted in two union-representation elections, both lost by the UFCW. Management used such extensive intimidation tactics that the votes were thrown out by the National Labor Relations Board (NLRB). In 1997 the head of plant security, Danny Priest, told local sheriffs he expected violence on election day. Police in riot gear then lined the walkway into the slaughterhouse, and workers had to file past them to cast their ballots. At the end of the vote count, union activist Ray Shawn was beaten up inside the plant. Three years later Priest became an auxiliary deputy sheriff, and plant security officers were given the power to arrest and detain people at work. The company maintained a holding area for detainees in a trailer on the property, which workers called the company jail. (Smithfield gave up its deputized force and detention center in 2005.)

Keith Ludlum was fired in 1994. In 2006 the NLRB forced Smithfield to rehire him and pay $1.1 million to him and others fired for union activity. In 2007 QSI settled NLRB charges that it had threatened workers with arrest by immigration authorities to dampen union activity. These were victories for the union, but for Ludlum's coworkers on the line, the lesson was also that Smithfield lawyers kept a union supporter out of work for over a decade, in violation of federal law.

Today the UFCW supports a labor law reform proposal called the Employee Free Choice Act, which would increase penalties for companies who fire workers for union activity, and make it easier for workers to organize. Until the law is changed, however, the union seeks ways to organize workers without labor board elections. Non-NLRB strategies require much more from supporters than signing a union card, voting on election day, or going to a few meetings. People have to lose their fear, show open support for the union, circulate petitions demanding changes, and form delegations confronting supervisors and managers.

In 2003 QSI contract workers began to challenge the atmosphere of fear in the plant. According to Julio Vargas, who worked for the company at the time, "The wages were very low and we had no medical insurance. When people got hurt, after being taken to the office they made them go back to work and wear pink helmets [to humiliate them]. We were fed up." Led by Vargas, the cleaning crew refused to go in to work. "We started talking to people as they arrived. Those who were in agreement stopped the other workers on their line." The company negotiated, and workers won concessions. The following week, however, those identified as ringleaders lost their jobs. "They fired me because they thought I was one of the organizers," Vargas recalls proudly. "And I was."

UFCW organizers understood the importance of that work stoppage: they knew the government couldn't and wouldn't guarantee an election free of union busters, labor law violations, and intimidation. Organizing a union at Smithfield would require a non-NLRB plan to organize workers in a different way. So the union set up a workers' center in nearby Red Springs, holding classes in English and labor rights. Vargas and other fired workers went to work for the UFCW, organizing discontent over high line-speed and its human cost in workplace injuries. Workers even stopped production lines to get the company to talk with them about health and safety problems. "This has not been a traditional campaign," explained Peña. "We're not going to give the company a chance to use union busters. We're asking workers to take direct action on the plant floor to improve their own conditions."

Immigration status itself became an issue for collective action. In the spring of 2006, as immigrant protests spread across the country, three hundred Smithfield workers stayed out of work on April 10, the first day of national demonstrations against proposed anti-immigrant legislation, HR 4437. Instead they marched through the streets of

Wilmington. Then, on May 1, when immigrants from Los Angeles to New York boycotted their jobs on May Day, Smithfield workers paraded with thousands of Latinos in Lumberton. Most of the plant's immigrant workers were used to the idea of demonstrating on May Day, a working-class holiday in their countries of origin. According to Gene Bruskin, director of the UFCW's Justice at Smithfield campaign, "The company tried to convince them to come to work, saying it would provide a place to write letters to Congress urging immigration reform. But when May Day arrived, only a skeleton crew showed up for work." Smithfield took no action against those who were absent.

Company representatives decline to be interviewed, but it's not hard to imagine that managers must have looked at the marches and the rising wave of collective activity with alarm. In late spring or early summer Smithfield enrolled in the IMAGE program—the ICE Mutual Agreement between Government and Employers. A July 26 press release from the Department of Homeland Security calls IMAGE an effort "designed to build cooperative relationships between government and businesses to strengthen hiring practices and reduce the unlawful employment of illegal aliens." Homeland Security secretary Michael Chertoff said the government "must partner with employers, educate them, and provide them with the tools they need to develop a stable, legal workforce."

The program requires employers to verify the immigration status of all employees, checking their documents against the ICE database. Employers must "establish protocols for responding to no-match letters from the Social Security Administration," and "establish a tip line for employees to report violations and mechanisms for companies to self-report violations to ICE." As Peña commented bitterly, "They saw an opportunity. With the organizing going on, they knew they could use it. They may not have expected the loss [the day after the raid], but it was probably worth it. They achieved their goal."

The IMAGE and other ICE workplace programs are designed to enforce employer sanctions, the provision of the 1986 Immigration Reform and Control Act that prohibits employers from hiring undocumented workers. Smithfield workers saw the first effects of cooperation between ICE and their employer on October 30, 2006. The human resources department sent letters to hundreds, saying the Social Security numbers they'd provided when they were hired didn't match the Social Security Administration database. Just a month after Woodfin Suites said the same thing to its employees, Smithfield's letters gave workers fifteen days to supply valid numbers. They'd be terminated, the company warned, if they didn't.

"Human Resources called me on November 8," said Pedro Mendez, "and said my Social Security number was bad. I told them I'd been working for nine years with that number, and asked them why they'd never said anything about it before. They knew I couldn't verify it, and they fired me the same day. They called security to throw me out of the plant. It was very humiliating."

Mendez asked to see a copy of the no-match letter from SSA listing his name, and said they refused to show it to him. If the company did have such a letter, it would have contained the paragraph cautioning Smithfield not to construe a discrepancy in numbers as evidence of lack of immigration status. Further, an operating instruction issued to immigration agents under the Clinton administration says they shouldn't cooperate with employers during labor disputes or use document checks to punish workers for demanding their rights. But what saved Pedro Mendez's job wasn't the law, but the collective action organizers had been pushing. "On November 13 [2006], the time given workers to come up with new numbers started to expire," recalled Peña. "By that time, a couple of hundred people had received letters. Over thirty were escorted out of the plant, and those still at work could see new workers hired to replace them. Many felt they had nothing to lose. On Thursday [November 16] they walked out."

Jose Osorio was one of the leaders of the walkout. "I and a group of about twelve workers began to organize our other coworkers to walk off their lines that day," he recalled. "When nine thirty a.m. came around we began to shut down our lines. When some asked, 'What's going on?' I said, 'This is because they have been terminating workers for their Social Security cards.' We moved down to the smoking cafeteria, and to my surprise the kill floor and conversion [workers] were arriving at the same time. We decided to move outside because there wasn't enough room for all of us. We said we wouldn't go in until we had a solution, so that employees would not continue being terminated for their Social Security cards." Osorio and his coworkers even walked back into the plant to get more workers to come out.

Taken by surprise, supervisors and even corporate vice president Larry Johnson tried to talk people into going back to work. None did. That evening a group of workers met at a local hotel and came up with a list of demands. "They decided to stick to the issue of immigration," Peña said. "Their idea was to go back in with something that would protect them, and show other workers the power of collective action."

At the request of the workers, representatives of the local Catholic diocese met with the company the following day, and Smithfield agreed to a sixty-day extension, to rehire those already terminated, and not to retaliate against anyone. Mendez was among those rehired. "Even the English-speaking workers were excited by what had happened," Peña remembered. "It's hard to imagine how empowered people felt. This wasn't some leaflet, it was the real thing."

Soon after the action at Smithfield, in December 2006, ICE carried out raids at six Swift & Co. plants, detaining over thirteen hundred workers for deportation. Meatpacking workers in companies including Smithfield began to fear the same fate. Nevertheless, the feeling of collective strength in the plant was still high. African American union supporters at Smithfield, where the workforce was about half Latino, 40 percent African American, and 10 percent white and Native American, asked the company to give employees the day off on January 15, the birthday of Rev. Martin Luther King Jr. The week before the proposed holiday, a delegation of workers went to the human resources office, bearing petitions with the signatures of four thousand people. Peña said that Smithfield vice president Johnson refused to accept them, arguing the company couldn't cancel the lunch trucks contracted to sell food to workers.

Despite the refusal, about four hundred workers from the first shift didn't come to work on King's birthday. The UFCW's Bruskin said this slowed down the livestock-handling department, where the animals are first taken into the plant, an area where African Americans are concentrated. The same thing happened on the second shift, he said, although the company disputed this in an article in the industry journal *Meatingplace* (meatingplace.com).

Nine days after the January 15 action ICE agents came out to the plant. According to *Meatingplace,* ICE gave the company notice of the raid the day before. Agents arrived with a list of workers, and company supervisors escorted them to the room where *la migra* was waiting. "We didn't want to do anything to upset our employees," Smithfield spokesperson Dennis Pittman told *Meatingplace* reporter Tom Johnston. Later the company announced it would run the plant the following Saturday, to make up for the production lost the day after the raid. Keith Ludlum said he heard a company spokesperson on the radio on Thursday, asking people to come back to work.

The no-match terminations and the immigration raid made workers feel insecure and fearful for their jobs, and Smithfield hadn't even needed to violate the National Labor Relations Act. "People are very scared now," said Julio Vargas. "They're afraid of more raids and more checks of Social Security numbers. People with ten years at work are thinking of quitting. It's hard to get them to come to meetings now." According to Vargas, people saw immigration enforcement as a kind of reprisal. "They think it's happening because people were getting organized," he said. To Ludlum, "It totally set us back. We spent a lot of time educating people, and now they're getting rid of lots of them."

According to Peña, "It takes years of convincing, of educating people, to develop this kind of trust and activity. The union has become part of the community, and backs up what workers want to do. People went from feeling they had no rights to looking their foremen in the eye. Immigrants in particular were taking bolder actions even than citizens." The raids and firings hit at the heart of this effort. "Now people are concerned about basic survival," he said. "The message they've gotten is that they're nothing. They can be taken from their families, arrested, and deported at any time. They wonder who will take care of their kids if the government comes for them. It's hard to think about workplace injuries if that's the big question on your mind."

The union, however, began turning the tables, using the violation of workers' rights to mobilize customer pressure against Smithfield. Bruskin and a crew of community organizers focused on the Harris Teeter store chain, collecting thousands of signatures on petitions asking managers to find another pork supplier. At the end of March 2007, religious and human rights leaders demonstrated outside twenty-four Harris Teeter stores across North and South Carolina, Virginia, and Tennessee. The union and the North Carolina Council of Churches asked the Food Network's Paula Deen, southern cuisine chef, to sever her relationship as a Smithfield spokesperson. The City of Boston decided to stop purchasing Smithfield pork products.

Inside the plant, the union reorganized, with African American workers becoming more active in the absence of many Latino leaders. In August, Jose Osorio, who led the original walkout over the no-match letters, was fired. The company accused him of excessive tardiness, although he said he'd reported to work on time. A human relations representative told him, he said, "that you have to be at your work station five minutes prior to the start of your shift, anything after that is considered late." No one is paid for that five minutes, Osorio said.

Despite the fear, union supporters collected the signatures of about half the plant's workers, demanding that the company agree to recognize the union without an NLRB election, and presented the petitions at a company shareholders' meeting at the beginning of September. That's when ICE agents came out again. Twenty-nine workers were detained, according to ICE spokesperson Jamie Zuieback, as a result of Smithfield's review of its own records. But this time ICE didn't just hold them for deportation. Twenty-five were charged with identity theft for having presented to Smithfield at the time they were hired Social Security numbers belonging to other people. "The theft of an individuals' identity where one assumes another person's name,

Social Security number, or other critical information compromises our security and can cause untold problems for the real owner of that information," U.S. Attorney George E. B. Holding said in a news release. "It is particularly troubling when individuals come to this country illegally and then prey upon others while here."

On January 31, 2008, three of the workers picked up in the raid were sentenced to a year and a half in federal prison, followed by deportation after they'd completed their sentences, for using false Social Security numbers to get jobs at Smithfield. Another fifteen were being prosecuted for that same crime.

No evidence, of course, was presented of any alleged harm to the original cardholders, since there was none. The real damage was perpetrated on the detained workers and their families, and once again ICE had intervened at a critical moment in the union's organizing efforts to protect the company.

Workers paid the price.

Two

WHY DID WE COME?

Flight from Oaxaca

Luz Dominguez, Marcela Melquiades, and each immigrant room cleaner at the Woodfin Suites Hotel had complex reasons for setting out on the road to Emeryville. Pedro Mendez arrived in Tar Heel with other migrants from the same constellation of towns in the Mexican state of Veracruz. Each had his or her individual motivation for making the journey to Smithfield. But common threads run through all their stories. Similar economic and political conditions make up the terrain on which individuals and families decide to leave home.

In 2006 Mexico was in turmoil. Dramatic political and economic conflicts uprooted and displaced thousands of families. Teachers struck in Oaxaca, and after their demonstrations were teargassed, a virtual insurrection paralyzed the state capital for months. Some of the world's largest mines and Mexico's only steel mill were paralyzed when workers occupied their worksites and refused to leave. Accusations that the July presidential election was marred by fraud brought Mexico City residents into the streets, where they camped for weeks in protest.

Economic desperation is at the root of these political and social movements, and is a major source of pressure on people to migrate. Repression brought to bear on those movements also leads to migration. It's no accident that Oaxaca is one of the main starting points for the current stream of Mexican migrants coming to the United States. And the miners of Mexico's northern states not only share family ties with miners on the U.S. side, but often have no choice but to join them when their unions are attacked or their jobs eliminated.

To understand the impact of U.S. immigration policy in Oakland's Fruitvale neighborhood, or at the Smithfield packing plant, one has to start by looking farther south.

About 30 million Mexicans survive on less than thirty pesos a day—not quite three dollars. The minimum wage is forty-five. The federal government estimates that 37.7 percent of Mexico's 106 million citizens—40 million people—live in poverty, and 25 million, or 23.6 percent, in extreme poverty. In rural Mexico, over 10 million people have a daily income of less than twelve pesos—a little over a dollar. Mexican income is falling faster than that of any other Latin American country, according to the International Labor Organization.

Poverty in Mexico, however, is no more evenly distributed than it is in the United States. According to EDUCA, a Mexican education and development organization, 75 percent of Oaxaca's people live in extreme poverty, making it the second-poorest state in Mexico, after Chiapas. Among Mexican states, Oaxaca has the second-highest concentration of indigenous residents—people who belong to communities and ethnic groups that existed long before Columbus landed in the Caribbean. Raquel Cruz Manzano, principal of the Formal Primary School in San Pablo Macuiltianguis, in the Zapotec region, says this concentration of poverty among indigenous people caused the uprising that shook Oaxaca in 2006. Of its 3.4 million residents, she says, only nine hundred thousand receive formal healthcare, while the illiteracy rate is 21.8 percent. Oaxacans speak twenty-three indigenous languages, yet "the educational level in Oaxaca is five-point-eight years of study, against a national average of seven-point-three years. The average monthly income for nongovernmental employees is less than two thousand pesos [about two hundred dollars] per family, the lowest in the nation, which means that seventy-five thousand children have to work in order to survive or help their families."

Oaxacan poverty is a result of Mexican economic development policies. For more than two decades, under pressure from the World Bank, the International Monetary Fund (IMF), and conditions placed on U.S. bank loans and bailouts, the government has encouraged foreign investment while cutting expenditures intended to raise rural incomes.

Oaxaca is a state of small farmers, whose main crop is corn. For many years, Mexico's state-owned CONASUPO grocery stores purchased corn at high subsidized prices, turned it into tortillas, and sold them, along with milk and other basic foodstuffs, at low subsidized prices in cities. Economic reforms and the North American Free Trade Agreement, however, led the Mexican government to dissolve the CONASUPO system and end subsidies. Prices were decontrolled and rose dramatically on necessities like gasoline, electricity, bus fares, tortillas, and milk. In 2006 a gallon of milk sold in Mexican grocery stores for more than three dollars—a higher price than its equivalent in many U.S. supermarkets.

NAFTA lowered customs barriers that historically prevented large U.S. corn producers from dumping corn in Mexico. U.S. grain production is large-scale and highly mechanized, with large inputs of fertilizers, pesticides, and, more recently, genetically modified seeds. Its production costs are lower than those of smaller Mexican producers, and in addition are subsidized by the U.S. farm bill, although NAFTA prohibited the Mexican government from paying subsidies to its farmers.

According to Juan Manuel Sandoval, a professor at Mexico's National Institute of Anthropology and History and a leader of the Mexican Network on Free Trade, once the agreement went into effect it became cheaper for large Mexican corn growers to buy U.S. corn and resell it than to grow corn themselves. For the vast majority, however, like Oaxaca's small farmers, the price for yellow corn (the first variety on which import restrictions were dropped) simply couldn't cover the cost of growing it. When farming families couldn't sell enough to buy food and supplies for the coming year, many had to look for another way to survive. Migration meant survival.

Oaxacan poverty has always been higher than the national average, and the state's residents have been seeking work outside their state for decades. Oaxacans traveled first within Mexico itself, starting in the late 1950s, when government policies of rural development and credit began to fail. In nearby Veracruz they first found work cutting sugarcane and picking coffee for the rich planters of the coast. Then Sinaloa's and Baja California's new factory farms a thousand miles north, growing tomatoes and strawberries for U.S. supermarkets, needed workers. Soon growers began recruiting indigenous migrants, and before long, trains were packed with Oaxacan families every spring. Over the last twenty years, the state's indigenous farmworkers moved north through Mexico and eventually began crossing the border into the United States.

Today thousands of indigenous people leave Oaxaca's hillside villages every year. And as they find their way to other parts of Mexico or the United States, the money they send home becomes crucial to the survival of the towns they leave behind. In 2005 Mexican president Vicente Fox boasted that Mexicans in the United States—often working for poverty wages—sent home over $18 billion. In 2006 the remittance total reached $25 billion. "Migration is a necessity, not a choice," explained Romualdo Juan Gutiérrez Cortéz, a teacher in Santiago Juxtlahuaca, in Oaxaca's rural Mixteca region. "There is no work here. You can't tell a child to study to be a doctor if there is no work for doctors in Mexico. It is a very daunting task for a Mexican teacher to convince students to get an education and stay in the country. It is disheartening to see a student go through many hardships to get an education here in Mexico and become a professional, and then later in the United States do manual labor. Sometimes those with an education are working side by side with others who do not even know how to read.

"Migration helps pacify people," he added. "Poverty is a ticking time bomb, but as long as there is money coming in from family in the United States, there is peace. To curb migration our country has to have a better employment plan. We must push our government to think about the working class."

By 2006, however, the social peace supported by remittances could no longer be sustained in Oaxaca. Poverty and migration provided the economic and social fuel for that year's uprising, which began with teachers and mushroomed into a virtual insurrection demanding the resignation of the state's governor. According to Jaime Medina, a reporter for *Noticias,* an independent newspaper founded in 1978 that became the voice of the Oaxacan rebellion, "Something had to give. It sometimes seems like Oaxaca and southern Mexico aren't even part of Mexico, the way we're ignored by the federal government until a crisis erupts."

If poverty supplied the fuel, the conditions of teachers were the spark that ignited the blaze. "The federal government is always raving about its educational system," Medina explained, "but here in rural parts of Oaxaca, a typical school consists of four poles and palm leaves for a roof. Students sit on rocks, logs, or anything else they can find. The country's educational department does nothing to improve these conditions. A typical teacher earns about twenty-two hundred pesos every two weeks [about $220]. From that they have to purchase chalk, pencils, and other school supplies for the children. The life of a teacher is very difficult, so the demands they are making are fair. Unfortunately we have a deaf and blind government. We are fed up with the promises made every election, because we get nothing afterwards."

In 2005 teachers demanded changes. When the state administration turned them down flat, they struck to force improvements. "The government's denial infuriated them," Medina said. "They almost didn't complete the 2005 school year, but teachers have such a love for their students they decided to return and finish out the term. They stopped the strike. But when government tried to force them to do the same this spring [in 2006], the teachers refused."

In early May 2006, teachers struck again for higher salaries and an end to growing human rights violations. Oaxacans charged Governor Ulises Ruiz, elected in 2004, with jailing so many activists that Amnesty International sent a delegation to the state to investigate. As popular resentment grew and the strike wore on, thousands of teachers occupied the main square in the state capital, camping with their children on the cobblestone streets. In a Mexican *planton,* or street occupation, people live in the streets as a form of social protest, cooking and eating out of doors, sleeping in tents. The teachers' *planton,* the largest in

Oaxaca's history, filled the *zocalo* at the center of the city's historic downtown. One demonstration during the occupation brought out more than 120,000 people. On June 11 Ruiz met with business leaders and pledged to use the *mano dura,* or heavy hand, against teachers and their allies. Oaxaca's wealthiest citizens, who benefited from the economic reforms, had a big stake in suppressing advocacy of political and economic alternatives. They gave Ruiz a green light.

Early in the morning of June 14, the twenty-fourth day of the *planton,* helicopters began to hover overhead. Police wearing helmets and flak vests and armed with automatic rifles filled the streets. People began to run, frightened at the crump of tear gas shells and the billowing clouds of suffocating smoke. Then the police opened fire. By the end of the afternoon, city hospitals confirmed that five people were dead—three teachers and two children. Hundreds of others were injured by beatings and bullets; some had broken limbs. One pregnant woman miscarried.

Ruiz underestimated the teachers, however. They retook the square at the end of the day, and the next morning some three hundred thousand people marched through Oaxaca demanding his resignation. In the following weeks, teachers and other groups calling for Ruiz's removal formed the Popular Assembly of the Peoples of Oaxaca (APPO). Doctors and nurses shut down clinics, while in a desperate reaction, police stepped up violence against protestors. One state university professor was killed in the street, and the husband of a striking teacher, José Jiménez Colmenares, was gunned down during a protest march. Pistoleros shot protesters guarding the transmitter for the Channel 9 radio station, after it had been occupied by demonstrators and used to broadcast news of the uprising. Gunmen fired on reporters from *Noticias.*

APPO supporters "were being assaulted and shot at by police in plainclothes," Medina recalled. "Finally a U.S. reporter, Brad Will, was killed in Santa Lucia del Camino, a neighboring town, when demonstrators were fired on. The protesters defended themselves with what they could. After that, thirty-five hundred federal police arrived with tear gas, water cannons, and pepper spray, and attacked the residents protecting the teachers in the plaza. The protesters held off tanks, their rocks and sticks against the guns. During this confrontation, a nurse was killed by a tear gas shell. Federal officers dislodged those occupying Channel 9, and a sixteen-year-old protester was killed."

According to Raquel Cruz Manzano, a member of the executive committee of Section [local union] 22 of the National Union of Education Workers, and active in the national union's progressive caucus, the National Coordinating Committee of Education Workers, teachers agreed to end the strike in October. Nevertheless, she said, the state government didn't allow many to return to their jobs. During the strike, Governor Ruiz hired strikebreakers with no certification as teachers, in direct violation of the law. "There are still three hundred schools where this is a problem," Cruz explained in an interview six months later. In the course of the repression 23 people were killed, she said, citing a report by the International Civil Commission for Human Rights Observation, which took testimony from over 420 victims during a four-week investigation. In addition to the deaths, Cruz accused the government of responsibility for "over five hundred arrests, and an undetermined number of people forced to flee, or 'disappeared,' not counting an enormous number who were assaulted physically and psychologically."

A year later Oaxacans remained defiant: "A true uprising took place," Cruz declared, "an authentic insurrection they were unable to defeat. We have not surrendered, nor will we ever surrender."

Oaxaca has many dangerous teachers like Cruz and Gutiérrez. In the 1970s and 1980s, more than a hundred teachers there were killed in the struggle for control of Section 22. Today it is one of Mexico's most militant unions. In many villages teachers are community leaders and popularize Mexico's most progressive traditions.

One afternoon a year before the uprising, Gutiérrez stood at the back of a classroom in rural Santiago Juxtlahuaca, dapper in a pressed white shirt and chinos. Two boys and two girls, wearing new tennis shoes undoubtedly sent by family members working in the North, stood at the blackboard, giving a report and carefully gauging his reaction. As they recounted the history of Mexico's expropriation of oil in 1936, a smile curved beneath Gutiérrez's pencil mustache. The expropriation was a high point in Mexican revolutionary nationalism. "Education is a very noble field, which I love," Gutiérrez enthused. "But today it means confronting the government. You have to be ready to fight for the people and their children, and not just in the classroom."

Gutiérrez was elected to Oaxaca's state legislature in 2000, in a partnership between the Indigenous Front of Binational Organizations (FIOB), which he then headed in Oaxaca, and the left-wing Party of the Democratic Revolution (PRD). Following the end of his term, he was arrested and jailed by Ruiz's predecessor, Governor José Murat. "Before my arrest I thought we had a decent justice system," he said. "I knew it wasn't perfect, but I thought it worked. Then I saw that the people in jail weren't the rich or well educated, but the poor and those who work hard for a living." In prison Gutiérrez met members of a local union who had been jailed for months. "There are over two thousand complaints of political oppression in the state that have not been investigated," Gutiérrez charged, months before the 2006 uprising.

News outlets that expose these abuses also find themselves in the government's crosshairs. In 2003 *Noticias* exposed public works fraud in the Murat administration. In that fall's gubernatorial election, the paper supported the left-wing PRD candidate, who lost amid charges of vote rigging. On December 1, the same day Murat's successor, Ulises Ruiz, took office, hooligans broke into the *Noticias* building and threatened reporters. More provocations followed. Six months later state police and dozens of thugs belonging to the Revolutionary Confederation of Workers and Peasants (CROC) surrounded the office. CROC is a labor federation founded in the early 1950s by the Institutional Revolutionary Party (PRI), the party that governed Mexico for over seventy years and still rules in Oaxaca. In some areas the CROC functions as a normal union, but in others it is a vehicle used by the PRI to intimidate political opponents.

Amnesty International reports that 102 of *Noticias*'s 130 employees belonged to CROC, but in 2004 CROC leadership called a strike "against the express wishes of the *Noticias* workforce." In a cynical use of the provision of Mexican labor law that prohibits an employer from operating during a strike, the Ruiz administration ordered the paper to stop publishing. "Three hundred people came in to take over," Medina recalled. "Thirty-one of my coworkers stayed behind. Some were getting ready to print the paper, while other reporters were finishing up last-minute stories. The editor and assistant editor also stayed behind. All of them were basically kidnapped. We could see them through the windows as they were being assaulted. They were held for thirty-one days."

Facing a news blockade in Oaxaca, the imprisoned journalists hit the phones. From inside the besieged newsroom, reporter César Morales got on the radio in Fresno, California. He was interviewed by Rufino Domínguez, the FIOB binational coordinator, and journalist Eduardo Stanley, cohosts of a bilingual program for Mixtec migrants on community radio station KFCF. Morales described "an assault by more than a hundred plainclothes police, and thugs brought in to beat us." He called for help, and letters and faxes from California deluged the governor's office in Oaxaca. On July 18 the journalists were released by military personnel, but were beaten again on their way out.

After the PRI evicted the journalists it closed the paper's offices, and for over a year *Noticias* was written, edited, and printed elsewhere. "Even though it was very expensive to produce, it came out daily," Medina recalled. "The newspaper would arrive in Oaxaca between one and three in the afternoon, and people would form lines to buy it. We were very thankful to the people of Oaxaca because they helped us survive." A year after the 2006 uprising *Noticias* was once again distributed in Oaxaca. Meanwhile, Oaxacans in California had discovered an ability to use media in their binational campaigns for human rights at home.

In the 2006 presidential campaign, the FIOB supported the PRD candidate, former Mexico City mayor Andrés Manuel López Obrador. Leoncio Vásquez, communications director for the FIOB in Fresno, said Mexico faced a clear choice in political direction. "López Obrador declared openly that he'd put poor people first. He's against corruption and corporations who violate workers' and human rights." Raising rural income was López Obrador's answer to the problem of migration.

During the campaign, violence in Oaxaca escalated. On May 19, three weeks before the assault in the *zocalo*, Moisés Cruz Sánchez, a PRD activist in the Mixtec town of San Juan Mixtepec, was gunned down in front of his wife and children as he left a local restaurant. The two gunmen fled, and police couldn't seem to find them. That month in Fresno the FIOB organized demonstrations against a planned visit by Governor Ruiz to California. Response to the protests revealed increasing cooperation between U.S. and Mexican authorities targeting dissent. After receiving a copy of a letter sent to the Mexican consulate objecting to Ruiz's visit, Fresno police detective Dean Williamson paid a surprise visit to the FIOB office on Tulare Street. "It's an official procedure," he claimed, "in which we're trying to clarify possible threats affecting public security."

When the state's teachers struck, indigenous community organizations, including FIOB, became heavily involved in APPO. In the Mixtec region, protestors occupied the Huajuapan de León city hall. Ruiz issued arrest orders for fifty APPO leaders, including three FIOB officials. Dominguez warned that "Mexico is approaching a situation of ungovernability, spreading to all parts of the country. A tiny group is trying to hold on to power by increasingly violent and illegal means."

By organizing across the border, the FIOB and other Oaxacan organizations sought to reduce that threat and defend its victims. Binational pressure freed Gutiérrez from Murat's jail, where local efforts alone might not have succeeded. Other human rights violations in Oaxaca over the last decade have resulted in similar cross-border resistance, and the FIOB was at the heart of many of these protests. Gutiérrez believes that a successful challenge to Oaxaca's elite must involve the state's residents living on both sides of the U.S.-Mexico border. If indigenous migrants raise their voices, he says, they may be able to help force a change in the political structure at home, and thereby influence migration abroad.

Medina believes poverty and political repression in Oaxaca "definitely affect the U.S. because we are such close neighbors. If the United States spent more money on the poorest neighboring regions instead of on war, we wouldn't need a fence to divide us," he asserted. "What is dividing us is the economy. It's incredible that so many of our people get an education here only to spend their days working as farmhands in the U.S. Mexico makes millions of dollars exporting petroleum to other countries, yet its people don't see that money. If that money was spent for our benefit, we wouldn't see the need to migrate elsewhere."

"Indigenous people are always on the bottom in Oaxaca," concluded Vásquez. "The rich use their economic resources to maintain a government that puts them first. Big corporations control what's going on in Mexico, and those who criticize the government get harassed constantly, with arbitrary arrest and even assassination. That's one of the reasons why people from our communities have been forced to leave to find a means of survival elsewhere. The lack of human rights itself is a factor contributing to migration from Oaxaca and Mexico, since it closes off our ability to call for any change." For Oaxaca's indigenous residents, greater democracy and respect for human rights are the keys to eventually achieving a government committed to increasing rural family income. That in turn might make it possible for people to make a living at home, instead of heading for California.

Battles in the Mines

In its natural state, Cananea's copper ore is part of a sagebrush-covered mountain, in the middle of the Sonoran Desert seventy miles south of Arizona. To extract the metal indispensable to computers, automobiles, and iPods, that rock is first blown out of the mountainside with high explosives and loaded onto huge dump trucks, the tires of which would each dwarf a basketball player. The trucks then dump their loads—small boulders, in effect—into the first crusher at the top of the hill overlooking the mine's concentrator. When the crushed rocks pour out down below, into tunnels deep in the hillside, they're still about the size of watermelons. The next crusher breaks them into smaller pieces, and then enormous mills below grind them down even further, until they are no longer rocks at all, or even pebbles, but a steady stream of fine sand.

Rock dust in parts of this huge complex is so deep that it rises up over the boot tops of the miners. In the dark tunnels where rubber conveyor belts normally carry the ore from crushers to mills at break-neck speed, the fine powder mounts up against the machinery in drifts. "When the mine is running," says Victoriano Carrillo, a member of the mine's health and safety commission, "you can't even see more than a few feet in front of you."

Mine dust is more than just uncomfortable or inconvenient. It's deadly. Superfine particles lodge in the lungs, so tiny that the cilia, the small hairlike projections that expel most foreign substances, can't get them out. Miners who breathe it year after year suffer a variety of lung diseases, but the most dangerous is silicosis. In mine communities from Cananea to Tucson, on both sides of the border, generations of copper miners have died from it.

In a well-run mine, dust is sucked from the buildings covering the crushers, mills, and conveyor belts by huge vacuum cleaners, or dust collectors. Outside the hulking buildings of the concentrator complex in Cananea, those collection tanks and their network of foot-wide pipes are five stories tall. But since 2005, many of the tanks have developed rusty holes in their sides the size of a bathroom window. And the pipes, which should lead into the work areas, instead end in midair.

The dust should have been sucked up by the collectors, but wound up instead in miners' lungs. There are other dangers as well. Many machines have no guards, making it easy to lose fingers. Electrical panels have no covers. Holes in the floor have no guardrails. Catwalks high above the floor are slippery with dust, and often grease, and are criss-crossed by cables and hoses. In 2006 one worker tripped and fell five stories to his death. Safety lines running alongside the conveyors, which can stop the speeding belt in the event of an accident, have been cut so that they can't be pulled, or are simply absent.

"We know what's safe and what's not," one miner said bitterly, "but they never want us to spend time fixing problems—just get the production out. If we tried to stop the line for safety problems, we would lose our jobs." He did not give his name, out of fear of being fired.

On July 29, 2007, miners at Cananea struck against the dust. The union for Cananea miners, Section 65 of the Mexican Union of Mine, Metal and Allied Workers, sought to force the mine's owner, the giant Grupo México corporation, to abide by the safety protections in the union contract. In response, Grupo México sought to replace the seventy-year-old union with a more friendly one that would let it run the mines as it likes.

Strikers charged that the vacuum apparatus to suck dust from the complex had been disconnected and inoperable for two years. In an effort to weaken the union, they said, Grupo México had eliminated the jobs of workers who were in charge of maintaining the dust collectors and brought in a private, nonunion contractor to do the work. When the union objected, the company disconnected the ventilators.

In Cananea, the healthcare system doesn't help workers assess their physical condition. In the union office, files are filled with letters signed by Dr. Alfredo Parra Ybarra, director of the Hospital Ronquillo, where the company pays for miners' medical care. The forms repeat a few stock phrases. Miners with fifteen or twenty years on the job are told they've either had a "normal medical examination," or are given diagnoses of problems unrelated to work, such as "overweight" or "poor eyesight." Recommendations amount to simply "Consult the medical service." The Hospital Ronquillo was built over a century ago, and though over a thousand miners, their wives, and children all get their care there it still has only one bathroom for men and one for women.

In October 2007 a binational delegation of health and safety experts from Mexico and the United States visited the Cananea mine and did preliminary health screening on sixty-eight of the thirteen hundred strikers. "We documented appalling working conditions in the open-pit mine and processing plants where workers are exposed to high levels of airborne silica, which can cause fatal diseases like silicosis and lung cancer," said Garrett Brown, a California health and safety inspector and network coordinator for the Maquiladora Health and Safety Support Network. "Ironically, the Mexican Labor Department's own safety inspectors found the same hazards in an April 2007 inspection of the facility and issued a laundry list of seventy-two 'corrective actions,' including fixing the cranes' brakes and reassembling the dust collectors. None of the mandated corrections, many of which had also been identified in previous inspections, had been completed by the time the workers went on strike over health and safety issues on July twenty-ninth."

The hospital's inadequacy led miners half a century ago to build a clinic of their own, the Clinica Obrera, with a beautifully equipped operating theater, a children's wing, wards with one bed and bathroom per room, and specialized prenatal care, obstetrics, and other services. The union contract required the company to pay its costs, and the workers ran it. In 1999, however, Grupo México and the state government reached an unusual conclusion. Comparing the larger, better-equipped clinic with the Hospital Ronquillo, they decided that the hospital was better. The company refused to continue paying the clinic costs, although Articles 146 and 147 of the union contract required it. After the clinic closed, Jose Luis Zamora, its last director, was kept from returning to his job in the mine for three years. "They were punishing me," he said, "for fighting to keep it open."

The company halted payments for the clinic, and forced workers' families back into the Hospital Ronquillo, a year after the union lost a disastrous strike in 1998, one of a long series of battles in which the union tried to resist the impact of the mine's privatization. The story of the privatization and the strikes that followed is also the story of migration from Sonora's mines to the United States—dislocation caused by free market economic reforms, uprooting families and setting them on the road north. These reforms not only drastically transformed workplaces, jobs, unions, and living conditions, but displaced a large portion of the country's industrial workforce. Like corn farmers and teachers, displaced miners saw little option for their families' survival other than migration to the United States.

Copper extraction began in the mountains of Sonora under the Spaniards in 1665. At the end of the 1800s Colonel William C. Greene, "the Copper King of Cananea," began large-scale industrial mining. In 1906 Greene almost lost the mine in an insurrection partially planned in the barrios of Mexican railroad workers in Los Angeles and St. Louis. The movement was organized by the brothers Ricardo and Enrique Flores Magón, Oaxacan anarcho-syndicalists with close ties to the Wobblies (the Industrial Workers of the World) in the United States. The Cananea rebellion was a precursor to the Mexican Revolution, which broke out in 1910, and the Flores Magón brothers were pursued by then Mexican president Porfirio Díaz. At his request they were arrested by J. Edgar Hoover, who headed the Federal Bureau of Investigation for decades, in one of his first forays as a U.S. federal policeman. The brothers paid for their radicalism with long U.S. prison sentences—Ricardo died in Leavenworth prison in Kansas.

In the 1930s the Cananea mine became the property of the Anaconda Copper Company, which owned many mines on the U.S. side as well. In 1971 the Mexican government took a 51 percent interest, in the waning days of its nationalist economic development policy, and in 1982 nationalized the rest.

Mexico has always been a mining country, and its copper mines in Cananea and nearby Nacozari were the jewels of its national industry—enormous open-pit excavations that are among the world's largest. The miners' union was a staunch pillar of support for the ruling Institutional Revolutionary Party (PRI) for decades. Its relation with the government and, by extension, the management of the nationalized mines, produced middle-class incomes by Mexican standards. In small mining towns, workers were given land and cheap loans for housing. A mining job was secure and many fathers saw their sons follow them into the pits.

Jesus Morales Tapia, a retired mine union leader in Cananea, recalled, "When I was young, the most moneymaking jobs were the mines. There were other jobs, but they were badly paid for that period. All of us tried to work for the company. There were many accidents, frequently fatal ones, but that was where you could earn the most money. At that time, it was shaft mining—subterranean work. All of us who were not scared went there."

Independent movements to democratize the union were ruthlessly suppressed, but workers were able to strike, and did so to win better wages and benefits. During the 1950s and 1960s, they even won conditions that were sometimes better than those in U.S. copper mines a hundred miles north in Arizona and New Mexico. Moises Espinoza, a miner in Cananea during those years, says silicosis was recognized as an industrial hazard in Mexico before it was in the United States. "We knew it was an occupational disease but it wasn't treated as one there," he recalled. "When I was in Denver, Colorado, I asked the engineers at the mine school why. They said that business was very powerful in the Senate and Congress, and they weren't going to allow consideration of it."

Espinoza was sent by Cananea's mine management to look at work methods in the United States. "When I was in Bisbee [Arizona], I met some young men who'd worked with me in Cananea," he remembered. Wages in the United States were better, although the difference was much smaller in that era than it is today. "The workers I saw were Mexicans, who worked first here in Mexico and used their experience to get jobs over there." It was not hard for Mexicans to get jobs in U.S. mines, and miners on both sides of the border often belonged to the same families. "Bosses in the United States always liked to hire Mexicans, because we were more willing to take risks. But we paid for it. My brother-in-law died in Superior [Arizona] from heart problems caused by silicosis. He worked for many years in the mines. My father died in Tucson from silicosis, too, but they wouldn't recognize it as an occupational illness."

Bosses may have liked hiring Mexicans, but they didn't like paying them the same wage as white, or U.S. citizen, miners. Winning equal wages for Mexican miners was a long struggle in both countries. Family connections became an important base of support for miners on both sides during strikes. "Despite the border, we've always had a lot of exchange of people between the mines on each side," Espinoza explained. Maclovio Barrajas, a leader of the U.S. union of the 1950s and early 1960s, the International Union of Mine, Mill and Smelter Workers, came from Cananea and grew up with Espinoza's family. "After we'd been on strike for a month or two," Morales Tapia remembered, "we sent out commissions to seek help. [Barrajas] arrived with half a dozen miners from the U.S. to give us support. There were people of Mexican descent with him, but also Americans. It was welcome help, if only for the fact that once the national leadership of our union knew that the miners in the United States were supporting us, there was more pressure on them to help too. Our movement was successful, in part because of the help the U.S. miners gave us. A year later there was a strike among the miners in the United States, which lasted a year. With the little that we were earning in that time, we were able to come up with a good amount of dollars to send them."

To Morales Tapia it was natural for miners on both sides of the border to support each other. "In the first place, we're both communities of miners. Plus, there are family relationships among people on both sides. But the main reason is that we all work in the mine. It's the same kind of work, regardless of which side of the border you're on. When we have problems, there are no borders. We all have to work to survive."

The government invested hundreds of millions of dollars in modernization, converting Cananea from shaft to open-pit mining, increasing output substantially. But in 1989 it declared the mine bankrupt, seeking to cut labor costs in preparation for privatization, and army troops expelled the workers from the mine. The conflict was so long, and miners' conditions grew so desperate, that the town's mayor hired strikers to pave the city streets, one reason Cananea's thoroughfares are still in much better condition than those in most border towns. To end the conflict, the mine was taken over by Financiera Nacional Azucarera, a national company in the sugar industry, which restarted operations.

That arrangement didn't last long. In 1988 Carlos Salinas de Gortari had become president, after an election viewed as fraudulent by many Mexicans. Salinas began a wave of wholesale privatizations, and

among the beneficiaries was one of Mexico's richest families, the Larreas. Their family business, Grupo México, eventually became one
of the world's largest mining corporations, buying numerous mines
that had previously been government property, at a fraction of their
true value. Salinas sold Cananea to Grupo México in 1990 for $450 mil-
lion, when its value was closer to $3 billion.

The Larreas, with their partner Union Pacific, the U.S. railroad
giant, also gained control of one of Mexico's main rail lines. Today
Grupo México's Southern Copper Corporation owns two copper
mines in Peru, even larger than Cananea, and it bought the American
Smelting and Refining Company (ASARCO) after it went into bankruptcy. ASARCO has two mines and a smelter in Arizona.

After the Larrea's Minera México SA de CV, a unit of Grupo México, took over ownership of Cananea, it began demanding changes.
In the years after 1991 the workforce was reduced from 3,300 to 2,000.
In 1997 Grupo México said it no longer wanted to operate the dam
and city waterworks. In Cananea, water and most municipal services
had been provided by the mine. The dam holds back a huge lake of
toxic runoff—if it were to fail, the human and environmental cost
would be enormous. Eliminating the 135 jobs in both areas threatened
the entire community, and on November 19, the mine's 2,070 workers
decided to strike to save them. Mexican labor authorities ruled the
strike illegal in January, and the company then announced it would
reopen the mine with strikebreakers. Strikers responded by sending
delegations north to Arizona and California, seeking support from
the United Steelworkers (USW), which represents copper miners
on the U.S. side. The USW and other Arizona unions sent truck caravans to Cananea, carrying food and supplies.

Conservative national leaders of the miners' union, however, allies
of the governing PRI, signed a back-to-work agreement promising
severance pay for those whose jobs were eliminated. Workers in
Cananea rejected the agreement, and on February 13, 1998, went into
the vast pit, concentrator, and smelter, to hold them against possible
replacements. Meanwhile, four convoys of Mexican soldiers began
moving toward the town. Over three hundred heavily armed mem-

bers of the state judicial police took over the streets. With violent confrontation in the air, local union president Manuel Romero, Cananea mayor Francisco Garcia, and police and army officers entered the mine. They walked from installation to installation, appealing to the miners to leave. Fearing an armed battle, the workers gave up the occupation and ended the strike.

In the days that followed, over 120 strike leaders were turned away as they tried to report back to their old jobs. Grupo México closed the smelter and began sending ore to the smelter at Nacozari. Hundreds were permanently laid off. Over the next few years, Grupo México contracted out many more jobs. By 2007 only 1,350 working miners belonged to the union, while another 450 people worked alongside them for contracting services, receiving none of the benefits paid to union members.

The company blacklisted Juan Gonzalez (whose name has been changed to protect his identity) for helping lead the 1998 strike and participating in the delegations to Arizona. When the conflict ended, the company posted lists for each department of the people they were accepting back. "When I went to look at the list, my name wasn't on it," Gonzalez recalled. "In my department, the two people they didn't take back were the two of us who participated in the movement." In the company office he was told by the labor relations coordinator that he was a *grillero*, a complainer. "He told me I'd never get a job anywhere in Mexico after that. They'd put my name on a flyer and sent it to other employers."

For a year, Gonzalez tried to find other work in Cananea, but with eight hundred other fired miners doing the same thing, it was impossible. His family survived only because his wife continued to work for the telephone company. "I had no alternative but to leave Cananea, to look for work in the U.S.," he said. "I still had my house and my family, so I really didn't want to leave, but there wasn't anything else I could do." Walking across the desert to Arizona was the only option. The line of applicants for visas, which would have allowed him to work in the United States legally, is many years long, and he'd already exhausted his family's resources.

"I don't have any papers, I really have nothing," he explained as he sat in a Phoenix warehouse. "But there's a group of us here from Cananea, friends, and we help each other. I'd like to go back, but there's nothing there for me. The only thing I can do right now is work here in the U.S." In the middle of the interview he began to cry. "My children and my wife are still in Cananea. We talk on the phone a lot. I go back and forth, but it's always a big risk. I'm hoping next year I'll be able to bring them. I don't think I'd go back to the mine, even if I heard they were hiring again. That part of my life is over."

When Napoleón Gómez Sada, the national president of the Mexican Union of Mine, Metal and Allied Workers, died in 2001, his son, Napoleón Gómez Urrutia, was elected union general secretary. The process in which powerful Mexican political figures pick their own successors, the *dedazo*, is normally a device to prevent change. Gómez Urrutia, however, was not like his father. Taking advantage of high world copper prices, he negotiated wage increases much higher than the limits the government sought to impose in its effort to attract foreign investment.

The miners' union established an education program in cooperation with the Technological Institute of Monterrey, formerly an elitist school for upper- and middle-class families, and seven hundred miners and their children enrolled in fifteen different degree programs. The union pressured the government housing program to build homes its members could afford. "We have recovered the dignity of workers and the union," Gómez Urrutia said.

Relations with the government became more strained when he began opposing two of its key economic policies. President Vicente Fox proposed to change Mexican labor law, weakening the right to strike. The law also gives workers the right to healthcare, protects job security, mandates strict hours of work, and imposes severance pay for laid-off employees. Fox sought to eliminate these protections, following recommendations made by the World Bank. Gómez Urrutia joined other leaders of the country's fractious labor movement in an unprecedented united front, spiking another Fox plan for a new tax on workers' benefits, which were previously exempt.

On February 19, 2006, sixty-five miners died in a huge explosion in the Pasta de Conchos coal mine in the northern state of Coahuila. That mine belonged to Grupo México's subsidiary, Industrial Minera México (IMMSA). The union found that workers on the second shift had complained of high concentrations of explosive methane gas in the shafts before the accident. "They told us that welding was still going on, even after the failure of some electrical equipment," Gómez Urrutia charged.

Of those who were killed, forty didn't actually work directly for Grupo México. Instead, they were employed by the network of smaller, private contractors who now supply personnel to larger employers. Union workers have the right to refuse dangerous work, and a labor-management safety committee will back them up if they do. But contract workers are often pushed harder, and economic desperation leads them to take more risks at work. At Pasta de Conchos, subcontracted coal miners were getting ninety pesos a day (about nine dollars) and regularly worked ten to twelve hours for it, beyond the legal eight-hour limit.

In a July 2006 report, the National Human Rights Commission found that the local office of the federal labor ministry had "clear knowledge" before the accident of the conditions that would set off the explosion. In 2004, labor safety inspectors had found forty-eight health and safety violations in the mine, including oil and gas leaks, missing safety devices, and broken lighting. Although Grupo México was given an order to remedy the illegal conditions, no compliance inspection was carried out until February 7, twelve days before the explosion. Only two bodies were ever recovered, and Grupo México abandoned recovery efforts in 2006. The widows of the dead miners launched a high-profile national campaign demanding that the government cancel the company's mining concession. Elvira Martinez, one of their leaders, called IMMSA "a socially irresponsible enterprise and a danger to Mexico."

Two days after the explosion, Gómez Urrutia accused the secretary of labor and Grupo México of "industrial homicide." Fox filed corruption charges against Gómez Urrutia less than a week later, accusing him of stealing $55 million that Grupo México agreed to pay miners when it took over the state-owned property. Labor Secretary Francisco Xavier Salazar Sáenz, with company support, appointed Elías Morales Hernández to replace Gómez Urrutia. Morales had been expelled from the union for his close relationship with the company.

In defiance of the government, miners reelected Gómez Urrutia twice, and then struck mines at Cananea and Nacozari, and the Sicartsa steel mill in Michoacán, to demand his reinstatement. At the same time that teachers were battling police in the streets of Oaxaca, two strikers, Mario Alberto Castillo Rodríguez and Héctor Álvarez Gómez, were shot and killed during the Sicartsa plant occupation. The strikes did not achieve their goal, however. At Sicartsa and Cananea, workers eventually returned to work, preserving their jobs and contracts. In Nacozari, the government permitted Grupo México to fire its entire workforce. It then selectively rehired about seven hundred union members and brought in another twelve hundred workers from southern Mexico, who were housed on the mine premises. The day Grupo México announced it was firing the Nacozari miners, an anonymous spokesperson for Scotiabank, one of Mexico's largest financial institutions, told Reuters that Mexican business welcomed the action. "This sets a precedent, so the workers will think harder," he threatened. When a group of fired miners marched to the mine in Nacozari to demand their reinstatement, one of them, Reynaldo Hernández González, was killed.

"Most of the miners who lost their jobs at Nacozari also had to leave their homes," explains Jorge Luis Morales, president of the Vigilance and Justice Commission of the union at Cananea. "I'm sure most of them are working in Tucson or Phoenix now, or even California. They are very skilled workers, but where else could they go?"

Gómez Urrutia also left Mexico to avoid arrest, and over the next year mounted a legal effort to win back control of the union. First, the labor secretary's decision appointing Elías Morales was overturned, when it was discovered that signatures on his petition to become union leader had been forged. A federal judge then dismissed corruption charges against Gómez Urrutia when a Swiss accounting firm, Horwath Berney Audit SA, went over the union's books and accounted for all the funds.

In the meantime, however, in November 2006 the federal Conciliation and Arbitration Board (JNCA), under the control of Fox's successor, President Felipe Calderón and the National Action Party, gave legal status to a new miners' union, the National Union of Workers in the Exploration, Exploitation and Benefit of Mines. The new union was headed by Francisco Gamez, a former contractor for Grupo México who once worked at Cananea. The federal labor board set up elections to allow it to take over representation rights in eight Grupo México mines. The Center for Labor Action and Reflection (CEREAL), a human rights organization based in Mexico City, charged that the election process was manipulated to get rid of the old miners' union. Fifteen workers were fired before one vote in San Luis Potosí, CEREAL said. In Nueva Rosita, Coahuila, miners on the first and second shifts were locked inside the coal mine for a day before balloting began, while three hundred federal, state, and municipal police surrounded the mine entrance.

At Nacozari, where fifteen hundred workers had been fired for striking in 2006, over nine hundred were denied voting rights. Workers brought in to replace the fired miners were told they would be fired themselves, evicted from company housing, and sent back to southern Mexico if the company union didn't win the vote there. Rita Marcela Robles Benitez, an analyst with CEREAL, charged that Grupo México "changed the working hours from eight to twelve per day, which has resulted in more accidents because of the lack of safety protection and training." The new union approved the change. The government and Grupo México were prevented from holding a similar election at Cananea because workers struck over safety violations in July 2007.

On January 11, 2008, the JNCA declared the strike illegal, and seven hundred agents of the Sonora state police and the Federal Preventative Police entered the mine as they had in 1989. Street fighting erupted between miners and police, in which twenty people were injured, several seriously, and five strikers went missing. "They dropped tear gas bombs on us from helicopters," said Jesus Verdugo, chair of the union's strike committee. "Dozens of us were beaten."

After the JNCA announced its decision, the union went before a Mexico City judge. Máximo Ariel Torres Quevedo, Sixth District Judge for Labor Matters, barred the JNCA from declaring the strike illegal. But in a highly unusual decision he then went on to declare that Grupo México could restart operations anyway, using either strikebreakers or strikers who "voluntarily" returned to work. Over twenty-five thousand miners across Mexico then walked off the job for a day on January 16 in protest.

Allowing a company to operate during a strike, and recruit strikebreakers under police protection, would make Mexican law much more like that in the United States, where companies legally use strikebreakers. Adopting that U.S. model was part of Fox's labor law reform proposals. His successor, Calderón, vowed to move those proposals forward, although neither president was able to win the votes for adoption in the federal Chamber of Deputies. In Cananea the government sought to accomplish by legal fiat what it was unable to win legislatively.

At the same time, by trying to break the strike, the company and government sought to install a company union as they had at Nacozari and the other Grupo México mines. With the union broken, its terminated leaders and activists would then likely have found themselves, like the fired veterans of earlier conflicts, in Phoenix, Tucson, or Los Angeles, hungry and desperate for work. In the weeks after Judge Torres's order, however, the miners continued to keep Grupo México from restarting operations at Cananea.

In the middle of the 2006 turmoil in Oaxaca and Cananea, Mexicans headed for the polls. The miners' union was one of many that supported the presidential bid of former Mexico City mayor Andrés Manuel López Obrador, candidate of the Democratic Revolutionary

Party (PRD). Miners, teachers, farmers, and others believed that López Obrador would roll back the conservative economic reforms of the past two decades.

Fox, a former Coca-Cola executive, sought to reassure Mexico's elite that the government would continue protecting them from popular upheaval. At the same time Fox seized control of the miners' union, López Obrador told the press that if he won, "There will be no intervention in the life of the unions. Workers can freely elect their own leaders." It was no surprise, therefore, that Grupo México and other large corporations poured money into the campaign of the National Action Party's Calderón, Fox's chosen successor. They funded commercials predicting chaos if López Obrador were elected, which dovetailed with news broadcasts of violence from Oaxaca and Michoacán.

Mexican voters faced the clearest choice they'd had since the night the computers went down in the 1988 vote count and Carlos Salinas de Gortari miraculously emerged the winner when electricity was restored the morning after. As president, López Obrador would hardly have been a radical on the order of Venezuela's Hugo Chavez, who declared his country's goal was socialism. That was Mexico's official ideal as well in the 1930s, but a socialist direction was not the alternative López Obrador had in mind. His program for redeveloping Mexico City's downtown was oriented toward business promotion, even to the extent of expelling the Mazahua indigenous street vendors there. "He adopted [former New York City mayor] Giuliani's 'zero tolerance' policy to improve personal security, at the cost of violating individual rights, and shelved the investigation into the death of [indigenous rights attorney] Digna Ochoa in the face of grave inconsistencies in police procedure," said Alejandro Álvarez, an economist at the National Autonomous University.

But López Obrador did propose a new immigration and economic policy. While Fox spent six years trying to negotiate a contract-labor program with the United States, López Obrador said the answer to migration was raising family income, especially for the poorest Mexicans in the countryside. "The rural social movements of the last two

years have been openly against NAFTA, and in the city, against privatization and the dismantling of the welfare state," noted Álvarez.
López Obrador hoped to ride this upsurge in popular sentiment into
office, making him a threat not just to Fox but to the Bush administration as well. Neither had a desire to see Mexico go in the direction
of Brazil, Ecuador, Argentina, Chile, Bolivia, or Uruguay, much less
Venezuela—rejecting the free trade model and economic control from
Washington.

Mexican employers, however, were losing interest in the country's
social contract, in which unions once had a place at the table so long
as they didn't upset it. They looked to Calderón to ensure the continuation of a favorable investment climate and control an increasingly
angry workforce. To Gómez Urrutia, "They think we're like a cancer
and should be exterminated. This is no longer a country that can be
called a democracy."

On July 2, the official count gave Calderón a two-hundred-
thousand-vote lead among more than 40 million votes cast. The political opposition, including the miners, called for a recount after
accusations of fraud threw the tiny margin into doubt. Huge national
demonstrations backed up the demand, and for weeks tent encampments of protestors along Mexico City's broad main avenue, the Re-
forma, threw traffic into chaos. In the end, however, the protests were
unsuccessful, and Calderón took office.

"What people want is justice," said Rufino Dominguez, binational
coordinator of the Indigenous Front of Binational Organizations. "To
us, democracy means more than elections. It means economic stability—our capacity to make a living in Mexico, without having to migrate. It means a halt to the continued violation of human rights in our
communities. It means having a government that attends to the needs
of the people. We're tired of governments which put other interests
first." No one understands the price of free trade policies better than
those who have paid it, leaving their homes and traveling thousands
of miles in search of work. "We know the reasons we have to leave,"
Dominguez asserted. "Over five thousand of us have died trying to
cross the border in the last decade."

The defeat of López Obrador was a setback to those aspirations. But it was very much part of the growth of the system of economic reforms, corporate investment, migration, and the exploitation of migrant labor.

Three

DISPLACEMENT
AND MIGRATION

Forcing People into the Migrant Stream

In the years since the passage of the North American Free Trade Agreement, critics have focused on the favorable investment climate it created in Mexico for large North American corporations. They've documented the treaty's high cost in labor rights, employment, and the environment, and the way it undermined laws and regulations protecting the social gains of working people in all three signatory countries, Canada, the United States, and Mexico.

Less attention has been given to the relationship between the treaty and migration. It's still a common critique that NAFTA freed the movement of goods and capital but not the movement of people. On the one hand, this seems quite an underestimation of the treaty's impact. During the years following NAFTA's implementation in 1994, a greater number of people moved from Mexico to the United States than in almost any other period in our history. On the other, it seems to suggest that NAFTA should have regulated migration just as it regulated trade and investment. In the current political environment, this would more likely have led to contract-labor programs than to the free movement of people.

In the one period in which a bilateral agreement between the United States and Mexico did regulate migration, Congress established the bracero contract-labor program, which lasted from 1942 to 1964. Today similar labor programs are popular once again among politicians in Washington and Mexico City. International trade negotiations have begun to discuss even more extensive schemes. The Mode 4 proposal made at the World Trade Organization talks in Hong Kong in 2005 would essentially create a new international guest-worker system, guiding the flow of migrants on a global basis to fulfill corporate labor needs.

Trade and immigration policy, especially in the post–cold war world, are part of a system that produces displaced labor and puts it to use. A close relationship does exist between U.S. trade and immigration policy, in which the negotiation of NAFTA played an important part. But it did not lead to greater freedom of movement for workers and farmers across the U.S.-Mexico border, nor did it give those migrants greater rights and equality in the United States.

Trade negotiations and immigration policy were formally joined together when the U.S. Congress passed the Immigration Reform and Control Act (IRCA) in 1986. Immigrant-rights activists campaigned against the law because it contained employer sanctions, prohibiting employers for the first time on a federal level from hiring undocumented workers. In their view, the proposal amounted to criminalizing work for the undocumented. IRCA's liberal defenders pointed to its amnesty provision as a gain that justified sanctions, and the bill did eventually enable over 3 million people living in the United States without immigration documents to gain permanent residence.

Yet few noted one other provision of the law. IRCA set up the Commission for the Study of International Migration and Cooperative Economic Development to study the causes of immigration to the United States. The commission was inactive until 1988, but began holding hearings when the United States and Canada signed a bilateral free trade agreement. After Mexican president Carlos Salinas de Gortari made it plain he favored a similar agreement with Mexico, the commission made a report to the first President George Bush and to Congress in 1990. It found, unsurprisingly, that the main motivation for coming to the United States was economic. To slow or halt this flow, it recommended "promoting greater economic integration between the migrant sending countries and the United States through free trade" and that "U.S. economic policy should promote a system of open trade." It concluded that "the United States should expedite the development of a U.S.-Mexico free trade area and encourage its incorporation with Canada into a North American free trade area," while warning that "it takes many years—even generations—for sustained growth to achieve the desired effect."

The negotiations that led to NAFTA started within months of the report. As Congress debated the treaty, President Salinas toured the United States, telling audiences unhappy at high levels of immigration that passing NAFTA would reduce it by providing employment for Mexicans in Mexico. Back home he and other treaty proponents made the same argument. NAFTA, they claimed, would set Mexico on a course to becoming a first-world nation.

"We did become part of the first world," Juan Manuel Sandoval says bitterly. "The backyard."

NAFTA was part of the corporate transformation of the Mexican economy—a process that began long before it took effect in 1994. That process moved Mexico away from nationalist ideas about development policy, which had been advocated from the end of the Mexican Revolution in 1920 through the 1970s.

Nationalist development became part of Mexico's official ideology in the 1930s. Nationalists advocated severing the ties most Mexicans believed held their country in bondage to its neighbor to the north. At the time the revolution began, U.S. companies and investors owned oil fields, copper mines, railroads, the telephone system, great tracts of land, and other key economic resources. To be truly independent, the nationalists believed, Mexico had to establish an economic system in which those resources were controlled by Mexicans and used for their benefit. The most important route to control was nationalization, intended to serve two purposes—to stop the transfer of wealth out of the country and to use state ownership to set up an internal market, in which what was produced in Mexico would be sold there as well. In theory, at least, the government had a stake in maintaining stable jobs and income, so that workers and farmers could buy back what they produced.

Mexico, under President Lázaro Cárdenas, established a corporatist system in which one political party, the Party of the Mexican Revolution (PRM), represented, or in practice controlled, the main sectors of Mexican society—workers, farmers, the military, and the "popular" sector (which included government employees and professionals). After World War II the PRM was reorganized and became the Institutional Revolutionary Party (PRI), which governed until 2000. In 1939 Mexican capital and the Catholic Church organized the National Action Party, which finally came to power six decades later.

PRI governments administered a network of social services. The social security system, IMSS, established in 1943, provided healthcare, while the government housing corporation, INFONAVIT, set up in 1972, built homes. The Mexican Constitution guaranteed economic and social rights, in addition to political ones, in a way the U.S. Constitution does not. Under Cárdenas, Mexico expanded the land reform begun in 1917, and redistributed haciendas in many parts of the country, although some vast cattle ranches and other landholdings were left intact. Land was considered the property of the whole country, and thousands of *ejidos,* or farming communities, were created, in which farmers, or *ejidatarios,* held the land they worked in trust. They could not legally sell, rent, or misuse it. Most foreign ownership of land was prohibited.

Cárdenas also nationalized Mexico's most important resource— oil—in a popular nationalist campaign. Even schoolchildren were encouraged to donate pennies to help compensate foreign corporations for the expropriation of their holdings. National ownership of oil, and later electrical generation, was written into the Constitution. Land redistribution and nationalization had a political as well as economic purpose—the creation of a section of workers and farmers who could be depended upon to defend the government and its political party, into which their unions and producer organizations were incorporated.

After World War II, Mexico officially adopted a policy of industrialization through import substitution. In this development strategy, enterprises were created or supported that produced products for the domestic market, while imports of those products were restricted. The purpose was to develop a national industrial base, provide jobs, and increase the domestic market.

Under that policy large state-owned enterprises eventually employed hundreds of thousands of Mexican industrial workers in mines, mills, transportation, and other strategic industries. It was not a socialist economy—large capitalist enterprises thrived. But for a while, the policy provided economic security to many workers and farmers. Foreign investment was limited, although after Cárdenas much Mexican capital operated in increasingly close partnership with U.S. and Canadian corporations. Enrique Davila, professor at San Diego City College and the Autonomous University of Baja California, summarizes that growing contradiction as "nationalism in rhetoric, selling out the country in practice."

Under successive PRI administrations, a vast gulf grew between those who were integrated into the formal sector, and farmers and indigenous communities who remained at the social margin, especially in the south. An even greater gulf widened between the political and economic elite, who managed the state's assets and controlled government policy, and workers and farmers in general. To protect this elite, the country's political system became increasingly repressive, especially toward those who wanted an independent political voice. Nationalist rhetoric often covered political crimes. Defense Minister Marcelino García Barragán, almost certainly on the orders of President Gustavo Díaz Ordaz, called out the army and killed hundreds of protesting students at Mexico City's Tlatelolco Plaza in 1968. Later, President Luis Echevarría conducted a so-called dirty war against Mexican leftists—in which hundreds were kidnapped, tortured, and "disappeared"—all while pursuing a "nationalist revolutionary" policy, as it was called in the official language.

Contradictions in Mexican development became sharper in the 1970s. To finance growth while the price of oil was high, Mexico opened up its financial system to foreign capital (mostly from the United States), and the country's foreign debt soared. State enterprises still belonged to the government formally, but in effect were hocked by their managers to banks. Instead of plowing loans into modernization and efficient production, the money often wound up in offshore bank accounts. Managers of state enterprises like the oil company PEMEX ran private businesses on the side, along with politically connected union officials. Rackets and corruption proliferated while labor and campesino leaders who challenged the system were imprisoned or worse.

Meanwhile, in the 1960s, the first big dislocations from the countryside began. Ciudad Netzahualcóyotl at the edge of Mexico City became one of the world's largest slums, populated largely by uprooted farmers. The movement of people across the border with the United States grew as well.

The accumulation of debt, and the hold it gave to foreign financial interests over the Mexican economy, spelled the end of nationalist development. Oil prices fell, the U.S. Treasury jacked up interest rates, and in 1982 the system collapsed when Mexico could no longer make debt payments. The government devalued the peso in what is still infamous as the great "peso shock." Agustin Ramirez, studying to be an agronomist at the university in Michoacán at the time, remembers that "the value of the peso went from twelve to the dollar to five hundred sixty to the dollar in six months. The government not only froze jobs, but started laying people off. My promised job went down the drain. So if I had to choose between being poor in Mexico and poor in the U.S., it was obvious where I should go." The cutoff date for amnesty under IRCA, January 1, 1982, was timed to give legal status to those who came prior to the devaluation in February, but not to the huge wave displaced by the shock itself.

The "nationalist" commitment to popular welfare was already more rhetoric than reality by the 1980s. In the Constitution, Mexicans still had the right to housing, healthcare, employment, and education, but millions of people went hungry, had no homes, were sick and unemployed, and couldn't read. The anger and cynicism felt by many Mexicans toward their political system is in great part a product of the contradiction between those constitutional promises of the revolution a century ago, plus the nationalist rhetoric that followed, and the reality of life for most people.

The crisis was an opportunity for the PRI to weaken that rhetorical commitment even further. In a desperate attempt to generate jobs and revenue for debt payments, the government encouraged the growth of maquiladoras, first permitted under the Border Industrial Program, begun in 1964. To develop the northern border region, the government had allowed foreign corporations to build assembly plants within a hundred miles of the United States. The raw materials had to come from the U.S. side, and all the finished products had to go back north as well.

From 1982 to 1988 the number of border factories tripled, from five hundred to fifteen hundred, the number of workers they employed went from 150,000 to 360,000, and they accounted for 40 percent of Mexico's total exports. Encouraging their growth set a process into motion in which today more than three thousand border plants employ more than 2 million workers making products for shoppers from Los Angeles to New York. By 1992, the year before NAFTA took effect, they accounted for over half of Mexican exports, and in the NAFTA era maquiladoras became the main sector of the economy producing employment growth.

Maquiladora development encouraged foreign investment at almost any cost. It undermined the legal rights of workers and communities in the border area and the enforcement of environmental protections or other laws that could be viewed as discouraging investment. Mexico's future, in the eyes of the technicians who were reordering its economic priorities, lay in producing for the U.S. market rather than for consumers at home, whose income, after 1982, could not support much domestic demand anyway. That gave the government a growing interest in keeping wages low as an attraction to foreign investment, instead of high enough that people could buy what they were making. Other incentives to investors included a political structure in which official unions controlled restive workers rather than organizing them to win better conditions.

Protecting investors required changes in the system of land ownership, since companies were reluctant to invest in factories or other productive enterprises if their titles could be challenged under land reform and land tenancy laws. Salinas pushed through a drastic change in Article 27 of the Mexican Constitution, which had guaranteed land reform and established the *ejido* system. After the change, *ejidos* could sell land, and many did. About three thousand of thirty thousand *ejidos* were legally converted into co-ops, condominiums, partnerships, *sociedades anónimas* (Mexican private businesses), and joint-stock companies. It became a crime for landless people to settle and build homes on vacant federal lands. Reforms began the reconcentration of land in the hands of wealthy investors and agricultural companies, while many *ejidatarios* became agricultural wageworkers or left for the cities.

As a result of taking control of banks in the 1982 crisis, the Mexican government became the owner of foreclosed assets, which included mines and other private businesses. It quickly began to sell these properties off. By the early 1990s Mexico had sold not just mines to the Larreas, but its steel mill in Michoacán to another elite family, the Villareals, and its telephone company to the Mexican businessman Carlos Slim Helú. Former Mexico City mayor Carlos Hank González, who controlled the CONASUPO trucks and warehouses, drove the city's bus system deeply into debt and then bought the lines in the 1990s at public auction. Mexico created a whole new stratum of billionaires in this period.

Rich Mexicans weren't the only beneficiaries of privatization. U.S. companies were allowed to own land and factories, eventually anywhere in Mexico, without Mexican partners. U.S.-based Union Pacific, in partnership with the Larreas, became the owner of the country's main north–south rail line, and discontinued virtually all passenger service, since it was less profitable than moving freight. As the Larreas and Union Pacific boosted profits and cut labor costs, Mexican rail employment dropped from over ninety thousand to thirty-six thousand. In the 1950s the railroad union, under left-wing leaders Demetrio Vallejo and Valentin Campa, had been so strong that its strikes rocked the government. The two were punished with years in prison. But when railroad workers mounted a wildcat strike to try to save their jobs from privatization, they lost and their union's presence in Mexican politics became a shadow.

After NAFTA the privatization wave expanded. Mexico's ports were sold off, and companies like Stevedoring Services of America, Hutchison Port Holdings (HPH), and TMM now operate the country's largest shipping terminals. The impact on longshoring wages was devastating. In Manzanillo and Lázaro Cárdenas, the two largest Pacific Coast ports, a crane driver made $100 to $160 a day before privatization in the late 1980s. Today crane drivers make $40 to $50.

Slashing wages in privatized enterprises and gutting union agreements only increased the wage differential between the United States and Mexico. According to Garrett Brown of the Maquiladora Health and Safety Support Network, the average Mexican wage was 23 percent of the U.S. manufacturing wage in 1975. By 2002 it was less than an eighth, according to Mexican economist and former senator Rosa Albina Garabito. Former United Auto Workers representative Steve Beckman says that after the 1981 debt crisis the Mexican average dropped to a twelfth or fifteenth of that in the United States, depending on the industry—even during a period in which U.S. wages declined in buying power. Brown says that in the twelve years after NAFTA went into effect, real Mexican wages dropped by 22 percent, while worker productivity increased 45 percent.

Low wages are the magnet used to attract U.S. and other foreign investors. In June 2006, Ford Motor Company, already one of Mexico's largest employers, announced it would invest $9 billion more in building new factories. Meanwhile, Ford said it was closing at least fourteen U.S. plants, eliminating the jobs of tens of thousands of workers. Both moves were part of the company's strategic plan to stem losses by cutting labor costs drastically and moving production.

All these economic changes displaced people. This too is part of a long historical process. People were migrating from Mexico to the United States long before NAFTA was negotiated. Juan Manuel Sandoval emphasizes that "Mexican labor has always been linked to the different stages of U.S. development since the nineteenth century—in times of prosperity by the incorporation of big numbers of workers in agricultural, manufacturing, service, and other sectors, and in periods of economic crisis by the massive deportation of Mexican laborers back to Mexico."

From 1982 through the NAFTA era, successive economic reforms produced more migrants. *Ejidatarios* who could no longer survive as farmers found jobs as farmworkers in California. Laid-off railroad workers traveled north, as their forebears had during the early 1900s, when Mexican labor built much of the rail network through the U.S. Southwest. Again, the displacement of people had already grown so large by 1986 that IRCA established a commission charged with recommending measures to halt or slow it.

The IRCA commission's report urged that "migrant-sending countries should encourage technological modernization by strengthening and assuring intellectual property protection and by removing existing impediments to investment." It recommended that "the United States . . . condition bilateral aid to sending countries on their taking the necessary steps toward structural adjustment. Similarly, U.S. support for non-project lending by the international financial institutions should be based on the implementation of satisfactory adjustment programs."

Beginning around 1980, the World Bank and the IMF began imposing a one-size-fits-all formula for development, called structural adjustment programs. These required borrowing countries to adopt a package of economic reforms, such as privatization, ending subsidies and price controls, trade liberalization, and reduced worker protections. After more than two decades, there is no strong evidence that this approach has achieved its stated goal of stimulating growth, while the toll on working people has been staggering. The IRCA commission report acknowledged the potential for harm by noting that "efforts should be made to ease transitional costs in human suffering."

The North American Free Trade Agreement, however, was not intended to relieve human suffering. Mexico hoped to negotiate a commercial treaty, to gain access to U.S. markets for Mexican goods and raw materials, which had often been barred by protective tariffs imposed by the U.S. Congress. The United States and Canada sought, on their part, to make it easier for foreign companies to move money and goods across the border, to invest in Mexico, and to protect that investment. But in 1994, the year the treaty took effect, U.S. speculators began selling off Mexican government bonds. According to Jeff Faux, founding director of the Economic Policy Institute, "The peso crash of December 1994 was directly connected to NAFTA, which had created a speculative bubble for Mexican assets that then collapsed when the speculators cashed in."

The government devalued the peso, trying to prevent a flood of money back to the north, but also allowed bankers to freely exchange pesos for dollars. As businesses tried to repay debt with pesos worth only half as much, bankruptcies spread. According to Harvard history professor John Womack, the old "nationalists," many now private billionaires, took control of government policy. In the ensuing political crisis, the new president, Ernesto Zedillo, made a deal with U.S. treasury secretary Robert Rubin. Goldman Sachs and New York and Spanish banks took control of the Mexican banks, and were guaranteed payment for refinancing Mexico's debt. "I think about eighty percent of Mexico's finances now runs through New York and London," says Womack. "The new Mexican government surrendered, conceded, and abandoned all the protections for Mexican businesses and producers." The arrangement negotiated with Rubin, he says, "was much more about finances than about trade, much more about the movement of capital, the creation of debt and derivatives, and the pursuit of speculation than about the movement of commodities."

The U.S. government guaranteed the bailout, and in return President Bill Clinton demanded that Mexico use oil exports to guarantee debt payments to the banks. Mexico had historically used its oil income to finance government expenditures, keeping taxes extremely low for businesses and the wealthy, while starving the state oil company PEMEX of capital for modernization and expansion. Using oil income to pay debt made matters even worse. In 2006 Manuel López Obrador, the PRD's presidential candidate, said he would ease the pressure on Mexicans to migrate by raising the income of the poor in the countryside. But even if a popular government had been elected, as seemed possible that year, it would not have had Mexico's main source of income available for alleviating poverty, granting rural loans, rescuing dilapidated social security clinics, or raising teachers' salaries and building more schools in Oaxaca.

Mexico lost a million jobs, by the government's own count, in 1995. That experience was repeated in 2000–2001, when recession in the United States, and the decline in consumer purchasing, led to the layoff of over four hundred thousand workers in the maquiladoras. NAFTA became an accelerant, pouring gasoline on the fire of economic reform. Instead of creating prosperity, it displaced workers and farmers at an ever greater rate.

The economic reform process required the Mexican government to dissolve the CONASUPO stores. Mexican subsidies to farmers were ruled illegal, although the U.S. continued paying huge subsidies to its largest growers under the provisions of the U.S. farm bill, while buying enormous quantities of farm commodities. At the same time, CONASUPO's state-run stores were held a barrier to the entry of private companies into the retail grocery business.

The ability of U.S. producers to grow corn cheaply using intensive industrial methods affected Mexican growers long before NAFTA. In the 1980s Mexico became a corn importer, and according to Sandoval, large farmers switched to other crops when they couldn't compete with U.S. grain dumping. But with no price supports, hundreds of thousands of small farmers found it impossible to sell corn or other farm products for what it cost to produce them. And when NAFTA pulled down customs barriers, large U.S. corporations dumped even more agricultural products on the Mexican market. Rural families went hungry when they couldn't find buyers for what they'd grown.

It's no accident that the Zapatista National Liberation Army, based in poor indigenous communities in Mexico's southernmost state, Chiapas, planned the beginning of an armed rebellion for the day NAFTA took effect. The Zapatistas knew what would happen to indigenous communities in the southern countryside. And the final elimination of tariffs on white corn, beans, and other farm goods on January 1, 2008—the implementation of NAFTA's final chapter—was greeted by demonstrations across Mexico.

Mexico couldn't protect its own agriculture from the fluctuations of the world market. A global coffee glut in the 1990s plunged prices below the cost of production. A less entrapped government might have bought the crops of Veracruz farmers to keep them afloat, or provided subsidies for other crops. But once free market strictures were in place, those farmers paid the price instead. Veracruz campesinos joined the stream of workers headed for the Smithfield plant in North Carolina and points beyond.

Poor people in the cities fared no better. Although a flood of cheap U.S. grain was supposed to make consumer prices go down, the opposite occurred. With the end of CONASUPO and price controls, the price of tortillas more than doubled in the years that followed. Higher prices intensified urban poverty, increasing the pressure to migrate. One company, Grupo Maseca, monopolized tortilla production. On its board of directors are Federico Gorbea Quintero, president of Archer Daniels Midland México, and Ismael Roig, ADM's vice president for planning and business development. (ADM is one of the United States' largest corn producers and processors.) Carlos Hank Rhon, whose family formerly controlled CONASUPO, is now also a Grupo Maseca director. Meanwhile, Wal-Mart has become Mexico's largest retailer.

Under its former development policy, foreign automakers like Ford, Chrysler, General Motors, and Volkswagen had been required to buy some of their components from Mexican producers. Workers labored in the parts plants that produced them. NAFTA forbids governments from requiring foreign investors to use a certain percentage of local content in their production. Without this restraint, the auto giants began to supply their assembly lines with parts from their own subsidiaries, often manufactured in other countries. Mexican parts workers lost their jobs by the thousands.

"The financial crashes and economic disasters drove people to work for dollars in the U.S., to replace life savings, or just to earn enough to keep their family at home together," Womack says. NAFTA didn't reduce migration, as the IRCA commission predicted. Following the 1994 crisis, it produced it. More than 6 million Mexicans came to live in the United States in the thirteen years after the treaty went into effect. In just five years, from 2000 to 2005, the Mexican population living in the United States increased from 10 to 12 million, and the government predicted annual migration would soon reach four hundred thousand per year. With few green cards, or permanent-residence visas, available for Mexicans, most migrants were undocumented.

The Sensenbrenner Family Business

Economic reforms and NAFTA made a small group of investors in both Mexico and the United States rich, or richer. But when people were displaced by this process, where were they supposed to go?

Not to the United States. At least, not according to Wisconsin congressman James Sensenbrenner. In December 2005 Sensenbrenner convinced his Republican colleagues (and, to their shame, thirty-five Democrats) to pass one of the most repressive immigration proposals of the last hundred years. His bill, HR 4437, would have made federal felons of all 12 million undocumented immigrants in the United States, criminalized teachers, nurses, or priests who helped them, and built a seven-hundred-mile wall on the U.S.-Mexico border to keep people from crossing. The bill never passed the Senate, but its wide margin of approval in the House was a vivid demonstration of how deep congressional anti-immigrant hysteria had become.

Representative Sensenbrenner is more than just a leader of congressional xenophobes, however. His family is intimately involved in creating the conditions that cause migration, and they profit from the labor it makes available. The family's connections, in miniature, reflect the political economy of migration itself.

The Kimberly-Clark Company was incorporated in 1906, and James Sensenbrenner's grandfather Frank became its head in 1907. It became one of the world's largest paper companies, and the family trust remains an important stockholder. The company's Mexican counterpart, Kimberly-Clark de México, is a close associate of the Mexican mining giant Grupo México. One of KC's former executives, J. Eduardo Gonzalez, is Grupo México's chief financial officer. (Another Grupo México board member, Luis Téllez Kuenzler, sat on the board of the Carlyle Group, which included former president George H. W. Bush. Kuenzler resigned to become secretary of communications and transport in the Calderón administration after the 2006 election.)

In 1998 Grupo México provoked the strike in Cananea that cost more than eight hundred miners their jobs. Many were blacklisted and left for Phoenix and Tucson. In 2006 the mining giant did the same thing at Nacozari, and twelve hundred more were permanently discharged, replaced by workers brought from southern Mexico. With the border just a few miles north, they too had no alternative but to cross it to survive. Those terminations, replacements, and busted unions successfully cut labor costs while world copper prices were climbing. Company profits increased.

During the months when Nacozari mining families set out on their journey north, Congressman Sensenbrenner organized a series of rump congressional hearings on the other side of the border to defend his immigration proposal. As he and his Republican allies toured various U.S. cities, they fulminated against the undocumented, declaring they had no place in the United States and should leave. If they didn't, his bill would send them to federal prison. In order to house those detained crossing the border without papers, contracts to build new detention centers had already been given to Halliburton Corporation, the company formerly headed by U.S. vice president Dick Cheney.

One of those hearings took place in Arizona, but no one invited any of the Nacozari or Cananea miners to testify. No reporter or politician asked Sensenbrenner where he thought they should go, or if the family's business associates bore some responsibility for their displacement and subsequent migration.

Other voices in Congress criticized the congressman's draconian bill, arguing that the labor of migrants was needed in the U.S. economy. Some 24 million immigrants live in the United States with documents, and 12 million without them. If they all actually did go home, whole industries would collapse. Some of the country's largest corporations, completely dependent on the work of immigrants, would go bankrupt.

One of these dependent corporations is the Sensenbrenner family business. Every year, Kimberly-Clark converts tons of wood pulp into a leading brand of toilet paper and sells it in supermarkets around the world. Deep in U.S. forests, thousands of immigrant workers plant and tend the trees that produce that pulp. Every year, laborers from Mexico, Central America, and the Caribbean are recruited for this job. In towns like La Democracia, Guatemala, where the global fall in coffee prices has driven families to the edge of hunger, recruiters promise jobs paying more in an hour than a coffee farmer can make in a day. They offer to arrange visas to come to the United States as guest workers, and for their services charge thousands of dollars. Hungry families mortgage homes and land just to put one person on the airplane north.

In the United States, recruiters hand the workers over to labor contractors. They, in turn, work for land-management companies, who tend the forests for their owners. The landowners grow the trees and sell them to the paper companies. No worker gets overtime, regardless of the law. Companies charge for everything from tools to food and housing. Guest workers are routinely cheated of much of their pay. If they protest, they're put on a blacklist. Protesting wouldn't do much good anyway. The U.S. Department of Labor almost never decertifies a guest-worker contractor, and says the blacklist is legal.

The paper industry depends on this system. Twenty years ago, it stopped hiring unemployed workers domestically and began recruiting guest workers. As a result, labor costs in the forests have remained flat, while paper profits have soared. The low price of labor allows landowners to sell their trees for less, and Kimberly-Clark profits from the result.

In Latin America, economic reforms promoted by the U.S. government through trade agreements and international financial institutions displace workers, from miners to coffee pickers, who join a huge flood of labor moving north. When displaced workers arrive in the United States, they become an indispensable part of the workforce, whether they are undocumented or labor under work visas in conditions of virtual servitude. Displacement is creating a mobile workforce, an army of available workers that has become an integral part of the U.S. economy.

The same system that produces migration needs and uses that labor. Despite the claims of the IRCA commission and NAFTA's proponents, one of the most important effects of the treaty and of structural adjustment policies in general is the production of migration. "The economic interests of the overwhelming majority of [U.S.] employers favor borders as porous for labor as possible," the Economic Policy Institute's Faux says. But labor must arrive in a vulnerable, second-class status, at a price they want to pay.

The U.S. immigration debate needs a vocabulary that describes what happens to migrants before they cross borders—the factors that force them into motion. In the U.S. political debate, people like the miners or pine tree planters are called job seekers, not political refugees. But when teachers and farmers in Oaxaca were beaten in the streets for protesting the fact that their state's government can't and won't provide a viable economic future, and then had to leave southern Mexico as a result, they became both job seekers *and* refugees.

It would be more accurate to call these people migrants, and the process migration. The miner fired in Cananea or Nacozari is as much a victim of the denial of human and labor rights as he or she is a person needing a job in the United States to survive. But in the United

States and other wealthy countries, economic rights are not considered human rights. In this official view, hunger doesn't create political refugees. The whole process that creates migrants is scarcely considered in the U.S. immigration debate.

The key part of that process is displacement, an unmentionable word in the Washington discourse. Not one immigration proposal in Congress in 2006 and 2007 tried to come to grips with the policies that uprooted miners, teachers, tree planters, and farmers, in spite of the fact that members of Congress voted for these policies. In fact, while debating bills to criminalize migrants in 2007, four new trade agreements were introduced, each of which would cause more displacement and more migration.

No speeches on the House or Senate floor connected the dots, or explored real alternatives that would protect jobs and rights for working families regardless of what country they were born in. This is a kind of willful ignorance, in which flawed policy assumptions are treated as obvious truth and repeated endlessly in a skewed policy debate: "Trade agreements are needed to help increase investment abroad," despite the openly predicted "transitional cost of human suffering." "Economic reforms and foreign investment create jobs and prosperity." "Immigration should be regulated to ensure that corporations in the United States have an adequate labor supply."

Underlying these assumptions, however, is a harsh unspoken reality. Whether acknowledged or not, displacement has been indispensable to the growth of capitalism from the beginning. As early as the 1700s, the English enclosure acts displaced villagers by fencing off the commons where they raised sheep for wool. Together with cottage weavers who wove that wool into cloth, herders were driven by hunger into the new textile mills. There they became the world's first wageworkers. Laboring on the new industrial looms, they produced the wealth of the first British factory owners and became the first members of the British working class.

When Karl Marx called Africa of the eighteenth and nineteenth centuries "a warren for the hunting of black skins," he was describing the bloody and forced displacement of indigenous communities by the slave traders. Uprooted African farmers were transported in chains to the New World, where they became an enslaved plantation workforce from Colombia and Brazil to the U.S. South. Their labor created much of the wealth that made the growth of capitalism possible in the United States and throughout the Americas.

Displacement and enslavement produced more than wealth. As slave owners sought to differentiate slaves from free people, they developed and refined racial categories. Skin color and place of origin were used to divide society into those with rights and those without them, who became property themselves. When Mr. Sensenbrenner called modern migrants "illegals," he used a category whose roots go back to these divisions, and the system of unequal status they created. Displacement and inequality are just as much part of today's economic system as they were at its birth in the slave trade and the enclosure acts.

In the global economy, people are displaced because the economies of their countries of origin are transformed, to enable corporations and national elites to transfer wealth out. After World War II, the former colonies of the United States, Europe, and Japan sought to stop that export of wealth. From Iraq to Tanzania to the Philippines, they embraced national economic development plans like Mexico's, to encourage industries and enterprises producing for their own people. The economic reforms that followed the end of the cold war, imposed by wealthy countries and institutions like the World Bank and the IMF, destroyed those systems of national development.

An unjust order inspires rebellion and movements to change it, however, like the Zapatistas in Chiapas or the teachers in Oaxaca. In El Salvador, Guatemala, and Nicaragua, when people tried to upend that social order, they confronted not just the armies of their own elites but, often, U.S. military intervention. Those wars also produced displacement and migration.

At the end of his paean to late-twentieth-century capitalism, *The Lexus and the Olive Tree,* the *New York Times* correspondent Thomas Friedman makes clear the reason those wars were fought. "Markets function and flourish only when property rights are secure and can be enforced, which, in turn, requires a political framework protected and backed by military power," he says. "Indeed, McDonald's cannot flourish without McDonnell Douglas, the designer of the U.S. Air Force F-15. And the hidden fist that keeps the world safe for Silicon Valley's technologies to flourish is called the U.S. Army, Air Force, Navy and Marine Corps. And these fighting forces and institutions are paid for by American taxpayer dollars."

Smedley Butler, the Marine major general who led U.S. interventions in China, Central America, and the Caribbean from the turn of the century to the 1930s, said it better. In a 1935 article for the radical magazine *Common Sense*, he recalled, "I spent 33 years and four months in active military service and during that period I spent most of my time as a high class muscle man for Big Business, for Wall Street and the bankers. In short, I was a racketeer, a gangster for capitalism. I helped make Mexico and especially Tampico safe for American oil interests in 1914. I helped make Haiti and Cuba a decent place for the National City Bank boys to collect revenues in. I helped in the raping of half a dozen Central American republics for the benefit of Wall Street. I helped purify Nicaragua for the International Banking House of Brown Brothers in 1902–1912. I brought light to the Dominican Republic for the American sugar interests in 1916. I helped make Honduras right for the American fruit companies in 1903. In China in 1927 I helped see to it that Standard Oil went on its way unmolested. Looking back on it, I might have given Al Capone a few hints. The best he could do was to operate his racket in three districts. I operated on three continents."

Migrant Labor: An Indispensable Part of a Global System

Although displaced people are an indispensable and growing part of the workforce in this new world order, not all cross borders. The explosive growth of export processing zones (EPZs), where maquiladora factories produce for export, depends on migrant labor.

The creation of the original maquiladora program, the Border Industrial Program, on the U.S.-Mexico border in 1964, was conceived as a way to absorb thousands of unemployed contract laborers, who had been working in the United States during the twenty-two-year run of the bracero program. To avoid social unrest, the Mexican government needed to find jobs for those workers. To attract employers, it changed laws that had prohibited direct U.S. ownership of factories in Mexico, allowing investors to build plants taking advantage of lower Mexican wages, producing goods for the U.S. market. A new labor regime was put in place to attract foreign investment, including the brutal repression of independent unions or challenges to the low-wage model.

Measures to pull workers north to the border were just as necessary. Over the next four decades the maquiladora workforce was drawn from the south. Migrants were displaced by the same economic changes—privatization, rural poverty, job elimination—that permitted construction of the maquiladoras themselves. Cities like Tijuana, Mexicali, Juárez, and Matamoros, which were not much bigger than large towns in the 1950s, mushroomed into cities with millions of inhabitants.

Prior to the economic reforms, the U.S.-Mexico border was a remote area, with a very low population, far from Mexico's industrial base and workforce. Without the simultaneous dislocation of workers from privatized or bankrupt state-owned factories, or farmers from southern Mexico's impoverished countryside, there would have been no workers available to make maquiladora development possible.

This development model has since been reproduced in developing countries all over the world. In the early 1990s the U.S. Agency for International Development (USAID) financed the construction of industrial parks, or export processing zones, in rural Honduras. It then contracted with the accounting firm of Price Waterhouse to study ways of producing workers for their new factories. In 1993 the company prepared a report for USAID that concluded, "EPZ's labor demands could not be met by natural population growth." Satisfying labor needs, it said, required "an increase in the labor participation rates of young women." Many of those young women are at the point in their lives where they want to begin their own families. Price Waterhouse noted with disapproval that "the pregnancy rate among women of childbearing age was 4% in June 1992, up from 2.5% six months earlier. This is regarded as too high (3% would be the maximum acceptable)." It recommended mandatory distribution of contraceptives, and said a similar program in Mexican maquiladoras "claims spectacular results in higher productivity, lower staff turnover and training costs, reduced absenteeism and reduced costs for maternity leave . . . and medical care."

Its most startling recommendation noted that the percentage of women under twenty-one had risen from a third to half the workforce. One table showed the employment rates of workers age ten and over. Another showed that children between the ages of ten and fourteen made up 16 percent of the women either employed or seeking jobs. A footnote claimed "the legal minimum working age in Honduras is 15, but in the rural economy it is normal to work from ten onwards."

The poverty that drove these young women into the plants in Honduras and Mexico is the same poverty that drives them to cross borders. Poverty causes displacement and migration. Maquiladora workers often become migrants traveling far beyond the nearest EPZ. And when the maquiladoras are located a stone's throw from the border, crossing it is almost inevitable.

Migrant labor is even more important in developed countries. U.S. industrial agriculture has always depended on immigrants. The farm labor workforce in the U.S. Southwest was formed from waves of Chinese, Japanese, Filipinos, Mexicans, and, more recently, Central Americans. During the years before World War II it also included native-born workers from Texas and Oklahoma, economically displaced in the Great Depression. Today a growing percentage of farmworkers are indigenous people from Mexico and Central America, speaking languages other than Spanish, an indication that economic dislocation has reached far into the most remote parts of the countryside. On the U.S. East Coast, migrants come from the Caribbean, and join large numbers of African Americans displaced from rural, or even urban, communities.

In other industrial countries a rising percentage of the rural work-force is also made up of migrants. Industrial agriculture, based on migrant labor, has expanded to developing countries, where plantations owned or controlled by large corporations like Dole and Del Monte draw a workforce from displaced rural communities. In Colombia uprooted Afro-Colombians are drawn into nurseries growing flowers for U.S. supermarkets, or plantations growing palms for biodiesel fuel. In northern Mexico, vast industrial farms grow winter tomatoes and strawberries for U.S. consumers, drawing on families migrating north from Oaxaca.

Migrants are now a vital part of the service industry workforce in most developed countries. As the most recent job seekers, they begin in the most marginal and contingent jobs. Day laborers on Los Angeles or Long Island street corners arrive from Mexico and Central America. In Britain they come from Romania and Africa.

But migrant labor doesn't remain at the fringe of the economy. The world's oil industry is completely dependent on it. The oil kingdoms of the Gulf states—Kuwait, Qatar, Bahrain, Abu Dhabi—have many more immigrant workers than native-born ones. Migrant workers, in other words, make the world's vital oil industry function. It was no coincidence that Halliburton brought migrants from Bangladesh and the Philippines into Iraq in the wake of the advancing U.S. invading force in 2003, intending to use them to replace Iraqi workers on the oil rigs and pipelines. Only a strike by Iraqi oil workers forced Halliburton to retreat, and prevented the company from taking control of their industry.

Employers gain great advantages from this system, particularly lower labor costs and increased workforce flexibility. Large meatpacking companies in the U.S. Midwest, for instance, hire a workforce in which immigrants are a majority. Over the last twenty years, the industry's wages have steadily fallen behind the manufacturing average, a major accomplishment from the companies' point of view. According to the Bureau of Labor Statistics, 1980 slaughtering-plant wages were 1.16 times the manufacturing average. After twenty-five years, they are now .76 times that average. U.S. manufacturing wages certainly haven't soared—in fact, they've fallen behind inflation. But meat-packing wages, in relative terms, have fallen faster.

A steady stream of migrants crosses the border, finds its way to small meatpacking towns, and gets jobs. Companies depend on this river of labor—not just on the workers in the plants themselves, but on the communities from which they come. If those communities stop producing workers, their labor supply dries up.

But the cost of providing new generations of workers from tiny Mexican and Guatemalan towns is not borne by the employers who need and use the labor. At the same time, the government budget for healthcare or education in those home communities shrinks because of debt payments and economic reforms. In Guatemala's Santa Eulalia, which supplies workers for Nebraska slaughterhouses, the government does not provide any healthcare system for the town's residents. In its schools, parents and teachers must buy paper, pencils, books, and other materials—universally true throughout rural Gua-temala. When San Miguel Cuevas, a small Mixtec town in Oaxaca, needed a new road from the main highway, it couldn't expect a gov-ernment crew to build it. San Miguel residents, now mostly farm-workers in California, built the road themselves, contributing labor and money through the indigenous tradition of the *tequio,* or com-munal responsibility.

When the IRCA commission on migration said Mexico should take "the necessary steps toward structural adjustment," and that loans to its government "should be based on the implementation of satisfac-tory adjustment programs," it was proposing deep cuts in government spending. As a result of those recommendations, workers themselves now bear the cost of almost all basic social services in towns sending migrants to the United States. They pay for them through remittances sent back from jobs in Nebraska slaughterhouses, California fields, and New York hotels. As stated previously, in 2005 then Mexican president Vicente Fox boasted that his country's citizens working in the United States sent back $18 billion. Some estimate that in 2006 that figure reached $25 billion.

At the same time, the public funds that used to pay for schools and public works leave Mexico in debt payments to foreign banks. Remittances, as large as they are, cannot make up for this outflow. According to a report to the Mexican Chamber of Deputies, remittances accounted for an average of 1.19 percent of the gross domestic product between 1996 and 2000, and 2.14 percent between 2001 and 2006. Debt payments accounted for 3 percent annually. By partially meeting unmet, and unfunded, social needs, remittances are indirectly subsidizing banks.

Companies that employ migrant labor in the United States benefit from the huge flow of remittances as well. Meatpacking wages are low, in U.S. terms. When workers send money home to their families thousands of miles away, the cost to employers of sustaining them is much lower than it would be if they were living in Iowa or Nebraska. In the United States, employers don't have to pay as much in taxes to support local schools or services for workers whose families are elsewhere. In Mexico or Guatemala they don't have to pay taxes at all to provide those services for workers' families.

At the same time, companies dependent on this immigrant stream gain greater flexibility in adjusting for the highs and lows of market demand. U.S. employers historically have treated immigrant labor as a convenient faucet, easily turned on and off. In the depression of the 1930s, Mexican workers were rounded up and deported by the thousands when the unemployment rate went up. When World War II started, the U.S. government negotiated their return as braceros. Growers needed workers, but didn't want to raise wages to draw them from cities.

Today the global production system has grown even more flexible in accommodating economic booms and busts. Its employment system is based on the use of contractors, which is replacing the system in which workers were directly employed by the businesses using their labor. Today's pine tree planters don't work directly for Kimberly-Clark or the paper companies, for instance, but for labor recruiters. They appear when trees need to be planted, thinned, or harvested. When the work is over, they are sent away. The paper corporations control labor costs indirectly, through the price they pay for harvested trees or wood pulp, and through the contracts signed with labor contractors.

Displaced migrant workers are the backbone of this system. Its guiding principle is that immigration policy and enforcement should direct immigrants to industries when their labor is needed and remove them when it's not. As President George W. Bush put it, the government should "connect willing employers with willing employees."

Contract labor offers important advantages to employers. The businesses that use it determine how much it's paid through arrangements with contractors, and have less and less responsibility for the actual conditions of employment or for what happens to workers when work ends. When demand is high, contractors recruit people and they're put to work. When demand falls, those people have to find other jobs. In the case of migrants on temporary-employment visas, if they don't find new jobs, they have to leave the country. Workers injured at work can't stay in the community around the plant where they were hurt, making demands for treatment. They have to go back to hometowns where there is often no medical care at all. Employers don't usually have to provide compensation for those forced out of the country.

As global production lines are tuned more and more closely to changes in the market, employers use the flexibility of the contract-labor system to adjust quickly. Capital has to be flexible, able to move where it can earn the greatest return, and permanent employment only gets in the way. When a garment goes out of fashion, or a piece of medical or electronic equipment becomes obsolete, the workers who produce it become expendable. Production of new product lines requires new workers, often in completely different locations.

This flexibility exerts a downward pressure on workers' living standards. Garment manufacturers, for instance, travel the world comparing wage rates. Their contractors are forced to undercut each other from country to country, competing for orders by cutting labor costs. What garment production remains in the United States is done almost entirely by contractors employing migrant workers. The factories owned directly by companies like Levi Strauss were closed years ago.

This has been the employment model in the agricultural, garment, and janitorial industries for decades, and it is completely dependent on migrant labor. This system is expanding to other industries. In the 1970s, production workers in Silicon Valley electronic plants worked directly for big manufacturers. Today, women working on the line assembling printers for Hewlett-Packard mostly come from the Philippines, South and Southeast Asia, Mexico, and Latin America. But now they work for Manpower, a temporary-employment agency with an office in the plant. Sometimes they do the same job they did when they worked for HP directly, but now without healthcare or other benefits. They're paid a lower wage, and they can be terminated at any time.

The Profitability of Undocumented Labor

In May 1994, five months after NAFTA went into effect, the Urban Institute estimated, in its report *Immigration and Immigrants: Setting the Record Straight,* that the Immigration Reform and Control Act had already failed to reduce the undocumented population of the United States, one of the law's stated goals. Just before the act passed in 1986, it noted, the number of undocumented people living in the United States was between 3 million and 5 million. After IRCA's amnesty program, which allowed many individuals without papers to normalize their immigration status, the undocumented population fell to 1.8 million to 3 million. Since only those people who had been living in the country since 1982 could qualify, a considerable number of people remained undocumented. By 1992, that population had rebounded to 2.7 to 3.7 million, roughly the same level it had been twelve years earlier—2.5 to 3.5 million people.

IRCA's amnesty recognized the basic reality that millions of people without status were living in the United States. It took a humane approach by giving them a permanent-residence status that corresponded with that reality. People were working and productive, had become part of the communities around them, and had put down roots. Giving them permanent-residence visas recognized this. The effect of the amnesty on those who qualified was profound. People gained confidence in exercising their labor rights at work, and millions began the long process of becoming U.S. citizens in order to gain political rights as well.

IRCA's other major provision, however—employer sanctions—had a very different effect. They were touted as a means to force those who didn't qualify for amnesty to go home, and to discourage others from migrating across the border without documents. Sanctions did not produce the predicted results, and the number of undocumented immediately began to rise. Those economic forces uprooting people, particularly in Mexico, were just as strong after IRCA was passed as they had been before. IRCA's Commission for the Study of International Migration and Cooperative Economic Development recognized that reality. But its recommendation—the negotiation of NAFTA—provoked a huge increase in undocumented migration, not a decrease. By 2007, thirteen years later, there were as many as 12 million undocumented people living in the United States—more than ever.

Producing undocumented migration is not a politically acceptable goal in the United States or in any of the other industrial countries to which that migration flows. The U.S. immigration debate, and the legislation it has produced in Congress, places great emphasis on the distinction between "legal" and "illegal" immigration. While members of Congress disagree about the socially beneficial effects of legal immigration, they almost all claim that the entry of undocumented people into the country has a negative effect. Claiming that undocumented immigration is out of control, they argue over tactics for suppressing it (except, of course, reducing displacement, which is ruled out of the debate from the start): is it better, for instance, to halt undocumented migration by denying medical care and education to children, or by prohibiting undocumented immigrants from working, or by militarizing the border, or by increasing the number of immigration raids and deportations?

The terrain of debate between most Democrats and Republicans is over these measures for increasing enforcement. Republicans argue for the most extreme proposals. In California in 1994 they supported

Proposition 187, which would have denied medical care and education to people without papers. Similarly, the Sensenbrenner proposal, HR 4437, would have made being in the United States without a visa, currently a civil violation rather than a criminal one, a federal felony. Mainstream Democrats have countered with proposals to increase enforcement on the border, and to beef up employer sanctions.

In fact, however, undocumented immigration has become economically embedded in U.S. society, and it produces important benefits, especially for industries that have come to rely on it. In 1994, the year NAFTA went into effect, the National Immigration Forum's *Guide to Immigration Facts and Issues* estimated that undocumented immigrants paid about $7 billion annually in taxes. Those payments included $2.7 billion to Social Security, and $168 million to state unemployment-benefit funds. In California, which accounted at that time for 43 percent of the nation's undocumented population, undocumented immigrants paid an additional $732 million in state and local taxes, according to Michael Fix and Jeffrey Passel in a study for the Urban Institute. The state, in turn, spent $1.3 billion on education for undocumented children, and $166 million for emergency-room care for their families (the only kind of state-provided medical care for which they qualified.)

Undocumented children are as much a resource of U.S. society as any of its other children. They are part of its future workforce, and will take their place in all aspects of social, cultural, and political life. Inasmuch as society has an interest in investing in the future of any of its children (and there are certainly those who question this), it has an interest in all of its children. It has a similar public health interest in providing emergency medical care, preventing the spread of medical problems from immigrants to the rest of the population and vice versa.

But leaving this argument aside, expenditures on the education of undocumented children, or on emergency medical care for their families, is not a net economic drain. Undocumented immigrants pay income and sales taxes into the government's general funds. They pay property taxes either directly or through rent paid to landlords. They make payments for Social Security and similar state-mandated programs. Yet for the most part, they cannot by law receive the services and benefits this money pays for. The Social Security fund is, in effect, subsidized by payments made by people who will never collect retirement or disability benefits. Undocumented people paying taxes for services they can't use subsidize tax cuts promised by politicians to middle- and upper-income voters. Federal and state enforcement proposals that bar undocumented immigrants from even more services and benefits will shift the burden further.

A study by the North American Integration and Development Center at the University of California, Los Angeles, *Tracking the Economic Impacts of North American Integration: Trade, Capital, and Migration Flows,* estimated that undocumented workers annually contributed approximately 7 percent of the $900 billion gross economic product of the state of California, or $63 billion in the mid-1990s. That contribution undoubtedly increased greatly in the following years, as the undocumented population grew rapidly.

In 1994 the Urban Institute estimated that about 1.4 million undocumented people lived in California, 43 percent of the nation's total. The gross economic contribution by each undocumented immigrant to the state economy was therefore about $45,000, including children, the unemployed, and those too old or ill to work. Their precarious status kept their wages near the legal minimum, $4.25 per hour at that time, which produced an annual income of $8,840.

The labor of undocumented workers pumped tens of billions of dollars into the state's economy—$45,000 per person—but the workers themselves were paid only a small percentage of it—$8,840 each. They received a much smaller percentage of the value they produced than that received by workers who were either citizens or legal residents. This difference is a source of extra profit for industries employing a largely undocumented workforce—agriculture and food processing, land development (including the residential construction and building services industries), tourism (including the hotel and restaurant industries), garment production and light manufacturing, transportation, retail trade, healthcare, and domestic services.

Undocumented workers, considering whether to organize a union to win better wages, have to take into account the possibility of being fired. Other workers also risk being fired, an important obstacle to all union efforts. But undocumented workers must weigh employer sanctions in the balance, which make finding another job harder and riskier. Any period of unemployment is likely to last longer. Because sanctions also disqualify the undocumented from unemployment benefits, food stamps, or other public services, fired workers are under pressure to take any job available, at whatever wage. And under federal court rulings, an employer who shows that workers fired for union activity are undocumented is not obligated to rehire them or pay back wages. Undocumented workers who complain about unpaid wages and overtime, wages below the minimum, sexual harassment, or violations of health and safety laws run the same risk.

These draconian exclusions are intended to make life unpleasant for undocumented immigrants, who presumably are encouraged to leave the country. But by making them more vulnerable and socially isolated, the exclusions make their labor cheaper. Mexican academic Jorge Bustamante argues that U.S. immigration law has historically been used to drive down the price of Mexican labor in the United States. IRCA's employer sanctions, along with measures like Proposition 187 and HR 4437, ensured that undocumented workers, with fewer rights and less access to benefits, remained cheaper for employers, and more profitable.

Businesses often complain about the burden of complying with sanctions' paperwork requirements. But Jose Semperio, an organizer for San Francisco's Comité de Trabajadores Generales, a committee of day laborers, accused them of benefiting from the vulnerability of immigrant workers. "When we have accidents, the contractor just drops us off at the emergency room parking lot," he said bitterly as he campaigned against Proposition 187. "Now they even want to make it illegal for us to get medical care at all. San Francisco, Los Angeles, San Diego, and Orange County all eat because we work, but we have almost no chance to get out of the shadows."

Four

FAST TRACK TO THE PAST

Not Enough Workers!

In 1947, after reading a newspaper article about the crash of a plane carrying a group of Mexican migrant workers back to the border, Woody Guthrie wrote a poem, later set to music by Martin Hoffman. In haunting lyrics Guthrie describes how the plane caught fire as it flew low over Los Gatos Canyon, near the farming town of Coalinga, at the edge of California's San Joaquin Valley. Observers below saw people and belongings flung out of the aircraft before it hit the ground—falling, as Guthrie sang, like leaves.

While the *Coalinga Record* carried the names of the pilot and Border Patrol agent on the flight, no record was ever kept of the workers' identities. They were all listed on the death certificates as "deportee," and that became the name of the song. It was a protest against that imposed anonymity, the denial of the very identities of the people who were creating wealth for the growers. Guthrie takes the point of view of those who died. "Some of us are illegal, and some are not wanted," he sings. And he reveals the deportation as the expulsion of unwelcome intruders, once their labor was over: "They chase us like outlaws, like rustlers, like thieves."

Today, the word "illegal" is used to mean a person without immigration papers. But Guthrie uses it in the deeper sense of an earlier era—of being excluded. To him, it means someone who is not a real resident of the place where he or she works, not part of a community or accepted by the surrounding society.

For twenty-two years, an army of transient workers like these harvested U.S. crops, and for two years laid its railroad tracks as well. At the time, being illegal and being a bracero, or contract worker, was almost the same thing. People went back and forth between the two categories so often that the words were used interchangeably. The growers who sent these dozens to their death in a fireball were taking advantage of this fact. Workers caught without papers were often given the opportunity to be deported, and flown back to Mexicali, on the border. There they would be hired again and return, this time under contract. Some growers even dropped a dime on their own undocumented workers, a process they called "drying out wetbacks."

Today those who remember the bracero program are in their sixties and seventies. Rigoberto Garcia, whose memories of his bracero experience are still fresh, lives with his wife, Amelia, in a small trailer in the Palo Verde Valley, at the edge of the desert by the Colorado River. At sixty-eight years old he was still working in the fields, picking lemons and grapefruit. A few of the bracero camps he remembers remain standing on the outskirts of Blythe, California, not far from his trailer park. No one has lived in them for twenty years.

"I went as a bracero four times," Garcia recalls. "Each time we got on the train in Empalme, went all the way to Mexicali [both cities are in northern Mexico], and from there on buses to El Centro [in California's Imperial Valley]. Thousands of men came every day. Once we got there, they'd send us in groups of two hundred, as naked as we came into the world, into a big room about sixty feet square. Then men would come in masks, with tanks on their backs, and they'd fumigate us from top to bottom. Supposedly we were flea-bitten and germ-ridden.

"Then they'd send us into a huge bunkhouse, where the contractors would come from the growers' associations in counties like San Joaquin, Yolo, Sacramento, and Fresno. The heads of the associations would line us up. When they saw someone they didn't like, they'd say, 'You, no.' Others, they'd say, 'You, stay.' They didn't want old people— just young, strong ones. And I was young, so I never had problems getting chosen."

Memories of a vanished past? In 2004, when President George W. Bush finally introduced his administration's long-awaited plan for immigration reform, it sounded remarkably like the one Garcia recalled. Even the old practice of transforming deportees into braceros returned as a provision of the proposed reforms.

The United States still has a program for guest workers in agriculture, the H2-A program, much like the old bracero scheme. Every season, immigrant farmworkers in North and South Carolina, Georgia, and other East Coast and southern states pass through the kind of mass shapeup Garcia describes. While the delousing (probably with DDT, given the era), is no longer a feature, Bruce Goldstein, executive director of the Farmworker Justice Fund in Washington, D.C., says ten thousand workers are processed in North Carolina's centers every year—"parceled out among growers in a huge barn."

And while the H2-A program brought only about forty thousand people a year through 2006, out of an estimated 2.5 million workers in U.S. agriculture, it may become the centerpiece of vastly expanded schemes in other industries. Employers dependent on undocumented workers increasingly call for replacing them with a more predictable workforce of contract laborers. Garcia's memories could describe not just a distant past but a rapidly approaching future.

"We slept in big bunkhouses," he remembers. "It was like being in the army. We woke up when they sounded a horn or turned on the lights. We'd make our beds and go to the bathroom, eat breakfast, and they'd give us our lunch—some tacos or a couple of sandwiches, an apple, and a soda. When we got back to camp, we'd wash up and eat. Picking tomatoes, you really get dirty, like a dog. If we wanted to go into town, in Stockton there was a Spaniard who would send buses out to the camps to give people a ride. He was making a business out of selling us shirts, clothes, and medicine."

Since Garcia's bracero days, the housing situation for farmworkers has actually deteriorated. In most parts of California and many other states, growers no longer want to house workers who harvest their crops. At harvest time it's common to see cars parked on the outskirts of farmworker towns, families sleeping beside them.

The current H2-A program requires growers to provide housing to the contract laborers they bring into the country, and their barracks or trailers are inspected—in theory. But in the fall of 2000, in negotiations over expanding the program, agribusiness associations proposed scrapping this requirement. "With a big expansion it's unlikely there would be the resources for inspections," Goldstein predicted at the time. "Instead, they could give workers a housing allowance, if the government certified that there was no housing shortage." The barracks of Garcia's memory might be preferable to what such an allowance could buy. The housing supply is very limited in farmworker communities, especially during harvest, and its condition ranks at the bottom. In fact, grower insistence on eliminating the requirement might even backfire, according to Goldstein. "You can imagine that a lot of people in rural communities would freak out if growers simply dumped a contract workforce on the local housing market," he speculated.

Housing is one element of living conditions. Another is food. Garcia remembers that food in the camps was often bad. One year one of the workers in his crew died of food poisoning. "Something he ate wasn't good," he recalls, "but what could we do? We were all worried that what happened to him could happen to any of us. They said they'd left soap on the plates, because lots of us got diarrhea, but this boy died." According to Goldstein, "Things have improved a little. Today [H2-A] workers complain that the food often isn't culturally appropriate, but no one's dying of food poisoning. But if a much larger guest-worker system is reestablished, it really would look like what we had during the bracero program. How else could they manage such a workforce?"

Braceros did not always willingly acquiesce in their exploitation. California's legendary immigrant-rights campaigner, Bert Corona, recalls in his autobiography not only that braceros sometimes went on strike, but that local Latino communities would bring them food and try to prevent their deportation. Garcia also remembers strikes. "One of my brothers went on strike in Phoenix because they were picking cotton and the crop was bad," he says. "They threatened to send them back to Mexico, and put them on a bus to El Centro. He got strikes into his blood, and later worked with César Chávez [cofounder of the United Farm Workers] for many years. Me too. When the farmworkers' movement came along, we already knew how to organize from people who'd participated in those conflicts." But while some braceros fought to change conditions, and small rebellions raised wages temporarily, the threat of deportation was enough to stop any larger strike and union effort until 1965, the year after the program was abolished.

The H2-A program establishes a minimum wage rate, a little over seven dollars an hour in most areas in 2000, and about eight dollars by 2006. "If workers demand more," Goldstein said, "the employer can say, 'I'm offering all the Department of Labor requires. If you don't like it, I can get more workers.' In effect, the minimum standard becomes the maximum standard. The department says you can't fill a vacancy created by a strike with a guest worker, but they define this so narrowly that it's virtually impossible to enforce." Furthermore, H2-A workers cannot lawfully choose to leave their jobs and work elsewhere, giving employers even more leverage.

Despite low wages and bad conditions, however, Garcia did eventually find an employer who felt compassion for braceros. "In San Diego I worked for a Japanese grower named Suzuki, a good man," he remembers. "During the war they had put him into one of the camps. He told us, 'I know what your life is like, because we lived that way too, in concentration camps watched over with rifles.' So he got [permanent-residence] papers for all of us. That was the last contract I worked." According to Goldstein, some growers in Canada even go to the Mexican hometowns of their workers, to attend the local fiesta. One New Hampshire apple grower attempted to take over the local growers' association to raise the wages for H2-A workers, only to wind up losing his own seat on the group's board. "Occasionally there is a person who wants to be fair," he said, "but the economic forces at work are too powerful. You can't really go against them."

For Garcia, the bracero program was the route to establishing a life in the United States, but it was a hard one. He's glad his children won't face it. "When I fixed my immigration status, I decided I wouldn't go back, and would bring my wife here instead. I was tired of being alone. That was the hardest thing—the loneliness, even though you have the security of three meals, a place to stay, your job. I missed my land and my wife, but it was important to send my kids to school. That's what I was trying to do as a bracero. I wanted a real future, and we knew that we were just casual workers—we would never be able to stay. So I had to look for another way. Eventually I got my papers and now I live like anyone else. Those experiences were the beginning of the life I'm leading now. We survived, and here I am. But I always remember how I got here. Illegal, a bracero."

During the 1950s, growers' use of braceros as strikebreakers allowed them to undermine the ability of the farmworkers to demand higher wages. César Chávez, then an organizer for the Community Service Organization in Oxnard, California, organized protests over this practice. Ernesto Galarza, a labor organizer and former diplomat, lobbied against the program in Washington. Chávez later said that it was impossible to organize the United Farm Workers until Congress terminated the bracero law, Public Law 78, in 1964. The grape strike in which the union was born began the following year. According to the UFW's Marc Grossman, "Chávez believed agribusiness's chief farm-labor strategy for decades was maintaining a surplus labor supply to keep wages and benefits depressed, and fight unionization."

With this goal in mind, starting in the late 1990s growers began a concerted effort to expand the H2-A program. To justify their proposal they claim they face a dire labor shortage. According to Lucas Benitez of the Coalition of Immokalee Workers, a community-based project organizing farmworkers in South Florida, "It's a lie. Every day in the papers you read about the high numbers of unemployed workers. The problem is that most workers in this country do not want to do the work we do for the wages we're paid. We average seven thousand five hundred dollars a year and the conditions are so exploitative that any reasonable person would prefer receiving unemployment benefits. The answer is to raise wages and improve working conditions."

In a series of articles in the *New York Times,* however, reporter Julia Preston interviewed growers, agribusiness spokespeople, and agricultural economists who said that crops were rotting in the fields for lack of workers to pick them. U.S. agriculture would go to Mexico, they warned, if Congress didn't expand the guest-worker program. California grower Steve Scaroni told Preston that without guest workers, "I have no choice but to offshore my operation." Craig Regelbrugge, cochair of the Agriculture Coalition for Immigration Reform, claimed that "the choice is simple: Do we want to import workers or import food?" And agricultural economist James Holt told Congress that "the U.S. agricultural industry is in the midst of a labor crisis, the resolution of which will determine whether U.S. producers... are more than marginal participants in U.S. and global markets." None felt that raising wages would encourage more people to take farm labor jobs. "I would have raised my wages," Steve Winant, a pear grower, told Preston. "But there weren't any people to pay." Scaroni, moving his harvest to Mexico's Celaya Valley, explained, "I know beyond a shadow of a doubt that if I did that [raised wages] I would raise my costs and I would not have a legal work force."

The cry was taken up by the *Wall Street Journal,* which made incredible claims of farm losses: "The problem was bad enough last year that some 20% of American agricultural products were stranded at the farm gate," it asserted in a July 2007 editorial, which claimed California would lose 30 percent of its crops, and that "farmers in North Carolina lost nearly a third of their cucumber crop last year." North Carolina growers are probably the most active users of the H2-A program, but apparently the workers they brought in weren't enough.

Growers charge that the H2-A housing requirement is helping to cause the terrible shortage. "When you're having to pay housing costs, it's very difficult to survive and wait for the next agricultural season to come around," Jack King, head of national affairs for the California Farm Bureau Federation, told the *Times.* After the Bush administration's immigration-reform bill failed to pass Congress in 2007, Commerce Secretary Carlos Gutierrez promised to make guest-worker programs more attractive to employers. He proposed to eliminate the current H2-A requirement that growers offer jobs first to U.S. residents before bringing in contract labor from outside the country.

The same month that growers told Preston their pears were rotting on the ground in California's Lake County, farm laborers in next-door Tehama County were leaving in large numbers for the grape harvest to the south, because there was so little work picking olives. If growers' claims of a labor shortage were true, workers would have gone to nearby Lake County instead. Growers told Preston that 70,000 of the state's 450,000 farmworkers were missing. But Lake County's unemployment rate at the time of the articles, according to the state's Employment Development Department, was 7.2 percent.

Unemployment in rural California counties generally averages twice that of urban counties. San Francisco's unemployment, for instance, was 4.4 percent, and Los Angeles's 4.9 percent in the same period. In the Imperial Valley, next to the Mexican border, unemployment was 16.6 percent, and in the San Joaquin and Sacramento valleys, it ranged from 7.7 to 10.5 percent. Delano, birthplace of the United Farm Workers, had a rate of 23.2 percent, despite construction of two new prisons on the town's outskirts. Unemployment in Salinas, the state's vegetable capital, was 15.2 percent. In the careful gray language of the Congressional Research Service, "Trends in the agricultural labor market generally do not suggest the existence of a nationwide shortage of domestically available farm workers." The CRS report said rural unemployment "remains well above the U.S. average, and underemployment among farm workers remains substantial." As a result, it notes that agricultural labor earns "about 50¢ for every dollar paid to other employees in the private sector."

Abe Lincoln said that "labor creates all wealth," but farmworkers get precious little of it. Twenty-five years ago, at the height of the influence of the United Farm Workers, union contracts guaranteed almost twice the minimum wage of the time. Today, the hourly wage in almost every farm job is the minimum wage—$6.75 an hour in 2007 in California. And taking inflation into account, the minimum is lower today than it was then. Farmworkers are worse off than they've been for over two decades, while the supermarket price of fruit has more than doubled.

U.S. agriculture is addicted to a vast reservoir of cheap labor. Outside of the brief years of the Dust Bowl in the mid-1930s, farm work has been the labor of people of color. African Americans made up the rural labor force of the South for centuries, first as slaves, then as sharecroppers and tenant farmers, and finally as wage laborers at the bottom of the scale. In the highly developed, corporate agriculture of the West and Southwest, immigrant workers from Mexico, Latin America, and Asia constitute the rural labor force. Their wages are also at the bottom. In fact, everywhere in the world, rural standards of living are far below those in cities.

Contrary to predictions of huge crop losses caused by labor shortages, nationwide, planting of labor-intensive crops like cherries and strawberries has grown by 20 percent over five years, according to Philip Martin, an agricultural economist at the University of California's main agricultural campus in Davis. Income hasn't gone up nearly as quickly. Martin says farm wages average $9.06 per hour. This average is just ahead of the minimum wage, but it includes skilled, better-paying jobs like equipment operators and supervisors. By comparison, the average nonfarm wage is $16.75.

Wages make up only six cents out of every dollar charged for produce in the supermarket. Wages could double and consumers would hardly know the difference. This, in fact, was the point made by Florida's Coalition of Immokalee Workers, when it successfully convinced McDonald's and other fast-food chains to increase the price they were paying for tomatoes, and ensure that the raise was passed along to the pickers. The United Farm Workers made a similar proposal during their organizing drive in Watsonville, California, in 2000—"5¢ for Fairness." Here again wages could increase significantly if consumers paid a nickel more per box of strawberries.

Farm wages, however, rose only a tiny half-percent a year from 2000 to 2006. In California and Florida, which employ more farmworkers than other states, they went up even more slowly. If there was a huge labor shortage, it didn't inspire growers to pay better in order to attract more workers, despite what they told Preston. They wanted a larger labor supply, but at a price they were willing to pay.

In housing, low wages mean that families live in cramped trailers, or packed like sardines into apartments and garages, many people sleeping in a single room. Indigenous workers from Mexico and Central America have worse conditions than most, along with workers who travel with the crops. Migrants often live in cars, sleeping in the fields or under trees because their income is too low to rent anything better. It's not uncommon to see children working in fields in northern Mexico, but they work in U.S. fields too. Families bring their kids to work, not because they don't value their education or future, but because they can't make ends meet with the labor of adults alone. Teachers and their supporters fled from Oaxaca's violence in 2006 only to find conditions that were, in many cases, not so different from those they'd left behind.

The UFW pushed wages up decades ago, getting the best standard of living California farmworkers ever received. But growers have been implacably hostile to union organizing, and for undocumented workers, joining a union or demanding rights can mean not just termination but deportation. Tight labor markets usually encourage unions and workers to strike, since it is more difficult for employers to recruit strikebreakers. But the last big strike among California farmworkers took place more than twenty years ago. If growers gain much wider use of the H2-A program, strikes and union-organizing drives will become even more difficult. According to a report by the Southern Poverty Law Center, *Close to Slavery,* "In practice, there is little difference between the bracero program and the current H-2 guest worker program."

Modern-day Braceros
Julio Cesar Guerrero came north from Mexico in the spring of 2001 on an H2-A visa. Recruited by Manpower of the Americas, he was sent to North Carolina, where he began working on the tobacco farm of An-

thony Smith. After a few weeks, his fingers started to hurt, and then one by one his fingernails began falling off. Although Smith told him not to see a doctor, he went anyway. The doctor said his problem was possibly caused by working without gloves in fields sprayed with pesticides. So Guerrero called North Carolina Legal Aid, even though Smith had warned him not to.

Guerrero returned to Mexico at the end of the season. The next year, when he tried to get another job, he found his name on a blacklist maintained by Manpower and the North Carolina Growers Association (NCGA). Legal Aid protested, and Guerrero was sent to the United States again. That year he worked for a grower named Rodney Jackson, who kept workers' drinking water on a moving truck in the fields, forcing them to run after it with their mouths under the spigot. When Guerrero filed a complaint with the Occupational Safety and Health Administration (OSHA), Jackson gave him a warning notice and asked him to sign it. Guerrero refused, Jackson fired him, and a foreman took him to the bus station, telling him to go back to Mexico. Again Legal Aid intervened and got him assigned to another grower. Soon a growers' association representative gave Guerrero another warning notice, which he again refused to sign.

When the 2003 season began, Guerrero tried once more to sign up with Manpower, but the recruiter told him that he'd already been given a second chance. Guerrero had had enough. In 2004 he became a plaintiff in a racketeering suit filed in Wake County Superior Court by Legal Aid of North Carolina, charging the NCGA with maintaining an illegal blacklist.

Defenders of guest-worker programs argue that increasing labor protections can put a stop to abuses while ensuring that employers get the labor they want. Guerrero's experience, like that of thousands of others, raises serious doubts that these programs can effectively safeguard workers' rights. The NCGA handbook warned workers that any effort to "deliberately restrict production" or to "work slowly" would result in discipline or termination. Strikes or slowdowns are prohibited. For Andrew McGuffin, staff attorney for North Carolina Legal

Aid, "The problem isn't that we don't have worker protection laws. It's that with guest workers they're not enforced, and when workers try to use these laws, they're blacklisted."

The blacklist is not secret. The handbook calls it a "record of eligibility [that] contains a list of workers, who because of violations of their contract, have been suspended from the program." It says no one will be disciplined for reporting violations of their rights, but that happens all the time. The "1997 NCGA Ineligible for Rehire Report" lists 1,709 names. The reason for ineligibility is most often listed as abandoning a job or voluntary resignation. Legal Aid charges that when workers are fired for complaining, they're given a paper to sign saying they quit voluntarily. Other reasons for ineligibility include "mother sick," "death in the family," "lazy," "slow," "work hours too long," "work too hot and hard," or "slowing up other workers." In 2003 the list for just one Mexican state, Durango, had 517 names.

The U.S. Department of Labor, which certifies employers for the H2-A program, has never taken action to end the practice. Bush's first DOL solicitor general, who would have had to support such action, was former union-busting lawyer Eugene Scalia (son of Supreme Court justice Antonin Scalia). He was replaced by Howard Radzely, another management-side lawyer and former Scalia clerk.

Growers and Legal Aid have been squaring off for years. NCGA's booklet told workers not to talk to Legal Aid staff, calling them "enemies of the H2-A program" who are "trying to eliminate your job." In September 2004, a foreman for grower Chester Pilson informed guest worker Juan Villareal Abundiz that there was no more work for him because he'd visited Legal Aid. An NCGA rep told him he'd probably be denied a job the following season. Villareal was brought to the association office in Vass, North Carolina, a huge barn with a balcony along one side. As two hundred workers gathered below, a foreman named Santos and an NCGA employee instructed them to take Legal Aid's pink "know your rights" booklets out of their pockets and throw them in a trashcan in the middle of the floor.

According to Villareal, NCGA head Craig Eury and his assistants gave him a paper he couldn't read, and told him if he didn't sign it, he'd have to pay his own bus fare back to Mexico. Villareal signed.

In 2005 the Farm Labor Organizing Committee (FLOC) forced the NCGA to sign a union contract, largely through a boycott of Mt. Olive Pickles, made from cucumbers grown by NCGA members. FLOC president Baldemar Velásquez said that with the contract, workers gained a grievance procedure that put an end to the worst abuses in North Carolina fields. But when the union set up an office in Monterrey, Mexico, to begin monitoring hiring and eliminate the blacklist, the office was attacked. Then, on April 9, 2007, FLOC organizer Santiago Rafael Cruz was found tied up and beaten to death in the office. According to Velásquez, the killing was a reprisal for FLOC's ongoing struggle against corrupt labor contractors. "We have put up with constant attacks in both the U.S. and Mexico—including having our office broken into several times. Now the attacks have come to this." Although the union contract can eliminate much of the corruption, he said, the H2-A system should be scrapped in favor of one that guarantees workers more freedom and rights.

Abuse of the H2-A program isn't limited to North Carolina. The most spectacular suppression of guest workers' rights came on November 21, 1986, when Caribbean cane cutters stopped work on the Fanjul family sugar plantation in South Florida. The Fanjuls tried to pay a rate lower than that specified in the work contract, and 384 cutters refused to leave their labor camp. The family called in the cops, who used guns, batons, and dogs to force workers onto buses, some in their underwear. They were taken to Miami and deported. Workers called it the "dog war."

Nine years later, Okeelanta Corp., owned by the Fanjuls, agreed to pay 355 people $1,000 each for lost belongings, and $20,000 to Florida Legal Aid. The Palm Beach Circuit Court dismissed the claim for lost wages, although the Department of Labor eventually fined the Fanjuls for shorting workers' hours and underpaying wages. Okeelanta was also charged with cheating guest workers of $14 million because it paid $3.70 a ton instead of $5.30 from 1987 to 1991. The jury was never told the company had agreed, and found for the Fanjuls instead of the workers. Rob Williams, director of the Tallahassee-based Migrant Farm Worker Justice Project, told the *Palm Beach Post* that "the lasting lesson of all this is that our government will not voluntarily protect the rights of guest workers."

In Canada, guest workers had similar experiences. On April 29, 2001, Mexicans laboring in Mastron Enterprises' tomato greenhouses in Leamington, Ontario, stopped work over complaints of abuse by a foreman. The day following the protest, twenty-four were deported. Other workers told representatives of the United Farm Workers that they had been working twelve-hour days, six and a half days a week, without overtime pay, for seven dollars an hour. "What I've realized here in Canada is that employers don't hire us as human beings," one worker told the UFW. "They think we're animals. The first threat they make is that if you don't like it, you can go back to Mexico." Chris Ramsaroop of Justicia for Migrant Workers observed, "To change their situation, migrants must be guaranteed the right to form unions, the right to social and economic mobility, and, most important, the right to apply for citizenship in Canada."

If Canadian guest workers can't win these demands in a country where labor rights are more vigilantly enforced, how likely is it that U.S. guest workers will fare better? According to the American Federation of Labor and Congress of Industrial Organizations (AFL-CIO), workers are routinely fired in 31 percent of all U.S. union-organizing drives. Most then face disqualification from unemployment benefits because of the pretexts justifying termination.

For guest workers, simply being without a job violates the conditions of their visas and makes them subject to immediate deportation. In addition, they're strangers. It's more difficult for them to find support from unions, legal aid workers, or other community institutions. When Fernando Rodriguez Aguilar was brought to North Carolina in 2002 to work for tobacco grower Jeffrey Lee, he complained to a priest, Father Tony Rojas, that the crew leader was selling alcoholic beverages in the fields and cutting the hours of workers who wouldn't buy them. An NCGA representative told him, "If you keep going [to his church], you'll have problems." Sure enough, the following season Manpower put Rodriguez on the blacklist.

Often the most important factor for guest workers is debt. "More than the law, it's the dynamics of the [guest-worker] program in developing countries that's the problem," said Mary Lee Hall, from North Carolina Legal Aid. Debt, in fact, led to one of the worst accidents in the history of U.S. guest-worker programs, in which fourteen workers died.

At three o'clock in the morning at the end of the summer of 2002, Edilberto Morales's supervisor gave his crew a wake-up call. The phone rang in an apartment above a gun store in the tiny town of Caribou, Maine, where Morales and five friends shared three rooms. In the cold darkness they put on their work clothes and made their lunch, their breath puffing like smoke in the September air. Outside, the van picked them up a little before six. Nine people were already inside—they lived in the apartment of the driver, just a few minutes away. They stopped at the gas station to buy snacks, and the van pulled out onto the road. Its destination was a field of trees more than two hours away, at the end of a network of dirt roads in the North Maine woods.

At 8:00 a.m. the jolting of the van jarred Morales awake, and he saw they were barreling fast through the trees. They'd left early because rain had kept them from working the day before. Juan, the driver, was trying to squeeze a few more minutes into the workday, and in addition, workers don't get paid for time spent traveling to and from work. "I told him to slow down, but the others woke up and began teasing me, asking if I was scared," Morales recounted. "They all wanted as much time to work as they could get." Bumping and swaying against the men crowded around him, he fell back to sleep.

The next time Morales awoke, the van was speeding across a low wooden bridge. They were almost at the other side when he felt the back tire pop. With no side railing on the bridge, the van shot off the road and hurtled into the Allagash River below. "When I came to," he recalled, "we were at the bottom of the river, with the tires upward. The front windshield was shattered and water was rushing in. I took a deep breath, and I remember some of the other men crying out. I started pounding on a side window and I broke it—I don't remember if it was with my hand or something else. Then I felt someone tugging at my pants but I couldn't do anything for them because I couldn't breathe. I finally came up to the surface and took a breath."

In the freezing water, with no pants or shoes, Morales went under again to find his friends. He says he remembers touching someone's hand, "but they were dead." Somehow he swam to shore. "I looked toward the river," he said, "and saw the blood and gas come up to the top. I began to scream. The water was so cold and I was so scared I didn't know what to do." He stood there crying by the river in the middle of the frozen woods until a truck came by. Two forest rangers put him in the cab and turned on the heat full blast.

Morales was alive, but fourteen friends were not. He saw the van pulled from the water with their bodies still inside. The next day he identified them for authorities. Then he went back to the apartment and packed their belongings for the long trip back to Guatemala and Honduras.

"I still think about them when I go to sleep," he said in an interview months later, his voice shaky and uncertain. "I remember back to what happened and how I had to recognize all of the bodies. I think about why I was the only one who survived. Maybe we all should have died." Four were his neighbors in the tiny mountain town of La Democracia, Guatemala. One was Juan Selles, his nephew.

Edilberto Morales will probably never stop pondering the question of guilt and innocence, including his own. On the last day of December 2002, the U.S. Department of Labor gave him one answer. It fined Evergreen Forestry Services, his employer at the time, seventeen thousand dollars. While "in no way meant to place a value on the tragic loss of life," wrote Labor Department official Corlis Sellers, the department concluded that the company had failed to ensure the safety of the fifteen men. Then it moved to revoke Evergreen's license to operate. The problem of responsibility was not so easily resolved. Why was the van traveling so fast? The answer to this simple question reveals a system of contract labor in which those fifteen men and thousands like them come to the United States every year.

For the four drowned Guatemalans, the road to Caribou began in La Democracia, a small town on the Selegua River, which flows north into Chiapas, Mexico, a dozen miles away. Its steep hillsides are covered with coffee plantations where the men worked most of their lives. The streets into their neighborhoods are unpaved, and so steep that only a four-wheel-drive vehicle can make it up to their homes, and then only in dry weather.

There, twenty-seven years ago, Juan Mendez married Florinda Sanchez, who lovingly remembers him as "a playful man." In the late 1990s, after the price of coffee fell from 1,000 quetzals ($125) per hundred kilos to 350, Mendez could no longer find enough work to support Florinda and his children. He took out a 20,000-quetzal loan ($2,500) at 15 percent interest, and paid Silvano Villatoro, a local recruiter, to take him to the United States. "When he left," his wife recalls, "he said that if it was God's will, he would return. If not, everyone had to die sometime, and if he died working he would be happy. And that is how it happened."

Cecilio Morales borrowed 10,000 quetzals ($1,250) for the same purpose. When he left with Villatoro, his wife, Natividad Maldonado, had no money and no food in the house. Taking her twelve-year-old son to work with her, she began harvesting coffee beans until the first money orders arrived from the United States.

Edilberto Morales had the same dream of going north, but at first he tried to go on his own as an undocumented worker. He borrowed 10,000 quetzals and made two attempts. Each time the Mexican police picked him up before he'd even made it through Chiapas. Then he borrowed another 10,000 quetzals and asked Villatoro to take him. By the time the airplane took off from Guatemala City airport, he owed almost 30,000 quetzals ($3,750), counting interest.

When the men approached Villatoro, they were at one end of a complex labor-recruitment system. Villatoro himself had been coming and going between Guatemala and the United States for almost twenty years. In 1985 he left La Democracia, partly for economic reasons and partly because of Guatemala's civil war. For a decade he'd belonged to the civil defense corps, a right-wing paramilitary organization set up by the Guatemalan army to fight the guerrillas of the Guatemalan National Revolutionary Unity (URNG). He got to the United States in 1989 and began working without papers. Then he received political asylum in 1992. Two years later he began working for Evergreen Forestry Services, a large labor contractor that moved him from forest to forest throughout the Southeast, planting trees that would eventually be harvested to make paper.

In 1986 the Immigration Reform and Control Act created a new visa category—H2-B—that companies could use to bring seasonal workers to the United States for jobs outside of agriculture. Evergreen and Villatoro made a deal. He went back to Guatemala and brought his son and brother under the program. "When the company saw that Guatemalans work hard, they gave us an increase in the number of visas," he explains. "The next year we took ten people, and fifteen the next. Forty-five traveled in the group last year. This year [2003] we are up to seventy."

Traveling with Villatoro gave two big advantages to those he accepted. The price charged by a coyote, or smuggler, to take someone from Guatemala to the United States illegally was about 35,000 to 40,000 quetzals ($4,375–$5,000) in 2003. Villatoro said he only charged the expense of airfare and visa processing—about 8,000. For that sum, people gained temporary legal status and didn't have to hide in the U.S. immigrant underground. But the visa lasts less than a year, and they had to pay Villatoro every year they went with him.

Villatoro inspired both admiration and fear in La Democracia. He still had his old association with the paramilitaries, plus the added power to decide who could go to the United States to work. "First I got family and friends," he said. "I interview each person individually. If they are teachers or students, you know they haven't done hard labor. I tell them to stay here. I only sign up people who are willing to work." An indication of Villatoro's reputation can be seen in the reaction of one local who pointed out his house to this author while hiding under blankets in the backseat of a car, hoping to avoid being seen and possibly offending the Villatoros.

Villatoro said he didn't receive a bounty for recruiting workers, just his wages as a worker. But his whole family was working in the United States, and he spent most of his time transporting and moving his crew. Contracting made him enough money to buy his own coffee plantation. "I grew up working in the coffee fields, but I did not own any until I made those trips," he said. "I was able to buy land that way." Villatoro may not have charged workers for visas themselves, but other contractors do. The Southern Poverty Law Center's suit against Decatur Hotels revealed that its contractor, Accent Personnel Services, used recruiters in Peru, Bolivia, and the Dominican Republic. Workers brought to work in the hotels after Hurricane Katrina paid $3,500 to $5,000 for recruiting fees, visas, and travel costs, and couldn't make enough in wages to pay their living expenses, much less pay off the debt.

Villatoro's crew worked on the pine plantations, like most Guatemalans. One worker from Huehuetenango, a city two hours away from La Democracia, described this work: "Our job was to plant little trees. They gave us a tool, called a talache, and a bag made of sailcloth to carry the seedlings. You can fit six hundred pines in the bag—about sixty or seventy pounds. With one hand you open a hole in the soil with the tool. With the other you take out the tree and put it in. Then you cover the hole with soil and press it down with a kick of the heel. You plant a tree and take two steps forward to plant the next. It has to be fast. Otherwise you don't plant enough trees."

The work is paid by piece rate, and accusations of cheating by labor contractors are common. The worker from Huehuetenango, afraid he wouldn't be rehired if he revealed his name, was employed by Eller & Sons Trees Inc. of North Carolina. "They told us they'd pay twenty-seven dollars and fifty cents per thousand trees," he explained. "Sometimes we'd plant two thousand or twenty-five hundred trees, but to our surprise the [weekly] checks would only amount to one hundred dollars, because they deducted money they said we owed for the equipment we were using. Only a hundred! There was not one week that we received more. I was planting for two months . . . and they still told me I owed them."

Before sending anything home they had to pay for food and board. "They were charging forty dollars per week per person for the hotel where we were staying," he recalled, "and we had to share the room among five people. We were eating, but we couldn't send any money to the family here in Guatemala. We didn't have enough." The day the occupants of the van drowned, they were on their way to thin trees with power saws at the end of the work season, on piece rate. For most of their time in the United States they'd been planting trees, too. Morales remembered, "We were paid twenty-five dollars [per one thousand trees]. With all of the deductions, for the most part our checks would come to three to four hundred dollars every two weeks." Morales's apartment in Caribou above the gun store cost each worker one hundred dollars a month.

Workers described a ten- or eleven-hour day with no lunch break. Under the law, companies must pay overtime after eight hours, even on piece rate, but almost none do. Evergreen was investigated and cited many times by the Labor Department's Wage and Hour Division for unpaid overtime. One investigator, bemoaning "a lengthy and woeful history of noncompliance," noted that "regardless of the hours worked, the payroll indicated consistently forty hours." Other citations included using unlicensed vehicles for transporting workers, although in the case of the drownings no such accusation was made. Carol Brooke, staff attorney with the North Carolina Justice and Community Development Center, said Evergreen "was fined over and over for violations in the way they paid, not counting hours, unpaid overtime, housing violations, and using unlicensed farm-labor transportation."

While some inspectors at the Labor Department tried to enforce compliance with the Fair Labor Standards Act, other parts of the government were working against them. Despite the fines, Evergreen received the certification required for employing H2-B workers every year from the Employment and Training Administration (ETA), another part of the Labor Department. Brooke wrote to the Atlanta ETA office and the Immigration and Naturalization Service (INS) five times, objecting to the certification. Regina Luginbuhl, bureau chief of the Agricultural Safety and Health Bureau, wrote, too, and William Green, the state's monitor advocate, filed a complaint with the office of the inspector general.

Floyd Goodman, who was responsible for H2-B certification in the Atlanta office, wouldn't comment directly on Evergreen. But, he said, unless the Wage and Hour Division revokes an employer's license, he assumes any applicant is abiding by state and federal law, a requirement for H2-B certification. His office had never rejected an H2-B application for violations of the Fair Labor Standards Act, or state wage and hour laws. "We have no information that they're doing that," he said. When asked about the letters from North Carolina, he responded, "I have no way of knowing if the accusations are true or not." He sent a copy of every certification application to the Department of Labor's Wage and Hour Division. "If there are outstanding violations, they wouldn't get their contractor's license. If they've been fined, and paid their fines, that satisfies their legal obligation."

Lack of enforcement doesn't just protect labor contractors. Further up the food chain are much larger economic interests. Tree planters are workers in the paper industry, planting and cultivating trees that will eventually be harvested and taken to paper mills. And paper is one of the most monopolized industries in North America. International Paper alone is the largest private landowner in the United States, with more than 12 million acres of forest. Another big consumer of wood pulp is Kimberly-Clark.

Paper companies don't employ tree planters directly, however. They hire labor contractors such as Evergreen and Eller and Sons. The workers who died in Maine were even more insulated from the big companies. Evergreen had been hired by a land-management company, Seven Islands Land Co. Seven Islands was working for a private landowner, Pingree Associates. But in the end, the trees the men were going to thin that fateful day would have eventually wound up in a big paper mill, producing rolls of toilet paper sold in Safeway.

Paper companies have kept the price of labor low for twenty years through a system in which contractors like Evergreen bid against one another for contracts to plant or thin a given tract of land. In January 2001, the Florida-based Migrant Farmworker Justice Project and the Virginia Justice Center sued three of the largest paper conglomerates, Champion, International Paper, and Georgia-Pacific. They accused the companies of responsibility for their contractors' unpaid labor and overtime violations. In depositions paper company officials admitted that the price they were paying contractors for labor hadn't gone up in twenty years. To win those contracts, contractors who formerly hired people living in the United States began bringing in H2-B workers to cut wage costs.

The paper companies say they're not responsible, because they don't directly employ the workers who plant the trees. But the Migrant and Seasonal Agricultural Worker Protection Act specifically says that if a company has the power to control the work and employment conditions, it is responsible. Morales remembered that "a lot of [white] inspectors, who came in a company truck, would inspect our work. If they didn't like it they would send us back and have us do it again."

In 2003, however, a U.S. District Court judge decided that the companies were not responsible for employment conditions for guest workers. Farmworker advocates were very disturbed. "The [Migrant and Seasonal Agricultural Worker Protection] act was passed in 1983 specifically to establish grower liability, because they were untouchable before," said Cathleen Caron, former staff attorney at Florida's Migrant Farmworker Justice Project. And in the wake of the Maine accident, another form of damage control became evident. As Florida attorneys prepared lawsuits over the drownings, Evergreen stopped answering the phone at its office in Sandpoint, Idaho. Villatoro said he was cut loose. "The company I represented for six years no longer exists," he lamented. "It combined with Progressive [Forestry Services Inc], with another representative here in Guatemala, Karla Ponce."

How Corporations Won the Debate
on Immigration Reform

According to a 2002 study by the Pew Hispanic Center, 47 percent of all farmworkers lack papers—about 1.25 million people. Farmworker unions would like to get them amnesty, like the one in 1986. Gaining legal status would make it less risky for workers in the fields to organize and win better conditions, and would help their families. Even if the present H2-A program was relaxed slightly, they argue, it would be an acceptable price to pay if hundreds of thousands of people eventually got green cards. Pursuing that logic, Los Angeles congressman Howard Berman, a longtime defender of farmworkers, crafted a compromise in the late 1990s, in cooperation with the United Farm Workers and other farmworker advocates.

"Growers always scream 'shortage,'" Berman said. "In reality what they want is an oversupply of labor to keep wages down and discourage unionization." On one hand Berman's bill, the Agricultural Jobs, Opportunity, Benefits, and Security Act (known as AgJOBS), would help them by relaxing restrictions on the H2-A program. It would allow growers to pay a housing allowance instead of providing housing, and it would freeze the minimum required wage for a number of years. In return, in his original proposal, workers who perform 100 days of farm labor in eighteen months could apply for temporary legal status. If they complete another 360 days in six years, they would gain permanent residency. In addition, guest workers would be covered under the Migrant and Seasonal Agricultural Worker Protection Act, which covers all other farmworkers. The act, amended to include the right to organize, would then allow all farmworkers, including guest workers, to sue their employers in federal courts over labor violations.

That compromise almost became law in 1999. But after seeing the 2000 election results, growers decided they could get a better deal under President George W. Bush and backed out. Senator Larry Craig (R-ID) introduced a new bill, much more like the traditional bracero program. Guest workers would have no right to go to court or recognition of union rights. The bill required only the minimum wage, and the government would no longer have to certify a labor shortage to permit importing workers. Workers would have to labor 150 days per year in agriculture to qualify for legalization, a much higher bar for seasonal workers than that proposed in AgJOBS.

In the following years, AgJOBS proposals varied in detail, although the basic trade-off remained the same—relaxation of guest-worker requirements in exchange for some degree of legalization. The bill was incorporated into other immigration-reform proposals, and even briefly attached as an amendment to tort reform and defense appropriation bills. In Congress's extreme anti-immigrant fervor, however, it was derided as "immigration amnesty" and couldn't win the votes for passage. The debate over AgJOBS, however, sent a clear message to farmworkers—to get legal status they had to accept some form of temporary guest-worker employment, for at least some period of time. The Bush administration then sent the same message to workers far beyond the fields, as Congress debated other immigration-reform proposals. The AgJOBS debate prepared legislators, and even many immigrant-rights groups, for a similar trade-off strategy.

Although Congress repealed Public Law 78, which established the bracero program, in 1964, guest-worker programs in the United States never really ended. New laws created new visa categories to permit employers to import workers for temporary labor. Some cover agricultural laborers while others cover skilled workers in healthcare and high-tech. Employers complain about restrictions on all of them—on numbers, on wage and housing mandates, on rights, and on requirements that they show that U.S. resident workers aren't available for the jobs they want to fill.

Until George W. Bush was elected, their complaints were largely viewed as self-interested efforts to lower wages. But at the end of the 1990s, the country's largest employer associations formed a low-profile, shadowy group to change that perception. When the votes were counted (or not) in Florida in 2000, their fortunes began to rise. As a result, their efforts have brought the old bracero program closer to new life than it's been since Galarza and Chávez killed it in 1964.

The Essential Worker Immigration Coalition (EWIC) was organized in 1999, while Bill Clinton was president, after one of the administration's most celebrated enforcement plans, Operation Vanguard. For an entire year following the program's launch in December 1998, the Immigration and Naturalization Service went through the employment records of every meatpacking plant in Nebraska. Poring over the documents of 24,310 people employed in forty slaughterhouses, they pulled out 4,762 names. These individuals were sent letters, asking them to come in for a chat with an Immigration and Naturalization Service agent down at the plant. About a thousand actually did so. Of them, 34 people were found to be in the country without visas and were deported. Those 3,500 people who didn't show up for their appointments left their jobs, whether for immigration reasons or as part of normal turnover.

The INS declared victory, crowing that it had found a new, effective means of enforcing employer sanctions. Nebraska's governor Mike Johanns and the American Meat Institute (AMI) hit the roof. They accused the INS of creating production bottlenecks, and implied they'd been denied a necessary source of labor if Americans wanted to continue eating beef for dinner. Strangely, the INS agreed. One of Operation Vanguard's architects, INS district director Mark Reed, boasted that ridding the plants of undocumented workers would force employers to support guest-worker legislation. "It's time for a gut check," he declared. "We depend on foreign labor...How can we get unauthorized [undocumented] workers back into the workforce in a legal way? If we don't have illegal immigration anymore, we'll have the political support for guest worker." Operation Vanguard, he predicted, would "clean up one industry and turn the [jobs] magnet down a bit, and then go on to another industry, and another, and another."

Reed was a little ahead of his time in calculating that Congress would act quickly, but he did get industry thinking. In the operation's wake, Sherry Edwards of the AMI said that while guest workers were a good idea, packers needed more than the old bracero program. "We need permanent workers, not seasonal laborers," she explained.

The year following Operation Vanguard, the AMI and a group of corporate trade associations, in industries employing large numbers of immigrant workers, organized EWIC, which began lobbying for a new, greatly expanded guest-worker program. The phrase "essential worker" in the coalition's name referred not just to immigrants in general, but specifically to guest workers. EWIC announced that industry faced a huge labor shortage and that "part of the solution involves allowing companies to hire foreign workers." Quoting Federal Reserve chair Alan Greenspan, EWIC said prices would go up if its labor needs were denied. It denounced restrictions on existing guest-worker programs as "unnecessarily tedious, time-consuming, expensive, and many times unsuccessful."

EWIC's proposals sought to create a tier of workers with none of the rights and social benefits U.S. workers won in the New Deal. The group quickly grew to include forty of the country's most powerful employer associations, headed by the U.S. Chamber of Commerce. The National Association of Chain Drug Stores belonged. Wal-Mart, with two members on the Chain Drug Stores board, was sanctioned for employing undocumented workers. The American Health Care Association, the American Hotel and Lodging Association, the National Council of Chain Restaurants, the National Restaurant Association, and the National Retail Federation all joined. They too depend on a workforce almost entirely without benefits, working at close to minimum wage. The violently antiunion Associated Builders and Contractors belonged. In 1992 its members fought a yearlong strike by undocumented immigrant drywall workers throughout Southern California. But ABC's more union-friendly cousin, the Associated General Contractors, also belonged to EWIC. The American Meat Institute was there from the beginning.

The Clinton administration initially held out hope for the EWIC program. Henry Cisneros, after leaving the Department of Housing and Urban Development, promoted a package immigration deal including guest workers. In April 2000 he proposed that unions and immigrant-rights groups, which were seeking an amnesty for the undocumented, relax their opposition to guest-worker programs in return for limited reforms that would allow some undocumented workers to gain visas. The main administration objective was to neutralize objections to expansion of the H1-B visa program used by high-tech employers in Silicon Valley to recruit foreign engineers. Lifting the cap on recruitment was a major demand of the electronics industry, a heavy contributor to Al Gore's presidential campaign. Congress in the end agreed to higher recruitment limits.

After the Florida vote count, Bush fed EWIC's expectations, conducting a highly publicized series of meetings with Mexican president Vicente Fox over a set of immigration-law changes dubbed by then–Mexican foreign secretary Jorge Castañeda as "the whole enchilada." This deal proposed the same key trade-off—limited amnesty for a new guest-worker program. An August 2001 letter to Bush congratulated the president on his "historic initiative" and laid out requirements for a deal. "A temporary-worker program that emerges from this debate should be markedly different from the existing and past models," EWIC urged. "Some of the workers who currently come from Mexico and other countries to work in the U.S. do so with the intention of returning to their home countries. It is reasonable then to construct a temporary-worker framework that provides a role for such workers whose labor is needed in the U.S." In other words, people migrating to the United States would be given not permanent-residence visas but work visas tying their status to employment.

Republican senators Phil Gramm and Jesse Helms, while fulminating against legalization for people already in the United States, supported guest-worker proposals, and even went to Mexico to discuss them with Fox. "It is delusional," Gramm told Fox, "not to recognize that illegal aliens already hold millions of jobs in the United States with the implicit permission of governments at every level, as well as companies and communities." They proposed annual visas, like the bracero program.

Economic recession, however, and the attacks on the World Trade Center and the Pentagon brought that process to a halt. Immigrants across the board were scapegoated for terrorism. More than forty thousand airport screeners were fired from their jobs and refused rehire because they weren't citizens, as the federal government took over the baggage lines. Other immigrants were subjected to arbitrary screening and indefinite detention. In highly publicized raids dubbed

Operation Tarmac, the INS deported hundreds of fast-food and service workers in airports.

In this new political climate, EWIC recast its proposals, tying them to enforcement. Guest-worker programs, it said, were actually a means to track the names and identities of those who otherwise would sneak across the border. Terrorists thus could be identified and pursued. "September 11 means we have to look at all these issues through the lens of national security," said John Gay, EWIC cochair and vice president of the International Franchise Association. "We live in a pool of migrating people, and we have to control people coming across the border."

In 2002 EWIC joined forces with the Cato Institute, the conservative/libertarian think tank whose ideology framed much of the Bush administration's legislative agenda. Asserting that "America's border policy has failed to achieve its principal objective: to stem the flow of undocumented workers into the U.S. labor market," a Cato Institute report authored by Daniel T. Griswold called instead for an "open, integrated labor market."

"The experience of the bracero program," he alleged, "demonstrates that workers prefer the legal channel." To open one up, a temporary-work visa "should be created that would allow Mexican nationals to remain in the United States to work for a limited period. The visa could authorize work for a definite period, perhaps three years, and would be renewable for an additional limited period." About three hundred thousand visas should be issued at first, he suggested. Guest workers with temporary visas would be able to get into line for eventual permanent visas after years of work. It's a long line— an applicant at the Mexico City embassy with the lowest preference has to wait at least twelve to fifteen years to get a permanent-residence visa. Undocumented people already in the United States would also be allowed to apply to become temporary workers, and eventually get into the back of the line. This substitute for amnesty would "dry out the wetbacks," much as the growers were doing with those who perished in Los Gatos Canyon.

The Cato Institute report was issued on October 15, 2002, a year and a half before Bush finally made his proposal. When he did, the two were identical.

The Cato Institute is bankrolled by the Sarah Scaife Foundation, the Claude R. Lambe Charitable Foundation, and the Koch Foundation, key funders of the conservative movement. Cato provided an important bridge to part of the corporate world with less direct interest in immigration. The institute has waged campaigns against tobacco, utility, and pharmaceutical regulation, for privatization of government services, and it has supported media consolidation. Rupert Murdoch, owner of Fox News, the *New York Post*, HarperCollins Publishers, and Twentieth Century Fox, has been a board member since 1997. In 2007 he became owner of the *Wall Street Journal*, whose editorials warn of terrible labor shortages and call for guest-worker programs to deal with them. Cato's ties to the media helped guest-worker proposals achieve greater political legitimacy. The institute's assertion that industries like meatpacking and tourism face a labor shortage, rather than a corporate unwillingness to pay higher wages to attract workers, has been treated as fact by much of the media. Likewise, its assertion that the bracero program was a humane institution created an easily accepted, invented history.

Following the issuance of the Cato report, EWIC continued to emphasize national security. Saying that "authorities know very little" about the then-estimated 7 million people in the United States without papers, it warned that while most came to work, "those few who wish to do us harm find it easier to hide among their great numbers." No undocumented worker from Mexico or Central America has ever been connected with terrorism, and those who flew the planes into the World Trade Center and the Pentagon all arrived with visas. Nevertheless, an EWIC letter to senators asked, "How can the immigration status quo be tolerated?"

When President Bush finally issued his reform proposal in January 2004, it contained no broad-based amnesty for the millions of undocumented, unlike the compromise signed by Ronald Reagan in 1986. As the Cato report recommended, it focused entirely on establishing a new temporary-worker program. The proposal was immediately greeted by EWIC and its members. The National Restaurant Association warned that restaurants faced "a worker shortage of 1.5 million jobs" by 2014, and praised the plan, which it said "would give employers greater opportunities to fill these jobs, grow their business, and help grow the economy." R. Bruce Josten, executive vice president of the U.S. Chamber of Commerce, praised Bush for making "an effort to streamline the process by which employers who cannot find U.S. workers may hire foreign nationals through temporary-worker programs while ensuring that the workers would have appropriate labor protections." He, too, warned of dire labor shortages, and concluded that "expanded, practical temporary-worker programs will help meet this need."

EWIC and Cato won support from the conservative wing of the Republican Party. Congressional leader Tom DeLay announced, "It is vitally important this country have some sort of guest-worker program. It is only fair to those here in the United States who need the workers and it is doubly fair to the families, Mexicans that need the work." Bush's proposal, however, was not as warmly embraced by immigrants themselves. In a poll conducted by Bendixen and Associates for New California Media and the James Irvine Foundation, 50 percent of the undocumented workers surveyed opposed it once its provisions were explained, while only 42 percent supported it. Renee Saucedo, director of San Francisco's Day Labor Program, said that the city's street-corner laborers discussed the proposal extensively and rejected it almost unanimously. "They feel that a temporary visa status would make them as vulnerable to exploitation as the undocumented status most of them now share," she explained.

The organization of veterans of the bracero program, with chapters in both the United States and Mexico, was even more critical. "We're totally opposed to new guest-worker programs," explained Ventura Gutiérrez, head of Unión Sin Fronteras. "People who lived through the old program know the abuse they will cause." As one former bracero, Manuel Herrera, told Juliana Barbassa of the Associated Press, "They rented us, got our work, then sent us back when they had no more use for us." Thousands of former braceros are still trying to collect money deducted from their pay during the 1940s and 1950s, supposedly held in trust to ensure they completed their work contracts but never turned over to them. Bush's proposal contained a similar provision. "If we accept, then our grandsons and great-grandsons will go through what we went through," ex-bracero Florentino Larios told Barbassa.

The Bush proposal wasn't welcomed by the Left in Mexico for the same reason. "We remember the bracero program here," said Mexican senator Rosalbina Garabito of the PRD, "and it's not a good memory. Our people were treated like animals. This is a binational problem that the U.S. is dealing with unilaterally. There must be negotiations and reciprocity, where people in both countries benefit. If we don't attack the economic root, the problem will continue growing."

While expanded guest-worker programs were key elements in Republican immigration-reform proposals that predated Bush's, EWIC won their incorporation into Democratic proposals as well. The accepted wisdom on Capitol Hill came to hold that no reform was possible if industry didn't get what it wanted. In the 1986 amnesty, immigrants were required to show that they'd been living in the country since 1982. EWIC reframed the residency requirement, transforming it into the concept of "earned legalization." In the new Washington proposals, it was no longer sufficient to have lived in the United States for years—only participation as a "willing employee" in a new temporary-worker program, hired by a "willing employer" (in the terminology of Bush and the Cato Institute) qualified someone for eventual legalization.

In a January 2004 press conference just prior to Bush's announcement, representatives of the National Immigration Forum (NIF), the American Immigration Lawyers Association (AILA), and the National Council of La Raza (NCLR) outlined a joint proposal for immigration reform, which included "earned legalization," strengthened border enforcement, and more guest workers. Jeanne Butterfield of the AILA announced that "the essential worker sector, the service sector, needs these people in fields and factories." NIF director Frank Sharry described their proposal as "more market-sensitive immigration," and declared, "This is what immigrants want."

The proposal was eventually incorporated into a bipartisan bill sponsored by Senators Tom Daschle and Chuck Hegel, and finally into a Democratic immigration-reform bill introduced by Congressman Luis Gutiérrez and Senator Edward Kennedy. Nicknamed the SOLVE Act, it would have allowed people living in the United States for five years, who worked for two of them, to apply for legal status. At the same time, employers would be permitted to bring in up to 350,000 temporary workers annually, who could bring spouses and children and change employers after three months. EWIC must have savored its moment of legislative triumph—no matter which side of the aisle made proposals, they all included the centerpiece of its agenda. It now seemed self-evident in Congress that migration should be harnessed to provide labor to corporate employers.

For the next three years, until the final failure of the Bush immigration program in the Senate in August 2007, the EWIC trade-off was included in almost every "comprehensive" immigration-reform proposal. EWIC became the linchpin of a Washington, D.C., coalition that included a wide variety of organizations, including the National Immigration Forum, a leading Washington, D.C.-based advocate for immigration reform that helped to design the legislative strategy. EWIC head John Gay became the forum's board chair. The National Council of La Raza and the National Council of Catholic Bishops supported the EWIC compromise, along with the American Immigration Lawyers Association and two unions, the Service Employees and UNITE HERE. Conservative support was organized by Tamar Jacoby of the hard-right Manhattan Institute.

After the House of Representatives passed Sensenbrenner's HR 4437, the coalition portrayed itself as sponsors of the liberal alternative. Even Bush criticized HR 4437 because it had no guest-worker provision. Fear of Sensenbrenner's extreme proposals caused many Washington advocates to support another bill by Senators Ted Kennedy and John McCain. Like its predecessors, it embodied the guest worker/

legalization trade-off, along with a third essential compromise—increased enforcement, including beefed-up employer sanctions, deportations, and patrols on the border.

In the face of fire from other unions, and immigrant-rights organizations outside Washington, the guest-worker provisions were hard to defend. The "guest worker" phrase developed an ill repute, and was replaced with euphemisms—workers on "employment visas," "essential workers," or just "new workers." But employers didn't help. In the middle of the debate, prominent Republican Senate supporters—John McCain, John Cornyn, Jon Kyl, Larry Craig, and Chuck Hegel—voted unsuccessfully to repeal the federal minimum wage entirely. Rob Rosado, director of legislative affairs for the American Meat Institute, lobbied for guest-worker programs, but against a wage guarantee. "We don't want the government setting wages," he said. "The market determines wages."

HR 2330, the McCain-Kennedy "bipartisan" bill, would have allowed employers to recruit four hundred thousand guest workers under temporary visas every year. Undocumented immigrants could also have received temporary visas. Temporary-visa holders would have been able to apply for legal status after four or six years, but would have had to wait additional years "at the end of the line" before their applications were even considered.

Increased penalties were proposed for working without papers to prevent workers from doing as many did during the bracero era—walking away from exploitative jobs. The bills proposed harsh penalties for "document fraud." Social Security personnel would have abandoned their historic mission of distributing pension and disability benefits, and would instead have become the workplace police, making Social Security cards, in effect, national work permits. After the Senate bill failed in August 2007, and Homeland Security secretary Michael Chertoff began beefed-up enforcement of no-match letters, coupled with arresting workers for document fraud, he was simply implementing by regulation what the comprehensive reform bills proposed.

Progressive immigrant-rights groups warned that the political dynamic of the reform debate would lead to more conservative, repressive bills. When the McCain-Kennedy bill couldn't get the support of more than a handful of Republicans, it died and was replaced by others. One, introduced by Senators John Cornyn and Jon Kyl, would have allowed corporations to recruit workers under two-year temporary visas. Undocumented workers could have qualified for temporary visas also, but would have had to leave the country to apply, euphemistically called "touching back." Ten thousand new immigration agents would have enforced heavier sanctions, border restrictions, and no-match letters. Its proposal for prisons to house ten thousand deportees was also partially implemented later by executive action.

Ultimately, in a bid to win over anti-immigrant Republicans, the Bush administration even proposed scrapping the system of visa preferences for family reunification. That system, established by the Immigration Reform Act of 1965, was won by Chicano activists including Ernesto Galarza, César Chávez, and Bert Corona. It prioritizes families and communities, and replaced the bracero system that valued migrants only for their labor power. Family preferences, Bush said, should be replaced with a "merit system," allowing people to qualify for visas only if they possessed job skills desired by corporate employers. This ultimately cost the support of some immigrant advocates who had reluctantly accepted guest-worker and enforcement compromises.

In the 2006 elections, the most anti-immigrant Republican candidates for Congress, endorsed by the House Immigration Reform Caucus, almost all lost. Meanwhile, even mainstream media polls consistently showed majority support for some kind of legalization. But once the administration treated immigrants as a potential threat, and proposed repressive measures to deal with them, it could no longer effectively oppose even more right-wing members of Congress who only wanted enforcement. It became an article of faith among Republicans, and many Democrats, that winning the next election required support for more and more repressive measures. House Democratic leader Rahm Emanuel called immigration "the third rail" of politics. The strategy of using enforcement to win over right-wing members of Congress undermined not just compromise legislation but opposition to anti-immigrant hysteria generally. And in the end, as support eroded on both left and right, the corporate base for the bills proved too narrow on its own to win passage.

Behind the conflict over individual provisions, however, was a deeper divide over the purpose of immigration policy. Should it be shaped by the desire of employers for labor? Or should migration produce strong communities able to assert their rights? Rick Mines, former director of the California Institute for Rural Studies, pointed out, "There is no question that Mexican labor and the U.S. industries that rely on it are profoundly interdependent. This cannot and will not be changed with simple, unenforceable policies. The issue is not how to end this relationship, but how to lessen its negative effects." The Southern Poverty Law Center's *Close to Slavery* report warned that expanded guest-worker programs, instead of lessening those effects, would strengthen them. "The current H-2 guest worker program," it emphasized, "is inherently abusive and should not be expanded in the name of immigration reform."

"People [in guest-worker programs] are treated neither as guests nor as workers," said North Carolina Legal Aid attorney Andrew McGuffin, "but as slaves for rent." The *Close to Slavery* report agreed. "These workers . . . are not treated like 'guests,'" it concluded. "Rather, they are systematically exploited and abused . . . They are, in effect, the disposable workers of the U.S. economy."

The fourteen men who drowned in the North Maine woods, and the fourteen coffee farmers from Veracruz who died trying to cross the border through the Sonoran Desert the year before, and the nineteen later found dead in a tractor-trailer in Victoria, Texas, are all evidence of the deadly effects of the current immigration system. Reforms could give future migrants real rights, and protect their ability to truly belong to communities on both sides of the border. If reforms do this, those deaths will have meaning long after the names of those who perished have been forgotten, like those of the deportees in Woody Guthrie's song.

But it would be a terrible misuse of the fate of those workers if their deaths were used to justify a new system enshrining the abuses of the old.

Five

WHICH SIDE ARE YOU ON?

Paolo Freire on LA's Mean Streets

> *I'm going to sing you a story, friends*
> *that will make you cry,*
> *how one day in front of K-Mart*
> la migra *came down on us,*
> *sent by the sheriff*
> *of this very same place . . .*

The thumping bass strings of a bajo sexto punctuate a simple two-four rhythm as a couple of old guitars and a plaintive accordion carry the familiar chord changes of a Mexican corrido. Seven mournful voices ring across the parking lot on St. Andrews Place, belting out the Spanish words in traditional style.

   Surrounding the singers, dozens of men dressed in work clothes listen intently, crowding under a blue awning or standing out on the black asphalt, sweltering in the sun. The *músicos* proceed with their cautionary tale:

> *We don't understand why,*
> *we don't know the reason,*
> *why there is so much*
> *discrimination against us.*
> *In the end we'll wind up*
> *all the same in the grave.*

At the end of each verse, the listeners shout or whistle their encouragement. It's obvious that almost everyone knows the story, and that many have had the same experience.

The song relates the history of a famous 1996 immigration raid in the City of Industry, in Los Angeles County. One rainy winter morning, Border Patrol agents charged into a street-corner clinic where forty day laborers had lined up to be tested for AIDS and other sexually transmitted diseases. One worker, Omar Sierra, had just taken his seat at the examining station, where a clinic worker had tied off his arm and inserted the needle for drawing the first blood sample. As agents of *la migra* swarmed across the street and sidewalk, Sierra jumped up, tore off the tourniquet, pulled the needle out of his vein, and ran.

Sierra escaped and made it home. Shaken by his experience and determined never to forget his less fortunate friends, he committed their fate to music. Returning to the corner three days later, he sang his song to those who remained.

> *With this verse I leave you,*
> *I'm tired of singing,*
> *hoping* la migra
> *won't come after us again,*
> *because in the end, we all have to work.*

Omar Sierra's song is not just a history; it's an anthem. The seven singers in the parking lot—Sierra, Pablo Alvarado, Jesus Rivas, Julio Cesar Bautista, Paula de la Cruz, John Garcia, and Omar Garcia—are more than a group of friends performing for their own pleasure and profit; they're the day-laborer band Los Jornaleros del Norte. And singing Sierra's "Corrido de Industry" is no casual social event; it's a new way of organizing Los Angeles's mostly immigrant day-labor force.

"What do we do while we're waiting for work on the corner every morning?" asks guitarist Alvarado. "We're learning to live with each other, telling jokes and stories, playing games, arguing about football—

a hundred interactions. We're learning to organize ourselves to the rhythm of our happiness and sadness. We're creating a culture of liberation."

Survival hasn't been easy for Los Jornaleros del Norte. All its members—except Alvarado, who today is the full-time director for the National Day Laborer Organizing Network (NDLON)—earn their daily bread from the curb every morning. None of them owns a car, so getting together to practice is hard. And taking time off to perform doesn't help pay the rent at the end of the month. But when they play, their audience recognizes itself, not just in the words and music but in the clothes, the mannerisms, and the hundred details that make it plain that these musicians earn their living on the streets. The band is a living, singing demonstration that solidarity among day laborers is not just a possibility but a reality.

Organizing people who work on the streets in LA requires more than a sing-along and a common culture, however. At six on a gray morning beside the Home Depot parking lot at Sunset Boulevard and St. Andrews Place, a grittier reality is evident, as Alvarado and another organizer for the Institute of Popular Education of Southern California (IDEPSCA), Mario Martinez, approach a group of twenty men strung out along the sidewalk. The workers are wearing plain trousers and cheap work-shirts. Some lean against a cinderblock wall in small groups, talking quietly and smoking; others sit on the curb itself. They're all waiting for the contractors to pull out of the Home Depot parking lot.

At this time of the morning, a steady stream of small trucks drives away hauling building supplies. As the drivers load up and start to pull out, Alvarado hands each of them a leaflet showing the location of a new day-labor pickup site IDEPSCA has opened in a parking lot a few blocks away. The workers on the curb aren't happy about the leafleting. Every truck that goes to the new site represents a job lost to them. A group of half a dozen men forms at the corner of Sunset. Two or three are in their twenties; the others are middle-aged. As they move angrily toward the driveway, their voices get louder. Soon Martinez, who's walked over to meet them halfway, is faced with a wall of hostile faces shouting questions and threats: "I have a family to feed!" "Who's going to buy school clothes for my three kids?"

Alvarado joins Martinez, and the two organizers patiently try to convince the workers to come to the new site to look for work, instead of standing on the corner here. A couple of workers say they've tried to get work there, and that there weren't enough jobs. "The site's just starting up," Alvarado explains. "It will take a little time to convince the contractors to use it. That's what we're doing with the leaflets. But if we all go over there, the contractors will come too. They'll have no choice." The new site, Martinez tells them, has free coffee and plastic chairs for the workers to sit on while they wait. There's a blue awning to provide relief from the sun and shelter from the rain. And it has one other big plus: no raids.

"Before the new site, there were three big sweeps by the Hollywood Division [of the Los Angeles Police Department] here, with a lot of arrests," Martinez reminds the workers. "They came out here with guns drawn and made everyone lie facedown on the sidewalk. They put handcuffs on people. What will happen if they come again and arrest you? What will happen to your children then? Think about it."

A few heads nod in grudging acknowledgment. Some of the workers who have been yelling at Martinez remember the raids. The memory is bitter and humiliating.

IDEPSCA and the Coalition for Humane Immigrant Rights of Los Angeles (CHIRLA) started organizing this corner a year before this morning's confrontation. Once a core of workers had formed the committee that voted to organize a new site, CHIRLA and IDEPSCA persuaded Sears to donate the use of an old parking lot behind its store, and the city provided some funds for staffing the site. Located off the main thoroughfare, it's not an ideal location, but it's the best IDEPSCA could get. The workers who committed to finding work at the new location were frustrated, in their turn, when contractors continued to pick workers up on the curb across from Home Depot. The curbside workers were taking their jobs. They put pressure on the IDEPSCA organizers to do something.

"They had the same desperation at our site that these people have here on the corner," Martinez explains. "They confronted us, and we all decided to go out and leaflet the contractors. Last Saturday, forty-three people found work at the new site. Only two were left at the end of the day."

"I felt this competition for work when I first came here," Alvarado remembers. A stocky Salvadoran in his late thirties, he arrived in Los Angeles in 1990 and went out to the corner to find work. "I got my jobs at [the intersection of] Vanowen and Canoga," he recalls. "I didn't understand what was happening on the corner. When the police came down on us, I just thought they were repressing us like in El Salvador. I just wanted to work."

Like each of the thousands of immigrant laborers who get jobs on the curb at more than two hundred day-labor sites across Los Angeles every morning, Alvarado arrived in LA at the end of an arduous physical and psychological journey, one that started in the country hamlet of El Nispero. There Alvarado grew up, the son of a farmer in a region of El Salvador controlled by revolutionaries during the country's civil war. In the sixth grade, he saw his teacher killed by the army. After that, no teachers came to the village, so he became a literacy volunteer in the hard-fought region.

Alvarado learned the techniques of popular education, a way of teaching designed to organize the poor, developed by the great Brazilian educator Paulo Freire. It relies on relating to the personal experiences of the students, teaching politics while tackling the alphabet. "We call it teaching the word through teaching the world," Alvarado explains. Helping poor farmers learn to read in war-torn Central America was no more neutral than teaching slaves to read in the Old South. "Popular education teaches subversive questions," he says. "It asks—why is there a war going on? Why are some people rich and others poor?"

After the revolutionaries' 1989 military offensive, his family began receiving death threats—his brother was an urban guerrilla fighter. The family told Alvarado to take him north. "The journey wasn't bad," he remembers. "But once I was actually here, it was a different story. I had no money and no friends. Looking for work was humiliating. The employers would get out of their pickups and come over and touch me to see if I was strong. Each time I got a job, I felt I was taking bread from the mouth of a man with a family."

He recovered his humanity finding a use for the skills he'd brought from home. He started teaching coworkers to read and went on to hold classes, first at the YMCA in East Los Angeles and then with IDEPSCA. That was the beginning of the day-labor organizing project. It's no accident that CHIRLA and IDEPSCA start literacy classes at all their organized day-labor sites. It's another way, like the day-labor band, of organizing and teaching immigrants how their new world works.

In 1997 CHIRLA and IDEPSCA formed a partnership to operate the City of Los Angeles Day Laborer Program in North Hollywood and Harbor City. Today their program runs eight other sites across the city, but the longest-organized ones are those in North Hollywood and Harbor City—the original hiring halls set up by the City of Los Angeles in 1989. They provide a vision of what finding a day-labor job can be like. The North Hollywood site, off Sherman Way, has a drive-through area where contractors can pull up to do their hiring. Farther inside the big triangular lot, an open area with an awning shelters workers as they play checkers, talk, and drink coffee. A portable building provides space for literacy classes and a tiny office with computers. Rows of cabbages and onions hug the fence at the edge of the property. Chile seedlings poke through the light-brown soil. A few men in work clothes stoop among the plants, picking weeds and watering with hoses. Many day laborers were farmers, and this garden shows their love for the land.

On one morning in 2000, a blue pickup truck with a rack of two-by-fours on the back pulled into the lot. A young white man in paint-spattered work clothes got out. Some of the waiting laborers pointed to a counter under the awning, on which sat two plastic jars. In the jar with the yellow plastic lid, every worker had put an orange ticket bearing his or her name. In the other jar, with its green top, were the names of the workers who speak English. After taking a name from each jar, the contractor asked the site manager about the expected wages. He was told to talk to the workers. After a brief discussion, the contractor agreed to $8.00 an hour and the laborers climbed into the back of his truck. At the time the minimum wage was $5.25 an hour.

Gone are the days—at this and other CHIRLA and IDEPSCA sites, at least—when workers crowded around the contractors, clamoring for work. "If the contractor already knows who he wants to hire, we let him ask for specific people by name," explained Victor Narro, the CHIRLA staff member who managed the day-labor programs at the time. "Also, contractors can request specific skills, like carpenter, welder, or painter."

While the day laborers' first priority at the North Hollywood site is finding work, they find other things there as well, beginning with friendship and community. When it took over the city-funded hiring operation in 1997, CHIRLA and IDEPSCA brought more than additional resources and building materials for the portable structure in which English classes are held. Instead of just helping a few people get jobs, Pablo Alvarado, Victor Narro, and other staff viewed the day-labor program as a means to unite the workers. Once they were organized, workers themselves were able to take steps, like learning English, that could increase their earning power.

It wasn't an easy transition for the existing staff, which had administered the two city sites for years. "There's nothing wrong with the service philosophy in itself," explained Juan Carrillo, a veteran of the Harbor City site, "but I believe you also have to find a way for people to exercise more power over their lives."

Carrillo reached back to his own experience working in Latino theater groups as a student at UCLA. Such *teatros,* he reasoned, could be another tool for organizing, so he helped set up the first day-labor theater group. The program's first production, *The Curse of the Day Laborers,* grew out of improvisations by the workers. In the drama a hostile resident in a neighborhood near a pickup site puts a curse on the workers—in the person of a real-life sheriff in Los Angeles

County's Agoura Hills notorious for hassling day laborers. Finally, a *curandera* (an old woman who practices traditional medicine) finds a way to drive out the demon.

"We don't have a script with lines," Carrillo explained. "We have ideas we want to get across, but no written dialogue." When the day laborers first became actors, they started by telling stories of their own experiences on the corner. Then, when they performed, they moved among the workers in the audience, asking questions. "We don't want people to be passive observers," Carrillo said. "If you can demand your rights from an employer in a play, then you can do it in life."

Eventually, the theater moved beyond its original function as a forum for self-expression. The group took the show on the road, to all the corners and curbs and parking lots across the LA Basin where people line up for work. "This was the big change," Carrillo said. "The *teatro* began to work toward forming the union." They even began singing a song, "La Frasesita," about learning to read.

> *I went to study English*
> *because I felt I had to,*
> *so I could defend myself*
> *from an angry Anglo.*
> *There where I worked*
> *they tried to cheat me*
> *because of the damn English*
> *I didn't know how to speak.*
>
> *That white man told me*
> *in his angry English words:*
> *You wetback don't understand*
> *what you are supposed to do.*
> *You wetback don't understand*
> *what you are supposed to do.*

On the corner of Pomona and Atlantic in East Los Angeles, Agustín Moncada described how he was cheated of over half his wages. "I got picked up by a roofer at one o'clock on a Friday," he recalled. "As we were driving away from the corner, I asked for eight dollars an hour. I've worked as a roofer, and I know what I'm worth. The contractor said, 'OK, I'll see how you work.'" Moncada worked five hours Friday, and then nine hours daily for the next three days. On Sunday, he was paid one hundred dollars, much less than he'd actually earned. On Monday, he told his boss he was disgusted with the job's unpleasant conditions and that he wasn't coming anymore. But when the contractor dropped Moncada off that evening, he told him he didn't have enough money to pay the rest of his wages. He agreed to meet Moncada on the corner the following day. At the end of the week, Moncada was still waiting.

Agustín Moncada was fifty-three years old at the time of this incident, in 1999. When a contractor hires him on the corner, it's not his youth that gets him work but his experience and skills. His family still lives in Durango, in central Mexico, where he had a trucking business until he came north in the early 1990s. "Originally, I thought I might bring them north," he said, "but life is too difficult here. My wife is sick of having to be both mother and father to our kids, and she's afraid I'm finding a much more comfortable life here with a *gringa*. I'm going back at the end of the year."

CHIRLA began organizing the day laborers at this intersection. After spending weeks on the corner, organizer Mario Lopez convinced them to form a committee. In the popular stereotype, people who get jobs on street corners are transients, here for a little while, then moving on. But people have spent years on this corner. Jose Valencia and Jorge Aboites, two friends who sat smoking on the curb, had been coming for five and ten years respectively. Another veteran, Antoli Garcia, had spent nine years here providing a living for his family.

Garcia, who was elected to the site committee, saw two reasons for getting organized: "First, we need to put ourselves in order. We used to have a lot of trouble from the sheriffs, mostly because our people were drinking while they were waiting for jobs. Second, we need better pay and a way of avoiding the competition for jobs." The committee met with the sheriffs and the surrounding residents to negoti-

ate a set of rules for people seeking work. A stretch of curb was des-
ignated as an official pickup site, so contractors wouldn't cause traffic
problems as workers gathered around their vehicles. Other rules
banned drinking or pestering people passing by. A final rule was an
agreement to insist on a six-dollar-an-hour minimum.

On organized corners the committee's power of persuasion is
sufficient to win cooperation from most workers. In East Los Angeles,
however, the day laborers had only begun to organize, so workers occasionally ignored the site's boundaries or took a job at a lower wage.

"One of the first steps we take is to set up a soccer team," Alvarado
says. "It's something that the workers do anyway, playing while they
wait for work. We come in and organize the matches, encouraging
cooperation in this very competitive environment. In the morning the
atmosphere is tense. The workers see each other as rivals. By afternoon, after soccer practice, people are talking to each other about
what's happening on the corner." CHIRLA eventually organized a full-
blown league with ten teams.

In September 1997 street-corner committees across the city sent delegates to the first ever Inter-Corner Conference, to begin an organizing movement of day laborers. After five inter-corner conferences,
day-labor leaders organized a historic meeting to create the Day Labor
Union and elect officers. It's a nontraditional union because its purpose isn't collective bargaining, but it does attempt to set goals for
wages. When the union was first organized there were six-dollar,
seven-dollar, and eight-dollar corners all over LA, with minimums established by the workers themselves.

But starting in Agoura Hills in 1989, Southern California communities began to pass ordinances prohibiting people from getting jobs on
the street. The Agoura Hills ordinance was followed by ones in Costa
Mesa, LA County, City of Industry, La Mirada, Malibu, Laguna Beach,
Pomona, Glendale, and Gardena. The Day Labor Union believes looking for work on the street is a human right, and it became the workers' voice in debates over the issues, dramatically transforming their
relations with local residents.

In Topanga, locals greeted the first proposal for an organized day-labor site with hostility, turning out for town council meetings with banners that read, "No Hiring Site." Then in 1995 a fire swept through the hills, and day laborers stood on rooftops along with property owners, putting out sparks with garden hoses. Cooperation with the workers proved not only possible, but beneficial. It was a transforming experience. In 2000, when a deputy began rousting laborers, homeowners besieged the local sheriff's station demanding an end to harassment.

In nearby Agoura Hills, however, sheriffs from the Lost Hills substation were accused of systematic harassment for years. According to Narro, workers were chased by deputies yelling racist insults, even using helicopters. In a protest to Captain Bill McSweeney, Narro recounted, "The force of the helicopters lifted workers off the ground, causing them to lose their balance and fall down the side of the hill." McSweeney responded that "the law is clear and we are obligated to follow it."

Los Angeles: Class War's Ground Zero

Today millions of working people, immigrant and nonimmigrant alike, no longer have a secure relationship with a single employer. Economic and demographic changes have created questions about how to organize casual labor. In Los Angeles and elsewhere, the organizing of day laborers has begun to suggest answers. The Day Labor Union created stability and developed leadership in a situation in which every worker has to find a new job every day. Often shared immigrant culture acts as a powerful tool to help workers articulate their needs and build an organization from the grassroots. U.S. labor unions have started to pay heed, as they look for ways to unite a workforce that is more diverse and less secure than ever before.

CHIRLA and IDEPSCA organizers have trained day-labor organizers and provided help to community groups in Portland, Seattle, and other cities. That process led to the creation of the National Day Laborer Organizing Network (NDLON). On August 9, 2006, the AFL-CIO and NDLON announced a new partnership to work for greater enforcement of workers' rights, wage and hour laws, and health and safety protection. They agreed to support immigration reform that includes workplace rights, a path to citizenship, and political equality. Afterward, NDLON member organizations began to join local central labor councils, starting in Alameda County and Los Angeles in California, and AFL-CIO president John Sweeney spoke at national day-labor meetings. NDLON also signed an agreement with the Laborers' International Union of North America (LIUNA), a major change, since Laborers' locals have often viewed street-corner workers as potential job competitors.

The evolving relationship between day laborers and unions is one aspect of a much broader shift in U.S. labor away from cold war politics. From World War II through the 1980s most U.S. unions clung to an official ideology of partnership with large corporations and the government. They supported U.S. foreign and trade policy abroad, ignoring its disastrous impact on workers in developing countries. At its worst moments, labor's cold warriors, allied with U.S. intelligence agents, helped destroy militant labor movements, often at a terrible cost in lives and living standards. They refused to acknowledge that their actions in the developing world, and the free market policies they defended, produced forced migration whose impact was eventually felt in the United States as well.

Racism was built into those partnership ideas, which held that unions functioned to protect their members, often against other workers. Many maintained discriminatory policies toward women and people of color, viewing immigrants as job competitors. The age-old choice confronting the U.S. labor movement has always been between inclusion and exclusion. Those cold war ideas rejected the more radical traditions of U.S. unions like the Industrial Workers of the World before World War I, or the Congress of Industrial Organizations of the 1930s, which organized all workers and fought for equality. Even during the cold war, despite the AFL-CIO's conservative national leaders, progressive voices supported civil rights and opposed wars in Vietnam and Central America.

Nevertheless, in 1986 the AFL-CIO supported the Immigration Reform and Control Act because it contained employer sanctions, prohibiting employers from hiring workers without papers. If immigrants couldn't get jobs, the argument went, they wouldn't be competitors and would go home. Dissenters on the left predicted that sanctions would instead cause discrimination and give employers a powerful weapon to stop immigrants from organizing unions. Immigrant-rights advocates in unions of that era included older leaders like Bert Corona, and Humberto Camacho of the United Electrical Workers. A younger generation, brought up in the Chicano and Asian movements of the 1970s, included janitors' leader Mike Garcia, garment union organizers Cristina and Mario Vasquez, José La Luz, and Katie Quan, and hotel organizer Pat Lee. Other early labor immigrant-rights activists got their bruising education in the realities of immigration policy working for the United Farm Workers. They were allied with progressive lawyers and community-based organizations that had actively opposed the Simpson-Mazzoli and Simpson-Rodino bills, which eventually became law as 1986's IRCA.

They all predicted disaster if sanctions became law, and criticized them as a violation of a basic human right of all workers—the right to a job. Workers must sell their labor to survive, they argued, and denying immigrants work denies their right to live and support their families. They attacked the hypocrisy of conservatives who derided social welfare programs and praised work as a virtue, then punished immigrants for working. Sanctions, they said, were really a sweatshop subsidy to U.S. employers.

They were right. The law's impact was a disaster for unions trying to organize new members in industries like janitorial services and garment manufacturing, where employers used sanctions as a justification for firing union supporters. At the same time, however, the bill's amnesty provision had a positive effect on unions, as more than 3 million people gained legal status. When workers qualified for amnesty, many lost their fear of deportation. An upsurge in strikes and organizing drives swept through those areas of the country where immigrants were concentrated. In the 1990s, Los Angeles became ground zero for that upsurge. Pro-immigrant organizers in the AFL-CIO set up the California Immigrant Workers Association, running four regional centers to help people with amnesty applications. More than twenty thousand people used their help, which contributed to that wave of labor activity.

Anger among immigrants had been building for years over low wages. Goetz Wolff, a professor at UCLA and lead researcher for the Los Angeles County Federation of Labor, showed they were actually falling among the region's immigrant industrial workers. In women's apparel, he documented, the average hourly wage declined from $6.37 to $5.62 between 1988 and 1993, the years immediately after sanctions took effect. The impact was felt by tens of thousands of workers—at the end of the 1990s there were still 120,000 people employed just in the city's garment sweatshops, almost all immigrants, and mostly undocumented, according to the clothing union UNITE HERE. Wages were also falling in paper recycling, plastics manufacturing, textiles, and food processing—all industries with an immigrant workforce. In contrast, the average wage in aircraft production hovered around twenty dollars an hour, and actually rose slightly despite layoffs, recession, and the closure of many factories. Aerospace employed a mostly unionized, native-born workforce.

Immigrant workers fought to reverse that decline. Their militant strikes often forced unions to discard old, ineffective tactics, even to reexamine how they functioned internally. People coming from Mexico, Latin America, the Philippines, and Asia often brought militant traditions and a rich repertoire of ideas for fighting employers. The Day Labor Union that Alvarado and others had established was one place where those traditions were put to work, but it was by no means the only one.

The city's labor movement became home to many immigrant labor activists. Joel Ochoa, a student militant who fled Mexico City in the wake of the 1968 Tlatelolco Massacre, became an organizer with feet on both sides of the border. Yanira Merino, who fled her native El Salvador as a young activist and was then abducted by supporters of the Salvadoran military junta in Los Angeles, became a leading organizer for the Laborers' International Union, and later helped craft its alliance with day laborers.

In 1990, one of the first battles in this immigrant-labor war broke out when Macario Camorlinga and his workmates organized a rebellion in one of LA's largest foundries, American Racing Equipment. This small group earlier had been imbued with left-wing ideals of militant unionism in the Mexican city of Lázaro Cárdenas. They were blacklisted for their activity and forced to leave Mexico to support their families. In the foundry, many workers had no legal status, yet despite an immigration raid, almost one thousand went on strike. They won a union contract with big improvements and set up a large union local. The International Association of Machinists recognized Ochoa and Camorlinga's talents and put them both on staff.

American Racing Equipment wasn't an isolated experience. The city's janitors' union was rebuilt in a similar movement. In the mid-1980s, Service Employees Local 399 was driven out of the city's office buildings when contractors dumped their union workforce and hired immigrants then coming into Los Angeles, fleeing the wars in Central America. Local 399, together with the national organizing department of the Service Employees International Union (SEIU), organized the first Justice for Janitors campaign in response. Immigrant cleaning workers poured into the streets, confronting building owners and the LAPD in a famous battle in Century City. The union eventually won new contracts covering four thousand members.

Justice for Janitors became the union's national organizing strategy, and the Ken Loach movie *Bread and Roses* made it the most widely recognized campaign since *Norma Rae* romanticized textile-union drives in the South. Justice for Janitors became a symbol, not just of a new attitude toward immigrants but of a more combative stance toward employers. John Sweeney, then head of SEIU, campaigned to become president of the AFL-CIO by dramatizing his commitment to organize immigrants and low-wage workers. Sweeney's opponent, Tom Donahue, was the candidate of the cold war establishment. Just prior to the 1996 New York convention, Justice for Janitors blocked a bridge across the Potomac River in Washington, D.C., using civil disobedience to demand union recognition. Donahue announced he wanted to "build bridges, not block them." Sweeney responded that he was willing to get arrested to organize workers. Sweeney won the election.

The longest-fought rebellion in Los Angeles was the yearlong strike by Southern California drywallers, who put up the interior walls in new homes. In 1992 and 1993, from the Mexican border north to Santa Barbara, an area of five thousand square miles, these mostly Mexican immigrants stopped all home construction. Their strike, followed by a similar strike of framers three years later, electrified unions and workers.

Many strikers came from a group of small towns in Michoacán. They ran their movement democratically, from the bottom up. When they picketed, their lines often numbered in the hundreds, challenging old, ineffective strike tactics in which a few picketers would stand forlornly watching strikebreakers take their jobs. In contrast, drywallers displayed an almost missionary zeal, not wasting their time hurling insults from outside the job. Instead they walked onto building sites, talking nonstriking workers into putting down their tools. Employers tried to use the Border Patrol and Highway Patrol to stop them, pulling over their caravans as they headed to construction sites. Drywallers responded by walking out onto the freeways in rush hour, tying traffic into knots. In the framers' strike the Carpenters Union in Orange County hired buses to protect picketers from *la migra*. They finally forced building contractors to sign the first agreements covering residential construction in decades—the first union contracts won by grassroots organizing in the building trades for many years.

Documented and undocumented workers participated in this labor upsurge regardless of their legal status or lack of it. That simply reflected the situation in their families and communities, where people with and without papers are all mixed together. As a result of these battles many labor organizers began to see this upsurge as a way to rebuild their unions. They acquired a basic understanding of immigration law in order to help workers defend themselves against it. Unions and immigrant-rights organizations began distributing business cards advising workers of their rights when stopped by the Border Patrol, with a phone number for workers to call on the back. In union meetings they welcomed questions about legal status to show that the union was really committed to defending undocumented as well as legal immigrants. They translated leaflets and contracts into Spanish.

Defending the undocumented became a survival issue, because employers routinely used the threat of immigration raids to intimidate workers. Employer sanctions provided a legal justification for mass firings when undocumented workers began to organize. The National Labor Relations Act, which calls for reinstatement and back pay for workers fired for organizing, couldn't be enforced for the undocumented. In the *Sure-Tan* decision, the National Labor Relations Board held in 1984 that employers couldn't be forced to reinstate undocumented workers fired for union activity, since this would force them to violate employer sanctions. Then, in the 2002 *Hoffman Plastic* decision, the Supreme Court said that employers didn't have to pay back pay to those workers either. In theory, undocumented workers still had the right to organize. In practice, employers couldn't be punished for violating it. William Gould, African American legal scholar and NLRB chair under President Clinton, concluded that "there is a basic conflict" between immigration law and workers' rights, in which the courts gave immigration law priority.

Unions were forced to look for tactics to pressure employers to rehire fired workers, remain neutral during organizing drives, and sign union contracts without depending on the NLRB process. Today these strategies have become the bread and butter of most organizing drives, but they had their birth in the cauldron of labor wars in Los Angeles, the San Francisco Bay Area, and other areas where immigrants shook unions loose from their cold war past. Workers came from El Salvador or Guatemala, for instance, believing that the labor movement is a social movement, not just an insurance scheme in which workers pay dues for better wages and benefits. Others developed radical ideas in the United Farm Workers' strikes and boycotts of the 1960s and 1970s, also a movement of immigrants. New ideas and tactics and an increased militancy helped ground unions in local communities and made them more democratic. Changing demographics were not a cultural or economic threat, but a source of new strength.

The Story of Ana Martinez

Ana Martinez was one of those who helped give unions new life. For six weeks in 1993 she lived under a tree at the corner of Ninth and East End in Pomona. There, immigrant workers from Mexico and Central America had gone on strike against Pomona's largest factory, Cal Spas. Working for the United Electrical Workers (UE), Martinez helped them run their picket line. Her home under the tree was the end of a road she'd started in Ilopango, in her native El Salvador, fifteen years earlier. There she'd become a factory worker, a union activist, and a refugee fleeing for her life. Her odyssey had taken her through poverty and desperation in Los Angeles, and finally to Ninth Street as a union organizer, still dedicated to the ideals that forced her from her native land.

Cal Spas' products are symbols of the good life in Southern California. Their hot tubs conjure up images of tranquil evenings in the breeze on the patio, relaxing in warm soothing water. But the 530 workers who labored in the sprawling plant were far removed from suburban homes with patios. Earning close to minimum wage, with no holidays or vacations, most lived in cramped Pomona tenements.

The five-thousand-dollar price of a spa represented months of take-home pay for the workers whose labor produced it but who lived their lives on the bottom. They were the ones who created the luxury goods they could never hope to own, cleaned the hotels where they could never stay, and nailed up the drywall in the dream homes where they would never live. In Pomona, Martinez found a world with gulfs between rich and poor not so different from Ilopango. Immigrants furnished the labor for the attractive Southern California lifestyle. But they lived their lives in the slums hidden at the edge of the suburbs.

When workers at Cal Spas described the conditions in their factory, they talked about life on the edge. Alfredo Carabez, who helped start the union-organizing effort, said, "We had no paid holidays, no vacations, and no healthcare for our families. Our supervisors told us that we had to work twelve- and sixteen-hour days for months, and we were glad to get the overtime because our wages were so low we couldn't live on eight hours' pay." After Martinez and other UE organizers helped set up the strike kitchen under the tree, and strikers began cooking a hot meal for the picket line every day, they discovered it was the only food many had to eat. "They were tired of enduring those conditions," Martinez says. In her, the workers found someone who could help change things.

"I began as a worker like them, in 1974 in El Salvador," she remembered. She was nineteen. Along with a thousand others, Martinez worked for Texas Instruments, a giant U.S. electronics company that owned a plant in Ilopango, on the capital city's outskirts. The women on the lines there assembled computer chips, spending long hours at benches peering through microscopes, attaching tiny wires to integrated circuits. In 1976 her first son was born, and then another in 1978. The pressure of growing families led the young women on the lines to begin organizing a union. "Ninety-five percent of us were mothers, and we had no one to take care of our children," Martinez recalled. "We were risking our eyes working with the microscopes, and had problems with the chemicals." Their fledgling union made demands for wage increases, nurseries for the kids, and measures to halt the deterioration in their eyesight.

Those were dangerous years for unions in El Salvador. By 1980, many unionists had been killed by the growing death squads, bands of killers organized by the country's conservative elite to stop movements for social change. Two workers from the Texas Instruments plant were among those murdered. In response, Salvadoran unions called a general strike to protest. "On that day I was working in the calculator-assembly department. I kept asking myself what I was going to do, and how I was going to get my department to stop. I thought that if I went to each person and said 'Stop,' they would be too afraid to do it. My union *compañeros* didn't tell me how—they just gave me my assignment and left it up to me to find a way. Finally, I talked to the mechanic who worked on my line, and asked him where the buttons were that turned the machines off. I prepared my coworkers, and told them that at eight a.m. there would be a general strike, and that the whole country was ready. When the moment came, I pressed the right button and all the machines stopped. We looked around and saw that the workers in the other departments had stopped too. It was very emotional, and very scary, because the army came into the factory. They took the manager away in a helicopter. The head of plant security walked down the rows of machines, a pistol in each hand. Outside the factory, two workers from the printing plant next door, who'd come over to help, were taken by the soldiers and shot."

The day after, Martinez and her friends from Texas Instruments went to their union office to hold a memorial service. The army arrived and arrested everyone. "They shot up the office, and I don't remember if it was one or two *compañeros* who died that day," she recalled. Martinez was held by the soldiers for hours, and fired from her job for her role in organizing the protest. Three days later a death squad sent by Army colonel Roberto d'Aubuisson entered the national cathedral in San Salvador and assassinated Archbishop Oscar Romero. The civil war had begun.

Martinez called her union a "revolutionary union" because it had a vision of larger changes beyond the problems in the plant. "We learned not just to fight for our union in the factory, but for a more just society," she explained. "We learned that we had to control our own union, because we, the members, were the union." Her activity, however, not only cost her her job, but it made her a target. She decided to leave the country. "We had one foot on earth and one foot in the grave. We didn't know if the next day we would wake up alive or what would happen. It was a horrible trauma that marked all of my generation which passed through these things."

Martinez felt guilty about her decision to leave. "I wasn't strong enough to face the ultimate consequences," she said. "I had small children, and I was afraid for them. Others were hard enough to be able to say, 'I'm here, and here I'll stay.' Many made that decision, and many died. I thought I was more concerned with myself than with the struggle of our people. I called myself a coward."

The strike took place March 21, 1980. She left the country on April 21.

Martinez had to leave her children behind, hoping to bring them later. She arrived in Los Angeles, and not long afterward her sister followed. Together they helped each other through the hardest years. In her first job, sewing on piece rate in a garment factory, she made only five dollars a day. "I thought, My God, I'll never be able to live here." Then she got a job as a servant in a home. Cooking and cleaning for a family, she earned more than she could as a sewing machine operator, but still hardly enough to eat. "I went around taking all my clothes and possessions with me," she remembered. "I would go to the house of friends, and they would give me a place to sleep. Sometimes I would sleep in a closet. Sometimes there were five of us sleeping in the hallway."

She began to get jobs cleaning houses, but that had its dangers for women. She explained: "We were in a strange country where we didn't understand the language, and our culture was very different. When people offered to help us, we didn't know if they were honest or not, and we had such a great need to survive. Sometimes men, really bad men, would tell us they knew where there was work, and they would take us there. I had friends who were tricked by men who said they would find them work, who raped them. It was so dangerous, and we were so poor."

Martinez kept looking for other Salvadorans who were involved in supporting the movement back home, and finally met someone handing out leaflets in the street. She began to help. Eventually friends organized a tour for her to talk to unions in Los Angeles and Silicon Valley, recounting her experiences as an electronics worker, asking help for the unions back home. After four years of saving every penny, she found a way to bring her children to the United States.

Martinez's attempt to reunite her family in the United States was bitter, however, and ultimately unsuccessful. Her sons stayed with her for five years, living near MacArthur Park downtown. Then she sent them back to live with their father in El Salvador. "I tried to ensure the education they got was good for them," she explained. "But I began to see that Los Angeles wasn't a healthy place for them to grow up. I could teach them good values at home, but how could I control the corruption they were exposed to outside? The gangs, the drugs, how? Our neighborhood, in the center of the city, was a lost and corrupt place. I don't think any parent could do it."

As she visited union offices throughout Southern California, seeking help for unions back home, she began to make friends. David Johnson, an international representative for the UE, asked her to talk to workers at a local electronics plant. "I sympathized with the UE," she says, "because it seemed more like the unions in El Salvador, like a rank-and-file union run by the members. Some leaders of other unions I met didn't have much humility or modesty. When I went to their luxurious offices, I felt like I was in an office a boss has in El Salvador." The UE's office was a storefront in Compton.

As an organizer she had more success. Organizing unions in Los Angeles wasn't nearly as dangerous as it had been in Ilopango. Nevertheless, fitting in with the UE wasn't easy either. Martinez had been organizational secretary for her union at the Texas Instruments plant. She was used to a very disciplined way of working, and the UE's freewheeling style seemed chaotic to her. "I didn't find a plan. I was just told, 'We're going to sign up some workers,' and we went and did it." When she pressed for more organized methods, "they thought I had a swelled head. I think they even wanted to fire me, but I told them, 'If I was here for fun, I'd tell you to keep your job.' And they gave me a chance."

In the 1990s the UE was very active in organizing immigrant industrial workers. During the cold war it had been one of the few that advocated for immigrant rights, and its leader in Los Angeles, Humberto Camacho, was a hero among younger organizers. In one organizing drive in the early 1980s at the Kraco car-radio factory, the union and workers threatened to strike if the owner cooperated with immigration agents. For many years, more than half its organizers in Southern California were born outside the United States.

Martinez discovered that workers identified with her because of her experiences in El Salvador and as a worker in Los Angeles. She participated in more than a dozen UE campaigns, but said the strike at Cal Spas was the hardest. Alfredo Carabez, one of the first workers to join the union, was fired, and a few days later beaten up in front of the plant. Another union committee member was taken from the factory in handcuffs by the Pomona police, called by the company. Charges against him were later dropped. Outraged over Carabez's beating, workers struck the plant that June, and the company locked the strikers out in retaliation. Cal Spas workers then organized a boycott of company retail stores.

The workers had few economic resources, were often unaware of their legal rights, and had problems with their immigration status. But they tried to turn all that to their advantage. "The fact that many people lived together in the same house helped them support each other," Martinez argued. "While their economic situation was really bad, those same conditions united them and made them want to fight." Cal Spas workers went into Pomona's Latino community to explain the reasons for the strike, and to try to stop the company from recruiting strikebreakers. They organized a large march through the barrio with a rally at a city park. Car caravans wound their way through the neighborhood almost every day. "The strikers looked at the community as a source of support and protection," Martinez said.

Their ideas often came from their immigrant experience. During a legal strike in Mexico or El Salvador, labor law says the company must shut its factory down. Strikebreaking is prohibited. "In El Salvador, of course, the government would say that all our strikes were illegal," Martinez explained. "But because we believed that they were legal, we would ourselves take steps to close the factory down when we were on strike. Many workers come to the U.S. from Latin America and the Philippines with this same experience."

Eliseo Medina, vice president of the Service Employees International Union and a former farmworker leader, agreed: "When you come from a country where they shoot you for being a striker, getting fired from your job doesn't seem so bad. Some immigrants have a much more militant history than we do, and the more militant they are, the more the union can do."

"Workers would say to each other, 'If they fire me, I can get the same minimum wage somewhere else,'" Martinez added. "Conditions are the same everywhere. The factories where you find immigrants are the ones where you find the lowest wages, the worst conditions, and the worst treatment. And where there are workers who have no documents things are the worst of all."

In the end, the strikers' lack of resources forced them back to work after six weeks on the picket line. But Martinez didn't see it as a defeat. "In Pomona there are a mountain of factories like that. The fire will spring up in other places," she predicted. But after years of work for the union, she was still unsure about her own future. Was she a Salvadoran in exile, thinking of eventually returning, or had she become a permanent part of Los Angeles? "I don't know if I should go back or not," she said. "Like many others, we came, we learned, we got involved. We found that we could be useful here. But that doesn't help me see what my own destiny will be."

Immigration Enforcement Becomes a Weapon to Stop Unions

As Martinez, Ochoa, and Camorlinga led immigrant workers in strikes, they battled not only firings and deportations but indecision and conflict in the labor movement itself. Having supported employer sanctions in 1986, many labor leaders questioned whether organizing immigrants was a good idea.

U.S. unions have been in crisis since the Vietnam War, and by 2006 they represented only 12 percent of U.S. workers, down from 35 percent in the early 1950s. To maintain that percentage, given the growth of the workforce and structural changes eliminating many jobs, unions have to organize hundreds of thousands of workers a year. In 2007 membership increased for the first time in a quarter century, according to the Bureau of Labor Statistics, when unions organized 310,000 new members, mostly in California. To grow by just 1 percent would require hundreds of thousands more, and former AFL-CIO organizing director Kirk Adams said in 1996 that unions really needed a million workers in the pipeline, "because of the noise that creates."

Who, in the U.S. workforce, actively wants to join the labor movement? For many unions, immigrant workers have become at least part of the answer. "I am convinced that as the labor movement is the best hope for immigrants, so are immigrants the best hope of the labor movement," said Eliseo Medina. But as unions have sought to organize those immigrants, employer sanctions became one of their greatest obstacles.

The record of firings and broken organizing drives is long. Even as the first President Bush took office, three years after sanctions went into effect, employers had already found them an effective antiunion tool. In 1990 Shine Building Maintenance in Silicon Valley faced an organizing drive by immigrant janitors. The company told its workers they had to provide new documentation verifying their legal status. When workers couldn't produce it, they were terminated. The check eliminated prounion workers, yet the company was protected against federal charges that it had illegally terminated workers for union activity.

The tactic of a company informing on its own workforce received a legal blessing in a case two years later, in 1992. Workers at STC Knitting in Long Island City, New York, began an organizing drive with the International Ladies' Garment Workers Union (now part of UNITE HERE). Just before the representation election, the company attorney wrote to the Immigration and Naturalization Service telling the agency that undocumented workers were employed in the sweatshop. The INS conducted a check of the I-9 forms on which new hires have to declare their immigration status. Ten workers were arrested, including Gloria Montero, an active member of the union committee. When Montero appealed the use of immigration enforcement to terrorize workers and remove union supporters, a federal court ruled it a legal application of employer sanctions.

Organizing efforts among immigrant workers came up against the same problem frequently under the Clinton administration, which made the workplace its focus of immigration enforcement. According to then INS commissioner Doris Meissner, "Work is the incentive that brings illegal immigrants into our country." Preventing workers from entering the United States without visas, therefore, depended on removing them from the workplace in a strategy called "interior enforcement," enforcing immigration law away from the border.

Under labor and congressional pressure the Clinton administration was forced to agree to an "operating instruction" intended to deter immigration enforcement in the middle of labor disputes. But it often proved ineffective. In 1996 in San Leandro, California, Mediacopy, a video-reproduction company, used threats about immigration status to terrorize workers before a union election and reduce the number of eligible voters. That December, immigration agents used I-9 forms to identify undocumented workers. Although the INS knew workers were organizing a union, a major raid followed in January, in which 99 people were deported. Local 6 of the International Longshore and Warehouse Union nevertheless filed for a labor board election, but a month before the voting, Mediacopy announced it had received an INS order to verify documents for another 166 people. Many workers simply disappeared, while those who remained were convinced another raid was imminent. The union lost the election. The labor board eventually ordered Mediacopy to bargain anyway because of the threats, but after signing a union contract the company closed the plant, laid off the workers, and moved.

A year later in San Leandro, workers sorting recycled trash for Waste Management Inc. organized a wildcat work stoppage over safety issues, occupying the company lunchroom. Three weeks later, the INS showed up, audited the I-9 forms, and eventually deported eight workers. In nearby office parks about five hundred members of the Service Employees International Union Local 1877 lost their jobs when two large janitorial contractors were targeted for similar checks. The SEIU was preparing for coordinated bargaining for the first time, and the I-9 checks removed many leaders.

The INS developed new relationships with other government agencies. A memorandum of understanding with the Department of Labor required federal inspectors looking for minimum-wage and overtime violations to review I-9 forms and report discrepancies that could lead to deportations. A series of raids in Los Angeles garment sweatshops, Operation Buttonhole, came in response to tip-offs from DOL inspectors. Similar raids followed efforts by the Korean Immigrant Workers Advocates to enforce wage and hour laws in LA's Korean restaurants. At a Staten Island laundry plant, Launderall, employees earning $300 for a seventy-two- to eighty-hour week called in DOL inspectors. After workers claimed $159,000 in back wages the INS conducted a raid.

Finally, the Yale Law School Workers' Rights Project and the American Civil Liberties Union filed charges under NAFTA's labor side agreement against the DOL-INS memorandum of understanding. Explained Shayne Stevenson, student director of the Yale group, "If no one can complain about slave wages, sweatshop owners have a green light to ignore minimum-wage and overtime laws." An embarrassed administration then drafted a softer memorandum, but interagency cooperation didn't stop. The Los Angeles INS district began sharing information with agents from DOL, the Internal Revenue Service, the state Department of Insurance, and even the federal Bureau of Land Management, in a Worker Exploitation Taskforce. Workers with no immigration papers were "protected" from exploitation by losing their jobs.

The systematic use of Social Security no-match letters also began under the Clinton administration as part of "internal enforcement." In the late 1990s, employers were flooded with them. In Sacramento, California, SEIU Local 1877 accused building service contractors of using the letters to terminate high-seniority workers, in order to avoid paying costly new medical benefits. In New York and New Jersey thousands of immigrant asbestos-removal workers reorganized their industry, and revitalized the Laborers' International Union in 1996. Two years later contractors sent the union a no-match list including all the leaders of the union drive, saying they'd no longer hire them. Another Laborers' International Union drive, at New Jersey's KTI Recycling Co., was lost after the employer distributed a no-match list to workers.

The largest I-9 check came in Washington State in 1999. After checking the forms, the INS questioned the legal status of seventeen hundred workers in thirteen apple-packing houses. Over five hundred were eventually fired. For three years prior, those Yakima Valley sheds were the focus of an industry-wide organizing drive by the Teamsters Union. According to lead organizer Lorraine Scheer, mass firings created an atmosphere of terror, intimidating documented and undocumented alike. One employee, Mary Mendez, said an antiunion consultant for Stemilt fruit company told workers, "With a union, the INS is going to be around." The drive was broken.

That year, the INS audited the personnel records of more than one thousand employees of the Bear Creek Production Co., the world's largest rose grower, in Bakersfield, California. The INS demanded that the company terminate three hundred. Bear Creek was the largest company organized by the United Farm Workers in a decade. UFW president Arturo Rodriguez denounced the INS: "These workers have been here fifteen, twenty, twenty-five years. They have houses and families, and have paid taxes for years. Their kids are in school. They're members of their communities. But the INS demanded they demonstrate again their status in this country, and they lost their jobs."

In the heart of downtown Los Angeles, workers at a small furniture factory had the same experience. The seventy employees at RCR Classic Designs on Avalon Boulevard voted for the garment union UNITE (prior to its merger with HERE) by a 33–21 margin in 1998. Then they started getting called into the office. "The secretary told me I had to show my green card, along with my ID and Social Security," said Salvador Ruiz, a union activist. "I refused. I gave her my address and telephone number, and told her I didn't think what she was asking for was legal." Other workers weren't as brave. RCR claimed its interviews were required by the INS, although workers said they'd never seen any request. When Ruiz was hired there seventeen years earlier, right after getting to LA, "no one ever asked me for papers then. They didn't care until now."

The company's demands couldn't have come at a worse time. After the union election, workers had put together a proposal for wage increases and other improvements. Then they began trying to get owner Mike Cruz to bargain. But after the company started demanding that workers re-verify their immigration status, union support dropped dramatically. "Now people won't meet with us," Ruiz said. Once negotiations started, "we couldn't agree on anything." It was a simple tactic. Since workers couldn't pressure the company to raise hourly wages above the seven to eight dollars workers were earning, Cruz's profits didn't suffer, even with a union in the plant. "Immigration law is a tool of the employers," declared UNITE regional manager Cristina Vasquez, herself a former worker in LA sweatshops. "Companies use it as a weapon to keep workers unorganized, and the INS helps them."

Operation Vanguard

The biggest immigration-enforcement operation under Clinton, perhaps the biggest ever, began in December 1998 in Nebraska, when the INS subpoenaed the personnel records for every employee of every meatpacking plant in the state. Agents compared the employment information they supplied, including Social Security numbers, with the national Social Security database and other related records. Concentrating on forty plants with a workforce of 24,310 people, they sifted out 4,762 names. To every worker, agents mailed a letter requiring them to come in for an interview at the plant on a specified day. In Madison, a tiny town in central Nebraska, 258 of the IBP plant's 1,051 employees got the letters. One of them was Concepción Vargas.

Vargas grew up in Reynosa, Mexico, across the river from Texas, and followed a migrant path pioneered by her brother Alfredo. After receiving immigration amnesty in 1986, he set off across the country and wound up in IBP's huge pork-processing plant (now Tyson Foods).

He began working on the line for eight dollars an hour, sleeping in the park and his car until he saved enough to rent a place. Alfredo brought his sister-in-law, who brought her brother Doroteo, Concepción's husband. "It's like a chain," Vargas explained. "First one person comes, and then they bring someone else. And we all are looking for something better because the situation at home is so bad we can't survive. So three months after Doroteo left for Madison, he came back and got my daughter and me."

But Doroteo and Concepción Vargas had a problem—they couldn't get into the plant without a Social Security card and an ID with a picture on it. And while Doroteo did what work he could fixing cars, their four-year-old daughter began to get sick from the unaccustomed cold. They had no money for a doctor and stayed awake in bed all night, listening to her cough. "Doroteo didn't want me to get a job, but we made an agreement," Concepción remembers. "We would both try to get papers, and whoever got them first would go to work. In the end, that was me." A friend sold them a birth certificate and Social Security card for $650. "When you're Mexican here, and you have family, they know who to go to for papers," she explains. Her friend helped her to go to the motor vehicle department to get a picture ID. "The day it came in the mail, I went down to IBP and they accepted me right away."

In Reynosa her business administration certificate had qualified her for a position training other workers in a factory. In Madison, for six dollars an hour, she worked on a line processing bacon, ham, and cooked meat. "They put me to work in a freezing cold room," Vargas recalled. "I had to strip plastic bags off big legs of meat, frozen and hard as rocks. I put them in a big vat, and after there were a hundred or so, we filled the vat with water to thaw them." Wearing only a light sweater, she began to freeze. "The work was hard, and I felt humiliated. Finally, I got so cold I asked permission from the supervisor to go to the bathroom. When I left the line, I wasn't planning to come back. I went upstairs to the bathrooms, but my daughter's face appeared before me. I heard her coughing the way she had all night. I remembered how much we needed the money. I didn't go to the bathroom, and I didn't leave either. I just stood there, crying. Finally, I went back to work."

Manuel Flores also got a letter at IBP. Since 1992, he had been trying to relocate his family from a barrio named Paradise, in Tulancingo, Hidalgo, a town in central Mexico. There he was a truck driver, but his wages could only put rice, beans, and milk on the table for his wife and four kids, and pay a little rent besides. "It just wasn't enough for us to live," he said. Over seven years he brought his family to live in Madison, returning to Hidalgo twice but each time coming back because conditions at home were even worse. The family was divided for many years, with some children living in Mexico while Manuel and his wife, Lydia, tried to get established in Nebraska. The year before Operation Vanguard, their five-year-old son Mario got sick in Hidalgo, before they could bring him to the United States. Although they rushed back, "there was nothing we could do for him and he died," Lydia said.

In Madison the Flores family lived in one of several apartments carved out of an old home just off the main street. The original living room, large and graceful and lined with windows, was reminiscent of a time when a comfortable middle-class white family occupied the whole house. The Flores family filled it with two sofas and draped them with blankets to give all their children a place to sleep.

At first Manuel worked in nearby Norfolk using the papers belonging to a friend at IBP. At the Beef America plant in Norfolk there were a lot of injuries because the lines ran so fast—about one thousand animals an hour. "The supervisors would shout obscenities at us to make us work faster," he remembered. "Eventually I got fired because they found out my papers were no good," he explained. "Then another friend told me he could get me other papers. So I paid him two hundred dollars and he gave me a birth certificate and a Social Security card, which I've been using ever since. Today they'd cost me a thousand dollars." As soon as he could, he got a job at IBP in Madison. "In May, I got a letter from *la migra* and my supervisor said I was on the list. A lot of people were on it—even the supervisor. She said I had ten days to fix my papers or leave. I worked until the fifteenth, my last day at IBP."

After losing his meatpacking job, Flores found a few days' work, but not enough to pay the family's expenses. "I'm really scared," he said a few months later. "I was making four hundred and sixty dollars a week at IBP—ten ten an hour, working six days. We're paying three hundred thirty a month rent, our food bill is a hundred and sixty a week, and I still have to send money home for my children and family there. We have nothing to fall back on. I'm really desperate, but I don't want to go back to Mexico. I don't know how we'll live there either. We weren't doing anything bad to anyone. I'm just trying to support my family. If I don't work with bad documents, how can I work? We can't get green cards [legal residence permits]—if we could, we would."

Prying loose people like Flores and Vargas from their meatpacking jobs became the focal point of the Clinton administration's effort to end undocumented immigration. To INS district director Mark Reed, the Vargas and Flores families were the enemy, and he referred to them as criminal aliens. More liberal advocates within the administration viewed Operation Vanguard as a plan to punish employers by denying them access to an undocumented workforce they exploited mercilessly. But there was no way to punish the employers without punishing the workers first. In fact, employers felt relatively little pain, despite loud complaints in sympathetic newspapers. The real impact was felt by workers themselves, and by their efforts to organize.

The Farmland pork plant in Iowa was one of the few targeted outside of Nebraska. Dozens of local families left home and camped out in the county park twelve miles outside of town for a week, fearing the INS would pick them up for deportation. In Madison, Vargas said, "There was no one drinking in the bars or shopping in the stores here—so many people didn't have paychecks." In Omaha, activists had been organizing workers inside local nonunion plants, and the leaders of that effort were wiped out by the raid. Sergio Sosa, a Guatemalan community organizer for Omaha Together One Community (OTOC), had been patiently meeting with packinghouse workers, looking for cultural threads to unify a fearful workforce. "We were trying to find natural leaders among the workers themselves," he said, "and slowly put together a base in the plants and organize collective actions to change conditions. Operation Vanguard gave the companies a big gift. Almost all our leaders had to find jobs elsewhere.

"I don't think it's impossible to organize the undocumented," he declared. "They're often forced to be transient, so organizing has to go on constantly. But they have some tremendous talent, and they're very courageous, creating a life out of absolutely nothing." Two years later Sosa and OTOC helped the United Food and Commercial Workers (UFCW) win a successful campaign at Omaha's biggest packinghouse.

High-profile immigration raids in meatpacking failed to raise wages, however. According to the Bureau of Labor Statistics, in the year of Operation Vanguard the average beef and pork slaughter wages were $9.03 and $9.01 per hour respectively. The average hourly wage in U.S. manufacturing generally was a dollar an hour below meatpacking in 1979. By 1998 the manufacturing wage had risen four dollars above meatpacking, to $13.17.

According to Mark Nemitz of UFCW Local 440 at Farmland, union wages declined $1.54 to $9.00 an hour in 1982, after plant closures, restructuring, bitter strikes, and the destruction of the old industry-wide union contracts. Immigration enforcement did not increase those wages in subsequent years. Instead, raids helped keep downward pressure on wages by making workers fearful and vulnerable. The base rate in the Farmland plant during Operation Vanguard was $9.70, just 70¢ above what it had been sixteen years before. Meanwhile, Farmland had done very well, expanding from four plants to fourteen. Bill Buckholz, who headed the UFCW local at the Morrell pork plant in Sioux City, said the wage there had dropped from $11.42 in 1983 to $10.00.

Both Buckholz's and Nemitz's locals tried to organize nonunion plants in their communities. In both cases, they said, threats of immigration raids turned the tide against the union at the last moment. Although Nebraska and Iowa are right-to-work states where union membership is not compulsory, both locals had over a 90 percent membership in the union plants, signing up documented and undocumented workers alike. Meetings and documents were translated into Spanish.

Low wages, however, meant that for over twenty years young people in Iowa and Nebraska, who could find comparable or better pay elsewhere, didn't go into the packinghouses. Instead of raising wages to attract them, meatpackers sent teams to Los Angeles and other immigrant communities. They placed advertisements on radio stations along the Mexican border, and even sent buses to pick up recruits as they crossed over. "They're bringing people from El Paso, Durango, Zacatecas, and Chihuahua," said Roberto Ceja, a worker at Nebraska Beef's Omaha plant. "The companies are sending people out everywhere offering jobs."

Immigration enforcement did not stop this recruitment or open up jobs to long-term residents of local communities. Omaha's black neighborhoods, which supplied a large percentage of the city's meatpacking workforce in the 1950s, supplies just a tiny percentage today. But Operation Vanguard did not produce jobs for African Americans. "Operation Vanguard wants to drive the undocumented out of meatpacking," Nemitz said, "but it will just drive people further underground, and make it harder for them to organize. If they were legalized, or sanctions were ended, they would be less vulnerable."

Operation Vanguard ended after the Social Security Administration grew uneasy at the use of its records and told the INS it would no longer give the agency access. Without the SSA database, it was impossible for the INS to sift out the names of possibly undocumented people. Operation Vanguard was used, however, by the INS's Mark Reed and others, to produce political pressure for their immigration-reform proposals. Such use of immigration enforcement was not unprecedented. In the early 1980s, before the Immigration Reform and Control Act was passed, the INS conducted a long series of highly publicized raids called Operation Jobs. Agents would swoop down on a factory, and anyone found without documents would be deported.

Then agents would go to the local unemployment office and take workers, with reporters tagging along, to fill the jobs they'd "created." The campaign was intended to convince the public and Congress that employer sanctions were needed to create jobs for citizens.

Nine years after Operation Vanguard, Homeland Security secretary Michael Chertoff conducted similar actions. While the Bush immigration-reform proposal was debated in Congress, agents raided six Swift & Co. meatpacking plants, arresting thirteen hundred workers. A wave of other highly publicized raids took place around the country. Chertoff told the media that deportations would show Congress the need for "stronger border security, effective interior enforcement, and a temporary-worker program." Bush wanted, he said, "a program that would allow businesses that need foreign workers, because they can't otherwise satisfy their labor needs, to be able to get those workers in a regulated program." After the Senate failed to pass the reform bill in August 2007, Chertoff and Commerce Secretary Gutierrez proposed to make no-match firings mandatory because Congress had "failed to act." Then Gutierrez announced that the administration would relax restrictions on H-2 guest-worker programs to help employers replace the fired workers.

Some things never change.

Immigrant Workers Ask Labor: "Which Side Are You On?"

For over a decade, immigration activists in the labor movement opposed AFL-CIO support for employer sanctions, arguing that instead of trying to keep immigrant workers out of the workforce, unions should try to organize them. For many years that argument was far from the mainstream. But increased interest in organizing, the simultaneous growth of the INS workplace-enforcement program, and a more powerful voice among immigrants in unions finally led to change inside the AFL-CIO.

Debate in the early 1990s in union meetings and conventions in California, New York, and Chicago led the two garment unions (which later merged in UNITE HERE) and the Service Employees International Union to call for the repeal of sanctions. The California Labor Federation followed, and immigrant-rights organizations began to cooperate with the federation on programs like its annual day for lobbying the state legislature. Starting in 1997, a group of union organizers, most of whom were veterans of campaigns among immigrant workers, began meeting in the San Francisco Bay Area. They were joined by activists in the Northern California Coalition for Immigrant Rights and the National Network for Immigrant and Refugee Rights, formed after the passage of IRCA in 1986. Together they formed the Labor Immigrant Organizers Network (LION).

LION organized opposition to immigration raids at local companies like Mediacopy, and supported organizing drives like that at the Berkeley Marina Radisson Hotel, where prounion workers were threatened with no-match letters. LION mounted a series of demonstrations against the Social Security Administration protesting no-match letters, and called for the repeal of employer sanctions. In 1999 LION activists wrote a resolution asking the AFL-CIO to take a similar position. After the Alameda County Central Labor Council passed it, other councils from coast to coast adopted it and sent it to the national convention, set for Los Angeles. When it began to seem likely that it would lead to an acrimonious debate on the floor, AFL-CIO staff negotiated a process they hoped would avoid confrontation. When the resolution finally was brought before the delegates that October, an orchestrated procession of national union leaders joined the call for the repeal of sanctions.

Speakers emphasized that the demographics of the U.S. workplace had changed dramatically, with millions of immigrant workers in meatpacking, manufacturing, healthcare, and construction. If the intention of employer sanctions was to reduce undocumented immigration, they'd clearly failed, said John Wilhelm, president of the Hotel Employees and Restaurant Employees (HERE, prior to its merger with UNITE). Further, he declared, his own union's support for sanctions in 1986 was a big mistake: "Those who came before us, who built this labor movement in the Great Depression, in strikes in rubber and steel and hotels, they didn't say 'Let me see your papers' to the workers in those industries. They said, 'Which side are you on?' And immigrant workers today have the right to ask of us the same question. Which side are we on?" He brought the house down.

Frank Hurt, president of the Bakery, Confectionary, and Tobacco Workers, chaired the committee in 1986 that recommended supporting sanctions. Acknowledging that they had had no positive effect, he said, "Instead, they arm employers with additional weapons, often wielded with governmental complicity...They pit worker against worker, ally against friend, driving wedges between us when we should stand united." Immigrant leaders like Eliseo Medina joined Chicanos born in the United States, like the UFW's Rodriguez and AFL-CIO executive vice president Linda Chavez-Thompson. No one spoke in opposition. The following February the AFL-CIO Executive Council adopted a position calling for replacing employer sanctions with labor-law enforcement, for protecting the organizing rights of all workers, for a new immigration amnesty, and for continuing the immigration policy based on family reunification. The AFL-CIO had adopted a position opposing guest-worker programs in previous years.

The change at the Los Angeles convention, reversing a nativist position held since the cold war, was a victory for racial equality and inclusion. Two ways of thinking about immigrants have always contested within the U.S. labor movement. In one, unions sought to restrict the labor supply, trying to maintain control over the labor market and higher wages by excluding workers. Unions acted as clubs for a privileged few, defending only the interests of their own members. Racism, sexism, and anti-immigrant sentiment excluded other workers. These ideas made AFL-CIO support for employer sanctions acceptable.

In Los Angeles, labor took a big step toward a very different vision, in which unions seek to become part of social movements, trying to organize everybody. A century ago the Industrial Workers of the World often held union meetings in a dozen languages. The CIO mounted checkerboard marches, in which black and white workers alternated in line, to oppose race riots in the 1930s. The AFL-CIO's new position on immigration followed that tradition, based on the idea that labor should fight for the interests of all workers.

Yet in many ways labor support for immigrant rights was not based on ideology or morality, but on pragmatic considerations. Immigrants today are the backbone of organizing drives from the Smithfield pork plant in North Carolina to Houston janitors and Cintas industrial-laundry workers. The unions that are growing are mostly those that appreciate the willingness of many immigrants to fight and join. As a result, immigrants have gained a growing base in union leadership, and now speak out on political questions from the war in Iraq to immigration and labor-law reform.

This has not been an easy process. Often, newly organized immigrants found themselves members of established organizations that wanted their dues and numerical strength, but not necessarily their participation. Immigrant members have expectations, demanding membership meetings and contracts in their own languages and the right to vote on important decisions. After the victory of Justice for Janitors in Los Angeles, a bitter struggle broke out when a section of the union's new immigrant membership ran a slate of candidates for union office. When they won, the old leadership refused to step down and the local was eventually placed in trusteeship. Similar struggles took place in other unions, as the influx of members with a different culture, and often with a very activist experience, wanted power.

Adopting a pro-immigrant position at the AFL-CIO convention did not change the thinking of many union members and leaders. Especially in unions where immigrants are a small minority, leaders there often see immigration as a threat. In 2006 the International Brotherhood of Electrical Workers invited the anti-immigrant broadcaster Lou Dobbs to speak at its national convention, where his tirades rivaled James Sensenbrenner's.

The changed position of the AFL-CIO was generally greeted enthusiastically by immigrant communities and immigrant-rights organizations that previously viewed unions as hostile or uninterested. "The change by the labor movement made a whole new discussion possible," said Victor Narro. "Now we have a labor movement that's on the side of immigrants, rather than one bent on trying to stop immigration, as we had in 1986."

At the convention, the federation launched hearings to gather testimony about the ways immigration law had undermined workers' rights, and many labor and community activists saw this as an opportunity to build a new labor/community/religious coalition to change immigration law. As the hearings moved across the United States it was impossible to ignore the immense support they generated among immigrants by their call for amnesty. At the last hearing in Los Angeles, more than sixteen thousand people poured into the city's Sports Arena, chanting "Qué queremos? Amnistía, sin condiciónes!"—"What do we want? Unconditional amnesty!" Thousands more gathered outside, unable to get in through the doors.

In addition to unions, the LA hearing was sponsored by sixty churches and community organizations, from the Hermandad Mexicana Nacional (the National Mexican Brotherhood) to the Catholic Archdiocese. "Labor can open some doors," said Miguel Contreras, the first Latino secretary of the Los Angeles County Labor Federation, "but we need community allies and a grassroots base. We have to build a rank-and-file movement for amnesty, and this huge turnout shows not only that it can be done, but that politicians who want the Latino vote had better take note." Bert Corona, shortly before he died, was brought to the stage in a wheelchair, honored by a labor movement whose nativist views he'd battled most of his life.

Inside the arena a procession of workers recounted horrifying experiences. Maria Sanchez described firings at the Palm Canyon Hotel in Palm Springs, after workers joined HERE. When the hotel refused to put those who were undocumented back to work, the workers, both documented and undocumented, stayed off the job until everyone was reinstated. "I lost my house and my car. I sold some of my possessions so I could survive," Sanchez declared. "But we woke up!"

Ofelia Parra, one of the five hundred fired workers in the Teamsters organizing drive in Washington State's apple-packing sheds, declared to huge applause, "We contribute to this society just like the people who have papers. We need an amnesty so we can work in peace and organize to improve conditions."

The big question was, how to get it.

In rejecting legalization, President George Bush was looking over his shoulder at the right wing of his party, especially fellow Texans Phil Gramm, Lamar Smith, and Tom DeLay. "Anything that smacks of [amnesty] we'll oppose," warned Larry Neal, spokesperson for Senator Gramm. What gave those Texans nightmares were the elections in Southern California, where the votes of new citizens, radicalized by the anti-immigrant campaigning of the state's Republican Party, swept the party out of most state offices in the late 1990s. Even noncitizens walked precincts in the first mayoral campaign of Antonio Villaraigosa in Los Angeles, and finally helped him get elected four years later. In the early 1970s Villaraigosa had been an immigrant-rights activist with Corona, and later an organizer for the teachers' union. "We called people on the phone, we went door to door," recalled Douglas Marmol, a member of HERE Local 814. "It doesn't matter where you come from. We all have rights, and we need people in office who understand and respect that."

In conservative Orange County, members of HERE Local 681 at Disneyland helped to defeat right-wing Republican "B-1 Bob" Dornan, electing in his place Democrat Loretta Sanchez. Republicans were so infuriated over losing in their political heartland that they pushed the federal government to investigate longtime immigrant-rights activist Nativo Lopez, claiming he'd registered noncitizens. Instead, the investigation revealed Republican poll watchers had tried to intimidate Latino-looking voters.

Republicans were stuck in a dilemma. The industries that provided political contributions to their party needed immigrant workers to pick crops, nail drywall, and clean hotel rooms. But immigration with legalization carried the prospect of political upheaval. Bush's answer was to portray guest-worker programs providing workers with no political rights—as a form of legalization. He paired it with increased enforcement, both to keep workers in those programs and to win over the nativist right wing of his party.

HERE president John Wilhelm, UFW president Arturo Rodriguez, and other labor leaders went to Mexico City in June 2001 to talk to President Vicente Fox. "We said we were inalterably opposed to guest-worker programs," Wilhelm said later. "We don't want any program in which a worker's immigration status is attached to their job, and where there is no realistic path to legalization." Rodriguez's position was slightly different, reflecting the union's effort to pass the AgJOBS immigration-reform act for farmworkers. He told the press, "We've made it clear that without legalization there will be no new guest-worker program or revision of the current guest-worker program."

Wilhelm called guest workers "a terrible idea." A first-ever committee on immigration and civil rights reported to HERE's summer 2001 convention that "tens of thousands of workers would be [made] hostage, and ultimately destroy wage and working conditions in the hospitality industry." Instead, the convention called for a broad legalization and citizenship program, and for repealing employer sanctions. Wilhelm argued that defeating Bush's guest-worker/enforcement proposal was possible, especially if some employer groups took an enlightened view of their own self-interest. "Some have said privately that guest workers aren't the answer, just a temporary Band-Aid," he explained in an interview. "Everyone thinks the labor shortage will get worse over the next two decades, and there's no incentive to provide training, or even English classes, to guest workers. So if we can get a significant group of employers to reject the idea, we have a shot. Short of that, I'm very fearful."

Wilhelm was right to worry. The September 11, 2001, attack on the twin towers of the World Trade Center changed the political climate completely. Immigration enforcement immediately acquired a national-security justification, while broad reform proposals were off the table. Shortly after the attacks, the Social Security Administration sent out 110,000 no-match letters. "Concerns about national security, along with the growing problem of identity theft, have caused us to accelerate our efforts," said SSA commissioner Jo Anne Barnhart. The reluctance of Social Security to cooperate in immigration enforcement, which the INS had been unable to overcome in the wake of Operation Vanguard, disappeared overnight.

In airports across the country, the newly formed Bureau of Immigration and Customs Enforcement (ICE), which replaced the old INS, conducted a highly publicized campaign called Operation Tarmac, arresting more than one thousand workers. While federal authorities admitted that none were accused of terrorist activity, U.S. Attorney Debra Yang claimed, "We now realize that we must strengthen security at our local airports in order to ensure the safety of the traveling public." How firing workers for Social Security discrepancies protected travelers was unexplained. To SEIU's Eliseo Medina, however, whose union had organized many airport workers, "these people aren't terrorists. They only want to work."

Enforcement pressure on undocumented workers helped keep wages from rising, giving national security a pro-employer impact on the labor market. One raid at Seattle's Sea-Tac international airport led to the arrest of workers at the Sky Chefs facility that prepared onboard meals for airlines, in the middle of bargaining between HERE and the company. The union claimed immigration agents disguised themselves by wearing company uniforms, called workers to an employee meeting, and picked them up. Some had worked as long as ten years there.

Unions and immigrant-rights groups spent the next two years fighting raids, deportations, indefinite detentions, and the rest of the enforcement wave. Finally, in September 2003, HERE, UNITE, SEIU, the Laborers', Teamsters, and other unions involved in organizing immigrants kicked off the Immigrant Workers Freedom Ride. Three caravans of buses, carrying workers, community activists, union staff, and supporters traveled for two weeks across the country, winding up at big rallies in Washington, D.C., and New York City.

"It was inspired by the freedom rides of the civil rights movement," Victor Narro recalled, and it included some of the original participants. "It was a post-9/11 effort to change the terms of the debate and the political climate around immigration." The ride's five demands included earned legalization with path to citizenship, labor protections, family reunification, and restoration of civil rights and liberties. "It was the beginning of getting back on the pre-9/11 road to citizenship and full civic participation," Narro said.

In the wake of the demonstration, unions began to work again on getting Congress to pass immigration-reform legislation. But after Bush won reelection in the fall of 2004, fissures developed within the labor and immigrant-rights movements over the strategy for accomplishing that goal. Three of the unions most active in the freedom ride, UNITE HERE (after a 2004 merger), SEIU, and the UFW, joined the Washington, D.C.–based coalition formed to promote comprehensive immigration reform, combining guest-worker programs, enforcement, and legalization.

This coalition sought to unite labor and corporations across class lines, based on the idea that each would get some desired reforms. Unions supporting the comprehensive reform bills argued that legalization couldn't pass a Republican Congress without employer support, and that corporations would not support bills without guest-worker programs. To attract other Republican (and even Democratic) support, expanded and harsher enforcement measures were also necessary. Often, however, to defend what was at bottom a pragmatic joining of interests, coalition members supported employer claims of labor shortages, argued that immigrants didn't want permanent-resident status, and that "smart enforcement" would avoid the abuses of the past.

The AFL-CIO continued to advocate the position adopted at the 1999 convention, and refused to support a succession of bills over the next three years, which all revolved around the same guest-worker/enforcement/legalization trade-off. In the middle of this debate, the AFL-CIO split. Those unions that were the most active in organizing immigrants argued that the federation was ineffective in requiring its affiliate unions to take painful steps to organize more workers more rapidly. They urged the consolidation of small unions, and sought to require all unions, as well as the federation, to spend a larger percentage of their budgets on well-defined organizing projects. In a rupture prior to the 2005 convention, these unions left to form the Change to Win federation.

The three unions supporting the comprehensive bills, SEIU, UNITE HERE, and the UFW, were unable to convince the other unions in Change to Win—the Teamsters, UFCW, the Carpenters, and the Laborers'—to support their reform proposals. In a letter to the *New York Times*, UFCW president Joe Hansen cautioned that "historically, guest-worker programs have led to worker mistreatment. There's every reason to believe that an expanded guest-worker program would lead to increased worker abuse at a time when the current climate is to relax, if not outright ignore, labor protections in many workplaces." For the UFCW, "a constructive immigration policy would respect and provide a legalization process for the millions of immigrant workers already contributing to our economy and society, while protecting wages and workplace protections for all workers."

Teamsters Local 952 in Orange County, heart of the anti-immigrant offensive, was one of the most active in organizing labor opposition to the bills outside the Beltway. When the mayor of Costa Mesa told the police department to begin picking up immigrants who couldn't produce visas, the union joined with the Hermandad Nacional Latinoamericano, a grassroots organization of Latino immigrants, to organize street demonstrations. Led by Patrick Kelly and Ernesto Medrano, Local 952 brought other unions and community groups to meet with Loretta Sanchez to voice opposition to the Washington consensus on reform and enforcement. Kelly and Medrano went to the Teamsters national convention, and then to a national Change to Win meeting, arguing that the comprehensive reform bill in Congress "does nothing to remove the economic incentives that unscrupulous employers have to hire and exploit immigrant workers, and fails to really address the fact that we have 11 million undocumented workers in this country contributing to our communities." The union, they said, "opposes any form of employer sanctions because they have historically resulted in 'employee sanctions' in the form of firings of workers for union organizing and discrimination practices on the job," and "opposes guest-worker legislative proposals because such modern-day 'bracero programs' create an indentured servitude status for workers."

In Washington, AFL-CIO immigration program director Ana Avendaño argued that if Congress thought there were available jobs for four hundred thousand guest workers a year (as one Senate bill proposed), immigrants coming to the United States to fill them should be given green cards, or permanent-residence visas, instead. Guest-worker programs, she said, would only expand the section of the U.S. workforce excluded from the basic labor protections of the New Deal. Eventually, she warned, employers would try to expand that exclusion beyond immigrants.

When Senator John McCain, cosponsor of one of the Senate's guest-worker plans, tried to defend it to a building-trades union audience in his home state, he was jeered when he told the assembled workers that even at fifty dollars an hour they wouldn't be willing to pick lettuce. Needless to say, he didn't actually advocate any wage guarantee for guest workers, much less fifty dollars an hour, about five times what lettuce cutters normally earn. Comparing the Senate bill proposed by Pennsylvania senator Arlen Specter to the bracero program, AFL-CIO executive vice president Chavez-Thompson said reform proposals must provide a clear path to permanent residency and enforcement of workplace standards. "There is absolutely no good reason," she declared, "why any immigrant who comes to this country prepared to work, to pay taxes, and to abide by our laws and rules should be relegated to a repressive, second-class guest-worker status."

The conflict in labor over comprehensive immigration reform was as much over conflicting ideas about alliances as it was over specific proposals. U.S. unions are tightly tied to Democratic Party politicians, in an alliance based on trading votes and money for influence. Union lobbyists are under tremendous pressure to be a player at the table when bills are written. The table at which the comprehensive immigration-reform bills were written, however, excluded alternatives to the guest-worker/enforcement/legalization compromise. Arguments of "political realism" justified a refusal to consider alternatives: it was pointless to debate what a Republican Congress would not pass.

Bills like that proposed by Congresswoman Sheila Jackson Lee were excluded from consideration because they had no guest-worker provision and challenged the idea that immigration policy should serve the needs of large corporations seeking a cheap labor supply.

In March 2006 SEIU president Andy Stern spoke to an American Bar Association meeting in Acapulco. According to the Bureau of National Affairs, "Stern said it was important to deal with proposals that are 'on-the-table' when it comes to immigration instead of backing a position that was not politically realistic. 'We support McCain-Kennedy because we want to be a player,' Stern said." Many Washington lobbyists called the effort to propose anything else "making the perfect the enemy of the good."

That approach did not succeed in passing humane immigration reform, any more than it won full-employment legislation or other major reforms sought by unions and working-class communities. Outside the Beltway the comprehensive proposals met a rising tide of rejection among community organizations with a long history of working with labor. The East Bay Alliance for a Sustainable Economy (EBASE), which helped the workers at Emeryville's Woodfin Suites, adopted a statement calling for a change in direction. In New York City, the South Asian immigrant-rights organization Desis Rising Up & Moving and twenty other groups formed Immigrant Communities In Action, and condemned both House and Senate bills for not halting the wave of detentions and deportations visited on Muslim communities after 9/11. Another coalition included the National Day Laborer Organizing Network (NDLON), the National Mobilization against Sweatshops, the Chinese Staff and Workers' Association, and the Asian American Legal Defense and Education Fund. This group said, in addition to rejecting guest-worker programs, that Congress should repeal employer sanctions.

Because of their divisions, unions failed to formulate a bill that would have united workers across race and national lines, as many had hoped after the AFL-CIO's Los Angeles convention. There was no campaign by labor in Congress around an alternative bill or framework for immigration reform based on the 1999 convention resolution. Yet there was no lack of alternative ideas. Winning amnesty and greater rights for immigrants, for instance, could be linked to jobs programs to reduce unemployment, especially in black, Chicano, and white communities affected by free trade and plant closures. Winning organizing rights for immigrant workers could become part of more effective protections for all workers trying to form unions, like those in the Employee Free Choice Act, labor's proposal for labor-law reform. Winning radical reforms like these, however requires a social movement based in grassroots organizations and local communities, and a different set of alliances.

Ultimately, the division among unions over immigration reform reflected even more basic questions about their politics and role. Should unions try even harder to cooperate with employers to "build bridges," as Tom Donahue had said, rather than "blocking them"? Or is another strategic alliance possible, which can not only win immigration reform but provide a more progressive political direction for the country as a whole?

Six

BLACKS PLUS IMMIGRANTS PLUS UNIONS EQUALS POWER

Mississippi Battleground

In big U.S. cities, African Americans and immigrants, especially Latinos, often seem divided by a political calculation in which each community fears that any gain in jobs or political clout can only come at the expense of the other. In Mississippi, though, African American political leaders and immigrant organizers use a different algebra: blacks plus immigrants plus unions equals power.

Since 2000, all three have cooperated in organizing one of the country's most active immigrant-rights coalitions—the Mississippi Immigrant Rights Alliance (MIRA). "You will always find folks reluctant to get involved, who say it's not part of our mission, that immigrants are taking our jobs," says Jim Evans, the AFL-CIO's state organizer and leader of the Black Caucus in the state legislature. "But we all have the same rights and justice cause."

Evans, whose booming basso profundo comes straight out of the pulpit, remembers his father riding shotgun for Medgar Evers, the civil rights leader who, as field secretary for the National Association for the Advancement of Colored People (NAACP), was slain by racists in 1962. He believes that organizing immigrants is a direct continuation of such campaigns as Mississippi's Freedom Summer and the Poor People's March on Washington. "Elijah tells us to do the Lord's work," Evans says, referring to the biblical prophet. "To get to peace and freedom, you must come through the door of truth and justice."

Both Evans, who chairs the coalition, and his political partner, Bill Chandler, its executive director, believe social justice and political practicality converge in the state's changing demographics. Beginning in the early 1900s, Mississippi, like most southern states, began to lose its black population. Before the Ku Klux Klan terror began at the end of the 1800s, African Americans were a majority of the state's residents. The black exodus out of the South, in fact, was one of the largest internal migrations in the nation's history. Out-migration reached a peak in the 1960s, when 66,614 African Americans left between 1965 and 1970, while civil rights activists were murdered, hosed, and went to jail.

But in the following decades, the magnet of Midwest industrial jobs began to vanish as these jobs went overseas, the cost of living in northern cities skyrocketed, and the flow began to reverse. From 1995 to 2000, the state capital, Jackson, gained 3,600 black residents. In the 2000 census, African Americans made up over 36 percent of Mississippi's 2.8 million residents—no doubt more today. And while immigrants were statistically insignificant two decades ago, today they're over 4.5 percent of the total, according to news reports. "Immigrants are always undercounted, but I think they're now about 130,000, and they'll be 10 percent of the population ten years from now," Chandler predicts.

That's still behind Washington, D.C., and the four states where some combination of blacks, Latinos, Asians, and Native Americans make up the majority—California, Hawaii, New Mexico, and Texas. But MIRA activists see one other big advantage in Mississippi. "We have the chance here to avoid the rivalry that plagues Los Angeles, and build real power," says Chandler, who left East LA and the farmworkers movement decades ago to go south. "But we have to fight racism from the beginning, and recognize the leadership of the African American community." Erik Fleming, a MIRA staff member and former state legislator, believes "we can stop Mississippi from making the same mistakes others have made."

The same calculus can apply across the South, which is now the entry point for a third of all new immigrants to the United States. Four decades ago, President Richard Nixon brought its white power structure, threatened by civil rights, into the Republican Party. President Ronald Reagan celebrated that achievement at the Confederate monument at Georgia's Stone Mountain. "Funders and the Democratic Party have written off much of the South since then," according to Gerald Lenoir of California's Black Alliance for Just Immigration. But MIRA-type alliances could transform the region, he hopes, "and change the politics of this country as a whole."

MIRA is the fruit of strategic thinking among a diverse group that reaches from African American workers' centers on catfish farms and immigrant union organizers in chicken plants to guest workers and contract laborers on the Gulf Coast and, ultimately, into the halls of the state legislature in Jackson. Activists look back to changes that started when Mississippi passed a law permitting casino development in 1991, bringing the first immigrant construction workers from Florida. Employers in gaming then began to use contractors to supply their growing labor needs. Guest workers, eventually numbering in the thousands, were brought under the H2-B program to fill many of the jobs development created.

Chandler, who had been organizing state employees for the Communication Workers, went to work for the hotel union, UNITE HERE, and helped win union recognition in three Mississippi casinos. In discussions arising out of major HERE casino negotiations in 2002 and the huge 2004 Atlantic City HERE casino strike, Harrah's agreed to a card-check process for union recognition at two casinos the company owned in Tunica, Mississippi, and one destroyed and later rebuilt in Gulfport. It voluntarily recognized the union after a majority of workers signed union-authorization cards. Harrah's eventually signed contracts covering the three casinos there at the end of that year, although temporary, contract, and H2-B workers were not covered. The Employee Free Choice Act would write that card-check process into law. In 2007, however, the National Labor Relations Board, with a majority of Bush appointees, moved to make use of this voluntary process much more difficult.

Throughout the 1990s more immigrants arrived looking for work.

Some guest workers overstayed their visas, while husbands brought wives, cousins, and friends from home. Mexicans and Central Americans joined South and Southeast Asians, and began traveling north through the state, getting jobs in rural poultry plants. There they met African Americans, many of whom had fought hard campaigns to organize unions for chicken and catfish workers over the preceding decade.

It was not easy for newcomers to fit in. Their union representatives didn't speak their languages. When workers got pulled over by state troopers they found themselves not only cited for lacking driver's licenses but also, often, handed over to the Border Patrol. Sometimes their children weren't even allowed to enroll in school.

"We decided that the place to start was trying to get a bill passed allowing everyone to get driver's licenses, regardless of who they were or where they came from," Evans remembers. In the fall of 2000 labor, church, and civil rights activists formed an impromptu coalition, and went to the legislature. At its heart was the core of activists who'd organized Mississippi's state workers, and a growing caucus of black legislators sympathetic to labor. Evans, a former organizer for the National Football League Players Association, headed the group on the House side, while Senator Alice Harden, who'd led a state teachers' strike in 1986, organized the vote in the Senate.

Harden's efforts bore fruit when the driver's license bill passed the Senate unanimously in 2001. "But they saw us coming in the House, and killed it," Chandler says. Nevertheless, the close fight convinced them that a coalition supporting immigrant rights had a wide potential base of support, and could help change the state's political landscape. In a meeting that November, the Mississippi Immigrant Rights Alliance was born.

To build a grassroots base, MIRA volunteers went into chicken plants to help recruit newly arrived immigrants into unions. Mississippi is a right-to-work state, where union membership is not mandatory. Frank Curiel, a representative of the Laborers' International Union of North America (LIUNA) who'd worked with the United Farm Workers for many years, says, "MIRA put the LIUNA business manager and a UFCW [United Food and Commercial Workers] rep on the board because we wanted them to understand the role of the union in representing Latinos—they had contracts in chicken and fish plants." In one plant, Curiel signed up 80 percent of the newly arrived immigrants, while in two others a MIRA student volunteer from the University of Texas signed up every Latino worker in two weeks.

It wasn't just about fighting grievances or recruitment—immigrant workers had much bigger problems. "There was a pretty repressive system in Laurel, Collins, and Hattiesburg," Curiel recalls. "Plants had contracts with temp agencies, and all the workers were undocumented. It was very hard to get a new contract because of the surplus of Latino labor, and low membership." By building a combined membership of immigrant and African American workers, union negotiations in one plant forced the company to get rid of the temp service and hire directly. "That meant that African Americans gained access to those jobs too," Curiel emphasizes.

In the casinos, MIRA volunteers worked with UNITE HERE organizers. In Jackson, the coalition got six bills passed the following year, stopping schools from requiring Social Security numbers from immigrant parents, and winning in-state tuition for any student who'd spent four years in a Mississippi high school.

Then Katrina hit the Gulf. After the hurricane blew through Biloxi and Gulfport, contractors began pouring in to do reconstruction, bringing crews of workers with them.

Vicky Cintra, a Cuban American with a soft southern accent, was MIRA's first full-time organizer. She handed out ten thousand flyers with MIRA's phone number, and the calls poured in. Thirty-five workers abandoned by their contractor in dilapidated trailers got blankets and food. When two Red Cross shelters evicted Latinos, even putting a man in a wheelchair into the street, her defense of them was picked up by national news media. "For the next year we were just reacting to emergencies," she recalls. MIRA fought evictions and the cases of workers cheated by employers. "When we threatened picket lines, contractors would sometimes offer to pay Latinos, but we said everyone had to be treated equally. We got money for African Americans and whites too."

MIRA eventually recovered over a million dollars. "And this was while the federal government said it wouldn't enforce labor standards, OSHA, Davis-Bacon [the federal prevailing wage law] or any other law protecting workers," Cintra says. "Really, it had been like this for years, but Katrina just tore the veil away." The key to their success, she believes, was that "we engaged workers in direct action. Eventually the companies got the idea that workers have rights and were getting organized."

MIRA volunteers began to hear that guest workers were being recruited in India, not for reconstruction but for the main industry on the Gulf—shipyards. That work has always been dirty, dangerous, and segregated. Jaribu Hill, a MIRA board member, accuses the yards of putting "hundreds of black women into the worst cleaner jobs in the bottom of the ship. And when we get organized and outspoken, the boss starts looking for people who are more grateful, and more vulnerable."

In late 2006 three hundred guest workers arrived at the Pascagoula yard of Signal International, which makes huge floating oil rigs for the Gulf offshore fields. They'd been hired in India by a labor recruiter and given H2-B visas, good for ten months. Out of their wages, workers paid thirty-five dollars per day to stay in a labor camp Signal set up inside the yard. "Twenty-four of us live in a small room twelve feet by eighteen feet, sleeping on bunk beds," said worker leader Joseph Jacob. "There are two toilets for all of us and we have to get up at three thirty in the morning to have enough time to use the bathroom before going to work."

Signal put the Indians to work in the yard alongside U.S. workers doing the same job, and claimed it paid them the same wages. The guest workers say they were promised eighteen dollars an hour, but many were paid only half that after the company said they were unqualified. Signal CEO Dick Marler admitted the company had reclassified some workers after they'd arrived, from first- to second-class welders, and then reduced their wages.

Six were eventually told they were completely incapable, and Signal announced it was sending them back to India. Marler said he was willing to keep the unskilled workers on "fire watch," but that his lawyers said the company had to send them back. Marler claimed it was the fault of the workers. "The unskilled workers tried to game the system, and lied about their skills," he alleged.

Going home meant disaster for them. Some had paid Signal's recruiter as much as twenty thousand dollars for a visa, selling their houses in India to come up with the money. The recruiting contractor (and Signal's caterer), Global Industry, promised them the company would refund the payments they were forced to make. "I had to pay fourteen thousand," said Joseph Jacob. "I worked for years in Abu Dhabi and Saudi Arabia, and I spent all the money I had saved to get the visa, which the recruiter promised would be a permanent-residence visa. But that visa never came, and finally he said they could get us an H2-B visa. That would give us ten months of work, and if the company renewed it, we might get as much as thirty months. I thought that was the only way I'd ever be able to get back the money they'd taken."

Marler said the company sent observers to oversee recruitment and testing in India, but that they were unaware of how much workers were paying for visas. "We weren't in that part of the loop," he said. "But workers paid that money with their eyes wide open, and our recruiters tell us that's perfectly normal in India."

MIRA asked a Hindi-speaking organizer from the New Orleans Worker Center for Racial Justice, Sakhet Soni, to come to Pascagoula. Together they helped workers organize Signal H2-B Workers United. Jacob was fired "because I attended the meetings," he said. "That's what the company vice president told me." Marler denies this.

When the company announced the terminations, one worker disappeared. Another, Sabu Lal, slashed his wrists and was taken to the Singing River Hospital in Pascagoula. He told the *Mississippi Press* that dying would be better than being sent home. "Lal and I are from the same place in India," Jacob explained. "I knew he had sold his home and had no place to return to. He was only able to make back a small part of the thousands of dollars he paid to the recruiter, and he said he couldn't go home like that."

Company security guards locked the fired workers in what they call the TV Room and wouldn't let them leave. MIRA went to the Pascagoula Police Department, and officers went out to the yard and eventually freed the imprisoned workers. Outside the yard, dozens of workers and activists denounced the firings and mistreatment. MIRA organized picket lines, and its attorney, Patricia Ice, started a legal defense campaign with the Southern Poverty Law Center.

The company said it used the H2-B system because it couldn't find enough workers after the hurricane. Other contractors have used the same rationale. "We've learned about case after case of workers in Mississippi, Louisiana, and all along the Gulf in these conditions," Chandler said. "There are thousands of guest workers who have been brought in since Katrina and subjected to this same treatment. Mexican guest workers in Amelia, Louisiana, were held in the same way. They also got organized, and came to Pascagoula to support the workers here when they heard what happened."

Organizing guest workers is part of an effort to build a membership among immigrants themselves. MIRA members get an ID card and agree to come to demonstrations and help others. When the national immigrant marches began in the spring of 2006, MIRA mobilized thousands of people for a rally in Jackson, and even a march in Laurel, a poultry town of 18,393 people with a progressive black mayor. "There's still a lot of anti-immigrant sentiment here," Cintra says, "but when people give the police their ID card they get treated with more respect, because they know their rights and have some support." Curiel says the same thing. "In Kentucky, outside of Louisville, Latinos are afraid to go out into the street. In Mississippi it's different."

Not always that different, however. In Laurel and many other Mississippi towns police still set up roadblocks to trap immigrants without licenses. "They take us away in handcuffs and we have to pay over a thousand dollars to get out of jail and get our cars back," says chicken plant worker Elisa Reyes. And the way the state's Council of Conservative Citizens demonizes immigrants is reminiscent of the language of its predecessor—the white-supremacist White Citizens' Councils of the 1950s and 1960s: "The CofCC Not only fights for European rights, but also for Confederate Heritage, fights against illegal immigration, Fights against gun control, fights against abortion, fights against gay rights etc. SO JOIN UP!!!" its website urges. The state's chapter of the Federation for Immigration Reform and Enforcement brought Chris Simcox, head of the extreme anti-immigrant group the Minutemen, out from California.

During the 2007 Mississippi elections for governor and state legislators the Ku Klux Klan held a rally of five hundred people in front of the Lee County Courthouse in Tupelo. They wore the old white hoods and robes, and carried signs saying "Stop the Latino Invasion." Their presence was so intimidating that Ricky Cummings, a generally progressive Democrat running for reelection, voted for some of the anti-immigrant bills in the legislature. When MIRA leaders challenged him, he told them that Klan-generated calls had "worn out his cell phone."

The Klan's website says, "It's time to declare war on these illegal Mexicans . . . The racial war is among us, will you fight with us for the future of our race and for our children? Or will you sit on your ass and do nothing? Our blissful ignorance is over. It is time to fight. Time for Mexico and Mexicans to get the hell out!" The website has links to the site of the Mississippi Federation for Immigration Reform and Enforcement (the state affiliate of the Federation for American Immigration Reform), founded by the conservative state legislator Mike Lott.

In 2007 the Republican machine introduced twenty-one anti-immigrant bills into the state legislature, including ones to impose state penalties for hiring undocumented workers and English-only requirements on state license and benefit applicants, to prohibit undocumented students at state universities, and to require local police to check immigration status. Many were sponsored by Mike Lott.

MIRA defeated all of them. "The Black Caucus stood behind us every time," Evans says proudly. There are no immigrant or Latino legislators. Without the caucus all twenty-one bills would have passed in 2007, and nineteen similar bills in 2006. The caucus didn't just fight a "vote no" campaign. It proposed a series of pro-worker measures that would have abolished at-will employment (the doctrine that says employers don't need any justification for firing workers), provided interpreters, and established a state Department of Labor (Mississippi is the only state without one). While these bills didn't pass either, the difference in agenda was as clear as black and white, or, perhaps, black/brown and white.

Although the political coalition in which MIRA participates was powerful enough to stop the worst proposals, it wasn't yet powerful enough to elect a legislative majority. Changing demographics is one element of a strategy to change that political terrain, but numbers alone aren't enough. Chandler describes three factions in the Democratic Party—the Black Caucus at one end, white conservatives hanging on at the other, and "liberals who will do whatever they have to do to get elected" in the middle.

After some Democratic candidates campaigned in 2007 on an anti-immigrant platform, MIRA wrote a letter in protest to Howard Dean, national chair of the Democratic Party. Those tactics, it said, were undermining the only strategy capable of changing the state's politics. "The attacks on Latinos, initiated by Republican Phil Bryant a year and a half ago, and joined by other Republicans, are now being echoed by Democrats like John Arthur Eaves and Jamie Franks," the letter said. State party leaders who "would go along to be accepted, rather than show the courage necessary for positive change . . . are peddling racist lies against immigrants that violate the core of the party's progressive agenda. We do not need politicians whose only concern is getting elected. We need leaders who will represent the best interests of all the working people of Mississippi."

Anti-immigrant campaigning by Democratic gubernatorial candidate Eaves, and by Franks, the party's nominee for lieutenant governor, was unsuccessful. Conservative Republican Haley Barbour was returned to the governor's mansion and Phil Bryant was elected lieutenant governor. Democrat Jim Hood, however, was reelected attorney general, with a higher vote total than either Eaves or Franks. Hood was the only Democratic statewide candidate who did not mount an anti-immigrant campaign, and had earlier been convinced by Jim Evans not to support anti-immigrant bills in the legislature.

In December 2007 Trent Lott suddenly resigned his U.S. Senate seat only a year after being reelected to a fourth term. Barbour appointed a conservative Republican, Representative Roger Wicker, to fill the vacancy and set the vote to choose a permanent replacement for the general election of November 2008. Erik Fleming decided at first to run for the seat and then decided instead to contest Mississippi's other Senate seat, held by Thad Cochrane. "We can't rely just on the demographic shift to win," he says, explaining that a winning majority in Mississippi requires about 80 percent of the African American vote, 20–25 percent of the white vote, and all of the growing vote of immigrants and other people of color. "But demographics makes it a viable race. We live in a conservative state where people don't accept new ideas easily, so the challenge for progressives is that we have to campaign and educate people at the same time. If we want people to move out of their comfort zone, we need a powerful message." That message concentrates on jobs, healthcare, affordable housing, and the basic economic issues that affect working people in a state with one of the nation's lowest standards of living and social services. Immigration issues, Fleming says, are not some toxic issue to be avoided at all cost. "If we talk about it in the context of protecting jobs, wages, and rights for everyone, it's something that can bring us together."

Finding common ground between immigrants, African Americans, and labor is MIRA's long-term strategy. Jaribu Hill, another MIRA board member and director of the Mississippi Workers Center, launched her own bid for election to the legislature as a Democrat, and points out that winning in the South requires open discussion of race and civil rights, even if it makes established institutions, including unions, uncomfortable. Before starting any campaign in the fish plants where her Mississippi Workers Center is active, she says, "we have to talk about racism. The union focuses on the contract, but skin color issues are also on the table."

To organize a multiracial workforce, divisions between African Americans and immigrants need to be recognized and discussed, she says: "We're coming together like a marriage, working across our divides." Rhetoric calling the current immigrant-rights movement the "new civil rights movement" doesn't describe those relations accurately. "Our conditions as African Americans are the direct result of slavery. Immigrants have come here looking for better lives—we came in chains," Hill explains. "Today Frito-Lay wages in Mississippi are still much lower than Illinois—eight seventy-five to thirteen seventy-five an hour. This is the evolution of an historical oppression." Immigrants, when they too are paid that lower wage, are entering an economic system based on discrimination and tiers of inequality, which was established to control and profit from black labor. They inherit a second-class status that developed before they arrived.

Jean Damu, a writer and member of the Black Alliance for Just Immigration, also warns that drawing a parallel between the situations of blacks and immigrants has its limits. "After all, who would want to claim that deporting someone to Mexico is the same as returning them to slavery?" he asks. "But the similarities are powerful enough to convince many African Americans that it is in their self-interest to support those who struggle against black people's historic enemies."

Hill therefore sees a common ground of experience. "We're both victims of colonialism, we're both second-class citizens denied our rights. If people could see how African American people live here, they'd see it's like Bolivia or Jamaica. On the other hand, it's important for African Americans to understand why people come here—because of what's happening in the countries they come from. If people had a choice, if they could live like human beings, they wouldn't have to risk their lives to get here. I don't believe any human being can be illegal."

But, Damu cautions, "The movement for immigrant rights must do a better job of uniting with black America. And African Americans should be sensitive to the current conditions in which many immigrants find themselves—conditions not unfamiliar to us."

Katrina: Window on a Nightmare

Hurricane Katrina and the destruction of New Orleans highlighted relations between African Americans and immigrants. In their wake, both New Orleans mayor Ray Nagin and nationally syndicated columnist Ruben Navarrette played on growing insecurity on each side of the migration divide. "How do I ensure that New Orleans is not overrun by Mexican workers?" the mayor asked in early November 2005. Navarrette praised immigrants for "not sitting around and waiting for government to come to the rescue. They're probably living two or three families to a house . . . that's how it used to be in this country before the advent of the welfare state." African American politicians, he said, just want to "keep the city mostly black."

On the Gulf Coast the racial fault lines of immigration politics threatened to pit Latinos against blacks, and migrant laborers against community residents hoping to return to their homes. Community organizations, labor, and civil rights advocates looked for common ground in a reconstruction plan that put the needs of people first. But flood-ravaged Mississippi and Louisiana were also a window into a threatening future in which poor communities with little economic power fight each other over jobs.

Even before Hurricane Katrina hit, the unemployment rate among Gulf residents was among the nation's highest. According to a study commissioned by the Congressional Black Caucus, 18 to 30 percent of people in the region live under the poverty line, and among blacks in New Orleans, the poverty rate was 35 percent. After the flood, jobs for workers in the area simply vanished along with their homes. Thousands of residents were dispersed to shelters and housing hundreds of miles away. Businesses closed for lack of customers. With no taxpayers filling the coffers, cities and school districts faced bankruptcy. In New Orleans, blacks, concentrated in public-sector jobs and already reeling from the storm and flood, were hit again by massive layoffs.

With no sure job waiting for them, few families had the resources to simply go back and take a chance on finding new employment. The Bureau of Labor Statistics found in October 2005 that five hundred thousand of the eight hundred thousand people evacuated had yet to return home. Those who did wound up living in Federal Emergency Management Agency trailers, since very little of the city's public housing was rebuilt, while rents more than doubled. Then, two years later, FEMA began evicting trailer residents in the name of making them "self-sufficient." According to Jared Bernstein, an economist at Washington, D.C.'s, Economic Policy Institute, the average unemployment rate for evacuees was 24.5 percent—10.5 percent for those who'd been able to return, and 33.4 percent for those who hadn't.

To help New Orleans residents go back, the People's Hurricane Relief Fund (PHRF) came up with some simple demands. The federal government, it said, should provide funds to enable families to reunite, and make public the lists of evacuees maintained by FEMA and the Red Cross to help people find each other. Disaster victims needed the same kind of immediate relief the World Trade Center fund provided in New York City. Finally, to enable people to restart economic life, the PHRF demanded public works jobs at union wages. It called for putting community residents on the boards planning the rebuilding, and making their discussions public. Steven Pitts, an economist at the University of California at Berkeley, pointed out that "the fundamental question in reconstruction is the role of the displaced residents, both in planning the rebuilding itself and in the support given them by the government."

What actually took place, however, was far from this community-based vision. As the floodwaters receded, a host of wealthy contractors invaded the waterlogged boulevards. Federal agencies signed no-bid contracts, guaranteeing that what little money they were willing to spend on reconstruction would become a source of private gain for the politically connected. Dispersed residents got no help in returning to rebuild their homes and lives. When they tried to go back, they were treated as threats to law and order—impediments to potential gentrification.

The Gulf Coast became a playground for advocates of free market nostrums. The Davis-Bacon Act's protection for workers' wages was suspended—reinstated only after massive protest organized by the AFL-CIO and many community groups in the region. Affirmative action, which might have diverted a small percentage of those no-bid contracts to locally owned firms, was abolished. The meager budget a Republican Congress was willing to divert from the Iraq war became a justification for slices to food stamps and student loans.

In this vast enterprise zone, the welfare of workers and the poor was sacrificed to provide incentives for corporate investment. Contractors did come, sometimes bringing their workforce with them. Many migrants were also drawn to Mississippi and Louisiana on their own, by the word-of-mouth network that passes along news of any area where employers are hiring and asking few questions about legal status. Employers wanted workers, but workers without families, who needed no schools or community services. They wanted workers who could be housed in homeless shelters or packed into trailers like sardines.

MIRA's Bill Chandler describes the conditions for migrant workers on the Gulf: "We found instance after instance of workers sleeping outside," he said, "or in abandoned trailers or even school buses. There was no enforcement of any health standards, no safety gear, and no immunizations for people who could easily get tetanus from cuts or punctures. Migrants worked from sunup to sundown, without any benefits, and sometimes even without paychecks." MIRA and the Quaker social justice organization American Friends Service Committee wound up buying tents and setting up encampments in church parking lots for workers and homeless people evicted from shelters.

Inspectors for the U.S. Department of Labor's Wage and Hour Division waited in their offices for workers to complain. In Jackson, Mississippi, the Bureau of Immigration and Customs Enforcement has its office on the floor above the inspectors, and the detention center for deportees is in the basement. As one might imagine, the Wage and Hour office didn't get much walk-in traffic from undocumented immigrants. Instead, labor and immigrant-rights groups were the ones who gathered complaints and demanded enforcement.

The biggest contractors—Halliburton and its subsidiaries KBR and BE&K (a construction giant with a history of strikebreaking) and others—disclaimed responsibility. They hired subcontractors, who hired other subcontractors, who hired labor recruiters, who employed the workers. According to Chandler, while the original FEMA contract might have paid thirty-five dollars for the removal of a cubic yard of debris, the subcontractor who actually did the work probably got ten. Layers of middlemen absorbed the rest. Subcontractors sought to underbid each other by pushing wages as low as possible.

A family seeking to return to the area, needing a living income, couldn't make it on minimum wage. For migrants, the contract system imposed conditions of virtual servitude. The net result was the casualization of the workforce throughout the hurricane-affected area. Temporary jobs instead of permanent ones. Jobs for mobile, single men rather than for individuals supporting families. No protection for wages. Hiring through contractors and temporary agencies instead of a long-term commitment from an employer.

This system of casualized employment isn't confined to the Gulf. It's growing throughout the United States, and Congress's comprehensive proposals for immigration reform, with huge guest-worker programs, would reinforce it. The economic pressure of competing layers of contractors, recruiters, and labor agencies would inevitably exert the same constant downward pressure on wages and conditions. Contractors would simply have a more systematic way to recruit the same contingent workforce they used in the Gulf, but with the help of the federal government.

The Department of Labor, with its current lack of political will to enforce worker protections, would have a new charge. Together with the Social Security Administration, these agencies would be the immigration police, poring through employment records for those lacking guest-worker visas. Inspectors might indeed leave that office in Jackson, but to find and deport the undocumented. Workers without papers would become even more vulnerable, while their employers would have new leverage to demand unpaid overtime or impose bad conditions. The impact of those comprehensive immigration-reform proposals, as previewed on the Gulf Coast, would be intensified job competition at the bottom of the workforce.

The Common Ground of Jobs and Rights

Not all proposals in Congress took the guest-worker/enforcement approach, however. In response to the hurricane, the Congressional Black Caucus (CBC) sponsored HR 4197, to authorize funds for housing and new Section 8 vouchers, for increased healthcare, and for extended unemployment and assistance to needy families. It would have provided money to help returning residents rebuild their homes or seek new ones, and for schools to help relocated students. The bill would have created apprenticeship programs to develop good jobs, and required the president to present a plan for eradicating poverty. For University of California economist Pitts, this moved in the right direction. "You have to assure there's a floor under wages," he cautioned. "Both immigrants and African Americans need this. To ensure people can return, the government has to recognize the need for two kinds of income—wages from decent jobs, and money to cover the cost of relocation. Immigrants need a living wage too, as well as the right to organize and the ability to move freely, so they're not tied to an employer or contractor."

The CBC supported another bill in 2005, by Houston congresswoman Sheila Jackson Lee. HR 2092 provided a way for undocumented workers to gain permanent-resident status, and enforced migrants' rights in the workplace. Unlike the other comprehensive immigration proposals, it had no guest-worker program and didn't call for greater enforcement of employer sanctions. Jackson Lee's bill was a rallying point for community and labor activists who wanted a progressive alternative to the big guest-worker bills.

The key to finding common ground between African Americans and immigrants is to fight for jobs for everyone. Whether black, white, Asian, Native American, or Latino, native-born or immigrant, no one can live without work. Yet this basis for an alliance of mutual interest has largely fallen off the liberal agenda. Unions were the support base for the Humphrey-Hawkins Full Employment Act in the 1970s, which said that the federal government should provide jobs to eradicate unemployment. Today, however, they only pay lip service to the idea. In the Democratic Party, free market ideologues ridicule the idea that the government should guarantee employment, as it did during the New Deal. Instead, both parties propose to pile guest-worker programs, and increased enforcement of employer sanctions, on top of job competition. This is an explosive mixture in which no one has the right to a job, and everyone shares only increased insecurity.

Unemployment and racism in the U.S. economic system pit communities of color against each other, and against working-class white communities. Competition produces lower labor costs and higher profits. In its guest-worker proposals, the Essential Worker Immigration Coalition was simply pursing this economic goal.

Racial division is a powerful political weapon as well. For working communities, overcoming racial divisions opens up new possibilities for winning political power. In the early 1980s a black-Latino alliance defeated the Chicago political machine and elected Harold Washington the first African American mayor. In the spring of 2005 the same strategy elected a Latino, Antonio Villaraigosa, mayor of Los Angeles, where division between blacks and Latinos was used to keep conservatives in power for decades. The rebuilding of Biloxi, Gulfport, and New Orleans may forge a similar political coalition on the Gulf Coast. But it will require working-class communities to combine support for immigrant rights, civil rights, and economic progress for all communities.

President George W. Bush and many in Congress have insisted that the only way Mexicans can avoid the deadly and illegal trip across the U.S. border is to come as guest workers. In their view, the 12 million immigrants already living in the United States without visas must become guest workers to get legal documents. Jackson Lee's approach is fundamentally different. "These are hardworking, taxpaying individuals," she says. "My system would give them permanent legal residence." Instead of looking at immigrants just as a source of labor, Jackson Lee sees them as members of communities. "People are human," she explains. "They might have married, invested, or tried to buy a house. They might have children and roots here. It's very difficult to imagine that a person with a three-year pass [a guest-worker visa] would voluntarily leave, particularly if they faced an oppressive situation where they came from."

The Jackson Lee bill was unique for another reason—most of its cosponsors were members of the Congressional Black Caucus, including California's Barbara Lee and Michigan's John Conyers. For many years the caucus has outlined an alternative federal budget prioritizing social goals like eliminating poverty, reducing military spending, and protecting social services. This was the first time caucus members made a proposal on immigration. Jackson Lee didn't want her bill viewed as just an African American proposal; nevertheless, she referred to her cosponsors as "the conscience of America, the conscience of the Congress."

In the situation of immigrants she sees the historic discrimination against black people and women. "I had the benefit of the Thirteenth, Fourteenth, and Fifteenth Amendments, the 1964 Civil Rights Act and the 1965 Voting Rights Act, and the executive order signed by Richard Nixon on affirmative action. Without them, I would never have seen the inside of the United States Congress," she says. "The rights of minorities in this country are still a work in progress. Nevertheless, someone recognized that the laws of America were broken as they related to African Americans—that we had to fix them. Now we have to fix other laws to end discrimination against immigrants." Her bill therefore banned discrimination based on immigration status, prohibiting employers from threatening deportation when workers invoke their labor rights or worker-protection laws. The secretary of labor would have to conduct a national workplace survey, to determine the extent of the exploitation of undocumented workers.

Jackson Lee opposed temporary-worker programs because she believes they inevitably result in second-class status, preventing workers from enforcing labor rights or using social benefits. Temporary status also has a high social cost. "Who pays for their housing and healthcare?" she asks. "They pay into Social Security, but they're denied benefits. What rights do they really have?"

The social cost of guest-worker programs can also include the impact on the jobs and wages of other workers. "Certainly you're made to believe that one group [blacks and immigrants] hinders the other," she says. "That's absolutely wrong, and I believe in fighting against that idea." That's why her bill sought to find common interests instead, connecting legalization for the undocumented with job programs for the unemployed. When undocumented immigrants applied for permanent legal status, the money they paid in application fees would have funded job creation and training programs for unemployed workers. Creating jobs for the country's 9.4 million unemployed would require more resources than those fees would have generated. But the bill recognized that the issues of jobs and immigration don't have to pit immigrants and native-born against each other. Instead they can unite people in a common pursuit of jobs, legal status, and workplace rights. And it recognized that until immigrant workers have genuine legal status, and the security to fight for better conditions and wages, all low-wage workers will be harmed.

African American concern about unemployment and jobs can't be dismissed simply as nativism or selfishness. In 2004 a study by the Center for Labor Market Studies at Northeastern University found that between 2000 and 2004, jobs held by immigrants rose by 2 million. Meanwhile, the number of employed native-born workers fell by 958,000, and of longtime resident immigrants by 352,000. According to the report's authors, "The net growth in the nation's employed population between 2000 and 2004 takes place among new immigrants, while the number of native-born and established immigrant workers combined declines by more than 1.3 million."

Black unemployment nationally is at catastrophic levels, especially in urban centers affected by plant closures and industrial restructuring. It is consistently double the rate among workers generally. Very little is a result of direct displacement by immigrants, however. It's caused overwhelmingly by the decline in manufacturing and cuts in public employment, which have a disproportionate effect on black workers. Although African Americans are just 11 percent of the workforce, in the 2001 recession three hundred thousand of 2 million black factory workers lost their jobs to relocation and layoffs.

Bill Fletcher, former president of TransAfrica Forum and onetime education director of the AFL-CIO, says changing demographics in the U.S. population are a concern for African Americans. He recalls that when black political leaders condemned the Vietnam War and widespread poverty in the United States, even liberal politicians told them to confine their concerns to civil rights in the South. "We don't want to just react to demographic changes," he says. "As African Americans, we have something to contribute to this debate."

Changing demographics in the workplace became a fact during a period of massive industrial restructuring, which eliminated the jobs of hundreds of thousands of African American and Chicano workers in unionized industries. Through the postwar decades, those workers had broken the color line, spent their lives in steel mills and assembly plants, and wrested a standard of living able to support stable families and communities. In the growing service and high-tech industries of the 1980s, however, those displaced workers were anathema. Employers often identified their race with prounion militancy, according to sociologist Patricia Fernández-Kelly. She asked employers why they employed so few African Americans. They responded that they thought African Americans were too prounion and too demanding of their rights. By contrast, they said they expected that immigrant women would be more complaint.

Today, corporations in those same industries argue that they need workers to fill labor shortages to come, and promote guest workers as the answer. Fletcher argues, "If there are people in communities destroyed because the industry that employed them is gone, and a few miles away there are labor shortages in other industries, then displaced people should fill the void. Instead, we're hearing proposals for guest workers. If African Americans were moving from lower- to higher-level jobs, there would be no reason for fear, but that's not the case." Only one current guest-worker program, H2-A in agriculture, even requires employers to advertise for workers locally before bringing in contract labor.

Jackson Lee's bill tried to balance the interests of immigrants and the unemployed. Employers, she said, should press for real legalization instead of guest workers. "That would give industry a pool of legal permanent residents or those seeking that status," she explained. "Most work is not cyclical—restaurants don't close in the fall. They stay open. They need people in permanent jobs, not temporary workers."

According to Jackson Lee, U.S. foreign and trade policy often exert great pressures on people to migrate. She says the country should welcome the immigrants who continue to arrive, while attacking the poverty and oppression that uproots their home communities. "We would do better to build the economies of countries like Mexico," she concludes, "so people can live their own dream in their own nation. If we don't, we will continue to have people fleeing for both economic reasons and because they're being persecuted." Fletcher goes further, asserting that U.S. policy often makes migration necessary. "We don't look at the role of U.S. foreign policy in particular as an essential cause," he says, "the way the war in Central America forced the migration of Salvadorans, or the Vietnam War the migration of people from Southeast Asia. When we don't speak out on foreign policy, we don't consider the human cost."

The Jackson Lee bill didn't address foreign or trade policy directly, but it did seek to correct some of the inequities created when immigration policy is used as an instrument of political reward or punishment. The congresswoman pointed to the huge backlog of applicants waiting for visas in developing countries, while many European countries are entitled to far more visas than they ever use. For Europeans, whose standard of living is often higher than that in the United States, there's very little pressure to leave. But in Latin America, Asia, and Africa, the poverty created by war and neoliberal economic policies produces far more applicants than there are visas available. Jackson Lee proposed taking those differences into account, and increasing the number of available green cards from about 240,000 to 960,000, to reduce the long backlog of applicants—a major cause of undocumented migration. In 2007, a visa applicant from the Philippines, sponsored by a brother or sister, had to wait more than twenty years, and from Mexico eleven years.

She further sought to help Liberian and Haitian refugees. Haitians in particular are victims of a double standard that allows Cubans to become legal residents as soon as they step onto U.S. soil, while the Coast Guard returns desperate refugees from Haiti, fleeing repression in tiny boats, before they get to the Florida beach. If they somehow reach it, they're held behind barbed wire. "There is an inequality between those fleeing from one island and those fleeing another," the congresswoman comments dryly. Jackson Lee's grandparents were Jamaican immigrants, but she says today's immigrants face a broken system and pay a painful price.

The powerful constellation of organizations in Washington, D.C., that supported guest worker/enforcement/legalization bills did not encourage discussion of Jackson Lee's proposal. Instead, they sought to present their proposals as the only alternative to even more draconian legislation, like Sensenbrenner's HR 4437. Although Jackson Lee was the ranking Democrat on the Immigration Subcommittee of the House Judiciary Committee, she never got a hearing on her bill while the Republicans controlled Congress. When the Democrats won a majority in the 2006 election, Representative Zoe Lofgren, from Silicon Valley, where employers have historically pushed for H1-B guest workers for high-tech industry, became the immigration subcommittee chair. Jackson Lee's bill didn't get a hearing then either. Nevertheless, for immigrant and labor rights advocates around the country, it provided, as Fletcher said, "a long-term vision of what we really want."

Remedy the Past's Injustice

It's no surprise that native-born workers and settled immigrant communities look at the growth of casual, low-paid employment with alarm. It fosters competition among workers for jobs, while the section of the workforce with the lowest wages and fewest rights is the one expanding the fastest. People can certainly see this system's impact on their own lives, even if they can't always identify its cause. "The fear of job competition in the African American community reflects both myths and realities, and we should pay attention to both," Bill Fletcher says. "African Americans fear that the increase in Latino immigration poses a potential threat to their ever achieving equity, that they will become overshadowed by this larger block of people. The reality is that there is competition for jobs at a certain level, and in certain industries. It's hard to overestimate the impact of the reconfiguration of industry on African Americans, especially in large cities like Los Angeles and New York."

When some immigrant advocates in the last decade argued that immigrants are just taking jobs others won't do, they seemed to be saying either that the jobs had been abandoned or that unemployed workers were unwilling to do them. This often denied a reality workers could easily see—discrimination and unlivable wages. More important, advocates thus stopped making clear the real causes of migration, unemployment, low wages, and job competition, and no longer pointed to the system and corporations responsible.

"In some industries the workforce changed completely in just a few years," Fletcher says. "In the hotel industry, for instance, the hotel union has concluded that, in effect, hotels practiced ethnic cleansing in the 1980s. The same happened among janitors." In Los Angeles in the early 1980s, when the janitor's union was driven out of the city's office buildings, contractors dumped union workers who were mostly African American. But after the immigrant Central American workers who replaced them fought courageously, and successfully, to regain the lost contracts, African American workers didn't return. Instead, the black community faced a color line, despite the high black unemployment rate.

In San Francisco hotels a similar demographic transformation took place. There the percentage of African American workers fell as employment grew. By 2004 African Americans made up less than 6 percent of the hotel workforce, declining in each of the five years after 1999 except one. Blacks have a long history of fighting discrimination in San Francisco's hospitality industry. The Sheraton Palace Hotel was the scene of the city's most famous civil rights demonstration in 1964. Hundreds of activists sat in and were arrested in the lobby, as they demanded that management hire blacks into jobs in the visible front-of-the-house, where the color line had kept them out. Richard Lee Mason, an African American banquet waiter at the St. Francis Hotel, remembers, "African Americans had been kept in the back of the house for far too long. People wanted to be in the front of the house, and rightly so."

Employment prospects improved for black workers for some years, but the situation changed in the 1980s, when hotels began hiring increasing percentages of immigrants. "I suspect that because the industry had had a great struggle with African Americans, they thought we were too aggressive," Mason speculates. "A lot of us had come out of the civil rights movement, and we were willing to fight for higher wages and to make sure we were treated fairly." University of California labor specialist Steven Pitts says Mason's experience was not uncommon. "This perception by employers of African American workers is true nationwide," he says. "Blacks aren't perceived as compliant, and therefore when many employers make hiring decisions, they simply don't hire them."

The history in Los Angeles is similar, where black workers made up only 6.4 percent of the 2004 hotel workforce. Clyde Smith, a houseman at the Wilshire Grand, remembered that when he'd been hired thirty-five years earlier African Americans worked in virtually all areas. "There are significantly less today," he said, "often only one or two in each department, and sometimes none at all."

If the hotel industry hoped their new immigrant workforce would be more malleable, however, those hopes were not realized. Immigrants proved to be as militant as the workers who came before—all of San Francisco's big hotels were struck in 1980, and smaller strikes took place in the following two decades. The biggest confrontation came in 2004, when workers endured a two-month lockout, and then went two years without a contract.

In the middle of a bitter war with the hotels, their union, UNITE HERE Local 2, decided to begin remedying past discrimination. Local 2 sought to protect family healthcare from escalating costs. It wanted corporate neutrality in the face of workers' efforts to organize in nonunion hotels. The union proposed a contract expiration date that would allow it to negotiate at the same time that other UNITE HERE locals were bargaining with the same employers in other cities.

But the demand the hotels resisted most was a unique idea combining immigrant rights with a commitment to hire more African American workers. Local 2 already had a contract clause protecting the job rights of the immigrants who made up a majority of the workforce, which it sought to strengthen. It had also won an arbitrator's ruling that employers couldn't use Social Security no-match letters to fire workers. In 2004 it proposed a new section, requiring hotels to set up a diversity committee and hire an ombudsman, to begin increasing the percentage of African Americans they employed. In effect, the union began to negotiate over the rights of black workers who weren't in the workforce any longer, but who might again become part of it in the future. The Multi Employer Group, the group representing management of the San Francisco hotels, rejected the union's diversity idea. Even after the rest of the contract was settled, Local 2 continued to fight over this issue, and finally compromised on its ombudsman proposal plus increased protections for immigrants' job rights. Los Angeles's Local 11 and locals in Chicago, Boston, and other cities made the same demands as part of the union's national campaign, Hotel Workers Rising. "Some people would try to pit Blacks against Latinos," said Wilshire Grand's Clyde Smith. "I think we shouldn't blame any race or culture."

In 2001 the UNITE HERE convention in Santa Monica had made a broad commitment to find common ground between immigrant and African American members. Local 2 and Local 11 sought to transform that general political goal—uniting blacks and immigrants—into concrete enforceable agreements with employers. Their proposals pointed to a possible future in which affirmative action language could make it mandatory that hotels overcome the legacy of past discrimination.

Both UNITE HERE and Jackson Lee envisioned a new movement for rights, geared to a changed world of migration and globalization, fighting to prohibit discrimination against both immigrants and domestically displaced and unemployed workers. Their ideas shared the assumption that unions and high wages could be a powerful protection against job competition. To build a movement bringing together immigrants and the native-born, local unions and communities could take the Local 2 and 11 hiring ideas and translate them into proposals for local or national legislation. Jackson Lee's bill was one possible avenue.

Another might be adding local hiring requirements to living-wage ordinances. The national campaign for living wages has been based on local ordinances mandating wages that actually reflect the real cost of living for working families. In addition to directly raising the wages of workers like Emeryville's hotel room cleaners, they create political pressure for a higher national minimum wage. These ordinances could also require employers to hire locally, prohibiting recruitment of low-wage workers in distant areas for publicly financed projects. This would not discriminate against immigrants—after all, immigrants also live in local communities. But local hiring ordinances would stop the use of contract labor and guest-worker programs. Fair wages and hiring and rights ordinances could also combine local efforts in a movement for national legislation.

Fletcher saw the Jackson Lee bill as "an opportunity for a discussion between African American, Latino, and Asian trade unionists. The question is, are there leaders in the trade union movement ready to stretch out their hands and have a discussion about how to build unity. Unity is the central question for the future of the trade union movement, and race is the tripwire."

People in the Streets Want More

Although James Sensenbrenner's HR 4437 passed the House of Representatives in December 2005, the Senate never voted on it, and the bill eventually died, killed by a huge surge of opposition from immigrants themselves. Its threat to jail the undocumented as federal felons was an electric current that jolted communities into political activity. The shock was felt far beyond the huge barrios of Los Angeles and

Chicago. Even in the most remote communities, in areas of the country where immigrant neighborhoods have grown up only in recent years, HR 4437 became a daily topic for heated debate.

In the middle of the desert south of California's Coachella Valley, less than a hundred miles north of Mexico, a group of indigenous Purépechas from the Mexican state of Michoacán met to discuss the proposal. They live in the Duros and Chicanitas labor camps, huge trailer parks housing hundreds of farmworker families. Their endless rows of dilapidated mobile homes sit on the salt pan of the Torres Martinez Indian Reservation, just north of the Salton Sea. The Purépecha migration is bringing people from tiny indigenous communities in the hills of Michoacán, far from the nearest city. In California they also live in settlements on the margin, often speaking no Spanish, but a language old before Columbus arrived in the Americas.

The Purépechas told local labor advocates that they'd heard about Sensenbrenner's draconian scheme, and that Congress was also considering a new bracero program, like the one many remembered from decades before. After a half hour of intense debate in Purépecha, Jose Gonzalez, leader of the families in the trailer camps, asked the advocates in Spanish about the possible consequences if they refused to work on the day of the planned national demonstrations. They'd heard on the radio that people planned to stay home from work on April 10, 2006. Mexican DJs were calling it "A Day without Mexicans," taking the name from a popular movie. After listening to the advocates, Gonzalez and the Purépecha council decided to join, despite fearing they'd lose their jobs or that the Border Patrol might deport people marching in the streets.

On May 1, even larger demonstrations took place. Over a million people filled the streets of Los Angeles twice in one day, in two separate marches. It was the largest mass protest in the history of the city, and possibly the country. Hundreds of thousands more paraded in Chicago and New York, cities with Latino and Asian communities going back many decades. Dallas had a huge rally. In northern California people marched not only through the historical barrios of San Francisco's Mission and San Jose's East Side neighborhoods, but in half a dozen suburban communities in the larger metropolitan area. Many large rallies were also held in communities where immigrants had previously been almost invisible, like Louisville, Kentucky, and Nashville, Tennessee.

The core of activists and organizers was a minority in a sea of ordinary families, most of whom had never participated in any kind of protest before. Day laborers who line the sidewalks in front of suburban Home Depots, and then vanish at night into hidden tenements and homeless encampments, became suddenly visible. Coachella's Purépechas, whose labor produces California's famous table grapes but whose language is unknown even to the companies that employ them, found a voice. Immigrant families felt their backs against the wall, and came out of their homes and workplaces to show that they were no longer willing to be ignored or scapegoated.

This huge national movement was more than a reaction to a particular congressional agenda. According to immigrant-rights activist Nativo Lopez, "It was the cumulative response to years of bashing and denigrating of immigrants generally, and Mexican and Latinos in particular." Lopez helped organize one of the Los Angeles marches as president of the Mexican American Political Association and director of the Hermandad Mexicana Latinoamericana. "The protests seem spontaneous," he cautioned, "but they come as a result of years of organizing, educating, and agitating. This is the legacy of Bert Corona, who trained thousands of immigrant activists, taught the value of political independence, and believed that immigrants themselves must conduct the fight for immigrant rights. Many of the leaders of our movement today were his students."

The marches also rescued a tradition of May Day demonstrations that fell victim to cold war fear and repression in the early 1950s. Despite its birth in Chicago in 1886 in the fight for the eight-hour workday, May Day was labeled radical and communist in the United States, while unions and workers celebrated it in every other country of the world.

According to Lopez, protests were increasingly critical of the comprehensive immigration-reform proposals in Washington. "People poured into the streets," he said, "not to support them, but driven by fear of the harm they'd do." More street action would produce concessions, he predicted. "This movement makes demands that go beyond what they've defined as 'politically possible.' They told us not to stop work or leave school or boycott, yet it's obvious that the national debate changed only because we were willing to do those things."

The main demand of the hundreds of marches and demonstrations of 2006, and the ones a year later, was legalization of the undocumented. In response to Washington proposals for "earned legalization," requiring fines and enrollment in temporary-visa programs, Lopez declared that immigrants had already earned legal status. "They deserve it because of their labor," he argued. "The value they create is never called illegal, and no one dreams of taking it away from the employers who profit from it. Yet the people who produce that value are called exactly that—illegal."

Other organizations also mobilized people in the streets, worried at the increasingly rightward drift of the congressional compromises. Many unions and immigrant-rights groups began calling for a pro-immigrant alternative, to stop what they viewed as a slide into support for them. The National Network for Immigrant and Refugee Rights organized a series of conversations that produced the first of these alternative proposals in April 2006. Eighty-three organizations signed a National Statement to Support Human and Civil Rights for All Immigrants, including the AFL-CIO, the American Friends Service Committee, the Chinese Progressive Association, and more than a hundred individuals. It provided a way for local immigrant-rights organizations and unions to restate their agreement on proposals for immigration reform they'd supported for years, as a criteria for evaluating the proposals in Washington. In California, local central labor councils adopted it, as well as the East Bay Alliance for a Sustainable Economy. "It was a constructive way to go about healing our divisions and recommitting ourselves to a positive agenda, rather than simply react to a negative one," said one participant, who still worried about being identified as an opponent of the Washington consensus.

The statement called for legalization of all undocumented immi-

grants, halting indefinite detention, no expansion of guest-worker programs, ending further militarization of the border, ending employer
sanctions, supporting family reunification, and expanding legal immigration opportunities. Senate proposals for a "path to citizenship," it
said, amounted to "a massive temporary-worker program without
worker protections . . . designed to force and keep wages down to compete with cheap labor suppliers globally." The statement called on
Congress to change economic and trade policies causing migration.
"Increased enforcement does not address this complex issue," it
warned. "Employer sanctions and beefed-up border security have been
in place for decades as deterrents to migration, yet the number of undocumented continues to grow."

Because of its experiences with guest workers brought into the Gulf
States in the wake of Hurricane Katrina, the Mississippi Immigrant
Rights Alliance announced it was opposed to Congress's compromise
reform bills. "Organizations that are fighting for the rights of workers
should be totally opposed to these programs," MIRA executive director Bill Chandler declared. "The conditions are so exploitative they're
even worse than those of undocumented workers." MIRA turned the
general principles in the network's statement into concrete proposals
for a new immigration-reform bill. "All people living in the U.S. without legal immigration status can apply for permanent-residence status
upon passage of this bill," it began, and stated that "all immigrants
living in the U.S. for at least five years should be eligible to apply for
permanent-residence status." To account for future flows of migration it proposed increasing the number of permanent-residence visas
for new migrants, as Jackson Lee had.

Other provisions proposed to abolish employer sanctions and reinforce organizing rights. MIRA proposed no new guest-worker or temporary-visa programs, and that the number of those visas be held at
present levels. It too called for creating "sustainable economic development policies in developing countries, instead of promoting free
trade policies which lead to the displacement of communities and
their forced migration." It incorporated Jackson Lee's proposal for job
training and creation, and a general statement of rights, in which "all

legal residents, including newly legalized people, would have the same labor and civil rights as the general population, in accordance with the U.S. Constitution."

As Congress seemed unable to break its internal stalemate, other efforts sought to create an even wider base of support for positive reform proposals. One, the "Unity Blueprint," gained the support especially of unions in Los Angeles that had supported the comprehensive bills. Local labor councils, like the one in Silicon Valley, also adopted their own proposals.

In northern California, a group of African American activists formed the Black Alliance for Just Immigration. "Our first efforts are to go to churches, barbershops, and other places in our community where people talk, and just listen to begin with," said the organization's Phil Hutchings. "But then we try to inject our point of view into the discussion. There is competition between communities, and U.S. immigration policy is infused with racism and inequality, so our goal is to organize our own community to challenge it. We defend the ideals we've always stood for. We also want to make sure that organizations in immigrant communities get a better understanding of racism here, and how it affects them."

The congressional compromise ultimately failed, but it provoked a wide variety of much more positive proposals. It sparked an upsurge of activity among unions, churches, African Americans, and, most of all, in immigrant communities themselves. Hope for progressive immigration reform depends on organizing and expanding that movement, and coming to agreement on a common ground of goals that can unite it.

Meanwhile, however, Mississippi governor Haley Barbour signed Senate Bill 2988 into law in March 2008, making it a state felony, punishable by one to ten years in prison and a $1–$10,000 fine, for an undocumented worker to hold a job. MIRA charged it was intended to drive immigrants from the state and prevent its political transformation; other states also passed laws further criminalizing work for the undocumented. The need for an alternative program for immigration reform could hardly be clearer.

Seven

ILLEGAL PEOPLE OR ILLEGAL WORK?

Pérdido en el corazón / De la grande Babylon
Me dicen el clandestino / Por no llevar papel.

. . .

Soy una raya en el mar / Fantasma en la ciudad
Mi vida va prohibida / Dice la autoridad.

Mano negra clandestino / Peruano clandestino
Africano clandestino / Marijuana! ilegal!

Lost in the heart / of the great Babylon
They call me clandestine / Because I have no papers.

. . .

I'm a line on the ocean / A ghost in the city
The authorities say / My existence is forbidden.

Black hand—clandestine! / Peruvian—clandestine!
African—clandestine! / Illegal! Marijuana!

—Manu Chao, "Clandestino"

Illegal Means Not European and Not White

A few days before Christmas in 1995, one of the last of a generation of Filipino labor organizers died in a hospital bed in Bakersfield, California. Pete Velasco was a veteran of the wars in the fields that created the United Farm Workers. With other Filipino leaders Philip Vera Cruz and Larry Itliong, he started the great grape strike of 1965 in which the union was born. In the years that followed he became one of its leaders.

Velasco was called Manong Pete, *manong* being a term of respect given to older people in Filipino culture. But along the Pacific Coast "manong" was more than an honorific—it was the name of a generation, the radical first wave of immigrants from the Philippines. Between 1920 and 1929, 113,144 people, mostly men and mostly farmers, left their lands and villages in the islands. Filipinos were first recruited for Hawaii plantations by the Hawaii Sugar Planters Association in 1906, just a few years after the end of the war in which the United States annexed the Philippines. In the early 1920s they began migrating from Hawaii to the mainland, and later many Filipinos came directly to the mainland from the Philippines. Like Velasco, who came in 1931, they were driven by hopes for education and advancement, crossing the Pacific Ocean to America when it was a voyage of weeks. But here they found no promised land. Instead, they found hard labor, bad conditions, and discrimination.

For the next five decades, Filipinos sailed in rusty ships to Alaskan salmon canneries so isolated that no roads led there. They traveled through the desert valleys of the Southwest, migrating from field to field, labor camp to labor camp, picking everything from grapes to asparagus. They sweated in the hot kitchens of restaurants, returning in the small hours of the morning to hotels for single men scorned by polite society as skid row. "When we walked the sidewalks in the early days," Velasco remembered, "they shouted at us, 'Hey, monkey—go home!'"

"The manongs who came in the 1920s were children of colonialism," explained Abba Ramos, an organizer for the International Longshore and Warehouse Union (ILWU), who was born into the generation that followed. From 1898 to 1946 the Philippines was a U.S. colony, and even in the most remote islands, children were taught in English, from U.S. textbooks, and often by missionary teachers from Philadelphia or New Jersey. Students studied the promises of the Declaration of Independence before they knew the names of Emilio Aguinaldo and Andrés Bonifacio—the general and revolutionary who led Filipinos in their own independence war against the Spaniards and, later, the Americans. "The manongs were radicalized because they compared the ideals of the U.S. Constitution, and of the Filipinos' own quest for freedom, with the harsh reality they found here," Ramos said.

For Philip Vera Cruz, who became a UFW leader like Velasco, that promise of equality "was in the books, and in the mouths of the American teachers in the Philippines. But it did not work that way. When Filipinos got to the U.S. they found that they were only wanted for their service, their labor."

Al Masigat, who came in the 1920s, recounted his experience in a master's-thesis study by Lillian Galedo, executive director of Filipinos for Affirmative Action, of the growth of radical ideas in that first generation of Filipino migrants, "The Development of Working Class Consciousness." "They made us stay in the stables," he remembered, "just put our straw in there, put our blankets in there with the horses and mules. When they told us to work in the morning I said to the owner 'No, we are not going to work.' In the Philippines, you do not sleep with the horses, no matter how poor you are."

The Filipinos arrived just in time for the Great Depression. Wages had been low all through the 1920s, because the industries in which they worked—agriculture and fish canneries—used the contractor system. "The owner tells the contractor, 'Supply me with twenty-five men, and I will pay them fifty cents an hour,'" Masigat explained. "But instead of paying you that fifty cents, the contractor will say to you, 'I'll pay you thirty cents,' so he gets the rest."

Once the Depression hit, Filipinos' conditions became even worse. Masigat traveled from farm to farm, sharing his poverty with five other young men from the islands, worried that the money he'd saved to get back home was almost gone. "Whenever we had nothing I took some of the money that I had and spent for all six of us, so on December of the first year of the Depression I only had a hundred dollars left and that was too low! I even sweat a cold sweat . . . But we couldn't complain. As long as we had a small place to hide when the winter or rain came, that was good because we could see people wondering where and when they were going to eat, or where they could get a small room to stay. . . We survived by helping each other. If you had no shoes to wear, you could not work in the fields. So we contributed to each other and bought shoes."

In Alaska's salmon canneries, conditions were no better. "Before you got overtime you had to put in twelve hours, from six to six," Masigat remembered. "In the morning maybe they gave you two pieces of bread, no butter, no eggs, no bacon, no nothing. At noontime they gave you only fish heads and mongo [beans]. For dinner, they gave you fried fish again, and you worked till four or five in the morning! I now wonder how I did it." Depression farm wages dropped from 30¢ an hour to 15¢, to 12.5¢ for field work. California's minimum wage in canneries fell from 33.5¢ to 30¢ to 27¢. But Velasco's and Masigat's generation refused to be docile labor sweated for pennies. Between 1930 and 1939 a Senate investigation counted 140 farm strikes in California alone, involving 127,000 workers.

What the manongs found in America made them hard. They became a generation of union organizers and political radicals, men conscious of their class status, not just as workers but as immigrant workers on the bottom of American society. They led strikes and founded unions; they wrote books and edited newspapers. And they stood as outsiders looking in, matching professed ideals of justice and equality with reality as they found it.

The manongs were mostly single men, some for economic reasons, others because the law often denied them the right to a family. Dean Alegado, professor of ethnic studies at the University of Hawaii, says many of the first Filipinos didn't bring their wives to the Hawaiian sugar plantations, because "they were paid the lowest, compared to . . . other workers on the plantations, and the housing camps they were assigned were in bad condition." Women did come, however, as part of that first wave. The larger wave that followed to the West Coast found more organized discrimination. When Filipinos danced with white women in the taxi dance halls, they were called a threat to white society, and antimiscegenation laws in California and the West prohibited the marriage of Filipino men and white women. A few of Velasco's countrymen traveled a thousand miles to the states of the Midwest to find a legal wedding, and Velasco himself only married long after those laws were struck down. The 1922 Cable Act even threatened the U.S. citizenship of any woman who married an Asian. In the eyes of employers and politicians, the Filipinos' reason for being in America was simply to work, not to have families and raise children. Not to belong.

The treatment of Filipinos as a mobile, vulnerable workforce, circulated from labor camp to labor camp, was not new on the Pacific Coast. Their inferior status was inherited from other workers imported from Asia before them, the Chinese and Japanese. While their legal situation was slightly different because they came from a U.S. colony, they shared with their predecessors a second-class social status. That simple sign in many businesses, "No Filipinos Allowed," made their status clear. They were the illegals of their moment in history— people whose labor was needed but whose inferior status denied them the rights others could take for granted.

The first group of people recruited from Asia to work in the United States came from the Toishan area of China's Pearl River Delta. They were brought by contractors to build the Transcontinental Railroad, and furnished brute manual labor in conditions not far removed from slavery. Later their labor and technical knowledge was used to drain the huge Sacramento and San Joaquin river delta, creating vast new areas of farmland.

U.S. immigration policy was the mechanism that defined their status. The inferior status of the Chinese and the Asians who came after them, and the undocumented workers of today, developed out of slavery. Chattel slavery created a society divided into human beings with rights and human beings without them. Its purpose was to supply labor at the lowest possible cost to the owners of the South's plantations. The ideology of the racial superiority of white people was developed to justify this brutal system, while racial categories developed to determine who could be enslaved and who could not.

Those racial categories, defining unequal status, were enshrined in the Constitution at the nation's birth when it counted people from Africa—slaves—as three-fifths of a human being. Free blacks had to be prepared to prove their legality—otherwise it could be assumed that they were runaways and reenslaved. Fugitive-slave laws established that runaway slaves were illegal from the moment they left their masters, and could be rounded up and returned to them, even if they were captured in the North, where slavery was supposedly not legal. In the Dred Scott decision the Supreme Court decided that no people of African descent could ever be citizens, whether slave or free. The country's first law defining citizenship, the Naturalization Act of 1790, allowed people to exercise the rights of citizenship only if they were "free white persons." That definition was held to eliminate women, slaves, freed blacks, and later others defined as nonwhite.

In the decades before the Civil War, Black Codes were passed to further define illegality. Those states admitted to the Union as "free states," or states in which slavery was not permitted, also made the mere presence of African-descended people illegal. Indiana's Constitution of 1851, for instance, said, "No Negro or Mulatto shall come into, or settle in, the State, after the adoption of this Constitution." In Illinois, the Black Code of 1853 also forbade black people from immigrating into the state.

At the end of the Civil War, the former slave states passed other Black Codes before the Union Army took away their powers. Their open purpose was to control the labor of the former slaves. According to historian Ellis Paxson Oberholtzer, in *A History of the United States since the Civil War* (1917), Mississippi's Black Code said that "Negroes must make annual contracts for their labor in writing; if they should run away from their tasks, they forfeited their wages for the year. Whenever it was required of them they must present licenses (in a town from the mayor; elsewhere from a member of the board of police of the beat) citing their places of residence and authorizing them to work. Fugitives from labor were to be arrested and carried back to their employers. Five dollars a head and mileage would be allowed such Negro catchers. It was made a misdemeanor, punishable with fine or imprisonment, to persuade a freedman to leave his employer, or to feed the runaway."

In 1866 the newly elected Republican government imposed a military occupation on the South, the Black Codes were repealed, and Reconstruction governments of black and white people were elected. When Reconstruction ended, however, and the troops were withdrawn, racist governments returned black people to an unequal social status, denied political and labor rights.

Following the Civil War, labor was needed to develop the railroads and agricultural areas of the West, and waves of workers were recruited to provide it. Immigration law then became one important means to define who was legal and who wasn't—that is, who possessed the legal right to live and work in the United States, and under what conditions. Ironically, the laws passed to guarantee the legal status of freed slaves were used to deny it to others. When the Civil War ended, the Fourteenth Amendment overturned the Dred Scott decision. To implement it, Congress passed the Naturalization Act of 1870, which limited citizenship to "white persons and persons of African descent."

Chinese contract laborers had already been working in the United States for twenty years by that time. In 1870 a third of the people living in Idaho were Chinese, but under this law, none could ever become citizens, nor their children. Then, in the 1880s as successive economic crises provided a fertile ground for the growth of racist hysteria fueled by fears of job competition, Congress passed laws barring the further immigration of people from China. Those who came after were then illegal, unless they could provide some kind of document showing they or their parents had come before the cutoff date.

"A hundred years ago my grandfather and his brother crossed the Mexican border into California illegally, buried in a hay cart," remembers Katie Quan, who today cochairs the Center for Labor Research and Education at the University of California in Berkeley. Then the fire that followed the earthquake of 1906 burned down San Francisco's City Hall, destroying the immigration records of the city's Chinese residents. The whole community became undocumented. And when everyone was undocumented, anyone could say they had arrived legally and had their papers go up in flames. Quan's grandfather became a legal resident as a result of claiming that incinerated records showed he had come before passage of the Chinese Exclusion Act in 1882. Other immigrants brought relatives from China, claiming they were "paper sons" of legal immigrants, or those whose documents had perished in the fire. "That is the way a very high percentage of Chinese Americans came to the U.S., including my mother's family," Quan says. "The Chinese Exclusion Act brings bitter memories for Chinese Americans to this day, because it barred Chinese, and only Chinese, from entering the U.S."

In the middle of San Francisco Bay, Angel Island became the detention camp for hundreds of Chinese would-be immigrants, who arrived on ships but could not produce paper-son documents or any written basis for being admitted. While they waited for such documents to come from China, some were held for years in barracks, carving poems into the wooden walls, pouring out their loneliness and frustration. At the same time, hundreds of thousands of white immigrants boarded freighters in Europe, crossed the Atlantic, and landed at Ellis Island in New York Harbor. There they were given a health examination, asked a few questions, and then admitted. There were some pitfalls. Would-be immigrants who admitted that they had been recruited and promised a job were denied entry. If they were sick, they were quarantined. But no one was required to have permission to enter, and visas didn't exist.

From the beginning, U.S. immigration laws defined legal status and assigned it to people on a racial basis. A Chinese worker who entered the country after 1882 without paper-son documents was illegal. An Italian who entered the same year at Ellis Island was not. Enforcing illegality was not a peaceful process. Anti-Chinese riots burned out entire communities up and down the West Coast. All the Chinese were driven out of Idaho by 1910. The creation of Chinatowns in San Francisco, New York, and other cities was not just the product of people's desire for community, but of segregation laws as well as the need for self-protection.

Denied Chinese labor in developing agriculture, western growers next recruited immigrants from Japan, whose horticultural expertise helped establish industrial-scale fruit and vegetable cultivation in California, Oregon, and Washington. When they began to buy land and start their own farms, however, Alien Land Laws were passed prohibiting land ownership by people of Asian ancestry. White growers not only wanted to prevent competition but ensure the continuation of a vulnerable labor force not tied down by land and family. Meanwhile, the 1924 Immigration Act said no further immigration would be permitted by anyone who could not become a citizen, and Asians were barred from citizenship by racial exclusions.

Al Masigat, Leo Lorenzo, Pete Velasco, and Philip Vera Cruz were all part of the next wave of Asian immigration, recruited by growers taking advantage of the colonial relationship between the United States and the Philippines. Because they came from a U.S. colony, they were not classified as "aliens" under the 1924 act. The first Puerto Ricans also came to California at that time as a result of recruitment based on Puerto Rico's colonial status. Both groups became important parts of the agriculture and food-processing workforce in Hawaii and on the Pacific Coast, along with a wave of migrants recruited earlier from India.

One Indian immigrant, Bhagat Singh Thind, tried to claim U.S. citizenship. The U.S. Supreme Court then held, in 1923, that Indians were Asians, and therefore not white, and not eligible. White was not just a color, but denoted European ancestry. A worker from southern Italy, for instance, might have skin as dark as Bhagat Singh Thind's, but Italians were considered white because they were Europeans, and therefore "readily amalgamated," as the Court said. The Indians already in California fields didn't disappear, of course. But they were prevented from becoming equal, put into a social category—illegality—defined by race and national origin, in which they had no political rights and were subject to vicious discrimination.

The Filipinos, the Chinese, and the Indians all organized as exiles against colonialism at home. Indians formed groups like the Ghadar Party that returned to take up arms against the British for independence and freedom. More than a hundred were arrested after their arrival from California in 1914. Filipinos in the United States agitated for Philippine independence, as well as for better wages and conditions. And the statue of Chinese revolutionary leader Sun Yat-sen in a park at the edge of San Francisco's Chinatown honors him for forming the Nationalist Party in exile, prior to the Revolution of 1911.

In 1934 the Tydings-McDuffie Act stopped further Filipino immigration and Filipinos were reclassified as "aliens" until the Magnuson Act was passed in 1943. Then the United States lifted the racial barrier to citizenship for most Asian immigrants, to encourage their participation in the war against Japan. On the West Coast, however, Japanese immigrants and even their children born in the United States were interned in concentration camps until the war ended. This was an extreme expression of illegality, again defined by race and national origin.

By the 1940s, Chinese and Japanese communities had become settled and left the agricultural labor force. Immigration from the Philippines had been cut off. The late 1930s was the only period in which a significant number of white people, mostly Dust Bowl migrants from Oklahoma and Texas, worked in the fields on the Pacific Coast. But they too quickly became settled residents in rural communities. Meanwhile, the preceding decade of strikes had put pressure on growers to raise wages. Even though many organizers had been deported or imprisoned, unions became strong in the fields and canneries. In 1942, in the middle of World WarII, the U.S. and Mexican governments set up the bracero program for the systematic recruitment of Mexicans, who'd been part of the farm labor force in the Southwest from its earliest days.

"The idea of a stable, locally rooted labor force was not an encouraging development for agribusiness," said Ernesto Galarza, the bracero program's greatest opponent, in Galedo's study. "While agribusiness might not have formulated a conscious long range plan for preventing farm labor insurgency, they had at least learned that the age old policy of keeping people on the move was much preferable to a labor force with roots from which a strong union could grow. To frustrate the danger, the industry realized that the roots must be cut and perpetual mobility reintroduced as a way of life for harvesters."

Fighting Second-Class Status

The history of unionism in farm labor is one of repeated efforts to bring together migrant workers from many countries, speaking many languages. In 1903 Japanese and Mexican workers united against low wages and bad conditions in a strike in Oxnard, California, against local pea growers. They formed a union, and turned to the socialist leadership of the Los Angeles labor federation for help. After they'd won their fight with the support of LA unions, they applied for a charter from the American Federation of Labor. Samuel Gompers, AFL president, refused to admit the new union unless it rid itself of its Asian members.

In the late 1920s and early 1930s Filipinos also began to organize and press for higher wages. At first they launched spontaneous strikes— "Not yet a union, but like a union," Masigat recalled. Filipinos created their own associations, because the AFL "did not want to have Filipinos with them," according to fellow manong Leo Lorenzo. Independent, left-led unions then brought together workers of different nationalities and mounted huge strikes in the Imperial, San Joaquin, and Salinas valleys. Eventually, Lorenzo said, more progressive trade union leaders, willing to organize Filipino, Mexican, and black workers, made a break with the old AFL. "That's when the CIO [Congress of Industrial Organizations] came into existence," he said.

After World War II, cold war hysteria in the labor movement destroyed the CIO's farmworker union, the United Cannery, Agricultural, Packinghouse, and Allied Workers of America. At the same time, the bracero program, as Galarza had warned, made it impossible for farmworkers to strike effectively. But in 1964 Galarza, Bert Corona, César Chávez, and others convinced Congress to repeal the bracero law, Public Law 78. In California the following year Filipino workers began striking, knowing that growers would have trouble finding strikebreakers to cross their picket lines. After walking out in Coachella and Arvin, the Filipinos and their union, the Agricultural Workers Organizing Committee, appealed to Chávez and the National Farm Workers Association, whose members were mostly Mexican. The two groups united in Delano, creating United Farm Workers. In his song "Huelga en General," Luis Valdez, the founder of the Teatro Campesino, a theater group organized at the beginning of the farmworker movement, celebrated the unity that made the strike possible:

> El dia ocho de septiembre de los campos de Delano
> 　　salieron los Filipinos
> Y después de dos semanas para unirse la batalla salieron
> 　　los Mexicanos
> Y juntos vemos cumpliendo con la marcha de la historia
> 　　para liberar al pueblo.
> ¡Viva la revolución!
> ¡Viva nuestra asociación!
> ¡Viva la huelga en general!

> *On the eighth of September the Filipinos walked out of the*
> 　　*fields in Delano*
> *And after two weeks to unite in the battle the Mexicans*
> 　　*walked out.*
> *And together we're now part of the march of history to liberate*
> 　　*the people.*
> *Long live the revolution!*
> *Long live our association!*
> *Long live the general strike!*

"America is not a land of one race or one class of men," asserted the Filipino writer Carlos Bulosan in 1943, in *America Is in the Heart: A Personal History.* "We are all Americans who have toiled and suffered and known oppression and defeat, from the first Indian that offered peace in Manhattan to the last Filipino pea pickers." At a time when the Philippines was still a U.S. colony, he declared, "America is not bound by geographical latitudes. America is not merely a land or an institution. America is in the hearts of men that died for freedom; it is also in the eyes of men that are building a new world."

"Bulosan wrote articles encouraging his countrymen to wake up," Masigat remembered. " 'Do not just give yourselves like dogs!' he told us." Bulosan's generation established a tradition of radicalism and trade unionism among Filipinos and farmworkers, and they kept that dream alive even during the difficult years of the cold war.

Abba Ramos's mother and father worked on Hawaii's giant sugar plantations in the 1930s and 1940s, when unionism was in the air. "It was an apartheid style of life," he remembered, "where workers were held hostage to the mill owners." Hawaii organizing drives during those years made the International Longshore and Warehouse Union (ILWU) the most powerful political force in the islands. "The union revolutionized the whole democratic process," Ramos explained. "Before sugar workers had a union, five families ran everything. Afterwards, every politician who wanted to run for office had to come talk to the workers, and their union decided who got elected." Hawaii's farm laborers were mostly Filipinos and Japanese, with smaller numbers of Puerto Ricans, Portuguese, and Chinese.

Ramos was one of the first children of sugar workers to attend the University of Hawaii. On graduation, he got a job in a nonunion hotel, the King Kamehameha, hoping to help workers organize. Ramos listened to Filipino ILWU leaders. "I admired them. They told me, 'If you want to be an organizer, show us what you can do. Go into the workplace and unite your fellow workers.' " Ramos took up their challenge, and spent his life working for the ILWU. "Filipino workers," he said, "are often still on the bottom. We make the beds. We work in the restaurants, the electronics plants, and the fields. We need to accept the fact we are a working-class community. If we want to advance, we have to unite with other workers like us. That's what we learned in Hawaii."

At the height of the cold war the Un-American Activities Committee of the U.S. House of Representatives held hearings in Hawaii and California, calling ILWU leaders to testify about their radical activities. The committee demanded they name members of the U.S. Communist Party; for immigrants, such membership was grounds for deportation. Federal authorities tried for years to deport the union's president, Harry Bridges, an Australian immigrant, accusing him of being a Communist. Many immigrant union leaders facing the same accusation, like Humberto Salas, were deported. Others, like Bridges and California cannery union organizer Lucio Bernabe, successfully fought deportation. The Committee for the Protection of the Foreign Born, an immigrant defense network of the 1950s, fought to defend them all. Ramos remembered that agents of the FBI came to his parents' home on a Hawaii plantation and told them their union was led by Communists. "My father said, 'If winning better wages and making us equal here is Communist, then we are too,'" he laughed.

Filipino labor activists not only organized unions, but fought to make them clean and democratic, responsive to the needs of their members. Seattle's ILWU Local 37 was organized by Filipino left-wingers Chris Mensalves and Ernesto Mangaoang in the Alaska fish canneries in the 1930s and 1940s. But during the 1950s and 1960s it fell into the hands of racketeers. Union leaders sold jobs in the union hall and ran gambling operations to fleece workers. Meanwhile, bad conditions in the remote canneries went unchallenged.

In 1977, labor leader Richard Gurtiza, just out of college, got a dispatch to Alaska. "I found segregated housing and mess halls," he remembered, "and discrimination against Filipinos in promotions and jobs. We had no upward mobility, and lived in decrepit bunkhouses. I felt like I was living in the past." Two older friends of Gurtiza's, Gene Viernes and Silme Domingo, filed suit against the canneries. They built a rank-and-file movement among the local's members and were elected dispatcher and president. Then they went to the Philippines and made friends with the radical May First Movement union federation, which was challenging the martial law regime of dictator Ferdinand Marcos, a strong U.S. ally.

Marcos sent agents to the West Coast, where they formed a covert alliance with the ousted corrupt officials. One of them, Tony Baruso, then hired assassins who shot and killed Domingo and Viernes in the union hall in Seattle in 1981. "I decided to help finish what Gene and Silme started," Gurtiza says. "We defeated the murderers because instead of scaring people into silence, more workers came forward." A celebrated trial convicted Baruso and documented the complicity of the Philippine government. Gurtiza was later elected local president.

The first generation of Filipino unionists shared the vision that a strong union movement in the United States might help people back home. The idea of freedom is contagious, said Vera Cruz. The United Farm Workers owed a lot to the civil rights movement. "Farmworkers saw on television that blacks were succeeding in the South," he recalled. "Some of their children even went there and came back. If it could be done there, they thought, it could be done here too." The idea could spread back home as well, he hoped: "The idea will travel. It will reach the Philippines because it goes all around. What we do here will be an invitation for other people to struggle and win their freedom."

The manongs didn't see themselves as romantic freedom fighters, however. Velasco was proud of simply opening up the Filipino Community Hall in Delano at 2:00 a.m. each morning during the first year of the grape strike that began in 1965. He made the coffee and set up the food bank for the strikers. After the UFW started the boycott, he stood in front of supermarkets passing out leaflets asking people not to buy grapes. The union recognized the contribution of Velasco's generation, because they'd kept alive the dream of unions in the fields through the hardest times. When the manongs grew too old to work, the UFW began construction of Agbayani Village, a retirement community on the union's Forty Acres headquarters in the heart of the San Joaquin Valley. A new generation of Filipino young people like

Gurtiza, radicalized by the civil rights movement and Vietnam War, traveled to Delano from all over the Pacific Coast to build it.

Migration from the Philippines did not end with the manongs. A second wave of soldiers and war brides came after World War II, and in the 1960s, a third wave began. In part it was the product of a liberalization of U.S. immigration law in 1965. But it was also produced by a precipitous decline in living standards in the islands, and the application of the same kinds of economic reforms that produced waves of migration from Mexico. Many Filipino migrants found their way to Silicon Valley. Much had changed in the United States since the manongs fought their battles, but one thing hadn't. Filipino workers were still on the bottom, in the worst jobs. And a new generation of union activists, some of them veterans of the Philippine labor movement, led efforts to organize them.

Silicon Valley's High-Tech Sweatshops

The railroad tank car sat for days on a siding at the Romic Corp. waste transfer station in Redwood City, a working-class town halfway between San Francisco and Silicon Valley. It was filled with chemical leftovers from the production lines of the valley's electronics plants. After they were pumped out, a sludge of toxic waste remained that was so thick, gravity alone couldn't drain it out. Poisonous fumes from the used solvents filled the air above it. John Moran, supervisor of the tank-cleaning operation, decided that someone would have to climb inside and push the sludge down to the drain valve.

His first choice, Luis Lopez, refused to use the company's breathing apparatus. For some time, the rig had been setting off alarms showing dangerous concentrations of carbon monoxide. Then Moran called Rodrigo Cruz. At 6:15 in the morning of February 15, 1995, Cruz reported to the Redwood City facility. He'd worked for Romic for two years, but at a yard in East Palo Alto, fifteen miles away. He'd never been trained to clean railroad cars or use the breathing apparatus. He was reluctant to go in, and looked at the coupling connecting the hose to the respiratory rig he would wear. It was wrapped in duct tape.

The supervisors knew about the tape and the alarms, but no one said anything to Cruz. He put a paper Tyvek suit on over his clothes, donned the apparatus, and went down inside. After pushing the sludge toward the drain for a couple of hours, he had trouble breathing. He came out and took a break, complaining he wasn't getting enough air. As soon as he went back in, his breathing problems increased. Suddenly, he could get no air at all, and a terrible smell and taste filled his nose and mouth. Cruz tried pulling on the escape cord, which should have signaled that he was in trouble. Nothing happened. Somehow, he didn't fall into the knee-deep sludge, where he almost certainly would have died. Instead, he managed to stagger back down the dark tank until he was under the hatch where he'd entered and caught the attention of someone above. They hauled him out.

After stripping off the breathing rig and his paper suit, smeared with the tank's waste, he still could hardly breathe. Finally, he lost consciousness and collapsed. Someone called 911, and the police took him away in an ambulance.

Cruz didn't die, but the effects of that morning will probably last the rest of his life. He had excruciating headaches and no sense of balance. His reflexes were poor. He couldn't drive or ride a bike. He had problems remembering things, and waves of depression swept over him. Doctors concluded he'd suffered carbon monoxide poisoning and oxygen deprivation down in the railcar. In addition, the fumes there contained xylene, benzene, methyl ethyl ketone, and trichloroethane, all dangerous solvents commonly used in electronics. Over time they can cause cancer and liver damage. Cruz had no way of knowing what he might suffer in years to come.

Cruz's story became a legend among Silicon Valley's Filipino workers, told in whispered conversations on the high-tech production lines. Families talked about it in the tiny Asian groceries that dot the home of electronics. "We understand why Rodrigo went into the tank when he could see the danger," said health and safety activist Romie Manan. "When he looked at the duct tape around the air tube, he was thinking of his family, of all the people he had to feed at home. We aren't stupid, but we'll do things despite our misgivings because of the consequences of losing our jobs."

In the popular imagination, Silicon Valley is the hub of the information superhighway. In reality, it is a huge industrial center with a workforce of over a quarter million people. In its heart, giant semiconductor plants manufacture chips, or integrated circuits, the brains of computers and electronic devices assembled in other valley factories. Chips are made in a process called wafer fabrication, where thin disks of silicon are bathed and baked in a large variety of extremely toxic solvents, acids, and gasses, to implant tiny transistors. The sludge at the bottom of the tank car is the "clean industry's" toxic residue. Until the city of East Palo Alto finally revoked its operating permit in 2007, Romic Corp. handled much of that waste.

Inside the plants, thousands of workers are constantly exposed to these chemicals at low levels. Asian immigrants do the jobs that bring the most chemical exposure and pay the least. In the high-tech workforce in the mid-1990s, they made up 30 percent of skilled production workers, 47 percent of the semiskilled, and 41 percent of the unskilled jobs. Of the many Asian nationalities in the plants, Filipinos were by far the largest group. Latinos constituted 18 percent of skilled workers, 21 percent of semiskilled workers, and 36 percent of unskilled workers. Together, however, both groups made up only 17 percent of management, and 25 percent of professional and engineering employees. Women were half of the production workforce, but only a small minority of managers and engineers. In 2007 that hiring pattern hadn't changed much.

In this race- and sex-stratified picture, African Americans are almost entirely absent. Although they are the majority of the residents of East Palo Alto and East Oakland, cities just north of Silicon Valley, African Americans constitute less than 7.5 percent of the electronics workforce in any category. It may be coincidence that William Shockley, co-inventor of the transistor, was also a strong believer that African Americans are genetically inferior. The de facto color line in Silicon Valley, however, is a demographic fact. Karen Hossfeld, a San Francisco State University sociologist who's studied women in high-tech industry, explains those demographics as a conscious choice by manufacturers. "Employers assume foreign-born women will be unlikely to agitate for pay hikes," she says.

Cruz's case was more than a symbol of racial stratification, however. For three months he ran a gauntlet of lawyers and social service agencies, looking for help. Romic fought his workers' compensation claim, and he was worried about how he would live, perhaps unable to work for the rest of his life. One afternoon he walked through the door of the Santa Clara Center for Occupational Safety and Health (SCCOSH), in an old house divided into crowded offices, across the street from the Santa Clara County Building.

SCCOSH was started by electronics workers and health and safety activists to challenge toxic contamination in the electronics industry. In 1992 the group alleged a connection between the high miscarriage rate among women in the factories and their job conditions. The Semiconductor Industry Association sponsored a study of eleven plants, and instead of refuting the claims, University of California experts found a direct link between miscarriages and the use of ethylene glycol. Lawyers working with the center filed numerous suits and workers' compensation claims for workers disabled by toxic exposure, against electronics giants like Intel, National Semiconductor, Hewlett-Packard, IBM, and Phillips. SCCOSH campaigns forced the industry to stop using 1,1,1-trichloroethylene, a carcinogenic solvent.

At SCCOSH, Cruz found two Filipino immigrants like himself, Raquel Sancho and Romie Manan. Both had roots in the anti-Marcos movement in the Philippines—Sancho as an organizer in Manila's women's movement and Manan as a trade unionist. Sancho used a grassroots organizing style, going to karoake bars and singing with workers, taking trips to the mall with their families, or going to picnics and potlucks. "In the Philippines we call this social investigation—getting to know the community," she explained. "I used to go from friend to friend selling Saladmaster, like people sell Amway or Tupperware. I used the same technique here."

Manan came to California from Manila in 1979, after a decade as a leader in the Telecommunications Workers Union, in one of Asia's most militant and turbulent labor movements. After martial law was declared in 1972, all the union leaders at Telefast PT&T, where Manan worked, were fired. He fought successfully for reinstatement, but was fired a second time. After that he worked as a full-time organizer. Facing the inevitability of eventual arrest, and possible disappearance, he decided to leave the islands. In Silicon Valley, Manan found a job at National Semiconductor's huge, ten-thousand-worker plant in Santa Clara. He soon became a leader of the Electronics Organizing Committee of the United Electrical Workers, a grassroots group trying to form a union. "From the beginning," he said, "we faced an industry-wide policy that fights any organizing effort." He wasn't just paranoid. Robert Noyce, who coinvented the transistor with Shockley and later founded Intel Corp., declared that "remaining nonunion is an essential for the survival for most of our companies . . . This is a very high priority for management here."

Manan recruited Filipino workers on the production lines, translating the committee's newsletter, the *Union Voice,* into Tagalog. "Every worker in Silicon Valley knows that if you try to organize a union, you will probably lose your job, even if we have that right on paper," he explained. "But in spite of our fear, we handed out the *Union Voice* in front of our plant. We pressured the companies to give us raises and to stop using dangerous chemicals. We passed around petitions when workers were terminated." Eventually almost all the committee's leaders were fired. Manan, however, held on to his job for another fifteen years. "Our union never won recognition and a contract," he said, "but we were the only voice calling for protecting the jobs of production workers in our industry, a large percentage of whom are Filipinos. We fought to improve life for the whole community."

When they met Cruz, Sancho and Manan had just organized a network of Filipinos, HealthWATCH (Workers against Toxic Chemical Hazards). They used popular-education techniques from the Philippines to recount their life histories and discuss the chemicals used at work. When Rodrigo Cruz showed up at the SCCOSH office, WATCH members were ready not just to listen to his story but to support him. The little network took Cruz's case into the plants. Workers brave enough to face company displeasure began wearing buttons or ribbons. In East Palo Alto, SCCOSH formed an alliance with the African American and Latino neighbors unhappy at living next to a toxic-waste dump. Together they organized joint demonstrations against company expansion plans, kept Cruz's legal case alive, and won an investigation of Romic.

California's Occupational Safety and Health Administration inspectors issued twenty-two citations for numerous health and safety violations, and twenty-five more over the railcar incident. Romic's community relations director Chris Stampoulis claimed the contents of the railcar were an "alternative fuel residue," because the sludge was burned as fuel in a kiln making cement. Eventually in 2007 a local coalition headed by Youth United for Community Action, a grassroots group of young activists, succeeded in getting Romic's East Palo Alto operation shut down.

Manan still believed that the only way to really improve the situation of Filipino electronics workers was to organize a union, but in his three decades in the industry, he didn't see much interest in the U.S. labor movement. While Filipinos don't face the same discriminatory barriers they did in the 1920s, they still didn't get much help. "Unions should make a long-term commitment to workers in the plants," he urged. "To electronics companies, we're cheaper. They don't have to spend money on the right equipment. They can just use an air tube wrapped with tape. If there's an accident, we'll pay the price."

Nevertheless, for Filipinos the giant semiconductor plants seemed at least a secure source of jobs in a modern industry. High-tech depended on them the way growers and fish canneries depended on an earlier generation. In some semiconductor factories, like National Semiconductor and Advanced Micro Devices (AMD), swing and grave shifts were known as the Filipino shifts. The community's dependence on the jobs became a liability, however, when companies began to move production out of the valley.

Maria Villanueva went to work at AMD's Sunnyvale plant in the

1980s, when there were fifteen wafer-fabrication lines. "Except for day shift, almost all of us were Filipino," she recalled. At the Plaza de Manila restaurant, just down the street from the semiconductor factories, Filipino customers formed long lines out onto the sidewalk at lunch break. When the companies began to relocate production in the 1990s, however, the tables at Plaza de Manila were deserted. Owner Mercy Sagun, who herself worked at Zycon Corp., a high-tech company in Santa Clara, lamented that "many old friends came in and told me they wanted to eat one last meal here because it was their last day at work."

According to Jeff Koller, an analyst at California's Employment Development Department, the semiconductor industry lost 30,000 jobs by the mid-1990s, dropping from 102,200 to 73,700 workers. Job losses fell much more heavily on operators and technicians than on engineers and management personnel. The companies kept their research-and-development capacity in Silicon Valley, but not production. "What this meant," said Manan, "is that Filipino workers lost their jobs by the thousands, more than anyone else." Howard High, a public relations spokesperson at Intel Corp., admitted that employment on the company's microprocessor-fabrication lines alone dropped from 2,000 to 600 after it built a new $1 billion plant in New Mexico. AMD kept one new fab line for research and development, and moved the others to Texas. The rest of the semiconductor companies did the same.

Vicente and Anita Angel lost their jobs at National Semiconductor's plant on Kifer Road in Santa Clara. After immigrating to the United States in 1979 they got jobs there at $3.25 an hour. They bought a modest home in Milpitas where they raised two children. "In our fab we were all friends," Anita Angel remembered. "We had potlucks and worked together like a team. Now we're worried we'll lose our home, since we don't have enough money for the house payment. We'll accept any job, but it's hard because we're older." At the time they lost their jobs in the mid-1990s, Vicente was sixty-one and Anita was fifty-seven. They'd been making more than eleven dollars an hour. "When our eighteen-year-old daughter heard that we lost our jobs, she joined the army so that she could get health insurance to cover us," Vicente said. "She knew we had no money for her to go to school anymore."

Maria Villanueva's mother worked at National for eighteen years as an operator, although she had a teaching degree from a university in the Philippines. "The company didn't honor her education, and in the end it didn't value the skills she acquired in the plant either," Villanueva said. In the transfer of production, almost no one was offered the chance to move with the work.

Like Vicente, many became security guards at local airports. Eventually almost all the baggage screeners in the Bay Area and other West Coast airports were Filipino. But that changed too after 2001. Close to thirty thousand screeners, working in every major metropolitan area, were fired after they were blamed for allowing terrorists armed with box cutters and plastic knives to board airliners on September 11. The items used by the hijackers were all permissible at the time, but baggage screeners made an easy target in the fearful hysteria that followed. Both Republicans and Democrats voted for the Aviation and Transportation Security Act, which called for replacing the existing workforce with a new, federalized one.

Federalizing the jobs could have benefited the existing workforce, bringing higher wages and greater security. But federal employees must be citizens. That requirement cost thousands of immigrant screeners their jobs. Erlinda Valencia, who worked at San Francisco International Airport, said, "I've done this job for fourteen years, but they're hiring people with no experience at all. You can fly the airplane if you're not a citizen, or carry a rifle in the airport if you belong to the National Guard. But you can't check the bags of the passengers." Only forty-five hundred of the original thirty thousand screeners were rehired, according to the Transportation Security Administration (TSA).

Ever resourceful, Filipino workers then migrated into airport jobs that didn't require citizenship. In Oakland and Los Angeles, they began a long effort that finally led to union recognition for security workers. Marina Neri helped start the Peoples Association of Workers and Immigrants, with the help of Filipinos for Affirmative Action. She became a leader of the local organizing committee for Local 1877 of the Service Employees. "It took us a long time," she said, "but as Filipinos we've never stopped trying to get fairer treatment here." In early 2007, however, TSA took over some of those jobs too, and Neri and other Filipino union activists were laid off.

"What Future for Our Children?"

Despite dangerous work, the lack of job security, and discrimination against those with professional degrees, about eighty thousand people migrate from the Philippines to the United States every year. The economic pressure pushing people out of the Philippines is very similar to that felt by workers and farmers in Mexico. The Philippine government has followed a development policy dictated by the International Monetary Fund (IMF) to encourage foreign investment. Although a strong popular movement won land reform when the dictatorship of Ferdinand Marcos fell, income in the countryside did not increase, and in some cases declined.

On the southern island of Mindanao, the undoing of land reform provoked a long struggle between banana workers and the U.S. corporations that employed them for decades—Dole and Del Monte. In December 1998 strikes finally erupted on many plantations. In the banana groves, formerly the property of Dole Corporation, outside of Davao, a large city in southern Mindanao, harvesting stopped when banana workers barricaded the roads. Roberto Sabanal was one of the strikers. "Most nights we went over to Diamond Farms, to beef up their lines and guard the roads," he recalled. At four-thirty one morning, as he and his friends were about to head home, a striker burst out of the darkness.

"He shouted that their lines were being attacked by soldiers and police on the other side of the plantation," Sabanal said. "We jumped onto the company fire truck and began rushing across the farm to aid our comrades." Shots came out of the trees, and Sabanal felt a numb sensation in his leg. "When I brought my hand up to my face, I could see it was covered in blood. On the main road soldiers trained their guns on us."

According to Antonio Edillon, a Diamond Farms banana harvester, more than five hundred armed men attacked one hundred people on the picket line that night. "We sat down at the edge of the banana grove and locked arms with each other," he remembered. "I was hit by an iron bar, and others were hurt as well. The soldiers pointed their Armalite rifles at us and told us they'd shoot." Edillon and Coronado Apusen, an attorney from the National Federation of Labor, identified the attackers as members of the 432nd Infantry Battalion of the Philippine Armed Forces. The army operated in tandem with local police and private guards from Timog Agricultural Corp., a division of Dole Asia Inc. Asked if the strikers also had arms, Edillon laughed. "We don't even have enough money to eat. Where would we get the money to buy guns?" The picket line was broken, and armed guards entered the plantation. Dressed in camouflage fatigues, they said they worked for Stanfilco, a division of Dole Philippines Inc.

For weeks Dole's armed paramilitaries refused to allow banana workers to set foot on the land, yet since 1996 the workers' cooperatives had been its owner. Before that, the banana harvesters had been employees of Dole subsidiaries Stanfilco, Checkered Farms, and Diamond Farms, and had belonged to the National Federation of Labor, one of the Philippines' most militant unions. Their wages had started at 146 pesos a day (the dollar was then worth about 40 pesos), and the company paid for medical care, pensions, vacations, and sick leave.

In 1996 workers petitioned the national government's Department of Agrarian Reform for redistribution of four Dole plantations. The Philippine agrarian reform law was passed during the upheaval that toppled Marcos in 1986. The workers set up cooperatives, but in the negotiations that followed, Dole insisted it would buy bananas at a price so low that in the first years workers earned only 96 pesos a day and lost all of their previous benefits. "The company reduced its labor costs by no longer employing us directly," explained Eleuteria Chacon, head of the co-op at Checkered Farms. "The company promised we would make big profits if we produced over three thousand boxes of bananas a day, but even after meeting that goal, our co-ops lost money. We didn't really understand how to compute our costs, and the company said they wouldn't negotiate with us if we brought in experts from our union." Dole withheld the workers' legally mandated severance pay until they signed the price agreement, and the co-ops were quickly in debt. The Diamond Farms co-op lost 30 million pesos the first year, and Checkered Farms 11 million, according to Apusen.

The co-ops were in a weak bargaining position because Dole kept ownership of the plantation roads, the packing sheds, and the complicated network of cables needed to support the trees and transport the bananas. Without those assets the co-ops couldn't produce bananas. When they suggested a clause in their agreement to allow them to sell bananas to other companies, Dole said it would refuse to let them use its infrastructure. Workers owned the land, but Dole controlled access to the export market, where the bananas were sold. With operations in eighty countries, it is the world's largest grower of fruit and vegetables, and the largest producer of bananas.

Amansueto Agapay, information officer for the Department of Agrarian Reform in Davao, admitted that the arrangement gave Dole an unfair advantage. "It allowed them to set the condition that they would be the sole buyers," he said. "But legally we had no power to force them to sell these assets." Dole Philippines and Stanfilco officials would not be interviewed.

One Diamond Farms worker, Felix Bacalso, had to pull all but two of his ten children out of public school, no longer able to afford the small tuition and the cost of uniforms, food, and transportation. Bacalso spent eight years with his family in a two-room home on the plantation, and sent some of his children to live with relatives. Eventually Dole agreed to increase its price to $2.60 a box. Still, the situation of the workers changed very little. "I'll have to send my children to work," Bacalso feared.

The fear wasn't unfounded, since that happened on other plantations producing for Dole. During the 1990s the company imposed an arrangement on other Mindanao growers similar to the one it negotiated with the co-ops. In 1992 Stanfilco convinced 108 small rice farmers in San Jose Campostela to pool their land and set up a banana plantation, Soyapa Farms. It signed an individual contract with each grower to buy their bananas at the same low price. While workers were striking in the co-ops, every morning on Soyapa Farms children huddled in a circle at one side of the plantation packing shed. There they flattened out sheets of plastic inserted between banana bunches to keep them apart as they grow. The kids, eleven to seventeen years old, were paid 2 centavos for each sheet, making up to 50 pesos a day. Next to them, Benjamin Libron, fifteen, threw bananas discarded for minor imperfections onto a truck for transport to local markets. He was paid 60 pesos a day. In the banana groves, Dini, fifteen, Jane, eleven, and Alan Algoso, nine, cut dead leaves away from the stems of the trees with large knives. The two younger children made 50 pesos a day, and Dini made 71. "My mom works here on the farm," Jane said, "and my grandparents have land here."

The children in the shed and the Algoso kids were still going to school. They worked for two hours in the morning and went back for another four hours after classes. Benedicto Hijara, fifteen, completed the sixth grade in 1994 and then started working. The youngest of five brothers and three sisters, they all worked with their parents for Soyapa Farms. Benedicto tied tree trunks to an overhead cable, propping them upright so they wouldn't fall over under the weight of the bananas. To earn 71 pesos daily, he had to tie up 105 trees.

Danilo Carillon, sixteen, stopped going to school after the third grade. For 86 pesos a day he climbed a bamboo ladder, pulling a plastic bag over each bunch of bananas, bagging 160 bunches a day. The bags were treated with a pesticide, Lorsban. Carillon wore a simple dust mask over his face when he unrolled each bag, not one capable of filtering out chemicals. "The children on this plantation work because their families can't survive without the wages they earn," explained Nenita Baylosis, a Soyapa Farms employee and member of the Associated Labor Unions (ALU). "When we started to campaign against child labor here, the parents got very angry, fearing the kids would lose their jobs."

One parent, Ludy Quinio, supported four children as a disease-control worker earning 71 pesos a day. To supplement his income, the family raised pigs and made tuba, a kind of coconut beer. His wife ran a tiny sari-sari store in the front of her home, selling a little bit of everything to their neighbors. That December, the value of the Philippine peso plunged from 30 to 46 per dollar. A coke in her store sold for 8 pesos—an hour's labor. "If Ernolie [his sixteen-year-old son] didn't work, he wouldn't be able to go to school," Quinio said. Despite working before and after school propping trees, and eleven hours on Saturday, he was second in his senior class in high school. "If I can keep on working, I'd like to go to college," he said.

The Soyapa Farms Growers Association employed 360 contract workers, adults and children. Because the workers were contract employees, they didn't qualify for even the lowest minimum wage in Mindanao, 96 pesos a day. "Stanfilco says it isn't responsible," said ALU representative Bebot Llerin, "since it doesn't employ the plantation workers directly." But Dole's low price traps growers in debt, who then have no money to raise wages for plantation workers, he explained.

On the other side of Mindanao, in Dapitan, children also work—on the docks. In late 1995, children started showing up on the Dapitan wharf, at first just a handful, but eventually more than seventy. The union contract, signed by the conservative Trade Union Congress of the Philippines, pegged longshore wages to the minimum wage in Mindanao for dock workers—96 pesos a day. The Philippine government estimates that it takes over 370 pesos a day to support a family of six, so the wages of adults on the waterfront were never sufficient to support a family. Occasionally dockworkers themselves would bring their kids to work, but the children did only light jobs.

Then the Dipolog and Dapitan Stevedoring and Warehousing Services Company began organizing a company union. Children began doing the work of adults. When a freighter carrying cement docked at the pier, kids would troop up the gangway and down into the ship's hold. Each would hoist a one-hundred-pound sack onto his shoulders and carry it up out of the boat. The boys were ten to seventeen years old, and for this heavy labor they received 80 centavos a sack. In a week, each might earn between 70 and 200 pesos.

The union's Flor Amistoso was given a grant by the International Labor Organization's International Program for the Elimination of Child Labor to organize the families. She befriended the kids, taking them fishing and on picnics, buying them a volleyball net for games between unloading boats. She held classes under a tree near the docks to teach them to read. She visited each of the parents, who lived in squatter communities without running water or electricity near the port, in homes made of cast-off materials. The boys complained of muscle pains, headache, fever, scabies, and respiratory ailments. Three had tuberculosis, and one started to cough up blood. A child fell to his death inside a ship.

But their families needed the income. "Their fathers asked me, 'Can you give us three meals a day?'" Amistoso recounted. "I'm not here to give them money or food, but to tell them what their rights are." Only one child wanted to go to school, and none of their families had money to pay for it. "The only way we can stop children working is if the port workers themselves take some action, like going on strike," Amistoso concluded. "They're afraid that if they act, they'll be fired and replaced. But if we don't act, we'll never be able to protect the jobs of the adults. And what kind of life will we be giving to our children?"

The Philippine labor code prohibits the labor of children under sixteen. Those between sixteen and eighteen can only work directly under their parents' supervision. The child labor in San Jose Campostela and Dapitan is clearly illegal, yet the local offices of the Department of Labor and Employment took no action to stop it. Under pressure from the IMF to make the country's economy attractive to investors, enforcement of labor-protection legislation, including the prohibition of child labor, has a low priority. Plus, an inexpensive labor force gives the Philippines a competitive advantage in the world economy.

In the wake of the economic meltdown in Southeast Asia at the end of the 1990s, the IMF urged the Philippines and other countries to provide greater incentives for foreign investment. This strategy led to declining household income in export agriculture, rising social conflict, an increase in child labor, and, ultimately, migration. Walden Bello, executive director of Focus on the Global South, says the Philippine government allows foreign investors to manipulate the country's legal process. "The government allowed land reform to take place, but then allowed so many loopholes that the former owners benefited from it more than the workers," he charges. "Dole actually lowered its costs, while appearing to comply with the land-reform process. Following the IMF's advice, the government is trying to help companies lower their labor costs to make the country's exports cheaper."

Growing poverty and child labor show what these policies mean to people. The United States is the largest stakeholder in the IMF, giving it the biggest voice in setting the policies it pursues. At the World Food Summit in Rome in November 1996, U.S. agriculture secretary Dan Glickman declared that "free and fair trade promotes global prosperity and plenty. The private sector is the great untapped frontier in the world war on hunger." In a letter of exception to the summit's final declaration, he wrote: "The United States believes that the attainment of any 'right to adequate food' or 'fundamental right to be free from hunger' is a goal or aspiration to be realized progressively that does not give rise to any international obligations."

"This inevitably has an effect on us," says Guy Fujimura, secretary-treasurer of Local 142 of the International Longshore and Warehouse Union in Hawaii. "We have contracts with Dole on three pineapple plantations with about five hundred members." Until the 1970s the union represented as many as six thousand pineapple workers, but most of that production went to the Philippines. "Lower labor cost wasn't the only reason, but it was a big one," Fujimura says. "It made the choice of moving production much easier. And the cost of labor is a function of the control of labor, which is what the banana strike was all about."

The same process affects sailors. Transnational shipping companies have dumped their high-wage U.S. and European crews on the beach, replacing them with seamen from countries around the Pacific Rim, especially the Philippines. Over 250,000 Filipinos now sail the high seas, more than any other nationality. High-paid European captains and a few officers still rule over these low-paid Asian crews.

Seagoing labor is sold and controlled through labor contractors, Philippine government agencies, conservative unions, and blacklists. The Philippine Association of Maritime Agencies shares lists of troublemakers among its member shipowners and labor contractors. A Philippine government agency, the Philippines Overseas Employment Administration (POEA), also maintains a blacklist of workers who organize strikes and labor unrest, which make Filipino workers less attractive to foreign employers. Sailors say that their own union, the Association of Maritime Officers and Seamen's Union of the Philippines (AMOSUP), discourages job actions. "If you organize a strike, and later go to the union looking for a job, they'll ask you, 'Why did you do that?'" one dissident crewmember alleged after a brief work stoppage in the California port of Stockton. AMOSUP was organized with the support of former dictator Ferdinand Marcos.

The Philippine government's economic policy is based not only on encouraging foreign investment, but on encouraging the country's people to seek employment overseas. Today millions of Filipino families depend on remittances by overseas relatives to survive. Connie Bragas-Regalado, chairperson of Migrante International, a Filipino migrant-rights organization, says the country's economy is propped up by a heavy reliance on money sent back from overseas. "While some other countries also have large numbers of migrant workers, the Philippines is the most heavily dependent on remittances," she asserts. Bangko Sentral ng Pilipinas estimates that in 2006 remittances totaled $12.9 billion, about 10 percent of the Philippines gross domestic product, and predicted that in 2007 they would reach $14 billion.

Remittances on a global scale have reached astronomical levels, as the world divides into labor-importing and labor-exporting countries. According to the Transnational Institute for Grassroots Research and

Action (TIGRA), an organizing project for migrants in Oakland, California, the global remittance total in 2000 was $132 billion, and rose to $232 billion in 2005 and $301 billion in 2006. TIGRA criticizes companies like Western Union, and the money-transfer industry, for charging as much as $13.50 for every $100 sent home by migrant workers, a global total of $18.8 billion in fees. It proposes organizing migrants into a global remitters association and forcing the money-transfer industry to accept standards of social responsibility, contributing to a transnational community-reinvestment fund.

Remittances play an increasing role in the Philippine economy, contributing to an annual foreign debt payment of $5 billion. Antonio Tujan, research director of the IBON Foundation, a Manila research institute, traces the roots of the outflow to the Marcos dictatorship, "which in the late '70s consciously promoted the policy of labor export and established the POEA in order to promote migrant labor, as well as develop partnerships with and regulate private placement agencies ... This policy has an avowed objective of earning foreign exchange and easing the unemployment situation." Philippines president Gloria Macapagal-Arroyo told one overseas worker in a televised phone conversation, "Jobs here are difficult to find and we are depending on the people outside the country. If you can find work there, and send money to your relatives here, then perhaps you should stay there."

As of December 2001 there were 7.4 million Filipinos overseas, about half permanent migrants and half temporary workers. In 2006 Ely Manalansan estimated in *PMC Reports,* a Manila journal, that the total had reached 10 million, and an out-migration rate of 2,700 people per day. In 2006, 74,607 Filipinos legally migrated to the United States, where the number of Filipinos with visas now numbers 1.3 million, according to government statistics. A significant number of Filipinos are also undocumented, largely people who have overstayed temporary or tourist visas.

In the United States, Filipino migrants have become most visible as healthcare workers, especially nurses, and the POEA says there are now three hundred thousand nurses from the Philippines working abroad. One clear reason is the difference in the standard of living. According to Manalansan, a registered nurse in Manila earns about five thousand pesos (seventy-one dollars) a month, while in the United States a nurse's aide can earn eighteen dollars an hour. Facilitating migration is a network of agencies that send workers abroad. The Philippines' Technical Education and Skills Development Authority certifies over a hundred training schools for overseas work, and issues a certificate to workers that documents their skill level. Many Filipino doctors, who have trouble getting their degrees and experience credited in the United States, instead get certified as nurses to qualify under the Exchange Visitors Program run by the Philippine Health Department. Applicants pay as much as one hundred thousand pesos to job-placement agencies for fees, visas, tests, and other expenses.

The system produces enormous consequences in the Philippines, where many hospitals are understaffed as skilled professionals leave. Manalansan says that twenty-five of the thirty nurses at the Jose Reyes Memorial Medical Center have applied to work abroad, and 17 percent of the eight hundred nurses in another eleven hospitals have already left. Tujan calls the process "obscene," since the Philippines used scarce resources to give people needed skills, and then those skills are "lost forever as they end up working as aides and domestics in the affluent countries." A common Filipino lament is "Brain drain in the south, brain waste in the north." Tujan concludes that "this partnership is a phenomenon of globalization, an internationalization of contractual hiring, exploiting even cheaper migrant labor."

Tujan also alleges that those nurses depress wages in the United States, "because employers utilize the combination of discrimination, oppressive hiring and working conditions, effect of wage differentials in the sending and host countries, and social and cultural differences." Despite the intentions of employers, however, U.S. healthcare workers have been more active in organizing unions and raising wages than almost any other occupation. Filipinos have been leaders in that effort. As it has since the first manongs came in the 1920s, the U.S. labor movement is again benefiting from the influx of immigrants.

Eight

WHOSE NEW WORLD ORDER?

High Skills and Low Salaries

By 2000, employment in Silicon Valley had not only dropped, but conditions for workers in electronics plants had changed drastically over the previous decade. Thousands no longer worked directly for the companies that formerly employed them. Instead, they were hired through temporary-employment agencies, some of which even maintained offices in the plants themselves. And contract employment no longer affected just workers on the lines. In engineering positions, semiconductor companies increasingly relied on guest workers.

Kim Singh was a high-tech worker who got his job through the H1-B program. He left India on a temporary-work visa to become a contract employee in Silicon Valley, thinking he would find a good job in electronics. Instead, he found a modern sweatshop. Singh worked for three different companies. Each got him a job using his H1-B immigration visa, which allowed him to work in the United States as a software engineer.

The first company, he said, withheld 25 percent of the salary from each of its immigrant engineers. "None of us received the money after we left," Singh alleged. At the second company, "I worked seven days a week, with no overtime compensation. The only ones required to work on weekends were the H1-B immigrants." The third company rented an apartment for four H1-B engineers in San Jose, charging each $1,450 a month, while holding on to their passports. This company "threatened to send some back to India if they didn't get contracts.

The workers were in tears. They were nervous wrecks, ashamed to ask for money or help from their families back home."

"I've been here for twelve years," said Rajiv Dabhadkar, another HI-B engineer interviewed in 2007. "I went to school in the U.S. and then I worked. My experience is that there's no fairness for the HI-B worker. We're being subjugated. It's like a form of involuntary servitude." Dabhadkar described a common situation. Recruiters for software, semiconductor, and computer companies troll the graduating classes of U.S. engineering schools. Foreign students, whose visas to study in the United States expire when they graduate, are often desperate to find a job quickly with a work visa that will allow them to stay. When contractors offer an HI-B visa job, there are usually many takers.

The visa lasts three years and is renewable once. At the end, the visa holder can apply for permanent residence (unlike the H-2 visas). In many East and South Asian communities in areas like Silicon Valley, HI-B visas are often seen as a road to eventual legal status and family reunification in the United States. But the process can take many years, and in the meantime HI-B visa holders have to stay employed or risk being sent back. Often they don't work directly for a major employer, but for a "job shop"—a contractor who sends them from one place to another. "My issue is with the companies who are intellectual capital brokers," Dabhadkar explained. "They abuse the system and turn us into a commodity. Under the guest-worker program, they can just buy people in bulk from overseas who never have a real chance to live in the U.S. This creates visa hustling and visa scams."

Among the scams are promises by contractors who say they'll pay the prevailing wage in a low-wage state like Idaho, and then send the worker to a high-wage state like California. The California employer pays the job shop the higher wage, but the worker must survive in Silicon Valley, one of the country's most expensive housing markets, on the lower wage. "They would also make applications to place workers at a local company with a low wage, and then place them in a better-paying company and pocket the difference," Dabhadkar said.

H1-B white-collar engineers wind up living like Singh, in a high-tech tenement.

"Even though you can apply for a green card while on an H1-B visa, if you actually get one, the companies lose interest in you," Dabhadkar said. They want the vulnerability the H1-B visa imposes, which makes it hard for workers to refuse low wages and bad conditions. One ad by Reasonsoft of Nashua, New Hampshire, reposted on the brightfuturejobs.org website, specified, "We require candidates for H1-B from India." The H1-B scheme doesn't require employers to advertise for workers in the United States first. Employers claim a supposed labor shortage makes H1-B recruitment necessary, but show little interest in actually hiring domestically.

AFL-CIO executive vice president Linda Chavez-Thompson accused companies of using this program "to keep workers in a position of dependence. And because these workers are often hired under individual contracts, U.S. labor law says they don't have the right to organize." Despite their vulnerable status, however, Dabhadkar started the National Organization for Software and Technology Professionals (NOSTOP) and promoted a one-day sick-out after seeing the big marches and May Day strike by other immigrants in 2006.

In the late 1990s Silicon Valley electronics giants began pushing for more H1-B workers, since existing immigration law sets a cap on the number of visas available each year. As the presidential campaign of 2000 grew more heated, Congress bent over backward to give the industry what it wanted, proposing to expand that limit to more than two hundred thousand workers a year. Only South Carolina senator Ernest Hollings voted against industry's proposal in the Senate. The voice vote in the House, called late at night after the Republican leadership promised that no more votes would be taken, was unanimous. Both Republicans and Democrats wanted high-tech campaign contributions in an election year.

One of the biggest champions of the H1-B system is Bill Gates, founder of Microsoft Corporation. When Congress was considering its comprehensive immigration-reform proposals in 2006 and 2007,

Gates told senators they should eliminate the numerical cap entirely. "Even though it may not be realistic, I don't think there should be any limit," he testified. Since a desire to keep wages low might sound selfish, Gates made his appeal in the national interest instead: "The U.S. cannot maintain its economic leadership unless our workforce consists of people who have the knowledge and skills needed to drive innovation." Gates and other high-tech employers complain that U.S. engineering schools aren't producing enough graduates to meet their demand. "We simply cannot sustain an economy based on innovation unless our citizens are educated in math, science, and engineering," he said.

The claim that U.S. schools don't produce enough engineers is questionable, however. According to the American Society for Engineering Education, they graduate more than 100,000 BAs, MAs, and PhDs annually, a number rising every year. While the H1-B cap rises and falls, there are about 500,000 in the United States at any one time. Their education level varies considerably—in 2007, there were 132,000 applicants for 65,000 visas, of whom only 12,989 had an advanced degree.

There's a kind of sneer when Gates implies the U.S. workforce isn't competitive. He angrily criticized the Senate after it failed to lift the H1-B visa cap in 2007, and complained that "the whole idea [guiding Congress] is, don't let too many smart people into the country." Microsoft pays almost none of the taxes needed to finance the U.S. educational system. It paid no corporate income tax at all in 1999, and according to a 2002 report by the nonprofit research and advocacy group Citizens for Tax Justice: "Microsoft enjoyed more than $12 billion in total tax breaks over the past five years . . . Microsoft's tax rate for the past two years was only 1.8 percent on $21.9 billion in pretax U.S. profits." Jack Norman, research director of Milwaukee's Institute for Wisconsin's Future, announced that Microsoft paid no corporate income tax again in 2005.

Dabhadkar said the H1-B program "created a big divide between the American tech workers and those on the guest-worker program." African American and Latino engineers have waged a protracted effort to break down discriminatory barriers in high-tech hiring. Civil rights groups point out that increasing the number of H1-B visas makes it more difficult to open up jobs for engineers of color, in an industry where the percentage of African American and Latino engineers is very low.

In 2006 Senator Richard J. Durbin of Illinois and Senator Charles Grassley of Iowa introduced a bill that would have required U.S. companies making applications for H1-B workers to advertise the jobs domestically first. It also would have made the prevailing wage requirement more stringent, after a report by the Government Accountability Office documented many cases where employers paid much less. One company, Patni Computer Systems, was forced to pay over $2.4 million to 607 workers who'd received illegal wages, while studies at UCLA and Cornell showed H1-B wages 20 to 30 percent below prevailing rates. That downward pressure on salaries discourages young people from becoming engineers. According to Robert I. Lerman, former director of the Urban Institute's Labor and Social Policy Center, "A policy of expanding [H1-B] visas for IT [information technology] positions is potentially counterproductive because it can increase uncertainty and reduce the incentive to enter the field." Needless to say, high-tech employers opposed the bill.

Phil Hutchings of the Black Alliance for Just Immigration says the H1-B program "creates for people who come here a kind of gilded cage. They have what look like nice jobs, but they have no rights, no ability to form labor organizations, and they're put into jobs where, if corporations had to hire U.S. citizens, they'd have to pay more. But with the H1-B program, a whole group of people in this country are kept from applying. And given the underemployed and undereducated status of African Americans this is totally offensive." In African American and other working communities, where the lack of resources for schools is the sharpest, "there are not enough science and math courses, and people get sidelined into community colleges where they can't get the advanced degrees they will need," Hutchings added. San Francisco's Public Policy Institute issued a report in 2006 describing the disconnect between the needs of the high-tech economy and the state of the public education system.

In his book *Green Carrot: America's Work Visa Crisis*, Dabhadkar asks: "What kind of education will protect a U.S. software engineer or biotechnologist from someone who can easily study the same things, but earns much less? Why should a laid-off Java programmer in the U.S. spend 18 months and thousands of dollars getting an advanced degree in neural network programming, when he knows that the moment there is significant demand for neural network techies in the U.S., the top Indian or Chinese engineering institutes will rush to offer equivalent courses or degrees at a far lower tuition fee? Who wants to be 'transformed' from an unemployed Java programmer into an unemployed neural network developer with additional student loans? Education used to give developed-country professionals the advantage that let them enjoy a big income differential with respect to the developing world. Today, that educational edge is almost gone, regardless of whether developed countries pour more money into technical education. How long before the income differential goes too?"

For India, China, and the Philippines, the source countries for most H1-B workers, the continued loss of high-skilled engineers recruited by Silicon Valley contributes to the same brain drain felt in their healthcare systems. "These programs are selling our human potential," says Anuradha Mittal, Indian-born codirector of the Oakland Institute, a nonprofit research and advocacy institute in Oakland, California. "Our educational system produces highly skilled workers, who then leave to become the working poor in America, while breaking down our ability to industrialize our own country. We wind up subsidizing U.S. industry."

From Guest Worker to German Citizen

France and Germany saw an additional social cost of guest-worker programs through the 1960s and 1970s. France had a temporary-permit system in which Algerian and North African workers came on short-term five- or ten-year visas. The visas were renewable, but gave people no permanent-residence rights. Migrants wound up living in

France for decades, where their children were born. In the 1990s immigrant activists went on hunger strikes in Paris churches to demand changes in their status, and to protest police brutality and a rising wave of anti-immigrant violence. French left-wingers mounted a solidarity campaign called *touche pas mon pote,* or "don't touch my pal," when right-wing politicians like Jean-Marie Le Pen advocated mass deportations.

The children of those immigrants, living in the poor suburbs ringing Paris, felt the sting of continuing exclusion and racism. Extreme unemployment made it clear they were not equal participants in France's wealth and culture. Young women were punished for wearing the hejab (a scarf covering the head) in school. Youth anger over abysmal living conditions finally exploded in street demonstrations and riots. French society grew even more polarized, however. Nicolas Sarkozy, who as Interior minister vowed to crack down on immigrants with a heavy hand, was elected French president in 2007.

In Germany the first wave of guest workers arrived in the early 1960s, recruited on temporary contracts. Mahmut Aktas's father came from Turkey in 1963. When Aktas was growing up, his father, on his trips home, described Germany as a green land with big factories and wide, clean streets. "But the people didn't accept him," Aktas recalled his father telling him. Nevertheless, seventeen years after his father took his first labor contract, Mahmut Aktas went himself as a teenager. "At first it seemed great," he remembered. "But as I got into working life, I realized things weren't what they seemed." Until German naturalization law was finally changed in 2000, the child of an immigrant, born in Germany, was still ineligible for citizenship. Turkish communities, although they've existed for many years in German cities, are still isolated enclaves.

Another who came in that era was a young theology student, Manuel Campos, who fled Portugal in 1974, one step ahead of the secret police. Just before the fascist dictator Marcelo Caetano fell, Campos discovered he was about to be arrested. A priest got him out of the country, and Campos suddenly found himself in Germany with no prospects, few skills, and a head filled with radical ideas. He became an asylum seeker, welcomed at a time when German unemployment was low and the need for educated workers high.

He wound up in an auto plant. "The assembly lines were filled with immigrants like myself," he remembered. "The job was so hard I still wonder at the ability of people to come to work every day. When I came here there was nothing for us. We had either fled our countries like me, or we were looking for a way to send enough money home so that our families would survive. Lots of us were here for both reasons."

Mahmut Aktas, who works at a huge Daimler-Benz plant, said discrimination is still common. "I started out as a skilled worker, but to my foreman, I was just a foreigner," he said. "Officially, the company says discrimination doesn't exist, that we can go into any job in the factory. But if you want to get into a really skilled position, they discourage you. I'm a German citizen now, and they still see me as a foreigner. They don't like it if I have a more skilled and better-paid job."

Germany has a federal law that forbids discrimination, but according to Campos it doesn't protect immigrant workers, who are still officially regarded as foreigners. "It's almost impossible for immigrants to file complaints and get them enforced," Campos charged. "The court system is very conservative, and many judges are racists. When someone says 'Foreigner, get out!' judges call this free expression. As a result, it's much better for workers when we negotiate these agreements, which are then enforced by the works council in the workplace."

IG Metall, the big German metal-workers' union, negotiated agreements with four major German corporations, including Volkswagen, outlawing discrimination or harassment based on immigrant status, along with other forms of racial and sexual mistreatment. It also requires companies to provide training to workers (immigrant and nonimmigrant alike) in unskilled jobs at the bottom of the workforce, and then to hire them into new positions. "Hundreds of thousands of immigrant workers," Campos said, "are trapped at the bottom, in jobs that are likely to disappear."

In most German cities, immigrant workers have elected commissions that meet in union halls or the clubs and associations of various nationalities. Immigrants make up 7.1 million of Germany's 80 million people and 2.1 million of its 34 million workers. IG Metall is the largest union in the world, with 2.8 million members, but membership has been declining as industry leaves high-wage Germany. The number of immigrant members—about 275,000, however, has remained constant. Aktas believed IG Metall makes an effort to stop discrimination, "not least because several officers of the union now are foreign workers themselves. If a worker has a problem and goes to a steward, the odds are good that the steward will be Turkish or Kurdish."

Aktas is one of them—a chief steward at Daimler-Benz. Of the thirty-six thousand workers in his plant, only twenty-five hundred are Turkish or Kurdish. "If I or one of my Turkish coworkers want to become a spokesperson for our group in the factory, many of our German coworkers just would not vote for us," he said. Yet he's been elected steward three times, and believes he fights for the interests of all his fellow workers, of whatever nationality. "I've taken on their cause," he said. "My foremen and supervisors don't like this one bit. They don't like the union, and they particularly don't like the fact that I'm a Turkish shop steward."

"You can just leave, or you can stay and fight," Campos concluded. "That choice makes a lot of us fighters. We have the worst jobs, and the lowest pay. The jobs that are disappearing the fastest belong to us. But we remain union members in much greater numbers than others because we look at the union as our political home." As a result, immigrants make up a much larger percentage of the union's stewards than their percentage in the general membership.

IG Metall is a political home for another reason. Since the reunification of Germany in 1990, unemployment has soared, particularly in the former German Democratic Republic, or East Germany. Gangs of young neo-Nazis accuse immigrants of taking their jobs, and have burned the hostels where guest workers and asylum seekers live. To denounce these actions, every year the union mounts a campaign to coincide with the U.N. International Day of Action against Racism, in coalition with the German Intercultural Council and the Committee of Turks in Germany.

"The danger to immigrants in Germany is constant—you feel it in the streets every day," Aktas declared. "And the reason is that nothing is being done to counteract it. When the neo-Nazis organized a march in Berlin the judges allowed it. That's a sign to me that you have to watch your back every moment. I can't say the union is one hundred percent behind Turkish workers, but it's a lot better than anywhere else in German society." Campos was one of many IG Metall members who went to Berlin to demonstrate against the neo-Nazi march. "I don't think Germany is about to become fascist again," he said. "But these groups, although they're small, are very aggressive, and protected by the police. If there's no visible opposition, it's a signal that hating immigrants is acceptable."

Other German unions still see immigrants as a threat, however. In Berlin, when the federal government built the new city center as a capital for a reunited Germany, German unions were locked out of the country's largest construction project. Instead, a network of subcontractors hired an immigrant workforce primarily from eastern Europe, where unemployment is higher and wages much lower. These workers were almost all undocumented, and their conditions were very similar to those of the earlier guest workers. Until Poland became a member of the European Union in 2004, its border with Germany was a wage wall like the iron fence between Tijuana and San Diego. In Germany a worker could earn as much in an hour as someone might earn in a day in Poland. When some eastern European countries joined the European Union, their citizens were no longer undocumented when they worked in Germany. But the wage difference hasn't changed much. German sociologist Boy Leutje says unions in both Germany and the United States confront the same choice. "Are they going to fight a losing battle to keep immigrants out of their trade and their country, or are they going to see them as potential union members and try to organize them?" he asks.

The concept of equal status for immigrants doesn't exist yet, Campos said. "Instead of an immigration law, we have a law which calls us foreigners. We need the law to see us in a new way, to set out the conditions under which we can immigrate, and to spell out the rights the government guarantees us." Germany is only now beginning to see its immigrant population as permanent residents rather than as foreign workers who will someday go home. "My children were born here," Aktas says. "For us, our future is here in Germany."

As Swiss playwright Max Frisch said in 1965, when the guest-worker programs in Europe began, "We called for workers, and there came human beings."

Suppressing Asylum Seekers While Promoting "Managed Migration"

The debate over immigration has become global. According to Geneva-based Migrant Rights International (MRI), which advocates for migrant rights globally, more than 180 million people live outside the countries in which they were born. All over the world huge streams of migrants are fleeing war, repression, and poverty, journeying from developing countries to the industrial ones of the so-called global north. At the same time, the industrial economies have become dependent on the work of migrants, who form a subclass of people working in jobs with the lowest wages, least security, and most dangerous conditions.

On the surface, proposals for comprehensive immigration reform like that offered by the Bush administration in 2007 seem schizophrenic. On the one hand, they seek to end the spontaneous movement of undocumented people. On the other, they seek to channel migration into programs that would deliver migrants to industry as a contracted workforce. This duality is not unique to the United States. Throughout the industrialized world, similar proposals are being made for using the huge global flow of migrants as a source of labor, while at the same time restricting the ability of migrants to travel freely and decide for themselves where and when to live and work. Every industrialized country is experiencing the growth of political movements of the right, campaigning on platforms of ending migration, and attacking migrants themselves.

In 2003 Abbas Amini, an Iranian immigrant, sewed his eyes, ears, and mouth closed and went on a hunger strike in which he almost died, to protest deportation from Britain. He became a powerful symbol for immigrants who accused the British government of racism. Amini had been granted refugee status because he'd been imprisoned and tortured in Iran, but the British Home Office declared its intention to deport him nonetheless. "His case symbolized the government's drive to stop asylum seekers from gaining legal status," explained Milena Buyum, coordinator for the National Assembly against Racism, a leading British pro-immigrant organization. "The prime minister promised on television he would cut the number of asylum applications in half, and carry out thirty thousand removals [deportations] a year. They can't actually do this, so they stage high-profile public deportations, days before local elections. Abbas Amini was used as an example."

According to Buyum, "Deportations are an increasingly common approach to asylum in most of Europe. The rising number of asylum seekers reflects conflict and economic conditions that threaten the livelihood of millions of people. But governments are no longer concerned about individual cases, and say only a tough approach to asylum will stop the rise of far-right extremism. This fuels racism rather than stopping it. The ultimate aim of organized racists like the British National Party [BNP] and All White Britain is removal by force. How far is the government willing to go?"

The BNP, a far-right party that advocates deporting all immigrants, is winning local council seats in white-flight areas outside London. Its popularity is growing among those who've left London because the city has become more multicultural. Meanwhile, British structural racism gives a U.S. observer a sense of déjà vu. "Black people are more likely to get higher sentences than white people for the same crimes," Buyum said, referring to all people of non-European ancestry. "They are more likely to die in police custody, and are twenty-seven times more likely to be stopped and searched. There are only twelve black

MPs in Parliament, and only two Muslim MPs, although Islam is the second-largest religion. I'm not advocating religious representation, but I think communities under attack have a right to representation. I've lived in Britain for eleven years, and this is one of the worst periods that I've experienced as a black person."

While the government is taking a hard line on asylum seekers, it is also systematizing the importation of immigrant workers. In the late 1990s Prime Minister Tony Blair announced that modernized immigration policies would be based on recruiting immigrants to work in large numbers. According to Don Flynn, policy coordinator for the Joint Council for the Welfare of Immigrants, an independent advocacy group, "The guest-worker approach is very much what the government has in mind. About 150,000 to 170,000 people are admitted on that basis now, and they're talking about seasonal schemes in labor-shortage industries. Their stay will be less than twelve months, with no family reunification rights. Employers will round up workers on the completion of their jobs and send them out of the country."

In 1997 the Labour government said immigration would be part of the modernization of the British economy. "They said they wanted immigration policies based on the needs of British industry and commerce," Flynn said. "They call it managed migration. At the same time, the government is absolutely intent on ending all spontaneous migration, that is, people who arrive in the country on their own initiative. The biggest group in that category are humanitarian migrants, who rely on rights under the 1951 Geneva Convention. The government is intent on ending that system and reducing that migration to zero."

Flynn and Buyum described the growth of enforcement in Britain, which resembles that in the United States. "Until recently nobody thought it was a big deal if somebody's immigration papers were not entirely in order," Flynn said, "but that is changing. The government wants the population to think it is a significant issue if you haven't been given explicit permission to do one job as opposed to another, if you've had access to a public benefit, or if a member of your family has managed to join you. The government wants public support for seri-

ous punishment for these offenses." The British government established sanctions for employers of unauthorized workers in 1996, and
has begun to introduce a system of national identity documents.

According to Buyum, it's only realistic to recognize that the British
economy needs immigrant workers and should allow people to come.
"But giving work permits to carefully targeted skilled individuals
would not be good for the economies of the countries from which
they're recruited," she warned. "Public services in Britain are crippled
because we hire too few people with important skills, such as doctors,
nurses, and teachers. But there are people already here whose talents
are not used. The government should use that talent before it starts
seeking skilled individuals elsewhere."

"Contracted immigrants are paid below the minimum," Flynn said,
"with substandard conditions and no holidays, and are expected to
turn up at short notice to do extra shifts. Sometimes housing is provided on-site by employers—people crammed together in unsanitary
and dangerous situations. Discipline is imposed by gang masters."
Agriculture, construction, and the National Health Service are the
most dependent on this labor. "In addition, most substitute teachers
come from a largely immigrant labor force prepared to travel across
London at very short notice to do a week's work here and a week's
work there," he explained.

Immigrant workers fear their employers will retaliate against them
if they try to organize themselves, but such activity is growing nonetheless, aided by British unions. According to Flynn, resisting deportation has become part of the political agenda of many unions. In 2005
the U.K.'s most senior union officer, Bill Morris, a Jamaican immigrant,
was general secretary of the Transport and General Worker's Union.
The British Trades Union Congress, the umbrella federation for U.K.
unions, belongs to the National Assembly against Racism.

Mode 4 and the UN Convention on the Rights of Migrants

A political alliance is developing between countries with a labor-
export policy and the corporations who dominate the World Trade

Organization. Many countries sending migrants to the developed world depend on remittances to finance social services, provide capital for small enterprises, and keep the lid on social discontent over poverty and joblessness. Corporations using that displaced labor have a growing interest with those governments in regulating the system that supplies it.

On a world scale, the migratory flow caused by displacement is still generally self-initiated. In other words, while people may be driven by forces beyond their control, they move at their own will and discretion, trying to find survival and economic opportunity and to reunite their families and create new communities in the countries they now call home. That stream of labor is not all unskilled. Rajiv Dabhadkar describes "a significant new group of nations where the average citizen is poor, but the nation as a whole is technologically advanced and economically powerful, like China, India, Brazil, Russia, and Thailand. Technical education in these countries is both cheap and advanced, thanks to the Internet and the easy movement of ethnic technocrats between the developed world and their countries of origin."

The idea of managing the flow is growing. During the negotiations at the Hong Kong summit of the World Trade Organization in 2005, a proposal was introduced for the first time to begin channeling the movement of people along with the movement of capital and goods. As the WTO further regulated the modes in which services are provided in the world economy, it began to propose managing the movement of people themselves as the "providers of services" in what was called Mode 4. The Mode 4 program was originally proposed for skilled workers and executives, and included salespeople, corporate managers and specialists, foreign employees of corporate subsidiaries, and independent contractors like doctors and architects. Labor-exporting countries, however, have advocated expanding the range of jobs to include construction workers, domestic workers, and other less-skilled employees.

As in all guest-worker programs, the visas of these workers would require them to remain employed; they would be deported if they lost their jobs. Contractors would be allowed to recruit workers in one country and sell their labor in another. The visas of these workers would all be temporary, and they would not be able to become permanent residents. Countries contracting for these guest workers could regulate the number admitted and establish conditions under which they could be employed. The WTO opposes the establishment of minimum wages and conditions, or standards of employment, and says they should be regulated by the UN's International Labor Organization instead. Over many decades, however, the ILO has been unable to create any mandatory standards or wages, nor any enforcement mechanism to punish any countries or corporations that violate its voluntary standards.

The economic reforms that displace communities, like privatization and the end of subsidies, are all mandated by the WTO and international trade agreements. Displacement, therefore, will continue under this scheme, while protection for workers and migrants will be voluntary and ineffective. Essentially, it will produce migrant labor on a huge scale, and give corporations and compliant governments the freedom to exploit it without regulation or limits.

A number of U.S. human rights and immigrant-rights organizations issued a statement during the WTO negotiations opposing Mode 4, including the American Friends Service Committee, the National Network for Immigrant and Refugee Rights, the Committee in Solidarity with the People of El Salvador, Filipino Civil Rights Advocates, the Teamsters Union, United Food and Commercial Workers, Public Services International, and fifty-five others. They criticized the impact of the export of skilled workers on developing countries, and predicted that the scheme would violate the rights of migrants themselves.

Migrant Rights International also criticized the Mode 4 proposal. Genevieve Gencianos of MRI said global immigration policy should be based on protection of the rights of migrants, rather than regulating their movement in the interest of employers. "Trade and investment liberalization," she said, "have eroded basic human rights. These include the right to quality public services (such as health and education), jobs at home, sustainable agriculture, indigenous knowledge, self-determination, and human security for all. These violations . . .

have directly and indirectly driven people out of their home countries to become migrant workers abroad."

While sub-Saharan Africa needs 620,000 nurses to cope with the HIV / AIDS epidemic, she said, 23,000 health professionals leave the region every year for jobs in developed countries. Contract-labor programs, especially those employing women, have mushroomed in East Asia, and now include 242,000 domestic workers in Hong Kong, 674,000 factory, construction, and domestic workers in South Korea, and 120,000 caregivers in Taiwan. In defining them as service providers, "the migrant worker has been dehumanized and commodified," Gencianos said. "The WTO is effectively stripping the worker of his or her basic human rights." Because the impact is greatest on women, she predicted "irreversible negative social impacts to families left back home."

While this is a convenient arrangement for wealthy nations, it has severe disadvantages for poorer ones. The cost of maintaining and reproducing this international migrant-labor force falls on countries least able to afford it. The remittances of migrant workers become the main source of income for the communities from which they come. Large corporations and industries of wealthy countries get the benefit of this labor force, and workers themselves pay the cost of maintaining it.

Developing countries do, however, have an alternative framework for protecting the rights and status of this migrant population. Both Gencianos and the statement by rights advocates urged that instead of regulating migration through the WTO, countries ratify and implement the UN International Convention on the Protection of the Rights of All Migrant Workers and Members of Their Families. "Rather than reduce migrants to a factor of production, or a commodity to be exported and imported, migration policy must acknowledge migrants as human beings and address their dignity and human rights," the statement concluded.

The UN convention was adopted in 1990. It extends basic human rights to all migrant workers and their families, documented or undocumented. It supports family reunification, establishes the princi-

ple of equality of treatment with citizens of the host country in relation to employment and education, protects migrants against collective deportation, and makes both sending and receiving countries
responsible for protecting these rights. All countries retain the right
to determine who is admitted to their territories, and under what conditions people gain the right to work. The convention does not answer all questions posed by migration in a world economic system.
But it takes two basic steps that still paralyze the U.S. debate. It recognizes the new global scale of migration and its permanence. And it
starts by protecting the rights of people, especially those with the least
power—migrants themselves.

In the U.S. immigration debate, proponents of restrictions usually
argue that they are directed only at undocumented immigrants. But
maintaining this distinction between legal and illegal status has become a code for preserving inequality, a tiered system dividing people
into those with rights and those without. Guest-worker schemes set up
similar tiers—in effect, another form of illegality or rightlessness. Once
established, growing inequality eventually affects all immigrants, including legal or permanent residents. The 1996 debate over the Clinton immigration reform began by proposing increased enforcement
against the undocumented, but ended by denying even legal immigrants Social Security and other benefits and rights they'd previously
enjoyed. The effects of inequality spread beyond immigrants to citizens as well, especially in a society that has historically defined unequal status by skin color and sex.

Transnational Communities:
A New Definition of Citizenship

With or without temporary-worker programs, migration to the
United States and other industrial countries is a fact of life. Congress
is not debating the means for halting that migration because nothing
can. In an economy in which immigrant labor plays such an important
part, the price of stopping migration would be economic crisis. But
does that mean that U.S. immigration policy should be used to increase

corporate profits by supplying labor to industry at a price it wants to pay? Migrants are human beings first, and their desire for community is as strong as the need to labor. Or as the old shop floor saying goes, "We work to live; we don't live to work."

In proposing alternatives to Congress's failed immigration reform, U.S. immigrant groups insisted the solutions considered should include those proposed by immigrants themselves. "Why didn't they consult us?" asked Mireya Olvera, of *El Oaxaqueño*, published in Los Angeles by immigrants from the Mexican state of Oaxaca. "It's obvious they don't want to listen to us."

With 12 million undocumented people living in the United States, gaining legal status is obviously a central problem for immigrant communities. At the heart of many of their proposals is relaxing restrictions on the granting of permanent-residence visas. They would allow migrants to live and participate in community life in the United States, and move to and from their countries of origin. The Coalition of Guatemalan Immigrants in the United States criticized Bush's comprehensive immigration-reform proposal because it failed to include "a process through which immigrants can obtain permanent residence and eventual citizenship."

Citizenship is a complex issue in a world where migrant communities span borders and exist in more than one place simultaneously. Introducing their 2004 volume *Indigenous Mexican Migrants in the United States,* Jonathan Fox and Gaspar Rivera-Salgado observe, "Mexico is increasingly recognized to be a nation of migrants, a society whose fate is intimately linked with the economy and culture of the United States." This description emphasizes the movement of people in the relationship between Mexico and the United States, rather than the formality of state-to-state relations or their economic underpinnings.

For Fox and Rivera-Salgado, Oaxacalifornia, the nickname given by the tens of thousands of Oaxacans to California, their new state of residence "brings together their lives in California with their communities of origin more than 2,500 miles away." The authors might have equally referred to Pueblayork, the nickname bestowed on New York by a similar flow of indigenous migrants from the state of Puebla. Migrants from Guatemala don't yet call their Midwest communities Ne-braskamala, but there are enough living in Omaha and surrounding meatpacking towns to make such a nickname inevitable. This is a global phenomenon. The creation of transnational communities exists at different stages of development in the flow of migrants from Algeria to France, Turkey to Germany, Jamaica or Pakistan to the United Kingdom, the Philippines to South Korea and Hong Kong, and from developing to developed countries worldwide.

An increasing percentage of migration from Mexico to the United States is now made up of indigenous migrants, who share culture and languages spoken long before the Spanish conquest. They overwhelmingly belong to transnational communities, retaining ties to their communities of origin and establishing new communities as they migrate in search of work. They move back and forth through these networks, to the extent that the difficult passage across border allows.

Young men and women leave San Miguel Cuevas, a Mixtec-speaking town in Oaxaca, and travel to Sinaloa and Baja California in North Mexico, or cross the border to Fresno, California, or Woodburn, Oregon. In all these places they find people who speak the same language, eat the same food, and dance the same dances. Some are friends and family members. Indigenous migrants have created communities all along the northern road—in reality, a single expanding community composed of many different settlements. Their traditions become a rich source of experience migrants draw on as they seek work, social justice, and to preserve their culture.

But for indigenous communities, migration has complicated social costs and benefits. It threatens cultural practices and indigenous languages, which become harder to preserve thousands of miles from their towns of origin. Migration often seems, especially to the young, a more profitable alternative to education. It exacerbates social and economic divisions, as some families have access to remittances and others don't. But it has also become an economic necessity, and the families of those who take the road north often do benefit, although they risk danger and debt to receive its rewards.

The transnational communities they create pose challenging questions about the nature of citizenship in a globalized world. In her study of marginalized immigrant workers on Long Island, *Suburban Sweatshops,* Jennifer Gordon described a new framework for defining citizenship. "The right to seek social change through the political process —a right at the heart of the meaning of citizenship—can be claimed by people who by virtue of their presence and their work are in fact a part of the political community, although they are not yet officially recognized as such." In "The Blossoming of Transnational Citizenship," his contribution to *Indigenous Mexican Migrants in the United States,* Paul Johnston states that what is new "is not the emergence of cross-border social and economic networks, long a central part of the fabric of life in southwestern U.S. towns . . . the significant new feature is the expansion of citizenship with the entry of first-generation Mexican immigrants into public life."

Basing citizenship on political activity in pursuit of rights is the key to the experience of Fausto Lopez, a Triqui migrant farmworker from Oaxaca. While living in a bamboo and plastic tent in the reeds beside California's Russian River, Lopez became president of the Sonoma County chapter of the Indigenous Front of Binational Organizations (FIOB), helping to lead other community residents in demanding driver's licenses and an amnesty for undocumented immigrants. Living in conditions most people in the United States would describe as extreme poverty, even homelessness, these migrants saw themselves not as victims but as social actors, with a right to acceptance both in Mexico and the United States.

The desire for community is as important and necessary to survival as the need to find work, or to escape hunger and state violence. Community lies at the heart of the questions posed by migration. "Among indigenous Oaxaqueños, we already have the concept of community and organization," said Rufino Domínguez, the FIOB's binational coordinator. "When people migrate from Oaxaca, we already have a committee comprised of people from our hometown. We are united and live near one another. We have traditions we don't lose, wherever we go."

But preserving indigenous language and traditions in a transnational community is not easy. "My wife and I are trying to preserve our culture," Lopez said. "We teach our children Triqui as well as Spanish. Things are changing so much that young Triqui children are learning Spanish a lot sooner. [In Mexico] the television, radio, and music that surrounds them is all in Spanish, as well as the books and newspapers." To give his children a chance to inherit and practice their culture in a meaningful way, when Lopez crossed the border to look for work in California, "I left my wife and children in Ensenada. When the school year ended, I sent them back to Oaxaca, so that my kids would learn Triqui. Here in California that wouldn't be possible. In Ensenada they were taught some Triqui through books in school, but that isn't the same as an environment like Oaxaca, where people speak it. I want my children to learn Spanish, but also keep our traditions, which I feel that they are losing. I have spoken with Zapotec and Mixtec parents who feel the same."

Lopez was willing to pay a high price for passing his culture on to his children—living as an outsider in the United States, "an illegal, a bracero," in the words of Rigoberto Garcia. "I don't want to be apart from my family," Lopez said. "The fact of the matter is that it is necessary. I am here so that they have a better life. I want my children to go to school and hope to give them a home when they are older. I never had the opportunity to have a home as a child. I am doing all of this for my family."

Transnational communities created by migration face an enormous challenge. How can people maintain and re-create their identity when they become physically distant from the towns that are its source? As new generations grow up removed from their culture's point of origin, will they be willing to accept and reproduce the traditions of their parents?

The FIOB's organizing strategy is based on the culture of Oaxacan communities, particularly an institution called the *tequio*. "This is the concept that we must participate in collective work to support our community," Domínguez explained. "That understanding of mutual assistance makes it easier for us to organize ourselves. Beyond organizing and teaching our rights, we would like to save our language so that it lives and continues into the future. We want to live our culture, to ensure that it won't die." Part of this culture is participatory democracy, with roots in indigenous village life. The organization's binational assemblies are built around workshops that discuss its bylaws and political positions in detail, and which have removed leaders for violating collective decisions.

Even in Mexico, the survival of indigenous culture is at risk. According to Fox and Rivera-Salgado, "The experience of racism against indigenous people in Mexico, and against Mexican immigrants in the U.S., also played a role in the [FIOB's] formation. It enforced a search for cultural identity to strengthen the ability of communities to resist, which in turn created the possibility of new forms of organization and action." Centolia Maldonado, today one of the FIOB's principal leaders in Oaxaca, recalls living as a migrant in Mexicali, in northern Mexico. "We were 'Oaxaquitas'—Indians," she recalls. "People from the north were always valued more, but we were the ones who weren't afraid of work. There is terrible discrimination when people migrate. People even do it to themselves after a while."

But the experience of migration sometimes changes indigenous traditions in positive ways. Oralia Maceda, a twenty-six-year-old organizer from Oaxaca, came to Fresno to develop women's participation in the FIOB. "I believe it is women's responsibility to get involved and to find out how to participate," she says. "I use different tactics to get them to come. I'll ask, who wants to become legal in this country? We talk about very basic problems." Irma Luna, who ran the FIOB's women's programs before Maceda, said that it's even changed the status of women back in Oaxaca. "Now there's more support for women to report their husbands, and many women send their husbands to jail after receiving a brutal beating," she explained.

In Omaha, the culture of indigenous Qanjobal people from the Guatemala highlands was adapted by organizers like Sergio Sosa to aid campaigns to organize unions in meatpacking plants. But transnational communities don't exist in isolation. In Omaha's organizing ferment, people who participated in land-reform struggles in Mexico made common cause with Guatemalans who knew how to use popular-education techniques from their civil war experiences. In Fresno, Mixtecs, Zapotecs, Triquis, and other indigenous groups first cooperated to stage the traditional pan-Oaxacan cultural festival, the Guelaguetza, and formed the FIOB. Then they joined resettled Hmong refugees from Cambodia in a joint celebration of their common migrant experience in a new synthesis—the Tamejavi festival.

Residents of transnational communities don't see themselves simply as victims of an unfair system, but as actors capable of reproducing culture, of providing economic support to families in their towns of origin, and of seeking social justice in the country to which they've migrated. They have a lot to offer a larger world. But they need an opportunity to define their experience for themselves, and to propose solutions to problems that correspond to the real conditions of their lives. A sensible immigration policy, therefore, would recognize and value the communities of migrants, and see their support as desirable. It would reinforce indigenous culture and language, rather than treating them as a threat. At the same time, it would seek to integrate immigrants into the broader community around them and give them a voice in it, rather than promoting social exclusion, isolation, and segregation. It would protect the rights of immigrants as part of protecting the rights of all working people.

FIOB's political platform, adopted at its Oaxaca assembly in 2005, condemns the U.S. proposal for new guest-worker programs, arguing that they treat migrants only as temporary workers rather than as people belonging to, and creating, communities. "There is no guarantee of their labor and human rights," the assembly noted. Instead, the FIOB called for legalizing the status of undocumented migrants in the United States. It also called for extending the rights of citizenship, by finally implementing a decision made in 1995 by the Mexican government to allow its citizens in the United States to vote in Mexican elections.

According to Fox and Rivera-Salgado, "To study indigenous Mexican migrants in the United States today requires a binational lens." The emergence of a critical mass of Oaxacans in California, they argue, made possible distinctive forms of social organization and cultural expression. Unlike the hometown associations that preceded it, the FIOB is more active in pursuing social change, whether advocating for workers' rights in California, leading struggles for housing along the border, or organizing politically in indigenous Mexican towns for cultural preservation and economic development.

Transnational communities in Mexico are creating new ways of looking at citizenship and residence that correspond more closely to the reality of migration. In 2005 Jesus Martinez, a professor at California State University in Fresno, was elected by Michoacán residents to their state legislature. His mandate was to represent the interests of the state's citizens living in the United States. "In Michoacán, we're trying to carry out reforms that can do justice to the role migrants play in our lives," Martinez said. In 2006 Pepe Jacques Medina, director of the Comite Pro Uno, a Latino community organization in Los Angeles's San Fernando Valley, was elected to Mexico's Federal Chamber of Deputies on the PRD ticket with the same charge. Transnational migrants insist that they have important political and social rights, both in their communities of origin and in their communities abroad.

According to Martinez, "Mexico has undergone a process of democratic transformation since the 1980s, but it is still incomplete. Mexicans living abroad, who represent 16 percent of the electorate, still have not been granted the right to vote. That's part of the inclusion that has to take place." The PRI and PAN control the national congress, and while they voted over a decade ago to enfranchise Mexicans in the United States, they only set up a system to implement that decision in April 2005. They imposed so many obstacles, however, that in the 2006 presidential elections only forty thousand were able to vote, out of a potential electorate of millions. "It was limited," conceded Dominguez, "but it was the fruit of many years of fighting by organizations here in the U.S. It's not all we wanted, but it's a beginning. And most important, now that they've passed the law and started to create a process, there's no going back."

U.S. electoral politics can't remain forever immune from these expectations of representation, and they shouldn't. After all, the slogan of the Boston Tea Party was "No taxation without representation"—those who make economic contributions have political rights. That principle requires recognition of the legitimate social status of everyone living in the United States. Legalization isn't just important to migrants—it is a basic step in the preservation and extension of democratic rights for all people. With and without visas, 34 million migrants living in the United States cannot vote to choose the political representatives who decide basic questions about wages and conditions at work, the education of their children, their healthcare or lack of it, and even whether they can walk the streets without fear of arrest and deportation.

Their disenfranchisement affects U.S. citizens, especially working people. If all the farmworkers and their families in California's San Joaquin Valley were able to vote, a wave of living-wage ordinances would undoubtedly sweep the state. California's legislature would pass a single-payer health plan to ensure that every resident receives free and adequate healthcare. If it failed to pass it, San Joaquin Valley legislators, currently among the most conservative, would be swept from office.

By excluding from the electorate those who most need social change and economic justice, the range of possible reform is restricted, not only on issues of immigration but on most economic issues that affect working people. Immigration policy, and political and social rights for immigrants, is an integral part of a broad agenda for change that includes better wages and housing, a national healthcare system, a national jobs program, and the right to organize without fear of firing. Without expanding the electorate, it will be politically difficult to achieve any of it. By the same token, it's not possible to win major changes in immigration policy apart from a struggle for these other goals. To end job competition, workers need legislation like the 1970s' Humphrey-Hawkins Full Employment Act. To gain organizing rights for immigrants, all workers need Congress to pass the Employee Free Choice Act.

Anti-immigrant hysteria has always preached that the interests of immigrants and the native-born are in conflict, that one group can only gain at the expense of the other. In fact, the opposite is true. To raise wages generally the low price of immigrant labor has to rise, which means that immigrant workers have to be able to organize effectively. Given half a chance, they will fight for better jobs and wages, schools, and healthcare, just like anyone else. When they gain political power, the working-class communities around them will benefit too. Since it's easier for immigrants to organize if they have permanent legal status, a real legalization program would benefit a broad range of working people, far beyond immigrants themselves. On the other hand, when the government and employers use employer sanctions, enforcement, and raids to stop the push for better conditions, making organizing much more difficult, unions and workers in general suffer the consequences.

That vulnerability is only increased by the social exclusion and second-class status imposed by guest-worker programs. Delinking immigration status and employment is a necessary step to achieving equal rights for migrant workers, who will never have significant power if they have to leave the country when they lose their jobs. Healthy immigrant communities need employed workers, but they also need students, old and young people, caregivers, artists, the disabled, and those who don't have traditional jobs.

The global economy has turned insecurity into a virtue, praising it as necessary to increased flexibility and competitiveness. But working communities need a system that produces security, not insecurity. In evaluating proposals for immigration reform, security, equality, organization, and community should be the watchwords used by human rights activists. Proposals to deny people rights or benefits because of immigration status move away from equality. Yet most people living in the United States believe in equal rights and status, even if there is often a gap between rhetoric and the concrete measures and laws necessary to achieve them.

Ultimately, most migration in today's global economy is forced migration, a result of dislocation. Yet even in a more just world, migration will continue. We move and travel because we can—it is part of what makes us human. Curiosity and the desire to know our fellow human beings, even on the other side of the planet, makes us who we are. We admire those who speak many languages and who can move skillfully from community to community, communicating with a broad variety of people. Today the huge global movement of people has connected families and communities over thousands of miles and many borders, creating links between people that will inevitably grow. Immigration policy should make that movement possible, instead of seeing everywhere the threat of terrorism. Freedom of movement is a human right. But selling workers to employers should not be the price for gaining it.

The use of pro-corporate economic reforms and treaties to displace communities, to produce a global army of available and vulnerable workers, has a brutal impact on people. NAFTA and the free trade agreements between the United States and Central America, Peru, Colombia, Panama, South Korea, and Jordan not only don't stop the economic transformations that uproot families and throw them into the migrant stream—they push that whole process forward. Minor modifications to those trade agreements will not alter their basic effect. Instead, working people need a common front to scrap those agreements and to change the economic and political priorities they enforce.

The Salvadoran American National Network, an organization of Salvadorans living in the United States, points out that any long-term solution has to include "development and implementation of new economic and social policies in our home countries . . . thereby reducing migration flows to the United States." Changing corporate trade policy and stopping neoliberal reforms is as central to immigration reform as gaining legal status for undocumented immigrants. But doing no harm is not enough. The United States, Europe, and Japan are wealthy societies, with the capacity and responsibility for repairing globalization's social damage. A fund, for instance, to provide rural credit (without strings to big corporations) could allow Mixtec farmers to raise their productivity and stay on the land. It's not so far-fetched. The fair trade movement in wealthy countries already helps many rural producers form cooperatives, to gain access to the markets of developed countries at a fair price.

Beyond equality is solidarity. U.S. workers have been forced into a global labor market. They have a direct interest in helping workers in other countries to organize and raise living standards, and in stopping U.S. military intervention in support of the free trade system. Working people have a great advantage in the global economy. More than 180 million people, almost all of them workers and farmers, are part of a great migrant stream, creating a human bond that connects the countries of the developed and developing world. What more natural vehicle for solidarity is there than people themselves? Who knows more about the working conditions in both halves of the world than someone who has worked in each place? Who can see most clearly the operation of the global economy, and who has a greater stake in changing it?

Today working people of all countries are asked to accept continuing globalization, in which capital is free to go wherever it wants. By that token, migrants must have the same freedom, with rights and status equal to those of anyone else. People in Mexico, Guatemala, China, the United States, and every other country need the same things. Secure jobs at a living wage. Rights in their workplaces and communities. The freedom to travel and seek a future for their families. The borders between countries should be common ground where they can come together, not lines to pull them apart.